Creating Digital Spaces for Multilingual Writers

NEW PERSPECTIVES ON LANGUAGE AND EDUCATION

Founding Editor: Viv Edwards, *University of Reading, UK*
Series Editors: Phan Le Ha, *University of Hawaii at Manoa, USA* and Joel Windle, *Monash University, Australia.*

Two decades of research and development in language and literacy education have yielded a broad, multidisciplinary focus. Yet education systems face constant economic and technological change, with attendant issues of identity and power, community and culture. What are the implications for language education of new 'semiotic economies' and communications technologies? Of complex blendings of cultural and linguistic diversity in communities and institutions? Of new cultural, regional and national identities and practices? The New Perspectives on Language and Education series will feature critical and interpretive, disciplinary and multidisciplinary perspectives on teaching and learning, language and literacy in new times. New proposals, particularly for edited volumes, are expected to acknowledge and include perspectives from the Global South. Contributions from scholars from the Global South will be particularly sought out and welcomed, as well as those from marginalized communities within the Global North.

All books in this series are externally peer-reviewed.

Full details of all the books in this series and of all our other publications can be found on http://www.multilingual-matters.com, or by writing to Multilingual Matters, St Nicholas House, 31-34 High Street, Bristol BS1 2AW, UK.

NEW PERSPECTIVES ON LANGUAGE AND EDUCATION: 86

Creating Digital Literacy Spaces for Multilingual Writers

Joel Bloch

MULTILINGUAL MATTERS
Bristol • Blue Ridge Summit

DOI https://doi.org/10.21832/BLOCH0794
Library of Congress Cataloging in Publication Data
A catalog record for this book is available from the Library of Congress.
Names: Bloch, Joel- author.
Title: Creating Digital Literacy Spaces for Multilingual Writers/Joel Bloch.
   Description: Bristol, UK; Blue Ridge Summit: Multilingual Matters, 2021. | Series:
   New Perspectives on Language and Education: 86 | Includes bibliographical
   references and index. | Summary: "This book argues for the value of digital
   literacy in the multilingual writing classroom. It examines the relationship
   between digital and print literacies and addresses the design of literacy spaces for
   multilingual classrooms. The book will help teachers meet the challenges created
   by rapidly shifting technology"—Provided by publisher.
Identifiers: LCCN 2020036956 | ISBN 9781800410787 (paperback) |
   ISBN 9781800410794 (hardback) | ISBN 9781800410800 (pdf) |
   ISBN 9781800410817 (epub) | ISBN 9781800410824 (kindle edition)
Subjects: LCSH: Composition (Language arts)—Study and teaching. | Composition
   (Language arts)—Computer-assisted instruction. | Rhetoric—Study and teaching.
   | Academic writing—Study and teaching. | Computer literacy. | Multilingual
   education. | Educational technology.
Classification: LCC P53.27 .B58 2021 | DDC 808.020285—dc23
LC record available at https://lccn.loc.gov/2020036956

British Library Cataloguing in Publication Data
A catalogue entry for this book is available from the British Library.

ISBN-13: 978-1-80041-079-4 (hbk)
ISBN-13: 978-1-80041-078-7 (pbk)

Multilingual Matters
UK: St Nicholas House, 31-34 High Street, Bristol BS1 2AW, UK.
USA: NBN, Blue Ridge Summit, PA, USA.

Website: www.multilingual-matters.com
Twitter: Multi_Ling_Mat
Facebook: https://www.facebook.com/multilingualmatters
Blog: www.channelviewpublications.wordpress.com

The policy of Multilingual Matters/Channel View Publications is to use papers
that are natural, renewable and recyclable products, made from wood grown in
sustainable forests. In the manufacturing process of our books, and to further
support our policy, preference is given to printers that have FSC and PEFC Chain
of Custody certification. The FSC and/or PEFC logos will appear on those books
where full certification has been granted to the printer concerned.

Typeset by Deanta Global Publishing Services, Chennai, India.

Contents

1 Technological Spaces and Teaching and Learning to Write

You're too various, too gifted, too personal, to tie yourself down at this age to the dismal drudgery of teaching.
Edith Wharton – *The Reef* (1912)

From Cute Cats to Digital Spaces

The comment made to Sophy Varney about her future career as a teacher in this Edith Wharton novel highlights the lack of respect teaching has long received, particularly in the digital age when teachers are sometimes viewed as obstacles to technological development. Today, teachers are often faced with the challenge resulting from the continually changing technological ecosystem from which they can design their courses. These challenges frequently result from changes in literacy brought from outside the classroom. Ethan Zuckerman's somewhat facetious argument that the shift from Web 1.0 to Web 2.0 is a change from exchanging academic papers to posting pictures of 'cute cats', reflects how the Web can be used as a digital space to later be imported into the writing classroom. Whatever the intent of his metaphor, the change has highlighted the importance of the Web in creating a 'participatory culture' (Jenkins *et al.*, 2016) that could later be imported into the classroom.

The World Wide Web was intentionally designed to support this new creative culture. Berners-Lee (1999), its principal designer, argued that opening the internet as a creative space could support the design of digital literacy spaces. As Weller (2020) argues, the Web is the basis for all subsequent technologies that provide greater autonomy to their users. Gilster (1997) popularized the term 'digital literacy' as the ability to use various modes of expression. What exactly, however, is meant by 'digital literacy' has never been clear (e.g. Secker, 2017). Nevertheless, the value of this critical change in the expansion of literacies in the writing classroom has not been lost on multilingual writing teachers who want to exploit their uses as writing assignments. The role of technology in multilingual writing has developed around two fundamental precepts: that technology can provide tools to help students write better and digital spaces where students can express both new and traditional forms of literacy.

1

There have been many examples of how new literacies can impact pedagogy. Groom (n.d.) places the burden for creating assignments on the students, which further shifts the teacher away from the center in digital spaces. Perhaps one of the most important developments has been how these literacies often have their origins outside the classroom and retain much of their features. Morris and Stommel (2018: para. 5) argue that these digital literacies 'pushes past the walls of the classroom and into the complicated practice of being human', thus reflecting how these literacies have changed the connections between the author and their texts. These literacy spaces – blogging, Massive Open Online Courses (MOOCs), flipped classrooms, open access spaces and even publishing – exemplify how these new technologies have impacted traditional approaches to teaching literacy.

The importance of digital spaces has increased as multilingual literacies have led to the greater globalization of literacy as the domination of English has spread and as new forms of literacy have gained in popularity. While the use of technology has often been inspired by changes in writing pedagogy, pedagogies have frequently been impacted by new technologies. Discussions about literacy have often adapted its terminology. In discussing the shift toward translingual pedagogies, Canagarajah (2018) utilizes terms popularized in discussions of technology, such as 'assemblage' and 'rhizomatic'. 'Assemblage', a term popularized in discussions of digital intellectual property (e.g. Lessig, 1999), refers to the ability of writers to connect different forms of semiotic materials, and rhizomatic, a term borrowed from postmodernism and popularized in discussions of MOOCs (Cormier, 2008b), illustrates the nonlinearity of learning found in digital spaces. Each space can be transformative for the literacy process, both by changing the nature of literacy and how it is learned.

Digital literacies have been constrained by the architectures of the technologies used with them as well as by the designs of the spaces in which they are learned. The internet has had a major impact on these literacies by turning what were once oral exchanges into written ones, beginning with email and text messages. Constraints, such as Twitter's limitations on the number of characters, may be valuable since they are more decentralized, more easily linked and thus can be incorporated for specific pedagogical goals. Crystal (2011) argued that these alternate forms of expression – tweets, texts, posts – have challenged conventional forms of language and literacy. The goal of this book, then, is to help teachers meet the challenges that these shifts have meant for literacy.

Technologically Enhanced Spaces and What it Means to be Literate

Underlying the value of these spaces is the changing meaning of literacy in academic writing classes. The introduction of digital literacy spaces has resulted from changes in how literacies are valued and has encouraged changes in the definitions of literacy in the classroom. The introduction of multimodality, for example, has added a visual and sometimes aural component to literacy while incorporating traditional pedagogical issues related to voice, textual borrowing, translanguaging, remixing and transfer, which are all issues long discussed in multilingual writing classes. Their impact has affected how literacy is viewed even in traditional writing classrooms.

These literacy spaces are continually changing, so new approaches to teaching literacy can be implemented, modified and assessed. Hafner and Ho (2020) propose what they call a process model based on the criteria used by teachers who include multimodal assignments. Each of these spaces reflects the growing importance of new types of texts, new forms of literacy, new approaches to learning and new ways of publishing and distributing information. Multimodality, for example, in the form of charts, diagrams, figures and images, has long been a part of academic writing (e.g. Kress, 2003). From using images in blogs and digital stories to accepting web texts as a form of publishing, multimodality has impacted how literacy is considered. Often, implementations overlap in different spaces. Ball *et al.* (2018) argue for the growing importance of multimodality in publishing as illustrated in their journal *Kairos* (http://kairos.technorhetoric.net/), which publishes multimodal web texts instead of traditional text-based papers.

Multimodal pedagogies incorporate various issues related to teaching multilingual students, including translanguaging, remixing and rhetorical transfer. Teachers can make these technologies interoperable by connecting them to the pedagogical issues. Blogging, for example, developed on the internet and was considered too informal to be a form of academic writing but could still be used for textual borrowing. Multimodality assignments could, in some cases, replace print assignments. Shipka (2013), for example, found multimodality to be a promising space for translanguaging, an argument somewhat supported by Canagarajah's (2018) use of terminology borrowed from multimodal literacies.

Digital storytelling, for example, illustrates this connection between literacy and social context. It was developed for social action groups (www.storycenter.org) and later used as an alternate form of literacy for outside school activities. Hull and associates (e.g. Hull & Katz, 2006; Nelson *et al.*, 2008) used digital storytelling in inner-city learning centers as an alternative to classroom writing. Soon, teachers began to see the potential for digital stories in the classroom, particularly with multilingual students who may struggle with traditional print assignments (Bloch, 2015).

The traditional forms of academic writing, which have dominated the teaching of writing from pre-freshman writing classes through publishing, often incorporated the institutional requirements found in genres taught in other classes or journals. None of these literacies developed in monolithic ways. MOOCs, for example, developed in different ways, sometimes combining the goals of the traditional classroom with new approaches to networked education, but in other cases with new and innovative approaches. Flipped classrooms were often structured around remediating the problems in existing classrooms. Even publishing spaces have been impacted by the development of new attitudes toward open access to challenge the traditional goals of publishing, evaluating, archiving and distributing research, intermixed with new concepts of openness and new technological tools for supporting these goals. These new forms of literacy, in turn, have led to new approaches to teaching and learning in spaces for all forms of academic literacies, from introductory writing through publishing courses.

These changes in classroom literacies have reflected how students have been using multiple forms of literacy, reflecting their experiences both inside and outside the classroom, as Heath (1983) described. These traditional classroom literacies have been 'disrupted' by the proliferation of Web-based literacies, although as Weller (2018a) notes, the term 'disrupted' may be too strong a word since many of the traditional forms and values attached to them remain highly valued, which has meant that traditional and digital literacies are often taught together. As Weller points out, technologies from outside of education, such as blogs and digital stories, have been repurposed for use inside the classroom. Weller argues that such disruptions, which are sometimes found in the business world such as when a traditional corporation such as Blockbuster is replaced by one such as Netflix with newer technologies, have not occurred in the teaching of writing where pedagogical growth has been more incremental.

Heath (1983) addressed the potential of disruption in valuing different literacy forms, both inside and outside the classroom. Web development has provided an impetus for implementing these new literacies, whether they include user-generated content (e.g. Jenkins, 2006) or social communities such as Snapchat, Instagram and Facebook that dominate outside the classroom (e.g. boyd, 2014). Open access has disrupted many of the traditional ways that research has been conducted, evaluated and distributed. Many, but not all, of these new contexts have impacted teaching and learning, but all have the potential to change the nature of literacy. The New Media Consortium's 2017 Horizon Report on digital literacy argues for a greater focus on creativity and collaboration for promoting digital literacies than traditional classroom-based literacies have presented – an argument supporting such activities as digital storytelling (see Chapter 4).

The Web has been one of the main contributors to current developments in literacy. Its biggest contribution to the development of literacy spaces may be seen in the increasing numbers of people contributing to their development. Gone are the highly centralized designs found in the development of previous technologies. Dear (2017) describes how its development was dominated by a small group of mostly male technologists working in a few places. They created a highly bureaucratic, though sometimes efficient, educational system where students sat in front of a screen as they might do when using a textbook.

These challenges have existed since the personal computer was introduced into the classroom. Its history has followed a similar trajectory to other technologies in developing and supporting these connections (e.g. Wu, 2010). With the personal computer came changes in learning that served to decentralize the process. Papert (1980) introduced the LOGO computer language for children where mistakes led not to crashes but to new creative patterns. In the field of writing, further changes resulted from linking these computers to first local and then larger networks. During this period of growing centralization that Dear described, Papert (1980) designed his programming language to respond to, not dictate, the input of its users. These spaces allow students to create their own flexible environments, which can be a model for any form of literacy space.

The introduction of new literacies, however, has necessitated new designs and tools for writing classrooms. Designing technological literacy spaces incorporates various practices related to literacy that can be adapted to the needs and goals of different multilingual writers, as well as new approaches related to the affordances of these technologies, about which teachers must become reflective. Such changes are consistent with historical research showing that what it means to be literate is always changing (Resnick, 1990) without providing the rewards often promised for mastering them (Graff, 1991).

How these technological spaces will be valued depends on how teachers use them and how, along with their students, they respond to the challenges of these new designs. One element is whether students have the required technological skills for their use. Are these 'digital natives' (Prensky, 2001) who grew up with the internet developing their digital wisdom for using these various spaces? The intense debate over the term 'digital natives/immigrants' metaphor illustrates how much disagreement there has been over the backgrounds of these writers and their familiarity with technological tools.

The determinism can also be impacted by the affordances each technology brings to the classroom. Since the design of these spaces often requires using technological tools, it is useful to consider Norman's (2007, 2013) research on the affordances of tools since this work requires teachers to reflect on how the tool can both constrain and help the development of a space as well as how the tool will be used in that space. To use Norman's framework for design, these spaces can reflect the teacher's sense of what is good pedagogy, provide students with functional activities and, perhaps most importantly, help students feel engaged, motivated and autonomous in their learning.

These affordances can both support and constrain these new literacies. Norman (2013) describes how the affordances of every object, whether teapots or computers have three aspects: a visceral aspect that incorporates the aesthetics of the object; a behaviorist aspect incorporating its effectiveness; and a reflective affordance supporting the emotional responses of the users and supporting the goals of storytelling, and a cognitive dimension for a more critical view of the effectiveness of these spaces.

Often, these digital spaces require new ways of thinking about the pedagogical potential of each technology. For many writers, for example, blogs are no longer simply digital diaries but have become a means of distributing their ideas to a larger audience; what Veletsianos (2020: 64) called 'literacies of participation', where audiences with varying backgrounds can be addressed with online identities. With any of these spaces, questions regarding privacy increase as the audience grows. Zoom, which has become a popular platform for online meetings, has been criticized for harvesting participants data often without their knowledge (Searls, 2020), for which its creator apologized and vowed to fix. Other platforms, such as ResearchGate, have been similarly criticized. As with any technology, there will be trade-offs. The structure of blogs provides greater freedom over what is written and the choices of language to write in as well as the ability to quickly address current concerns. As they have moved into the classroom, blogs, for example have retained these features but can also be adapted for classroom goals, such as being a heuristic for generating ideas. With changes in their valuation as an academic literacy, these materials can be valued as texts to be borrowed for the same purposes as traditional texts.

For teachers, designing digital spaces to exploit their affordances can be shaped by the definitions of literacy. In some cases, such as with digital stories and blogs, there are issues surrounding how different literacies from outside the classroom are to be valued inside the classroom. Batson *et al.* (2008) argue that these connections can provide an even greater abundance of materials to be brought into the classroom, which is consistent with Canagarajah's (2018) use of the term 'bricoleur', as a writer who can draw upon whichever materials feel most useful for the construction of the texts.

Multimodality provides the opportunity to integrate tools and materials in developing projects. Hull and associates (e.g. Hull & Katz, 2006) have examined the potential of this approach in their discussion of the semiotics of the materials available for digital storytelling. How students use this abundance, whether for transformative remixing or for challenging intellectual property laws, can constrain the use of alternative materials, as Hafner (2015) discusses in his use of digital stories with science students to support writing technical reports. It is interesting to note here that compared to Bloch (2015), Hafner used the same multimodal literacy but with a different assignment, one that promoted more collaborative work. This difference illustrates how the teacher can utilize literacy to create the desired social context.

In such approaches, there are questions about defining open access and therefore how such stories are to be copyrighted. Designing flipped classrooms or using MOOCs can incorporate various literacies along with their underlying assumptions about literacy. Similarly, issues surrounding publishing focus on the social context for writing and how differences in contexts can impact the role of literacy. In spaces such as MOOCs and flipped classrooms, the choice of tools could have far-reaching impacts on the literacies that emerge from these spaces.

Underlying these choices in digital spaces has been the debate over the deterministic impact of technology (e.g. Feenberg, 1999). These literacies may be seen as having a deterministic impact not only on the goals of the teachers and students but also on the institutions, communities of practices and societies where the technologies are implemented. These changing forms of literacy, however, are not detached from the social contexts in which they developed. The extent of such determinism has also been limited for developing literacy skills by the constraints of the technologies. Users continually design new usages that can bypass the constraints in the design of these spaces. With the personal computer and the World Wide Web, the determinism of these new technologies has been constrained by the social context into which they have been introduced.

Thus, digital spaces can impact writing pedagogies in two ways. First, traditional pedagogies can be seen from alternative perspectives in these spaces. The purposes of textual borrowing in establishing an argument or the ethos of the author may be similar regardless of the types of texts being borrowed. As Bawarshi and Reiff (2010: 4) argued, teaching about genres entails 'how formal features ... are connected to social purposes and ways of being and knowing in relationship to these purposes'. These genres can evolve as they are connected to these literacies for various purposes and contexts from both inside and outside the classroom. At their essence is how the languages brought to these spaces are valued. Hessler and Lambert (2017) argue that digital storytelling supports the expression of experiences that parallel traditional written texts, so one literacy can become a bridge to another.

Second, these spaces can support new approaches to literacy and pedagogy, such as translanguaging, by allowing students to value their own experiences and language in the institutional context of a writing classroom. This approach blends multimodal and traditional forms of academic discourse. However, these digital literacies can also stand on their own. Horner *et al.* (2014) argued that there should be no distinctions between multimodal language and other linguistic forms, an approach to literacy that can provide theoretical support to implementing new forms of literacy.

The Development of New Literacies for Classroom Use

In the design of these new spaces, it is important to recognize their connections to previous designs. Often, their designs may reflect traditional problems that, as Wiley (2019) has argued, have been addressed previously. They may also result from an analysis of the needs of the participants and how these spaces can address such needs. However, he laments how proponents of these new technologies rarely acknowledge their history, resulting in a recurrence of the same problems, what Watters (2013b) refers to as 'zombie ideas' for solving educational problems that persist regardless of which technologies are implemented, an argument she attributes to Larry Cuban (2001).

The controversies surrounding implementing technologies in writing classrooms have existed from the time computers were first introduced as a tool for teaching. In early studies on computer usage, Daiute (1985) argued that even the blinking cursor was an inducement to write. The impact of the personal computer was most evident on the revision process. Papers could be revised without retyping, whether from hard copy or directly on screen, which made multiple rewrites, an inherent focus of process writing theories (e.g. Flower & Hayes, 1980), easier to implement. The ability to link computers into first local and then wider networks impacted how students and teachers could connect. The design of the internet and later the World Wide Web further, and often in dramatic fashion, impacted by greatly expanding participation and connectivity among both teachers and learners.

Along with research on the affordances of designs (e.g. Norman, 2007, 2013), there was similar interest in the impact of computer hardware design on writing. Haas' (1989) research on screen size was important in shaping how teachers could respond to student writing as well as on the impact of technology on how papers could be read on a computer screen. The layout of computer classrooms, the changes in hardware and the development of new tools have similarly changed pedagogies for literacy.

Diwanji *et al.* (2018) argue that the impact of digital technology today is as important in addressing this isolation by spreading information as the invention of the printing press was hundreds of years ago (see Eisenstein, 1980). Digital literacies have been seen as instrumental in developing learning networks as well as in addressing long-standing pedagogical issues in the writing process, such as the role of the audience or the social context of argumentation. Wiley (2019) discusses its role in extending literacy to the internet, a topic repeatedly addressed. He argues that the internet has been as transformative as the printing press and writing itself. Blogging (see Chapter 2), for example, illustrates how new technologies can address old problems in multiple ways: by providing a tool for heuristics, extending the audience and creating new texts to be borrowed and valued for traditional argumentative purposes.

Most digital literacies come from outside the classroom while most academic literacies, which have predominated in the multilingual writing class, have developed inside the institution or the disciplinary communities. However, despite these differences, the affordances of multimodality often match traditional concerns with print-based pedagogies – a concern with adapting to audiences, the development of an authorial voice and using textual borrowing. However, they are still pushing the boundaries of literacy pedagogies. As Belcher (2017) argues, teachers must continually rework their pedagogies with changes in these literacies as well as in the backgrounds of students.

This approach can also be applied to the technology spaces discussed here. No space has received more hype than the flipped classroom; after the initial hype, which included the influx of funding from the Gates Foundation to promote college-level writing, MOOCs have been strongly criticized for lacking openness. Although there has been a tremendous increase in the number of MOOCs in countries like China, MOOCs have never lived up to the expectations for the personalization of writing that the Gates Foundation had envisaged, but they still provide important spaces for participants from all over the world to study literacy.

The Evolution of Technologically Enhanced Literacy Spaces

Blogs supported new perspectives on the importance of user-generated materials, which reflected more the personal concerns of the designers than the domination of classroom-based assignments. Such a shift sometimes had a transformative effect on the design of literacy spaces. New spaces for teaching and learning reflect this transformation from flipped classroom as a technological space to flipped learning as a form of active learning (Davidson, 2012).

The role of technology in writing classrooms can vary a great deal. Flipped learning does not solely rely on using technology, but many approaches, particularly implementing literacies from outside the classroom as well as stimulating discussions, which involves exploiting the affordances of these technologies. The design of MOOCs can create new technology-enhanced spaces that differ from the traditional lecture spaces, particularly impacting the decisions students make about their own learning processes and the roles of teachers in areas such as evaluating student work and presenting content. They often offer various practices for students to connect to each other, peer review their writings and seek new methods of learning that differ from those found in the classroom.

The challenges in designing new spaces with new technologies require an understanding of the affordances they provide. As Norman (2007) argues when discussing the spaces and objects encountered daily: 'we are all designers'. Thus, the greatest impact of the introduction of these technologies has been on teachers to become designers. Today, teachers are neither sages nor guides but must be a designer first. By providing students with more autonomy and diversity, teachers themselves must develop new skills and pedagogies. The development of these spaces highlights the need for teachers to reconceptualize and remediate their existing approaches to thinking about education. Lieberman (2018) has discussed how changes in technology have impacted educational change. However, he found that controversies and resistance to these changes have highlighted the problems with the new student and teacher roles, which can further complicate the challenges teachers must address.

One challenge is integrating diverse literacies brought to the classroom. Students can be optimistic about digital literacies. Students often expect more technology in their classes than previous generations and that teaching writing must include using these spaces to better engage them. Students were initially seen as dichotomized from their adult counterparts in their use of technology. Terms such as 'digital natives' and 'digital immigrants' (e.g. Prensky, 2001) have been the subject of much controversy (Bennett & Kervin, 2008), which has complicated how teachers view the technological skills their students are bringing to the classroom.

However, this controversial 'digital immigrant/digital native' dichotomy has been largely replaced by the more neutral 'digital wisdom' (Prensky, 2011) metaphor. Despite the criticism over the flawed dichotomy, students may still occupy these spaces differently than their teachers. Anyone with a child may find some merit in these differences. For example, I learned how to use a mouse when I was 30; my daughter when she was 2. She is more visually communicative than I ever was, favoring sending images via Instagram. Sites such as Facebook, which are mostly populated with digital immigrants, are largely scorned by immigrants.

However, there can still be differences between teachers and students in how they view and use technology. The most obvious example is in the differences in how intellectual property and privacy are viewed. The late John Perry Barlow (1994), the former songwriter for The Grateful Dead and founder of the Electronic Frontier Foundation, had written about the differentiation between how parents and their children used technology, particularly in areas of copyright, arguing for a new view of open access on the internet. With the controversies over Napster and music sharing, Lessig (2002) wrote that the fight over intellectual property was a conflict between the young and old, an issue sometimes seen today in discussions of online privacy.

However, the dichotomy between age groups failed to capture the subtleties in how technology spaces were navigated by different age groups. Prensky's (2011) revised metaphor 'digital wisdom' has proved valuable for describing the types of literacies currently addressed in some classrooms. The value of providing spaces for bringing outside literacies into the classroom, such as digital storytelling, has expanded both as new forms of literacies and as bridges to existing forms. In digital storytelling, for example, students write their stories and then remix related images, which require new skills such as mixing texts, images and music.

New forms of literacy require not only additional technical abilities but also the rhetorical abilities to mix these different tools. Moreover, since this literacy relies on both textual borrowing and the expression of the students' voices, it seems complementary to the text-based forms of literacy that are transferable in both directions (e.g. Perkins & Salomon, 1988). The introduction of such literacies responds to Lea and Street's (2006) call for a greater pluralization of academic literacies, so writers can move between the different forms in different social contexts.

A Framework for Discussing Literacy Spaces

Designers and students can draw upon many sources of free or inexpensive materials from outside the classroom for designing these spaces. The Digital Story Center, as does the Global Flipped Network, for example, offers free resources but charges for workshops and books as well as soliciting donations. As will be discussed in Chapter 6, open access journals have sought institutional support to provide free open access in comparison to the more expensive forms of access provided by publishers.

However, there is also a counter trend in the need for funding to make open access sites sustainable (Poyndor, 2019). Sustainability has been a major concern in open access, in relationship to both institutions and consortia of institutions and publishers. In the past, as Dear (2017) showed in his discussion of PLATO, support came from businesses and government, while some educational institutions balked at the high costs While, initially, MOOCs received grants from agencies such as the Gates Foundation and the US State Department, today corporations and institutions developing MOOCs (see Chapter 4) have been developing business models, whether for creating profits or alternative degree programs, that often have limited access, pushing the spaces away from their initial purposes.

Although the decentralization of the network has sometimes exerted downward pressure on costs, the pedagogy of digital literacy often involves monetary costs. Many of the tools teachers may have used have begun to charge fees or have reduced their free services. Scoop.it, a valuable site for curating articles on topics related to these spaces, has begun to limit the number of articles that can be posted for free to pressure users to upgrade their membership. Scoop.it is useful for providing choices in texts, which could counter the concern some teachers have of students sharing papers. In some cases, alternative tools can be found as free substitutes. Screencast-O-Matic, a useful tool for creating inexpensive videos for flipped learning, has implemented a 'freemium' model that charges teachers for some features that used to be free. MOOCs that used to be free have similarly begun to charge participants, sometimes depending on the levels of participation desired or on the number of courses the participant wishes to take. Accessing published research has similarly undergone tremendous changes as new business models are implemented and ongoing conflicts between publishers and academic institutions continue.

The flipped classroom has exemplified the impact of commercial pressures. On the one hand, teachers can avail of free or inexpensive resources and professional organizations for personal training (e.g. the EVO) and connections (e.g. Coombes *et al.*, 2020). On the other hand, many of the training resources that used to be free, now cost money to use. Other resources can be developed inexpensively or use inexpensive equipment. Creating videos, for example, can be developed inexpensively using tools such as Screencast-O-Matic, but can also involve investing large amounts of money in cameras, software and editing devices. Such decisions may involve the determinism of teachers on the quality of the desired videos.

Beyond the material costs of implementing digital literacies are the pedagogical challenges that confront teachers and students with the often new affordances of these spaces. The affordances these digital spaces contain can help teachers directly address traditional classroom problems. A teacher who feels that technologies can provide a stronger sense of audience (e.g. Ong, 1982) may also have to consider current discussions of technology on privacy, the lack of anonymity and even intellectual property law. Many issues with data collection can be problematic in the classroom, especially as data collection outside the classroom has become more controversial. For example, students who spend much time connected to their technologies outside the classroom may be disconnected inside.

Immersion in these technologies can also make teachers more aware of the associated problems. As Mary Shelley noted in *Frankenstein*, teachers, as is true for everyone, should be concerned with the pervasiveness of technology in education. The importance of technologically enhanced spaces has been accompanied by a fear that technology will take over from teachers. Warner's (2019) critique of algorithmic-based evaluations is part of a concern for how technologically enhanced tools are taking over roles, such as providing feedback and evaluating papers, that teachers may still perform better.

Chapter 6, for example, addresses how research in the global knowledge economy can be affected by how knowledge is created and distributed in these academic networks. Although the publishing space may seem rarified, questions about how knowledge is created, distributed and used are fundamental issues that designers of these spaces must face. These spaces have largely been created at the corporate and institutional levels, so teachers and students must understand how to negotiate their affordances as they might try in any technological space: How information is created, distributed and copyrighted, and how teachers teach and how learners learn have been affected by changes in technology.

The implementation of digital literacies in multilingual classrooms has been highly controversial. Casanave (2017), for example, argues that although she initially did not discuss digital literacy, she now admits that it has become an important, though still controversial, part of teaching. As many teachers have found, she questions whether digital literacy is really writing, as well as what burdens it places on teachers. The problems with these spaces have accompanied every introduction of a technology into the classroom. In my previous book on technology and multilingual writing (Bloch, 2007b), I focused on how writing pedagogies incorporating new forms of literacy have expanded along with the technologies that have been imported into the classroom. The designs of these new literacy spaces may be more complex, placing more burdens on, as well as opportunities for teachers to address.

More than ever, therefore, teachers need to prepare for how the growing complexity of these spaces affects how they teach and what they are teaching. These issues mirror discussions concerning many technologies. Many technologically enhanced spaces require that every user – students, teachers, IT personnel and even administrators – must negotiate the affordances of these spaces. Even the apparently simplest of these contexts can present various design challenges. Norman (2008) gives the example of the inside of a car, which can contain various technologies to foster different activities including listening, eating/drinking and talking. Some activities such as talking with another person in the car require no additional technologies but, as with technologically enhanced activities, require new facility with skills, such as multitasking, which can limit using these technologies. A simple blog can be a literacy space, but it can also be a heuristic for developing ideas, a multimedia artifact, a social space for interactions and a text for remixing – all depending on the context in which it is implemented.

Designing digital spaces can be equally challenging. The complexity challenges both the design and teaching of these new literacies. Speaking of game design, Will Wright, the creator of *The Sims*, argues that good game design involves 'the balance between the technical aspects of the game's implementation (the game's technology) and the model of the game as rendered in a player's mind (the games psychology)' (cited in Dear, 2017: 299). As in any game, all the players or users must share the same knowledge for the game to proceed in a fair manner. In a classroom, both teachers and students similarly understand the possibilities and constraints to best exploit their potential for literacy development.

In these digital spaces, both teachers and students share a responsibility for meeting their goals. Multilingual composition teaching has often focused on preparing students for the forms of writing they may encounter. Therefore, the transfer of what is learned in one space needs to be transferred to other spaces. How well students can transfer from their multilingual writing classroom to their other courses, or even from one assignment to another, has long been controversial (e.g. Leki, 2007; Spack, 1997). New approaches that use technology to address these problems have isolated many teachers from other teachers who do not share their interests. However, these technologies have been used not only to connect students with other students and their audiences, but also to connect teachers who share the same interest in digital spaces. The Flipped Learning Network produced a webinar to address the isolation of teachers using flipped learning. This isolation puts more pressure on instructors to assess their work in ways that may influence their colleagues.

A framework for discussing digital literacy spaces can begin with an expanded value for new literacies inside the classroom. For example, blogs and digital stories illustrate how outside literacies can be brought into the classroom. There has long been a frustration with the traditional classroom, what Raymond (1999) might refer to as a 'cathedral' as a space for learning. This 'cathedral' metaphor has been used to describe the traditional lecture. Teachers can also be challenged by the continual changes in the design of digital spaces. Changes in designing digital literacy spaces have been influenced by a frustration with the traditional classroom as captured, for example, in Michael Wesch's popular YouTube movie 'A Vision of Students Today' (https://www.youtube.com/watch?v=dGCJ46vyR9o) on the sterility of the lecture classroom, which highlighted the need for creating new learning spaces.

In this cathedral-like classroom, students gather in one space supposedly attentively listening to a 'sage on the stage' and taking notes. In Wesch's movie, however, the students deconstructed these classrooms by silently raising signs about whether they were learning or even whether they bought or read the textbook, an issue that has become important in the development of flipped learning and open educational resources (OERs). Often, technologies simply provide more efficiency for learning with few or no disruptive changes to this context, such as with the app for better organizing notes, whose popularity indicates that students are still being lectured to as always.

These spaces illustrate how this framework can respond to this decentralization. MOOCs were originally designed to be spaces where participants from all over the world could learn on their own time. Their sources in the Open Courseware initiative from MIT (https://ocw.mit.edu/index.htm) and the Open Learning initiative from Carnegie Mellon (https://oli.cmu.edu/) highlight their open origins. In a flipped classroom, more traditional classroom spaces can be reorganized using different approaches to make learning more active. Classroom activities needed to be rethought and rearranged to best exploit their potential as digital literacies.

While flipped classes are primarily designed around isolated classrooms, simply moving some intellectual property outside the classroom, often into videos, has meant that teachers can consider the consequences of such openness. In the flipped classrooms, learning spaces can occur both in the classroom and anywhere students can access course materials. While the flipped classroom was initially developed as an alternative to the large lecture classes, it can model smaller, language learning classes (e.g. Arfstom, 2013). A flipped class may begin with the teacher rearranging activities both inside and outside the classroom for individuals and groups of students, which can evolve into new activities and new forms of interactions.

Although flipped classes can be taught using various methods, they are often designed as blended learning spaces combining classroom spaces with technologically enhanced ones, although the ratio between the two is not clearly specified. Technology, although not required, has played an increasing role in their creation. Short lectures, for example, can be easily recorded and posted on YouTube so that students can view them anytime, anywhere and as often as they like. The flipped classroom predated the development of MOOCs, an approach credited to Eric Mazur over 20 years ago, but its popularity has grown in the teaching of writing. Initially, flipped classrooms in universities were designed in response to the types of criticisms about engagement seen in Wesch's videos; however, now they have been applied to various learning spaces. Although flipped classes can be taught in different ways, they are often designed as blended learning spaces combining classroom spaces with technologically enhanced ones. Their origins in university often focused on making large lecture classes more interactive by moving the teacher lectures outside the classroom. A flipped class may begin with rearranging activities for both individuals and groups of students and then creating new activities and new forms of interactions.

All such spaces reflect changes in the social contexts for multilingual writing, as the relationship between literacy inside and outside the classroom illustrates. Changes in open access (see Chapter 6) have led to changes in publishing (see Chapter 7). Greater pressure on graduate students to publish has increased the value of publishing spaces to be integrated into writing programs. The context for publishing has also become more complicated. What constitutes being published and how publishing is changing have been evolving differently across different disciplines and even different journals. The publishing process has been affected as technology has impacted the publishing space. Changes, for example, in how papers are evaluated through peer review can impact how the papers are written.

An important contribution of MOOCs to literacy pedagogy was providing more diverse peer reviewers. By moving the writing process outside the classroom, both teachers and students must better understand intellectual property laws and different criteria for judging intellectual integrity than they faced in their classes. The result has been a closer relationship between the affordances of the technology and how students are expected to write. Graduate students are under more pressure to publish, which necessitates a greater need for understanding the publishing space and how it is being disrupted both positively and negatively, which could relate to the rhetorical structures of the paper or to the rhetorical implications of publishing terms such as 'reject but resubmit' or how to evaluate predatory journals.

The importance of these publishing spaces was further enhanced by changes in traditional methods of mentorship and advising where students traditionally learned such distinctions. The role of the teacher may not only be a designer but also a 'broker' (Curry & Lillis, 2006) or 'sponsor' (Brandt, 2001) who can add a level of personal support to the publishing process. Sometimes, that means mediating between a student and an advisor. For example, a Turkish student asked about writing a book review for a journal his advisor did not want to write. The broker may have to respond to his concerns as well as various problems, such as grammar concerns, technological tools and intellectual property issues, all with an awareness of the local nature of these concerns, often including the personal successes and failures of the broker.

These new spaces have allowed for a different, and possibly more collaborative, relationship between teacher and student and among students. New developments in technology have changed how research is evaluated, distributed and sometimes published, not always at the same pace across disciplines. The rise of open access and predatory journals has meant that students and even teachers need to take more care in determining legitimate places to publish. We began, for example, by implementing multimodality as a means of reaching students who were struggling with traditional rhetorical forms (Bloch, 2015). MOOCs could play a more macro-level role by providing educational experiences to students wherever they are located if they have access. As will be seen with MOOCs, the flipped classroom highlighted the role of active learning in the design of the space.

Although language learning and writing classes were seldom as large as lecture classes and did not feature the traditional 'sage on the stage', teachers still found that learning could be changed by introducing these alternate technologically enhanced spaces. Active learning in the classroom has become associated with flipped learning, which highlights this relationship between pedagogy and the digital space. Although flipped learning does not always require an offline or out-of-class space, it has become an important example of this hybridity between in-class and out-of-class spaces.

Digital literacy and technologically enhanced spaces can vary a great deal, and what literacy means globally can vary even more. The 2017 Horizon Report discussed several perspectives on these questions from developed and developing countries that reflect the need for new teaching strategies. These attempts at new strategies have drawn upon practices in related fields such as first language writing but often adapt them to the needs and goals of multilingual writers.[1] The social, economic and political position of multilingual writing teachers have their own goals for using digital spaces and digital resources. Teachers use these resources to improve student learning by creating or finding authentic materials, and by better integrating current research into classroom design. To best implement these spaces, then, both groups must understand how these issues are incorporated into their designs.

Implementing these literacies challenges both students and teachers to understand using these digital spaces for teaching literacy. The choice of which space to use, however, is critical for matching the pedagogical goals. Technologies are not neutral; each choice impacts while not controlling the forms of literacy taught. These spaces may not be as deterministic as Plato and Carr (2011) have argued for the last 2000 years, but how they are implemented can impact the types of literacy that are taught. Since many of these digital spaces were developed outside the classroom, teachers must choose those most appropriate for their goals. The growing importance of open access has also had an impact on classroom pedagogies.

These spaces will continually change as new technologies are developed. Newer technologies, such as blockchain ('Building Your Blockchain Advantage', 2019), can be used for building networks and connecting these technologies in areas such as peer review (Rosenthal, 2018). Older technologies such as data mining can be repurposed for use in finding linguistic and rhetorical models. The 2019 Higher Education Edition Report identifies three critical technological spaces that have been important in higher education – adaptive learning, augmented and virtual reality, and gamification – that have entered into the digital spaces but have not been developed fully, which has been especially true with the digital literacy spaces. Although the 2019 Higher Education Edition Report (2019: 14) differentiates between 'digital fluency' and 'digital literacy', future research may deal with both aspects in these digital spaces, although to varying degrees.

Such rearrangement of activities across digital spaces and tools illustrates the possible roles of learning spaces, both physical spaces such as classroom design, and virtual spaces such as in Second Life or with virtual tools such as Google glasses, Oculus, or the next generation of wearables, in the writing classroom. Initial failures with these technologies could be remediated through changes in the technology or in the development of new pedagogies for using them in writing spaces.[2] These tools may disappear, be modified or made more expensive or less accessible. These relationships have long existed in the design of technological spaces. Dear (2017) describes the development of competing programs – PLATO and TICCIT – as spaces defined by the development of technologies in different institutional contexts. While these programs may not be relevant today, they remain important for understanding how technology has developed. As writing processes evolve, new spaces are needed. The choice of these tools and literacy spaces, therefore, needs to be grounded in an understanding of the writing process.

However, the history of technology illustrates how the development of new spaces often requires tools for providing additional affordances for course goals. The Open University added tools to enable sharing among teachers and students. There are freely accessible digital resources, as well as a few proprietary ones, such as Socrative (https://www.socrative.com), Menti (https://www.mentimeter.com), Poll Everywhere (www.polleverywhere.com) and Top Hat (www.tophat.com), all of which can be used to facilitate class discussions by having students respond anonymously to questions they can later discuss collaboratively.

Digital storytelling requires its creators to contextualize the vast amount of materials available on the internet for themselves and their audiences. As with any form of multimodality, it forces teachers and students to learn new skills and use new technological tools, which often requires more collaborative forms of learning by both teachers and students. The development of MOOCs for teaching writing, often with large numbers of participants, has raised additional pedagogical questions regarding how such spaces should be designed to meet course objectives. Early MOOCs on literacy sometimes adapted pedagogies similar to those used in the writing classroom. The first MOOCs to teach writing, such as one from Stanford University on scientific writing, used traditional lectures about writing along with recorded interviews with journal editors.

As these spaces developed, new approaches to teaching writing were developed, which often required different designs and different affordances for different tools. As new uses for MOOCs developed, new spaces had to be designed. Using MOOCs for teaching writing was boosted by the Gates Foundation, which provided funding for four American institutions, three universities and one community college, to design writing courses that would prepare students for university-level writing, primarily in the United States. The MOOC instructors did not seem prepared for the large number of participants who were not native-English speakers. Often emulating the traditional writing courses illustrated the need for different pedagogies and approaches to learning models.

These criticisms on digital literacies have focused on how they have been implemented in multilingual writing courses, often focusing on whether students improved their writing. Casanave (2017) questions the role of these literacies in improving writing. For example, she has been critical of these writing spaces in developing the language ability of students, as in this quote about an article I wrote on blogging (Bloch, 2007a):

> Bloch was honest that there was little evidence that Abduallah [the student focused on in the study] or other students improved their control of grammar. (Bloch, 2007a: 74)

This critique of my use of blogging – that there was no evidence of improved student language use – highlights differences in both my pedagogy and epistemology that reflect how I chose to use the technology. This analysis illustrates a reluctance in 'proving' the efficacy of any writing space, something for which many teachers are looking. The ability to improve grammatical accuracy or use was not the purpose of implementing blogging. Her techno-skepticism has a long tradition in studying the educational use of technology (e.g. Cuban, 2001).

The hype surrounding using technology has impacted how it has been valued. The much-publicized Gartner Hype Cycle (https://www. gartner.com/smarterwithgartner/top-trends-in-the-gartner-hype-cycle-for-emerging-technologies-2017/) primarily focuses on the rise, decline and leveling out of many of the most popular technologies. New technological spaces seem to have followed this Gartner trajectory. A commonly discussed issue has been the rise and fall of Facebook as a tool for democratization around the world to one that violates norms on privacy. These changes can also be seen in how it can be used as a literacy space or a tool for use within a space. Assuming it survives, it may do so with different practices and more moderate aspirations. Other widely adopted technologies such as Twitter may follow the same pattern. Twitter, through its affordances from using hashtags, emerged as one of the foremost sites for creating online identities and communities (Weller et al., 2014). In these cases, it is not up to Mark Zuckerberg or Jack Dorsey but the teachers and students who use them to spur their development as a form of academic literacy.

A similar argument can be applied to the technology spaces discussed here. Watters (2018) focuses on the word 'personalization' as a concept in teaching that has grown in significance. No space has received more hype than the flipped classroom; after an initial period of hype, which included the influx of funding from the Gates Foundation to promote college-level writing, MOOCs have been strongly criticized for lacking openness. MOOCs may never have lived up to the expectations of the Gates

Foundation for developing learning spaces, but they still provide important spaces for participants from all over the world to study writing.

Despite lacking direct proof about their effectiveness, these spaces have been selected because no matter where they stand on the Gartner Hype Curve, they still offer viable and useful alternatives to traditional writing spaces. Casanave's critique highlights how spaces may be valuable for some aspects of teaching and not for others. Digital spaces can support traditional approaches to teaching writing. Belcher (2017) argued that today's interest in digital literacies continues the importance that process-orientated teachers and researchers have placed on the exploration of ideas. One concept she focuses on is 'voice', a topic that has been well discussed in print writing (e.g. Ivanič, 1998) but has just emerged in digital literacy (see Chapter 3).

Digital storytelling creates a space where voice becomes a major focus by having students begin their digital stories with a personal story and then voice them in a podcast that will be expanded upon through using images and sound (Lambert, 2020). Students can tell their own stories in their own voices, which can help them create their professional identities. Our use of blogging reflected, as Belcher (2017) argued, a technological extension of the process role for heuristics in developing ideas (e.g. Flower & Hayes, 1980). Blogging (see Chapter 2) can also support students developing their own voices as a heuristic to express their ideas later in their writing (Bloch, 2008b).

Bringing new literacies into the classroom has also challenged many teachers to rethink their pedagogies. Casanave (2017) was critical of the importation of these literacies, questioning what teachers can bring to teaching such literacies that students may have previously explored or even whether they were relevant for academic purposes. She cites a number of critiques of the internet, such as Carr (2011), who warned that the predominance of new forms of internet literacies can degrade traditional educational goals for reading and writing. His questions such as 'does Google make us stupid?' can challenge advocates of digital literacies to show their relevance to the goals of writing.

The potential value of including these literacies despite these concerns has been a fundamental premise of challenging conventional writing classrooms. The New London Group argued that literacy is a technology that can be valued differently in different social contexts, not simply as a set of additional skills for enculturating students into those contexts but also as an alternative form of writing (Cazden *et al.*, 1996). The Department of Education (2019) argued for the importance of these new social contexts, despite the potential for divisiveness among teachers, administrators and even students, such implications may cause. This social context, however, is not simply the goals of the teachers and students, but also those of the institutions, communities of practices and societies where the technologies are implemented and evaluated.

Therefore, it is no wonder that the technological spaces can control the literacies of the students, although as I have argued earlier (Bloch, 2007b) the growth in technologies, beginning with the personal computer and the World Wide Web, has loosened the control that any technology can exert and to its various constituents. The technologies discussed in this book contain underdetermined affordances that the designers of the spaces can exploit for their pedagogical goals.

Street (1984) argued that not all forms of classroom literacies are equally valued. Connecting these various forms of literacy can be important for understanding both their nature and their role across various contexts. Much like Feenberg's (1999) critique of technological determinism in the discussion on technology, Street opposed the deterministic view of literacy detached from its social context. The growth in digital spaces has disrupted some barriers between literacy inside the classroom and literacy outside of it. Shipka (2013), for example, discusses multimodality as a promising space for practicing forms of translanguaging, particularly their valuation. These 'enclosed' or 'gated' spaces may be constrained by course goals and how students can mix their own ideas, projects and artifacts with these goals, which has been important in discussions of translingualism (e.g. Guerra & Shivers-McNair, 2017) and its relationship to multimodality.

An important example of multimodality in composition pedagogy has been the use of digital storytelling (Bloch, 2015, 2018). Digital storytelling (see Chapter 3) is another outside-of-class literacy that can be adapted to the pedagogical goals of a course. The choice of digital storytelling, for example, illustrates the appropriateness of multimodality for a multilingual course on academic writing. The types of learning supported in these spaces have themselves been controversial. The students' ability to use artifacts from the internet, for example, incorporated different approaches to defining and distributing intellectual property that support openness to allow teachers and students to use, borrow and remix this property for new educational purposes with transformative results (Lessig, 2002).

Potential increases in active learning and engagement have been applauded despite the concerns about using traditional forms of reading and writing (e.g. Carr, 2011). They may resemble the approaches used in traditional spaces but still vary because of the nature of the technologies. In designing their courses, teachers must analyze the affordances of each space and how such affordances may support their course goals. Such decisions can affect the choice of technologies. Digital storytelling requires teachers to learn the skills related to recording and editing movies, although the technologies for use in these spaces are changing the requirements for deploying these skills. Digital storytelling has also required both teachers and students to learn new approaches to using intellectual property often found on the internet, whether licensed through Creative Commons (https://search.creativecommons.org/) or copyrighted through traditional legal means (e.g. Bloch, 2012). For students, using Creative Commons can be confusing because of the various licenses from which to choose. Teachers can also become confused from relying on fair use (Aufderheide & Jaszi, 2012).[3]

This choice is one of a number that teachers must make in designing digital spaces. Teachers can choose where a technology can be effectively implemented and where it cannot, a role that can require a deeper understanding of the affordances of each technology. Twitter, for example, has become popular, from politicians and athletes to teachers, to quickly communicate with their followers (e.g. Stewart, 2015), so it may communicate ideas and make connections but not necessarily as a literacy space for developing ideas or creating texts. Twitter provides a space to share shorter messages, initially limited to 140 characters although recently expanded, which could also have a different role in writing pedagogy. Although some teachers have found Twitter useful for exploring language and sharing ideas, it has never appeared to be as valuable as blogging for developing ideas in an academic writing class (c.f. Morris & Stommel, 2018). Other programs, such as Piazza (https://piazza.com/), can be used to create communities among students to ask and answer questions.

We chose blogging instead of Twitter (see Chapter 2) to help students better negotiate the messy connections between forms of literacies and specific rhetorical approaches, such as voice or textual borrowing. Students may have faced questions about valuing these spaces and whether the literacy forms are transferable. However, even such challenges may provide pedagogical opportunities for developing literacies. As students move from one digital space to another, this framework can disrupt their traditional approaches to writing, causing confusion that the teacher can explain.

The Role of Teachers as Designers

In these spaces, the teacher remains an integral part of the design, constantly tweaking or changing the space in response to the participants' representation and performance. Therefore, the concept of teacher as designer, rather than either a 'sage of the stage' or a 'guide on the side', both popularly used, is a more relevant and supportive concept. Since its inception, Weller (2018a) argues that the Web was marked by an almost yearly creation of new technologically enhanced spaces, which could be used for teaching writing.

The design of these spaces provides not only greater access to these literacies but also the ability to connect these spaces together to change collaborative pedagogies. In his history of the PLATO project, Dear (2017) shows that it was designed with the contributions of many creators often working independently but sharing what they had created. The history of the personal computer would follow a similar arc, although it would foster more 'personal computing' than fostered by PLATO (Watters, 2018). As Dear describes PLATO's development, such systems were often centralized, dominated by a few highly gifted individuals, and eventually controlled by large corporations.

The rise of personal computers was an important first step in creating greater roles for the teacher. The story of Jobs and Wozniak working in a garage to build the Apple computer illustrated the same patterns of individual work. The growing complexity of the technologies has led to greater collaboration among their developers. The Web expanded these opportunities for collaborative working for both groups and individuals by decentralizing the process. Such connectedness underlay the creation of MOOCs and the expansion of flipped classrooms. Instead of having knowledge centered in a few individuals, as Downes (2011) showed, knowledge lay in the 'connections' among them (e.g. Siemens, 2005). Such connections were designed to create new forms of emergent knowledge both within and across disciplines. Teachers could also play an increasing role with the development of open access and the related pedagogical developments.

This decentralization of learning has enabled a gradual shift to where today the teacher can be the primary designer of digital spaces. Large systems, as Dear (2017) describes, are no longer pushed out to teachers and learners. The Web expanded these opportunities by decentralizing the process to those who could access it. This connectedness underlay the creation of MOOCs (Siemens, 2005, 2012) and the expansion of flipped classrooms. Downes (2011) showed that knowledge has been decentralized through the 'connections' that both teachers and students can plug into.

The role of teacher involvement also developed as the economies of development have changed. There have been shifts in the economic structure in educational software development. Instead of dealing with a large corporation such as Control Data, as Dear (2017) discussed, teachers can now work with smaller companies that are more responsive to educational goals although often continually changing their prices and terms of service, sometimes making their use more difficult and sometimes even disappearing so that designers may have to scramble to find alternatives. These design choices are not simply technological but can also reflect the availability of financial and personal resources. Technologies often require financial expenditure, which can increase at a moment's notice, for new equipment or specialized training.

The complexity of these spaces and their impact on academic literacies have ensured that the teacher, with their understandings of the factors incorporated in the design of the space, is central in the design of the literacy space. Beyond designing the curriculum, the roles of teachers in this network are more fluid, which can challenge their traditional roles and the kinds of knowledge they require (e.g. Casanave, 2017). Therefore, teachers may no longer be either a 'sage' or a 'guide' but play an active role in designing these spaces by modifying the technologies and the networks to reflect their own goals and values as well as feedback from their students.

Both teachers and researchers must address the same social and cognitive issues related to learning and the implementation of these technologies. For both groups, are manifested, which have addressed many controversies in multilingual writing addressed in this book, such as digital literacy (e.g. Palmeri, 2012), publishing as a global enterprise (Curry & Lillis, 2018) and the significance of translingualism and multilingualism in writing classes (c.f. Atkinson *et al.*, 2015; Canagarajah, 2013, 2018; Matsuda, 2006).

As the example of implementing blogs illustrates (see Chapter 2), the teacher has remained important in remediating these issues and choosing the tools in response to the participants' representations, learning potential and performance. The concept of teacher as designer, rather than either a 'sage' or a 'guide', has provided a more relevant and supportive role for the teacher. Thus, Bergmann's definition of flipped learning as a means 'to reach every student' makes the role of the teacher even more significant in adjusting the space to meet these needs.

These spaces have often changed the forms of learning available to the different needs of the students, as illustrated in the various designs of literacy spaces. MOOCs (see Chapter 3) provide educational experiences to students wherever they are located, as long as they can access and choose which aspects of the MOOC to focus on. This ability has broken down the one-to-many learning usually found in lectures to more personalized forms of active learning. The flipped classroom (see Chapter 4) has evolved through multiple stages, currently exemplified by what Bergmann calls the '187 elements of effective Flipped Learning' (https://mail.google.com/mail/u/0/#inbox/Whct-KJVBBcZPpLFDkbTnSLdGrsPQqXQpnRgLDLfQpqZrzkClCWnd-DPgdWHjLFBsRkfvhlgB?projector=10). Although language learning and writing classes were seldom as large as lecture classes and usually did not necessarily feature the 'sage on the stage', designers still found learning could be impacted by introducing these alternative technologically enhanced spaces.

As discussed earlier, the role of teachers has long been impacted by economic considerations. These spaces have been impacted by the attempts of vendors to monetize their tools. Companies have attempted to impose business models often supported through fees to teachers and institutions. In some cases, teachers may appropriate corporate platforms to distribute their courses. Coursera, as well as other MOOC companies, have provided platforms for these new spaces; however, while the platforms can constrain their pedagogies, they cannot determine their usage, so teachers can still develop their course designs.

However, the economic realities of these platforms have impacted their use as the companies that have sponsored them have searched for business models to monetize their creations. At the same time, there has been a counter interest in open access that has allowed teachers to freely share their materials. These financial issues are not new. Dear (2017) discusses the financial issues in the attempts by Control Data to monetize the resources of the PLATO educational system. Later, other corporations, such as EXXON, tried to profit by developing programs that might help students with their writing. Today, the most publicized company in this area is Apple, which has been pouring resources into educational computing, often expecting returns in purchases of other products.

The expenditures for these resources could limit the number of teachers interested in becoming designers, which can result in their further isolation from their colleagues. Even teachers wanting to employ these technologies can be overwhelmed not only by their number but also by the economic problems associated with their implementation. While these technologies may not be deterministic on teacher-designed pedagogies, they are usually not neutral, often forcing teachers, as well as their students, to use the technologies while negotiating their constraints and affordances to 'make them their own'.

However, the Web has also countered some expenses by providing more opportunities for professional development. Organizations dedicated to professional development, such as the Flipped Global Network, which charges fees for teachers to become certified, or the EVO, which is free, have provided ongoing training and, more importantly, connections to like-minded teachers. The Flipped Global 3.0 Exchange (https://flglobal.org/hackingfl/) has been an attempt to provide teachers with the opportunity to exchange materials. Given the possible designs for digital literacy spaces, there is a need to critically evaluate whether a technological space is appropriate for course goals.

Digital Literacy Spaces and Openness

The design of digital spaces has often incorporated the various metaphors for describing the openness of the literacy space and the related learning processes. Raymond's (1999) 'bazaar' metaphor describes their multiple access points where students can learn wherever they are and however they desire and through whichever media they consider most important, which could be shared and repurposed. Learning spaces vary as to their degrees of openness, so who controls the distribution of intellectual property is highly contested – is it the copyright holder or the copyright user? – or how changes in the business model can impact openness, as illustrated by the limitations of posting articles in Scoop.

it or restrictions on downloading open books in Issuu, as well as how copyright laws can control the distribution of intellectual property. New apps such as Wakelet (https://wakelet.com/), with a different business model, can replace them. Such changes in the use of tools illustrate how they must be constantly evaluated as part of the digital literacy space.

Raymond's commons metaphor captures the concept of the abundance of tools and resources that students and teachers can use for both the design and use of these spaces. Creating a commons for sharing educational materials has been an essential influence on the use of materials from the internet, the publishing world or the spaces for teaching and learning themselves. The openness factor can be applied to various literacy spaces, whether it be open resources associated with flipped classrooms or open access publishing for both researchers and students. MOOCs can be open for some participants but locked down to other designers and potential participants. Even when the MOOC is open for learning, it may lock down teaching materials, so they cannot be used outside the MOOC, similar to the case with classroom learning management systems. Flipped classrooms are usually built around a closed classroom but the materials could be opened depending on the goals of the designer. For example, professional development sites, such as the EVO, are open for designing either locked-down or collaborative spaces.

These spaces often incorporate varying degrees of openness, although the trajectory across the spaces has been uneven. The intellectual property controversy in these literacy spaces reflects a general confusion over what the term 'open' means in relation to their affordances, which, for example, can impact their openness to support collaboration not simply among individuals but also between individuals and the surrounding artifacts. The pedagogical value of multimodal literacy forms such as digital stories, for example, can depend on resource availability and teacher attitudes toward openness. The stories themselves can be posted, so they are 'open' to their classmates or, if desired, posted on sites such as YouTube to become open to anyone with access.

MOOCs were originally designed to be spaces where participants from all over the world could learn whenever they wanted, although their degrees of openness would dramatically change. The peer review process was also opened up. One of the contributions of MOOCs has been what Fitzpatrick (2011) called a 'quid pro quid' approach to peer reviewing where if an author wants a paper reviewed, then that author has to review other authors' papers. This means that anyone can review a paper. In designing these spaces, teachers may be neither 'sages' nor 'guides' but designers who have a range of digital resources to draw upon.

The publishing process has been most dramatically affected by the development on the Web facilitating information sharing. The implementation of new technologies has affected paper submission and evaluation. Open access[4] journals have changed the access, so potential authors can have more access to the research. The old adage 'standing on the shoulders of giants' has evolved as authors from all over the world can access greater numbers of articles and therefore freely connect to other authors, in best cases creating an increased awareness of the issues considered important and the research needed to build upon and support new research.

While present to some degree in these spaces, the spread of openness has been limited. Journals today still resemble journals of the past, in the same way that lecture halls today resemble their traditional counterparts, although much different activities may be occurring within them. Changes in the more mundane areas of publishing, such as the length of an article, have occurred in some journals but not in others. The *Journal of Writing Research*, for example, now suggests a 10,000-word limit but does not make it mandatory.

Changes in research evaluation have similarly evolved with more articles being published and different approaches to peer review being implemented. In some areas of science, there has been an increase in publications giving more power to readers to decide their value. One change in publishing has been more open forms of review. Preprints, in particular, have helped these digital spaces by not only opening the peer review process but also allowing early reviews of new research. These early reviews, however, can complicate the publication spaces. These technologically enhanced changes have not affected all fields equally. Prepublication review, where articles are reviewed before being formally submitted, can mean that reviewers may know the names of the authors and vice versa.

As students cross literacy spaces, there is an increased need to understand the openness and constraints of each space. The result has been the creation of new spaces for teaching about publishing – courses, workshops, writing spaces and camps – to help prepare these new researchers entering the publishing space. These spaces address very specific topics such as the meaning of 'reject but resubmit' along with larger issues concerning what constitutes publishing and peer review. These changes in the demands for literacy often require new spaces to support potential authors, whether for publishing or intellectual property law. As more scrutiny is given to academic integrity, authors must acquire a better understanding of the ethical considerations of publishing beyond simply those related to plagiarism often taught in writing classes.

Changes in openness are not simply a response to changes in intellectual property use in response to changes in traditional pedagogy methods. Such changes may mitigate the problems that multilingual writers may have with publishing (c.f. Hanauer & Englander, 2011; Hyland, 2016a, 2016b; Politzer-Ahlesa *et al.*, 2016). The Web has supported an increase in the diversity of journals, providing more choices for publishing but often requiring more consideration in making such choices (e.g. https://thinkchecksubmit.org/). There have also been changes in the traditional ways of learning about publishing. Traditional forms of mentorship and advising have sometimes broken down while there have been increases in the numbers and types of spaces available for publishing, which has meant that students must make more decisions regarding publishing.

The commons metaphor (Raymond, 1999) reflects the ability to include various writing activities for both personalizing the space and providing more autonomy. Designers must decide among different variables which aspects of pedagogy are open and which are closed. Openness has many meanings in describing who can participate in the principles of creating and using academic artifacts. Often, their openness cannot be sustained. MOOCs, for example, were initially designed to be more open so that the more participants there were, the more knowledge could be generated (Downes, 2011; Siemens, 2005, 2012).

Technology has greatly impacted how everyone, including multilingual writers, negotiates the publishing space. Issues such as open access and preprints, for example, have changed who gets published, how long it takes to get published, how published research is accessed and, ultimately, how the research is evaluated. The proliferation of open journals has raised additional challenges for the publication, evaluation and distribution of information. The concurrent rise of open access and predatory journals has meant that students and even teachers need more care and practice in determining legitimate places to publish.

However, the variability of these places could also be surprising for their designers – who are the participants? who is visiting and who is participating? and what happens to texts created in a commons where they can become widely used? (Wiley, 2007). Such surprises illustrate how teachers cannot always control digital spaces, which can provide students more control over their learning. These technologically enhanced literacies can incorporate influences from both inside and outside the multilingual writing community. This is a bazaar where no one literacy space has emerged but rather a multitude of literacies has emerged, none of them dominant but all of them relevant.

Openness brings its own social contexts by challenging the legal constraints on the design and use of copyrighted materials. As OERs have become more available, alternative forms of copyright have been used to support the goals for using their materials, whether for the attribution, distribution or monetary potential of the materials. Early attempts to provide access to previously locked-down materials, as seen at MIT, necessitated changes in how copyright law was viewed. Creative Commons was designed for these purposes. Regardless of the constraints on using these materials, increased sharing can benefit teachers and researchers who have been excluded from a central position in their communities of practice.

Intellectual property law has played an important role in the design of literacy spaces in relation to issues of openness. The uses of intellectual property could conflict with established rules and laws. However, changes in how intellectual property was viewed contributed to the development of designing for openness. Creative Commons has allowed the creators of intellectual property to designate property use. Teachers could contribute to the OER movement by using Creative Commons to allow videos to be resourced, remixed and repurposed by other teachers.

Changes in intellectual property law could have a dramatic effect. Their roles in MOOCs, flipped classes and journals began with the Open Courseware movement (https://ocw.mit.edu/index.htm) which was an initiative of MIT and the Open Learning initiative of Carnegie Mellon (http://oli.cmu.edu), and exemplify the concerns with the removal of constraints on the distribution of intellectual property. Besides the decisions that teachers make about the origins of multimodal texts, their own materials could be either locked down or freely distributed.

The success of these approaches depended on the new perspectives of intellectual property, such as Creative Commons, that provided a better framework for designating how intellectual property could be used. Previous questions such as whether the copyright holder could block the educational uses of the user through legal means could be directly addressed by implementing Creative Commons. Teachers could base their designs on what they knew about the intellectual property status of the materials they wanted to use without having to go to court to retain their rights. At the same time, neither Creative Commons nor fair use could completely address the problems students had with the privacy of their writing.

The intellectual property controversy has further confused what the term 'open' means. MOOCs were originally designed to be spaces that decentralized the role of teachers. New forms were later introduced that allowed participants access to research, connect with others and ask questions. As has often been the case, the development of these new spaces required changes in how intellectual property was viewed. Along with the intellectual property issues, each new digital space creates new challenges for teachers. As MOOC designers struggled with completion rates (Ahearn, 2018), it became apparent that their designs were being appropriated by participants to learn how and when they wanted to. Some of these consequences spread to the classroom. In the bazaar-like classroom, students can learn wherever they are and through whichever media they consider most important. Teachers can design videos that can be viewed anytime, anywhere and as often as desired. These learning spaces, however, may not be purely 'open', as exemplified by the conflict over the ownership of intellectual property.

Openness can be impacted by the decisions to use found materials that carry some form of copyright. The choice of materials for multimodal projects can be constrained by the fair use doctrine[5] (in some countries) for determining restrictions or by using materials with Creative Commons designations or materials in the public domain that are not considered copyrighted and can be freely used. Using digital storytelling in a multimodal space, for example, can be constrained by the types of assignments and the materials required to create them. For example, to best exploit the openness of the internet, students can choose traditionally copyrighted materials and then decide whether their use is legal or appropriate. In these situations, students and teachers are not just exploring new literacies but are also learning about the rules and laws governing the borrowing of materials in these new contexts.

These examples illustrate that openness is not either/or but exists on a spectrum of possible degrees. Digital spaces such as MOOCs and flipped classrooms can combine an open space and a closed space where videos and other teaching materials can be used in different contexts. In the writing classroom, both spaces can be important for expanding the author's audience, a goal that many writing teachers have sought. Openness has economic benefits as well. OERs are often considered a means of lowering the costs of education and can also affect how spaces where materials can be readily shared are created for both teaching and research (Hegarty, 2015).

As is true in these spaces, the evolution of the publication process in both gated and open journals has been augmented with new technologies. Articles are often submitted online as are peer reviews. Publishers can exploit the online process by using copy-detection programs such as Turnitin.com to check for copying, plagiarism and prior publication (c.f. Morris & Stommel, 2017) in the same way that teachers can exploit the spaces in learning management systems for the same goal, although the trajectories of openness can be hard to control.

The design of open access journals, for example, was intended to spread research at zero or low costs. However, gated journals responded by creating various levels of openness with a high cost to the writer but still retaining free distribution. More threatening has been the predatory journals that have lower fees for publishing but without the traditional standards of editorial control or verification associated with traditional journals. These developments have resulted in spaces where authors, especially novices, may have difficulty negotiating the various constraints on literacy (e.g. Elbow, 2007).

Returning to Plato's arguments about the downsides of memory loss due to the dominance of written literacy, there will also be downsides that must be factored into decisions about using spaces. The downside of the development of open access has been its exploitation by so-called 'predatory' journals. Defining predatory journals can be difficult, but generally they are considered journals that lack transparency in their fees, as well as engaging in various practices including highjacking titles, making claims about publishing practices that are not true and threatening those who criticize them with lawsuits.

Predatory journals have raised important concerns in the publishing space. One blog reported on a predatory journal that disappeared, leaving 1500 previously published articles in limbo as to their publication status (RIP OAPL, 2018: para. 2). While admitting that there is no clear definition of predatory journals, *Nature* (2019) described them as 'a global threat'. While some journals have always charged fees, these predatory journals may now charge authors for publishing in disciplines that have never previously been charged fees, sometimes with shoddy peer review and unethical publishing practices including publishing articles without the knowledge of the author.

Openness supports connections for greater collaboration, which can affect both the creation and distribution of student and teacher work. One of the most popular models for this common space is Wikipedia, which combines a technological architecture where individuals can collaborate in creating and editing projects and a social structure that constrains their interactions by employing editors to review what is published. Wikipedia is itself a literacy space, which has illustrated how the openness of the internet can attract more contributors.

Questions of Assessment for Digital Literacy Spaces

Assessment has been one of the most controversial aspects of the design question since assessment can play multiple roles. Traditional means of assessment such as giving grades or even more technologically enhanced methods such as e-portfolios (Crusan, 2010; National Council of Teachers of English, 2015) may or may not be included in a digital space. However, in this framework, assessment refers more to the reflections teachers and students have on these spaces, a process Weller (2020) finds most beneficial about the use of technology. There have been questions regarding the learning outcomes that are most valued and whether these digital literacy spaces can accommodate these outcomes. Can students use these spaces in ways teachers intended? What does Bergmann's admonition to 'reach every child' mean in terms of the outcomes that the institution, the designer and the individual mean? There are three, perhaps contradictory, purposes for assessment: to demonstrate the value of a space, to remediate its weaknesses and to indicate progress for participants. Advocates of these approaches often show positive effects to build momentum for expanded usage.

There are additional questions over assessments as they are in traditional spaces. Curry and Lillis (2019) argue for the importance of research, particularly in the publishing space (see Chapter 7), where they suggest longitudinal research to determine whether students publish their research. Such research could be important in determining the value of a course; however, the resources required for such research can be expensive. A less expensive way, however, is to rely on more extensive lore from teachers who may or may not have successfully utilized the spaces or post-course assessments from students. There is also the student role in assessing their own experiences. Although this approach does not answer the questions that Curry and Lillis (2019) raise, this assessment can inform evaluating the effectiveness of the space and the remediation of its problems.

As Casanave (2017) argues, the value of some literacies may be questioned, especially when they require a great expenditure of resources by the teacher. Multimodal forms of literacy have grown in importance although they may not be a universally accepted form of literacy. Flipped learning has greatly depended on combining lore and research, although formal research has shown mixed results as to whether it improves learning. Setren *et al.* (2019), for example, found limited improvement in a study of economic classes at the United States Army Academy. While they recognize various limitations in their study, such research points to the difficulty not only in finding evidence but, more importantly, in generalizing its results to different learning contexts.

Assessment in digital spaces has always been controversial, particularly for guiding pedagogies. Should writing in digital spaces be assessed similarly to its assessment in print spaces? For both teachers and students, questions of assessment are becoming more complex, including issues regarding effectiveness, transferability across different genres and the social and political issues often resulting from its implementation. Assessment has become a central focus in the evaluation of design. Without having enough teachers or assistants to respond to every paper, peer review has emerged as a possible solution. While it is possible to work alone, designers have frequently created tools to foster collaboration. Therefore, peer reviewing, sometimes abetted by the introduction of new technologies such as one designed at Ohio State (Halasek *et al.*, 2016), has become the standard for writing assessment. The Open University added tools to enable sharing among teachers and students (Ferguson *et al.*, 2019). However, at least the potential for incorporating writing has made it clear that these spaces can also be used for teaching writing even if traditional teacher assessment cannot be implemented.

Another concern is that research may only evaluate accessible elements in the space, such as whether test scores or grades increase in digital spaces; however, in these spaces, these issues are often more complex, requiring alternative approaches for demonstrating their effectiveness. Issues such as completion rates, which may be important in a conventional writing course, may be less so in a MOOC where participants can better control their participation. Therefore, transferring assessments from one space to another has proved problematic; traditional assessments in print spaces may not be as effective in digital spaces.

Balancing the different needs for demonstrating effectiveness has been an important question in determining their relative value. The difficulty with assessment, particularly its role in encouraging implementation, has constrained the introduction of some technologies. There is still a concern for assessing each new literacy space. Tham *et al.* (2018) argue for continually examining the pedagogical importance of introducing each new technology. Such evaluation is particularly important with new and untested tools, which have not always been well received, despite arguments for their potential. Meadows (2019) reports on new directions in using augmented reality in publishing where integrating information makes it easier to access. Virtual reality can be promising spaces for creating relationships among teachers and students, but the most promising spaces, such as Second Life, never materialized because of both their high learning curves and their cost.

Other concerns reflect issues that have also developed outside the classroom. Artificial intelligence and its related algorithms were thought to reflect new ways of thinking, but current approaches have been scrutinized for how they reflect the social and political problems throughout society. They could impact, in both positive and negative ways, what kinds of writing are valued. Similar problems have been raised with even newer technologies such as chatbots. Chatbots, which are extensively used in business contexts to provide a more inexpensive way of giving information to customers, could be adopted to provide information to students, although it is not clear how that will be accomplished. Turnitin.com, which began as a technology to prevent plagiarism, has expanded to include feedback and evaluation functions, all of which may be as controversial as its original goal for detecting copying. The growth of metrics promises new ways of assessing students – how often do they watch a video, where do they pause the video – but these metrics may not reach the teacher or are difficult to understand. The debate over Facebook, once seen as an essential tool for supporting various social causes but now blamed for many of the ills of the current political discourse, has mirrored this cycle of hype and disillusionment. Even open access journals and materials have not always been well received because of questions about their quality.

One of the major roles that teachers play in the design of literacy spaces is in evaluating the teaching of these literacies. The challenges to teaching literacy that Casanave (2017) warned about have also long existed. We can return to Plato's famous observation that literacy itself is a technology (e.g. Ong, 1982) within a deterministic framework so that the choice of a tool or a literacy space can impact the writing that students produce. For example, the invention of the printing press influenced the Protestant Revolution as it was used to spread biblical literacy (e.g. Eisenstein, 1980), and a similar argument has been made for the development of the World Wide Web (e.g. Berners-Lee, 1999), with its decentralized access by large numbers of users and creators who can connect for sharing and developing their pedagogical ideas.

Both student and teacher resistance to these digital spaces has often arisen from lack of effective assessment (e.g. Lieberman, 2018). Such assessments are only part of the process of turning these designs into learning spaces where students can feel that they are creative, engaged and autonomous. These technological spaces have gone through phases of hype, disillusionment and acceptance connected to assessment. Many technologies have been introduced with a tremendous amount of hype and then, as the Gartner Hype Cycle would predict, periods of disillusionment and revision, and then more gradual growth, all of which point to the importance of assessment, despite the controversies, in designing and remediating digital spaces.

More Challenges in Using Technologically Enhanced Spaces

There have been numerous challenges in adapting these spaces for multilingual writing. The challenges have become more problematic because the evolution of these spaces has not been evenly distributed across disciplines; therefore, each change must be evaluated for its relevance to multilingual writing. Changes in one discipline may be manifested in another or may appear differently. This development has undercut the ability of designers in one discipline to share their research. There are also problems with how the promise of the spaces responds to the uneven access to the internet. While the technological spaces have in some, perhaps limited cases, increased access, they have failed to do so in other cases. This unevenness, for example, impacts the growing interest in open access journals.

Teachers and students lacking access to these technological spaces may create workarounds, including redesigning the class to incorporate the technologies in non-standard ways. Slow access or even no access can similarly impact learning in those digital spaces requiring faster access. These concerns pose challenges for teachers that can complicate classroom design to incorporate these new technologies. The 'in-class flip', for example, illustrates a workaround for flipped learning by incorporating all the technological resources within the classroom space (https://flippedlearning.org/syndicated/whats-class-flip).

While MOOCs may not have be intentionally designed for personalized learning, students can better control how they learn and what features of the MOOC they want to incorporate. While sometimes preserving the lecture format, MOOCs allow the students more flexibility and mobility in how they view lectures. The varying roles the teacher can play also challenge how different designs affect pedagogy and learning.

Many of these spaces were designed to create new roles for the teachers and therefore the students. For example, Hart-Davidson's (2014) argument concerning the values of MOOCs, which can also be true for flipped classes, has challenged the 'sage on the stage' model incorporating a 'one-to-many' model. The design of these spaces used several models: sometimes a 'sage' providing these one-to-many lectures, a group of 'sages' each providing individual lectures or a no-lecture model with knowledge contributed by the participants. Each model attempted to use Vygotsky's (1934/1986) zone of proximal learning model, for providing more personalized scaffolding to meet the needs of individual students.

All these literacy spaces have experienced challenges that literacy pedagogies must address, often being affected by the design of other spaces, the introduction of new technologies or changes in teaching methodology, as seen in the interest in translanguaging. Other spaces, such as multimodality, allow for different forms of mixing languages and texts. The flipped classroom was initially designed to provide teachers and students with more personalized learning, which could later be applied to teaching composition.

Videos could better engage their viewers by inserting questions that the viewers could answer (MacWilliam *et al.*, 2013) and by adding captions (Gass *et al.*, 2019; Perez *et al.*, 2013). The development of open access in publishing has changed both how research is published and distributed and how publishing is taught to new authors. The design of alternatives to the traditional classroom spaces has been captured in the metaphors used to describe these spaces. Raymond's (1999) 'bazaar' metaphor describes how these spaces can be decentralized, so learners can better personalize their learning, which has often conflicted with traditional teaching methods, especially in the areas of assessment.

The flipped classroom predates the development of MOOCs, but has grown in importance for teaching English and writing. Initially, flipped classrooms in universities were designed in response to the types of criticisms of traditional learning seen in Wesch's video. A flipped class may begin with rearranging activities for both individuals and groups of students and then by creating new activities and new forms of interactions. Flipped learning spaces can be designed as blended learning spaces combining classroom spaces with technologically enhanced ones. Their implementation in universities often focuses on bringing more active learning (Davidson, 2012) to large lecture classes by recording lectures in shorter videos to be viewed outside the classroom. Active learning has led to different pedagogical approaches in the writing classroom, such as the studio approach, which Sutton and Chandler (2018: 3) describe as 'a process for reflecting on, critiquing, and re-envisioning the way things are done'.

This evolution in design illustrates the potential for supporting different forms of active learning in these digital spaces, which can be enhanced with new tools. Such tools may disappear, be modified or made more expensive or less accessible. This process is not new; today's changes have historical precedents. Dear (2017) describes the development of competing programs – PLATO and TICCIT – as spaces defined by the development of different technologies in different institutional contexts. As is often the case, the internet has increased the availability of new technologies but with more complexity in their terms of use, which can affect their classroom use, as their creators search for ways to make them more profitable.

In part, the New London Group (Cazden *et al.*, 1996) wrote in response to conventional approaches that becoming literate can change both social and economic perspectives. Becoming a blogger or a digital storyteller may not bring the institutional social capital that more traditional forms of literacy bring, but it still has its own value in developing the identity of the writer/creator by resisting the enculturation process that the New London Group criticized. The growth of open access materials and the implementation of new publishing spaces can also respond to the issues surrounding the attainment of social capital as each of these literacies may impact where writers choose to publish and their perceptions of the process.

Not all changes have been positive. Today, the argument that 'Google makes us stupid' (Carr, 2011) assumes, as Plato argued 2000 years ago in *Phaedrus*, that new technologies can negatively impact abilities to read and write. Casanave (2017) echoes the question often asked of digital spaces in multilingual classrooms: Is what is occurring in digital spaces writing or language learning? My first attempt at multimodality was to redesign a banal writing assignment where students were expected to write three paragraphs about their past, present and future to explore the verb forms associated with each time frame. I blogged at the time:

> Since I doubted that this [the original assignment] was the type of assignment nobody would ever do, I thought about how creating these paragraphs and posting them on their own website with their own images could transform the assignment. The website was posted online so that their friends and family, and not just their teacher, could see what they have done. I'm not going to argue that this first attempt at multimodality was any more successful than my other attempts, it does illustrate how I still look at technology: as a way of transforming writing into ways that can extend both the creativity of the author and the potential audience for the writing.

Even this traditional approach to multimodality where texts and images are separated can prepare students for current and future forms of literacy. Belcher (2017) argued that implementing multimodality can prepare students for the types of literacies they may encounter outside the writing classroom. Newer forms such as multimodality, where texts and images are mixed, can play more complex roles in developing academic literacies

(Bloch, 2018), particular for students traditionally struggling with standard forms of language and rhetoric (Bloch, 2015).

The controversy over Plato's relationships between literacy and memory, moreover, is a reminder that there has always been a concern for the downsides of technology. This debate has been included in many aspects of second language learning, particularly the deterministic impact of language (e.g. Phillipson, 1992). The deterministic view of technology assumes that the technology can determine the pedagogical goals. Feenberg (1999) argues that this determinism assumes an autonomous view of technology, which contradicts how the values teachers bring to the classroom and the social contexts in which they teach can affect the development of these technological spaces. However, Feenberg's warning about this deterministic view of technology has been as much an issue for writing teachers.

These concerns are part of how technologies are introduced or repurposed. A discussion on the implication of providing all incoming students at our university with an iPad showed that the most popular app was still for taking notes, the process critiqued by Wesch in his videos.[6] For Watters (2013a), the most important goal for teachers is to have students control accessing these spaces from both inside and outside the classroom, supporting what Jim Groom (n.d.) calls 'a domain of one's own' (https://umw.domains/) where projects can be retained by students after leaving their course, in contrast to many learning management systems that lock out the students after their course is over ('7 Things You Should Know About ... Domain of One's Own', 2019). This Educause paper argues that these domains allow students 'to explore critical questions about digital literacy' ('7 Things You Should Know About ... Domain of One's Own', 2019: 2), which can be an important affordance to add to a digital literacy space.

The growing popularity of multimodality has been consistent with research on alternative forms of literacy that do not 'enculturate' students into the dominant forms of academic discourse. The New London Group discussed the social and economic perspectives in evaluating these different forms of literacy (Cazden et al., 1996). Heath (1983) had shown that different forms of literacy were valued in different cultures, some of which were not found in the classroom. Sweet (1984), a member of the New London Group, also wrote that new forms of literacy were not as valued in the classroom. The development of the internet as well as new forms of technology has added to both the number and the value of these new literacies.

The growing importance of these literacies and their potential for being transferred across contexts (e.g. Anson & Moore, 2017) have partly motivated designing these new spaces in conjunction with traditional print assignments and spaces. It is within this debate over the relative values of such literacies. In practice, however, the participants have much greater autonomy to negotiate this impact. As Feenberg (1999) shows, actors, such as teachers and students, can negotiate the determinism of the technology, so they can better control its implementation. As the technologies used in writing classes evolve, these debates have similarly evolved while issues such as determinism persist. The loss of the ability to remember (e.g. *Phaedrus*) has been dwarfed by the importance of literacy. Nevertheless, the controversies remain. Issues that have arisen in discussions over bias and privacy in artificial intelligence and robotics often raise similar deterministic questions on their introduction into literacy spaces.

Publishing spaces have similarly been impacted by new technologies supporting open access,[7] providing new technologies for publication that may both increase and lessen control over intellectual property. These approaches have led to the creation of new kinds of open access journals that have expanded the creation and distribution of research. The ambiguity of these technologies, however, has meant that openness can be easily appropriated by predatory journals that publish for a fee and traditional gated journals that provide openness for an even greater fee. Therefore, what is meant by 'openness' can be confusing.

The discussion of technological determinism is important for understanding the continually changing design of these spaces. The trajectories of technological implementation in writing classrooms have never been defined in both social contexts. This evolution has not increased linearly. It has been argued, for example, that the more nuanced development of flipped learning after the initial hype, as the Gartner Hype Scale (Panetta, 2018) illustrates, indicated that its trajectory was changing as more teachers became involved.

The same trajectory can be seen with MOOCs as they have become more controlled by institutional and corporate goals while flipped classrooms have evolved more from increased teacher initiatives. These numbers do not mean that the interest in these spaces is waning, but that they are not always achieving their initial levels of enthusiasm and hopes. These developments have always been a part of technological development, although often in various ways. In a series of blogs, Weller (2018a, 2018b) traces the history of their implementations and their impact on teaching and learning, showing that these technologies often address a narrow set of educational problems.

The biggest challenge is therefore to choose technologies that address the educational problems that teachers may find in their classrooms with the availability of more tools. Speaking of the increase in the number of tools for publishing, Whitehouse (2019) argues that tools are being developed more by corporations for more general internet purposes. Therefore, teachers and students have a greater responsibility for adopting them for classroom purposes. This growing complexity has resulted in a greater need for teachers and students to become connected in networks.

With the growing decentralization of these spaces, the challenges of this complexity can be addressed by students as well as teachers. Elola and Oskoz (2017) argued that multilingual students be involved in developing these spaces to better exploit the affordances that the tools offer. Bowen and Whithaus (2013) argue that new forms of multimedia have changed literacy in higher education as well as what it means to be literate in the world today. As Godwin-Jones (2018) argued, digital writing is the current and the future way that many multilingual students will express themselves.

There have been criticisms of the value of these spaces as well. Pedagogical and political issues that have permeated the debate surrounding using technology are as prevalent as they are throughout society. How these technologies can affect teaching writing has been widely framed by multilingual pedagogy and theory. Issues such as translingualism that are debated both within first language (e.g. Lu & Horner, 2016) and multilingual pedagogies (e.g. Atkinson *et al.*, 2015) will affect the future design of technological spaces. Thus, there are concerns that technological use must confront: issues such as distraction and multitasking, privacy, diversity, colonialism and user isolation have entered into discussions of technology in the classroom.

Privacy has been a concern with the controversies around Facebook and new technologies such as artificial intelligence. Using technologies in our daily lives has raised many personal issues, such as privacy concerns, related to teaching and learning about literacy. New technologies, those designed both for the public and for education, have challenged existing models of pedagogies. Teachers face a challenge in choosing from among a plethora of new tools, each with its own affordances, for designing new literacy spaces. Not all these tools have had an immediate impact. The growing interest in wearable technologies, including watches, glasses and various forms of augmented and virtual realities, has begun to impact changes in literacy while still not delivering the promised rewards (Resnick, 1990).

As Stephens (2018) argues, all design features involving technology include such concerns for privacy. Privacy concerns permeate many of the decisions that teachers make in creating digital spaces. Even long-valued classroom goals, such as increasing audiences, entail new concerns for the privacy of the student. However, this debate has framed the design of appropriate spaces and tools for responding to the pedagogical challenges from outside the classroom. Teachers have become the center of this debate, although they may not be rewarded or trained for these new digital literacy spaces. Casanave (2017), for example, has expressed concern over the importance of digital literacies on reading and writing long-form texts, a debate that has raged outside the institution.

The impact of these digital literacies on literacy, however, remains unclear. Carr's arguments about the disappearance of 'long-form' writing from college curricula, as it has in other literacy spaces, often raises consternation and derision about using technology. Some students may wonder why their teachers are not present in the classroom. Other students may question the value of these literacies in an academic context. An older graduate student asked about digital storytelling, 'Why are we doing this?' which forced me to rethink the assignment.

The social, economic and political positions of multilingual writing teachers can impact their usage as digital spaces. This new role as a designer, however, has not always been an easy one. Their choices may be impacted by departmental decisions, institutional values or economic concerns. Some technologies may be free or inexpensive because they are open-sourced, while others may cost money or require expensive yearly subscriptions. Teachers can use these resources to improve student learning, bring authentic materials into the classroom and better integrate current research into teaching. Teachers have many choices for deciding which literacy to integrate into their classrooms, although choices can make their implementation more difficult, depending on the flexibility and cost of the materials, as well as their confidence in their efficacy.

Some commercially available software may have free versions that can be used on a limited basis, but their use may become more limited as these companies attempt to push users to pay for services. These factors can impact the design of digital spaces as has the design of the technology itself. Moreover, as Casanave (2017) warns, teachers and students must face the complexity of these technologies, their poor design and the continual changes with their accessibility as companies struggle to find profitable business models. However, the growth of personal learning networks has responded to the perception of isolation that teachers and researchers often feel, as illustrated with the formal and informal networks surrounding flipped learning (see Chapter 5). The economics of the internet has also affected the design of these spaces. The companies that own the tools for designing have either limited the free affordances to try to push users to pay for more features (e.g. Issuu,[8] Scoop.it[9]) or have gone out of business (e.g. Xtranormal[10]). Continual changes in fee structure for platforms supporting the distribution of online materials can confuse and frustrate those interested in open spaces.

It is not just economic resources that teachers must invest in but also personal time, often without compensation, to learn how these technologies can be implemented. Creating videos for flipped classrooms, for example, can involve much time in scripting and recording the video as well as additional resources for selecting images, fonts and colors. Putting in subtitles so multilingual and hearing-impaired students can follow can be accomplished using free resources such as YouTube Studio, which still involves much extra time, or using expensive subtitling services that may involve less time but cost more money. The openness of the internet can also affect the costs of designing spaces. Publishing videos online can be shared and repurposed as are other open access materials, which can lessen the costs and resources but can involve losing control over one's intellectual property.

Many teachers are overwhelmed by the development of new technologies, causing what Hong calls 'digital duress'. Hong gives two reasons for this condition:

> The first is just feeling stressed due to a constant stream of interruptions combined with fear of missing out. The second, and far more important, is that engagement with this kind of content means that we are spending less time building and maintaining relationships with actual people. (Cited in Anderson & Rainie, 2018: 16)

This fear of 'missing out' can result from the hype of the new technologies introduced as well as the increased needs of teachers that Casanave (2017) discusses. These technologies often require evaluating the hype coming from both educators and corporations. The complexity of these technological spaces has forced teachers to become involved in what Turkle (2017) calls the design, transparency, usability and ownership of all forms of software, including the technological spaces discussed here.

Teachers must understand these debates over the role of technologies to implement them. The debate, for example, over whether cyberspace should be treated the same as the physical world is at the heart of many issues concerning the relationship between digital spaces and physical spaces, as are concerns over artificial intelligence and privacy. Designers of technological spaces may face the same economic pressures as are faced throughout society, in terms, for example, of who can access the internet and who may struggle with how digital resources are distributed. However, such access may be expensive.

As challenges to this use of technology are met, new challenges are continually arising. Research has shown the gaps in understanding the roles of technologies in education. A survey of university leaders in the United States found that 83% believed that they needed a greater understanding of technology in the last five years and that 74% felt that it was more difficult to make decisions about its use ('The Hard Choices of Academic Technology', 2019). The survey also found a gap in the perception that college leaders had about their teachers, often excluding faculty from decisions about technology. They rank faculty resistance second only to budget concerns as a stumbling block in implementing technologies. Teachers interested in designing these technologically enhanced spaces may face difficulty and anxiety in meeting the challenges for determining the value of implementing new technologies and porting their existing approaches to these new spaces. There may also be concerns that these technologies may reduce employment levels.

Teachers have learned that technology always serves pedagogy, not determines it, which means, however, that they must play a greater role in designing its outcomes. But there are also issues every teacher must face, reflecting the larger pedagogical issues that technology has raised. Resistance has always been a part of technological implementations. The UNESCO (2019) report on the adaptation of open access has shown a pervasive indifference among some groups of academics. Lessig (2002) gives an example of how John Phillips Sousa, the American composer, testified to Congress about how the invention of the record player would destroy the tradition of getting together for singing. Similar practices regarding both teaching writing and using technology have incorporated new technologies and new research and have met similar resistance. Flipped classrooms have been viewed skeptically by students, who are concerned with the decentralization of their teachers as have the potential of MOOCs to change higher education (e.g. Krause & Lowe, 2014).

The implementation of these technologically enhanced spaces can bring similar criticisms that the general use of technology in society has raised: a loss of privacy, a sense of alienation and isolation, digital divides in accessibility and the alienation resulting from potentially discriminatory algorithms. A Pew study on the internet and society (https://www.pewinternet.org/2018/04/30/declining-majority-of-online-adults-say-the-internet-has-been-good-for-society/) reports a growing disillusionment toward the internet (Smith & Olmstead, 2018). The controversy over Facebook, from being a tool seemingly essential for social movements to a violator of privacy, illustrates how technology is still playing a controversial role in our society.

The challenges teachers face cannot always be controlled as they are in traditional classrooms because they may involve corporate or institutional decisions so that teaching may require agility to adjust to the changes. Even the goals for these spaces cannot always be controlled by their designers. The funding from the Gates Foundation, for example, to create digital spaces to prepare potential students for college-level writing was undermined by the large number of participants who may not have shared that goal.

No technology is free from these innovations; all involve the issues affecting the roles that teachers and students play. A facilitator, a participant or a designer, therefore, must choose the design of the spaces to achieve the classroom goals. These choices have consequences for student learning and therefore must be continually evaluated for their pedagogical potential. Norman (2013) discusses the importance of interactive testing and revising for any form of design. No implementation can be perfect, so it must be remediated, which is referred to as being in 'perpetual beta'. As Norman argues, this approach can improve the usefulness of a design but not the emotional reaction inherent in the design, with which teachers and students may experiment.

In response to these criticisms, combinations of formal research and less formal personal learning networks have attempted to support creating these spaces. Teachers, in conjunction with their students, administrators, vendors and the designers of the tools they use, have become the 'deciders' over networks design. To implement these forms of learning, flipped learning has to pay more attention to the importance of teacher training, which is considered the 'fourth pillar' of flipped learning. Teachers can create their own personal learning networks to find greater support and share resources, including the creation of webinars such as found in the Electronic Village Online (EVO) both to introduce new teachers to flipped learning and to build a learning community around the methodology. Open access journals can be part of these networks, as are other forms of the open access knowledge creation, including OERs, open data, open courses including some MOOCs, post-publication platforms (e.g. ResearchGate, Academia.edu) and free streaming of conferences.

The Goal of the Book

The goal of this book is to assist teachers to take more control over their use of technology by helping them decide on the appropriate technology for the needs of their students, focusing on how technology has connected these aspects of the teaching and learning process. Teachers may first assess the literacy needs of their students. The spaces discussed in this book – blogging, flipped classrooms, MOOCs, multimodal assignments, publishing – all strive for the same balance, although instead of playing a game, the participants are learning about writing, and the teacher is the primary designer.

In the discussion of these new spaces, we have seen a shift in how teaching is viewed, what Bergmann referred to in an email as the shift from 'Bloom to Maslow', which reflects a shift from thinking about spaces for teaching individual skills, as exemplified in Bloom et al.'s (1956) taxonomy, to a concern with more macro-level processes and the individual as expressed throughout Maslow's (e.g. 1966) work. This shift allows designers to better consider what Dweck (2007) has called 'mindsets' or 'mindfulness', in terms of helping students consider themselves as writers and writing as part of a holistic self-assessment rather than simply an acquisition of skills. While such terms are often overused, they reflect how technology change may require even more dramatic changes in how teaching and learning are viewed.

These relationships between the technology, the teacher and the student are continually changing as the design of the spaces seeks to match the goals of participants just as the rules of a game are in flux to meet its goals and needs. These spaces are not new – all have been extensively discussed – but they are changing as new technologies, teaching methodologies and new approaches to language have evolved. There have been continual changes in technology and the introduction of new technologies that have shifted how teaching and learning are viewed. However, the assumption is that the interaction between the participants' psychologies and the teacher's designs will impact both the writing process and the relationship between teacher and student.

This book focuses on technological spaces that have continued to impact literacy teaching. These spaces – blogging, flipped classrooms, MOOCs, multimodal assignments, open publishing – have strived to balance the affordances of the technologies with the pedagogical goals of writing teachers. Although, instead of playing a game, the participants are learning about writing, and the teacher is the primary designer of the space. These technological spaces can refer to overlapping spaces. A flipped classroom, for example, can include changes in the physical spaces in how the classroom is designed and even the types of furniture used, as well as the technological changes in presenting information.

Therefore, the goal of this book is twofold: to develop a theoretical perspective for developing technologically enhanced spaces and classrooms for connecting multilingual writing and the implementation and remediation of digital pedagogies. As Belcher (2017) has argued, teachers have an important role in facilitating the introduction of digital literacies. Teachers should understand the potential of each space for the literacy development of their students before choosing the more appropriate one for the goals of the course and for the diverse approaches to students' learning. With this understanding, teachers can adapt the spaces to advance their own goals. It is the purpose of this book to address how understanding the affordances of these spaces can help teachers in their decisions.

This book not only discusses these approaches but also attempts to help them consider the technology as well as the possibility for innovation in the field of multilingual teaching and research. Teachers and students play increasingly complex roles. Designers must teach as well as design and often curate information for their students and their own personal learning networks. Students must adapt to these new approaches to take advantage of their opportunities. If these approaches cannot be adapted or if they are not presented in a meaningful way, the students may resist these approaches and possibly undermine their potential. Not every teacher can readily implement every technology, sometimes because of limited access.

This book is, therefore, not an evangelical tract uncritically arguing for implementing technological spaces, but an exploration of how these spaces can impact the interactions among students, teachers and a larger audience outside the classroom. My previous book reflected my personal journey with technology until then. However, since its publication in 2009, the evolution of these spaces has been enormous. But for me the same question arises on how these new technologically enhanced spaces can address the problems faced in the writing classroom.

The Organization of the Book

The remainder of the book examines the various literacy spaces that have been incorporated into writing classrooms. These spaces are interconnected and often overlap, thus addressing similar problems using similar tools but from differing perspectives.

Chapter 2 discusses blogging as an exemplary space for using social media for writing. I begin with discussions about blogging, an older digital space but one that has grown as a space for expressing ideas, as new platforms emerge. As Weller (2018a) argues, no other form has persisted or has evolved as blogging, an early instantiation of Berners-Lee's (1999) vision for the goal of the World Wide Web. Unlike other forms of social media, blogging allows authors to explore their ideas and voices, create new texts and reflect on classroom issues.

Chapter 3 examines the use of multimodality in creating new spaces for introducing multiple literacies. Matsuda (2006) had argued against monolithic literacies in academic discourse, and with the introduction of new forms of multimodality, the number of literacies in academic writing is expanding. The chapter focuses on using digital storytelling in a writing class where students use their life experiences and their choice of artifacts, particularly images and music, to develop their stories. The chapter discusses the relationship between multimodality and academic writing by focusing on shared threshold concepts in the two forms of writing and the potential for multimodality both as an alternative form of literacy and as a space for teaching related threshold concepts to support transfer with print assignments.

Chapter 4 discusses MOOCs as spaces for teaching and learning writing. MOOCs were to be the new direction for higher education. This chapter discusses the development of MOOCs, how multilingual writers use them for their own goals and how they have been adapted for teaching multilingual writing.

The earliest MOOCs were seen to be alternative spaces for a paradigm shift in learning, employing a connectionist metaphor where there was no central teacher but that each participant was a source of information. Metaphors such as 'rhizomatic' (Cormier, 2008a) were used to describe the connections. The later xMOOCs were often developed by large universities for sometimes tens or even hundreds of thousands of participants. Their popularity diminished as problems with completion rates (Ahearn, 2018) and new business models became more widespread, but today they still remain a potential digital space, often without the early hype or grand purpose, for learning about writing (Bloch, 2018).

MOOCs were especially important as writing spaces for non-traditional students who for various reasons could not obtain a traditional education. In this context, MOOCs attracted large numbers of multilingual participants regardless of the course content. They seemed to be a useful, though often controversial space for teaching writing (e.g. Krause & Lowe, 2014).

However, today, MOOCs seem to have abandoned these goals for more niche courses, such as FutureLearn courses on writing literature reviews that originated in Wollongong University in Australia. Their approach did not try to emulate the past approaches that had writing assignments, but focused instead on more limited discussions of the academic paper.

Chapter 5 discusses flipped classrooms and flipped learning in multilingual writing classrooms. Flipped classrooms can be separated into two learning spaces: a group space, such as a classroom, where students can interact with their teachers or classmates, and an individual space where students can work at their own pace, wherever and whenever they want to on class content. The goal of these spaces is to provide students with more opportunities to learn autonomously in different, often more personalized, ways.

Chapter 6 discusses new technological spaces for publishing. By publishing their research, students can enter global spaces for sharing research, but this poses new problems with assessment and audience analysis. This chapter discusses a digital space for publishing, developing a course for graduate students in publishing, and examines new technologically enhanced initiatives in publishing, open access and intellectual property. The chapter examines how students must evaluate these spaces for publishing their research to judge the journal's authenticity and value.

Chapter 7 concludes with a discussion of the implications of these designs on pedagogy. It is the goal that teachers, in conjunction with their students, can control the design of these spaces. It is not simply for their sake, but for the sake of the technologies themselves. Many technologies have failed because they have not considered these complex relationships. The growth in the number and sometimes complexity of these technologies has often made teaching more difficult.

The spaces discussed here raise questions about both teacher and student preparedness for acquiring literacy: What does it mean to be literate? What counts as literacies? What pedagogies best support teaching digital literacy? How do students and teachers prepare themselves to participate in these spaces? What does it mean to be a teacher or a learner in this digital environment? However, as the spaces for digital literacy evolve, finding answers is becoming increasingly important for both teaching and learning literacy in the digital age.

Notes

(1) The use of the term 'multilingual writer' is itself controversial and isused here as reflecting the current usage of the term.
(2) I encountered a problem with using voice threads as a tool for providing responses in a writing classroom after experiencing a medical problem. Although I consider my use a failure, it may not have been the technology but with my implementation that was the cause of the failure (c.f. Anson *et al.*, 2016).

(3)   For a somewhat light-hearted view of fair use, see https://www.youtube.com/watch?v=CJn_jC4FNDo&t=13s.

(4)   For an animated introduction to open access, see https://www.youtube.com/watch?v=L5rVH1KGBCY.

(5)   See https://www.youtube.com/watch?v=Tk2QqjkofoI for a discussion of fair use in publishing.

(6)   For a discussion of the use of iPads in the classroom, see https://www.youtube.com/watch?v=xwLiap74u7E.

(7)   For an introduction to open access, see https://ia802906.us.archive.org/21/items/PaywallTheBusinessOfScholarshipFinalMovieMastered/Paywall%20The%20Business%20of%20Scholarship%20Final%20Movie%20Mastered.mp4.

(8)   See www.issuu.com.

(9)   See https://www.scoop.it/topic/plagiarism for an example of using Scoop.it to collect articles on plagiarism for our writing course.

(10) See https://www.youtube.com/watch?v=8mrmyYmbeX0&t=199s for an example of using Xtranormal in designing videos for a hybrid course on plagiarism.

2 Bringing Students' Voices into the Public Sphere: Blogging in the Debate over Plagiarism and the Use of Intellectual Property

Blogging as a Literacy Space

In the updated version of Sherlock Holmes distributed by the BBC, Dr Watson blogs about Holmes' exploits rather than publishing a journal. Blogging can provide multilingual writers with alternative forms of language and literacy that can have various roles in a writing classroom (Bloch, 2010) since it provides the opportunity to use multiple forms of language that are not always found in classroom-based literacies (Schreiber, 2015). Blogging has been important for expressing ideas and connecting with an audience, sharing the goals found in the writing classroom (Doctorow, 2002). Winer (cited in Powers & Doctorow, 2002: 224) wrote 'Blogging really enables me to have a conversation with the audience'. As Weller (2020) argued, blogging has become as important a part of academic identity as have publications and grants, thus providing an important form of literacy, though one with fewer constraints, for use in writing classrooms.

Blogging is a literacy space, primarily developed outside the classroom, which is becoming a more acceptable form of academic writing. Berkenkotter (2012) identified blogging as illustrative of the changing nature of genres. Blogs can be seen as the latest attempt to increase the speed of publication and the audience for new ideas, which began with the first journals in the 18th century (Bazerman, 1988). Saunders *et al.* (2017), for example, argue that blogs are important for scientists in advancing their personal careers as well as their academic communities. McGlynn (2017) similarly argues that blogs have become an important communication form, especially for junior scientists, since they may be viewed more frequently than academic papers, particularly as they may have a greater distribution (McKenzie, 2018a). Such factors make blogs important in developing voices for writers across various social contexts.

Unlike other forms of social media, moreover, blogging can supply writers with a greater sense of authorship. Blood (2000) noticed that the 'blogosphere' can support 'authors' who have achieved fame as well as promoting a different type of authorship than do other digital literacies. Weller (2012) argued that blogging provides writers with a space for increased identity by expanding their networks and opportunities for interactions, both of which are important for teachers of academic writing. He perceives that these developments have been encouraged by universities interested in increasing the reputations of their faculty.

Therefore, blogs have gained greater acceptance in academic writing. Blogs such as Retraction Watch (https://retractionwatch.com) and The Scholarly Kitchen (https://scholarlykitchen.sspnet.org) publish discussions at the cutting edge of important discussions on academic writing on such topics as ethics and publishing, respectively. In these spaces, students can use the writing skills often associated with formal academic writing or their own favored forms of academic rhetoric. Steele (2016) found that African-American writers used a more personal, performative style, incorporating both traditional forms of predominately oral African-American rhetoric with contemporary adaptations to express modern arguments.

By providing this sense of authorship, blogging can play a more active role in designing digital spaces for academic writing (e.g. Martindale & Wiley, 2005). Murray (cited in Powers & Doctorow, 2002: 226) wrote 'Blogging also helped me rediscover my voice again'. The importance of voice is an important reason for using blogs in creating ideas. Wheeler (2017) gives reasons why blogging helps him clarify his thinking, think more creatively and become more engaged with his readers, all of which can motivate its use in writing classrooms.

While still not as valued as traditional academic papers, blogging has become more widespread among academic writers for expressing opinions to a larger audience. Holland (2018) argues that blogging gives students voices in public discourse, similar to Groom's (n.d.) A Domain of One's Own and our own goals for discussing plagiarizing. These changes in expression support a trend in pluralizing knowledge-making in academic communities of practice. Canagarajah (2018) used the term 'bricolage' to describe this shift in the voices available in the classroom (c.f. Elgort, 2017). Matzke and Garrett (2018) also used the term 'bricoleur' to describe their decentralized approach to studio classes. A *bricoleur* can use whatever materials that are readily available (Levi-Strauss, 1964). Using this metaphor for textual borrowing, blogs, those published both on the internet and in the writing classes, can be used to challenge the traditional role that texts play in academic writing. As scientific papers now address more specialized audiences (Somers, 2018), blogs are being directed at explaining and arguing to a more general audience. Topics that may be too new for publishing in scholarly journals may be addressed in blogs.

Knowledge can be made more accessible to audiences who may lack the background to read academic journals, in part because blogs can address issues using a less formal voice. A survey of academic writers voted blogging as an alternative to academic publishing (Taylor & Francis, 2014). Emerson (2016) finds that scientists are using blogging to write for broader audiences. She discusses a physicist who found that blogging gave her a voice she did not know she had. She cites another scientist who blogged to express his passion for his subject as well as to connect with other enthusiasts outside his community.

For these reasons, blogs provide an invaluable resource on current topics such as ethics and publishing, which may be more current and relevant than information found in academic papers. Therefore, they have been used in various literacy spaces both as texts for potential borrowing and as a heuristic for exploring the writing process: with digital storytelling to facilitate the reflection and transfer of threshold concepts; with Massive Open Online Courses (MOOCs) as a form of response to the lectures or discussions; and with flipped classrooms for creating individualized, active learning.

Blogging as a Literacy Space in the Academic Writing Classroom

What makes blogging even more important for the writing classroom is the sense of authorship it can engender. In-school blogging has produced similar personal expressions. Crowther (2017) found that blogs gave her students a stronger sense of their selves and persona in their writing. Similar forms of expressive, sometimes oral rhetoric, were found in the blogs of African multilingual students (Bloch, 2015). These factors may help student writers take greater control of their writing. Yancey (2004) found that online writing provided students with a space they could control even without the teacher, which illustrates blogging's potential for expressing ideas without the necessity to produce the 'correct' writing often entailed in formal writing assignments.

The affordances of blogging could also provide multilingual classroom teachers with a space where students can discuss and debate issues publicly, at least within the 'public' space as defined in the classroom and in whichever forms of writing they choose (c.f. Elgort, 2017). Providing such a space can impact the writers' sense of audience. The popularity of blogs for readers outside of their writers' traditional communities of practice enables them to become 'public intellectuals' in debates that go beyond their traditional audiences. The blog The Scholarly Kitchen, for example, is cited in chapters on publishing and open access since it is a source of controversy which the students addressed in their writings

(Bloch, 2008a). The permanent and public nature of blogs can contribute to creating in the classroom what Habermas (2001) refers to as a 'public sphere', which he defines as a place for debating the rules and norms of society that have generally been private.

> The bourgeois public sphere may be conceived above all as the sphere of private people coming together as a public; they soon claimed the public sphere regulated from above against the public authorities themselves, to engage them in a debate over the general rules governing relations in the basically privatized but publicly relevant sphere of commodity exchange and social labor. (Habermas, 2001: 27)

Blogging can emulate this public sphere inside the writing classroom by allowing participants to discuss publicly what Habermas calls the rules that govern the social activity of society, or what are referred to today as communities of practice (Lave & Wenger, 1991). Crowther (2017) found that blogging allowed her students to publicly discuss subjects about which they were initially apprehensive. This public sphere can be implemented in an academic writing class as a space where students can debate crucial institutional issues, issues they may be 'clueless' about (Graff, 2003).

The key affordance that blogging provides to these literacy spaces is its flexibility in addressing different audiences. As Myers (2010) has argued, blogging provides writers with rhetorical devices allowing them to consider their audiences in different ways. As Emerson (2016) found, bloggers can expand their audiences through links and images and better conceptualize the needs of their audiences for additional information. Therefore, these audiences can be more varied and complex than would be addressed in a classroom. The writers could incorporate ideas and arguments directly aimed at a specific audience. The audience, in turn, could later incorporate these arguments into their own papers, thus giving student voices and personal forms of English a greater role in classroom literacies.

Thus, a blogging space was designed to supplement the more formal writing spaces. Blogging had two purposes in our classroom: to generate well-developed ideas for their academic writing and to immerse them in the debate over textual borrowing and the rules that constrain its usage. The different ways that blogs can be used have encouraged us to expand their usage in academic writing classrooms. Although classroom-based blogging is not consistent with Habermas' (2001) definition since, in our classroom, the students were 'coerced' into blogging as part of their classroom grade, blogs were important spaces for contested speech forms, which the students could still benefit from by giving them a stronger sense of themselves as authors connected in a network (Shirky, 2009) with others on a topic that could impact their academic lives.

Equally important is the role of blogging as a traditional heuristic. Unlike its shorter contemporary forms such as Twitter or Facebook posts, the longer form of blogging lends itself to support the roles of the literacies of the academic writing classroom, particularly in its support of more reflective thinking associated with academic discussions. By reflecting on these issues first in their blogs, students could not only develop more complex writing skills but also navigate academic writing outside their writing classroom.

Plagiarism, Intellectual Property and Blogging

The goal for designing this space was to have students participate in the debate over the various issues surrounding textual borrowing.[1] The debate both inside and outside the academy regarding this relationship between intellectual property and plagiarism means that, despite its controversies, connecting these issues can be important not only for helping students understand the norms and rules underlying questions of plagiarism but also because the debate over intellectual property,[2] which affects teachers and students, is itself a topic of concern in the classroom (c.f. Bloch, 2008a; Pecorari, 2016).

Our institution, for example, made it clear that acts of copying or plagiarism would be punished. However, the complexity of these issues, along with the often harsh punishments for violations of the rules, has complicated an already complex learning environment. Blogging can provide a safe space for discussion of issues that students would deal with in their other classrooms (Yancey *et al.*, 2014). With its role both as an important form of social literacy and for developing the voice of the author, blogging could provide a safe space for discussing controversial issues, such as plagiarism and intellectual property.

Addressing these issues in a writing class is not new. Robillard (2008) has reported on several pedagogical approaches, including her own, to incorporate topics related to plagiarism into freshman-level composition courses. We started with a problem and then created a digital space to address the problem. Our implementation of blogging, however, was designed to address how problems regarding voice and authorship could impact how the students were using these forms of intellectual property. Given this complexity, therefore, blogging could be included in discussions on plagiarism that do not simply address rules on how much can be copied. Pecorari and Petrić (2014) have argued that pedagogies focusing on plagiarism should not simply provide advice but also engage the students in discussions on the issues regarding textual borrowing. Providing a digital space for these voices that have previously been excluded from such discussions (e.g. Graff, 2003) has also impacted the design of other literacy spaces, such as MOOCs (see Chapter 4), for discussions, interactions and the expression of ideas.

Blogging, therefore, can be used for developing students' ideas before writing a text. By focusing the blogs on a classroom-based assignment, the blogs could be remixed as are other texts, so the bloggers could become both creators and distributors of ideas and not just consumers, as Berners-Lee (1999) envisioned. Unlike how multimodality could be used as an alternative literacy (see Chapter 3), our use of blogging, at least initially, focused primarily on having students discuss and reflect on ideas from print texts. With multimodal assignments, students could also use blogging to explore the relationship between digital and print assignments, which might foster transfer (e.g. Perkins & Salomon, 1988). Thus, the goal was to develop their voices in the blogs before writing about the issues. However, it became apparent that with certain rhetorical functions, blogging allowed them to express themselves more forcefully. Therefore, writing a conclusion was found to be better suited to blogging, so students were often asked to cut and paste text suitable for the conclusion directly from their blogs to their print texts, which could also help demonstrate the value of the blogs.

Their print assignments included summarizing the texts (Hirvela & Du, 2013), evaluating and synthesizing the issues discussed and arguing about those issues. Students could use whatever form of English with which they felt most comfortable. This ability to explore their preferred forms of language was important in the design. Such freedom could be important to even the most experienced writers. Emerson's (2016: 54) physicist, for example, found that not being restricted to passive forms was not only fun but also made her feel 'more complete'.

The students often blogged on these issues, initially as a heuristic to generate ideas, and later to create texts for the students to borrow. Heuristics can be important in helping students generate ideas for their essays. Through both their print and digital texts, the students could participate in the often emotional debate over what constitutes plagiarism and how to deal with it.

The students entered a debate already populated with extensive research on plagiarism, often with contradictory findings, that provided an opportunity for students to express their own voices (c.f. Abasi *et al.*, 2006; Angélil-Carter, 2000; Buranen, 1999; Chandrasoma *et al.*, 2004; Deckert, 1993; Fox; 1994; Howard, 1999, 2007; Keck, 2010, 2014; Li & Casanave, 2012; Matalene, 1985; Ouellette, 2008; Pecorari, 2001, 2003, 2008, 2015; Pecorari & Shaw, 2012; Pennycook, 1996; Rogerson & McCarthy, 2017; Sapp, 2002; Shi, 2004, 2006, 2016; Sunderland-Smith, 2005, 2008). Many of these texts, or excerpts, were used to populate the digital space with various ideas and issues about which the students could blog.

This debate over copying and textual borrowing occurs across all academic, professional and even political communities and are discussed in staff workrooms, academic conferences, scholarly publications, as well as in various media – magazines, newspapers, television shows, movies and blogs – wherever there is a concern with the implications of this issue for our educational and creative lives. While the students did not read this research, it provided a plethora of issues that could be introduced into the classroom.

As new forms of literacy spaces have been introduced into the writing classroom, issues concerning intellectual property and plagiarism have grown more complex. The importance of multimodal literacy draws upon different approaches to borrowing and remixing different types of intellectual property that can be readily downloaded from the internet, whether it be under copyright, Creative Commons or in the public domain (Bloch, 2012). The popularity of MOOCs, which have great appeal for multilingual students (see Chapter 4), has raised questions relating to dealing with instances of plagiarism that were not initially considered (Young, 2012).

As the blogs were not shared outside the classroom, they provided only a limited voice to the debate often within the power structure of the institution, which could be seen as a limitation of the pedagogy. Institutional policies regarding plagiarism, on the other hand, tend to be absolute and universal. These policies can be implemented top down from the institution, so that students may or may not understand them but are still at risk of violations. Therefore, it is important that all participants understand the rules regarding intellectual property use to the same degree as those who enforce these rules (Bloch, 2012). However, this relationship is often misunderstood (Abasi *et al.*, 2006), much to the detriment of students who have difficulty understanding why they must cite sources, which could result in accusations against them of plagiarism with the possibility of punishment.

This imbalance in understanding not only places students at risk of institutional censure but also impacts the quality of their writing that relies on textual borrowing. In this approach, blogging played an important but secondary role to the print texts. After discussing the reading materials, the students posted on their own blogs on a class site, which was locked so only their classmates could read it. Each week, they posted at least 300 words primarily related to their class readings or personal experiences, as well as briefly responding to the other students' blogs. A few students had experience blogging in their own language; however, since the writing space in blogger.com was similar to that of any word processing program, only a short introduction about using links and inserting images was necessary. While having class blogs limited the students' ability to publish outside the classroom, they were easy for teachers to monitor and for students to access their classmates' ideas and arguments. The site Blogger.com (www.blogger.com) was primarily used to host the blogs. In the next part of this chapter, I will illustrate how the students used this digital space to develop their ideas and texts.

Discussion of the Students' Blogs

Reflecting on plagiarism

In this section, I will examine how students used digital literacy as a heuristic in conjunction with print literacy. The value of blogging can be seen in how the students' reflections are consistent with what is found in the research. One issue frequently discussed was 'Why do students cheat?'. In this blog, the students were asked to discuss whether they had plagiarized or knew someone who had plagiarized. This research indicates that students bring various attitudes to the classroom that shape their ideas and practices. However, often their voices were not incorporated into this discussion. The blogs illustrated how digital literacy could be used to remedy that problem. Here, for example, a graduate Korean student recalled an incident when she was an undergraduate.

> When I was college student, I took a course. It's a literature class about Romantic composer. ... In the midterm exam period, I got a new task from literature instructor. At that time, I was in panic, because I had another assignment and had to prepare to take an exam. So, I decided to get some help from the internet. On the internet, I searched about my task and copied it and pasted it into my paper. So, I made a new paper. Even, I didn't learn what plagiarism is and how can I avoid plagiarism. So, I didn't need to worry about plagiarism. Plagiarism didn't matter. Of course, I couldn't get a good grade, but it was not a poor grade, and I could spend more time to study for another exam.

Blogs allow students to discuss issues they may not feel comfortable discussing in a regular classroom. This student discusses her own motivation for plagiarizing: her feelings of helplessness, her lack of understanding of textual borrowing and the appropriate institutional responses to her alleged violations of the institutional norms. In one of the articles they read, Rose used the metaphor of being like a janitor at an art gallery to discuss his own feelings of isolation from the dominant institutional norms, specifically in this case regarding textual borrowing. This student's concern about feeling 'in panic', without knowing much about the topic of the assignment or how to avoid plagiarizing the texts, echoed the concerns both Rose (1989) and Blum (2009) expressed about contradictions between student and teacher values toward textual borrowing.

The relationship between the students' representation of textual borrowing and their strategies for reading and summarizing has similarly been explored in blogs. As Rose contended, the blog argues that plagiarism is a result of 'the culture of the university', which positions students where they may not know enough about the assignment to avoid copying information while lacking the knowledge of citation practices or the necessary skills for paraphrasing. The blogging space provided the opportunity to safely explore different perspectives or motivations for plagiarizing.

The Moral Dimension of Plagiarism

One of the goals of the writing assignments was to discuss the moral dimensions of plagiarism, so before writing their argument papers, students blogged about this connection with the moral dimensions of research, such as data fraud or the misrepresentation of information. Blogging supported student participation in various debates on the effect of plagiarism on the individual and on the integrity of the institution (e.g. McCabe *et al.*, 2001), fraudulent actions (Posner, 2007) or the degradation of classroom learning (Blum, 2009).

Blogging revealed the arguments that students perceived most important about the topic. While this moral dimension seldom appears in the research, it appears in arguments on how plagiarism can have a negative effect on individual development, an argument that was not discussed in the articles they read.

> The most reason why I think that plagiarism is bad is because it kills the creativeness of one person. Then, this results the decline of the creation. People should learn that creativity is the most fearceful weapon that we, human have.

Here, a Chinese blogger seems to take a strong moral position on plagiarism, as indicated in his term 'kills the creativeness', which emphasizes the negative effect of copying on individual development as opposed to its impact on society or the integrity of the university, which are often cited as reasons for institutional concern. The latter discussion is sometimes found in university handbooks and on websites discussing plagiarism along with discussions of its effect on the university and the student's classmates.

The underlying assumptions or warrants (Toulmin, 1958) regarding these arguments often reflected traditional concepts of rectification of moral deficiencies, frequently attributed to Confucius, where acting in a proper manner will both develop one's self and bring harmony to the community (e.g. Mao, 1995). As a digital literacy, blogs allow for students using their own language, Although the blogs may seem full of grammatical issues, they often contained the result of mixing rhetorical forms thought important in academic writing. Not only could students remix the linguistic elements with more formal English writing, but they could also use the rhetorical elements they were importing from their own cultures.

Intentionality versus cultural difference in plagiarism

Cultural issues, for example, are often assumed to be a major cause of problems with textual borrowing, as Redden's (2007b) story about plagiarism allegations at Duke University, indicated. This cultural component is often controversial. As the following student blogs show, plagiarism was not simply seen as resulting from cultural traditions but as much from pedagogies that have ignored it. As one student complains, 'I didn't learn what plagiarism is and how can I avoid plagiarism', echoing how Rose describes Marita's lack of the requisite skills for knowing how to cite sources to her lack of voice in expressing original ideas about a topic on which she knew little.

Although the argument that copying may be culturally acceptable in some non-Western cultures is no longer generally acceptable (Bloch, 2008a), culture remains a powerful meme in discussions about institutional attitudes regarding plagiarism. In response to a question about the importance of such cultural differences, a Turkish student who had been a teacher before entering graduate school reflects on her students' attitudes, as well as her own, that may cause such misunderstandings.

> I can say that as a student I did not take any training about plagiarism in Turkey. Because of that reason, students never think that it is wrong or in other words, they never think that copying assignments is stealing someone ideas. I believe that it is the main problem. I do not have any resources to support my ideas since these are my experiences. In my opinion, one reason may be the lack of sources of the teachers.

In this blog taken from Rose (1989), the Turkish blogger identifies cultural and developmental issues that seem to override a concern about the moral issues.

> She [Marita] had no idea about why the assignment was considered as a plagiarized work. She used outside sources because of two reasons. First reason is her father's sayings about expressing ideas and second reason is the lack of knowledge about academic work. She did cite but not all of them and she could not distinguish her work from the source. The event was a very good experience for her, and she must have learned a lot. Since she was a very motivated student, she would not do it again for sure… Therefore, school's response to Marita was right.

Although the cultural issues were not the primary focus of Rose's analysis of Marita's plagiarism, many students used their blogs to focus on the cultural consequences of Marita's father telling her not to speak unless she had something to say, an important cultural factor. The free form of blogging may have supported students exploring various arguments regarding plagiarism. This student, for example, not only dwells on cultural issues, but also connects these issues with the developmental problem of judging whether Marita's lack of quotation marks was an act of plagiarism (e.g. Pecorari, 2008).

Students could also use similar rhetorical strategies needed for the class, such as summarizing. Summarizing is sometimes a neglected skill in the classroom. Howard *et al.* (2010) found that summarizing can be difficult for L1 writers to understand, which is consistent with what Pecorari (2008) found about second language (L2) writers. The combination of not having the topic knowledge to understand the subject or the writing skills to avoid plagiarism seems to doom students to commit a violation.

The students often identified with the readings, so blogging provided a space for exploring the reasons for such identification. For example, they strongly identified with Rose (1989), who seemed to take a more positive pedagogical view since although Marita knew little about the topic of her assignment, she cared enough to consult an encyclopedia to complete it. Students often responded in similar ways, focusing on the personal dimension of Marita's story as opposed to the social context of the classroom. Students may not share that position but respond to what they see in her personal background as having a good and caring *ethos*. Despite these controversies, cultural differences are still a justification for discussing plagiarism, particularly as they impact educational practices. Here, for example, a Korean student attributes the difference in the importance given to plagiarism in different cultures.

> I think this is because of the culture difference, that we do not take plagiarism as a serious problem. We do think that taking other's work and pretending to one's own is cheating. However, when someone uses other's contribution without citing or without mentioning the original reference is not that serious, except in academic field... we consider many things as common knowledge, which we think that citing is unneeded.

> However, this loose attitude to plagiarism may lead information miss transferred. When people do not take serious about what they said, just using something they heard and transferring to others, they might pass the error information. If they do read the original document, the mistakes will be less.

Despite the controversies surrounding the importance of plagiarism, many composition teachers feel an overconcern with plagiarism is counterproductive (e.g. Pecorari, 2015), and while cultural differences were a reason for why the students were expelled from Duke University (Redden, 2007b), there was still a concern that the international students were more severely punished because of perceived cultural differences. Such differing opinions allowed for an open debate over the issue in the papers and blogs.

In the foregoing blog, the student responds to these controversies with a more complex argument than is sometimes found in the literature regarding culture: that while cultural differences may be an issue, particularly in deciding about the citation of common knowledge, such cultural differences do not necessarily exonerate the students. Her reference to 'common knowledge', a topic often discussed in class, raises several complex issues related to distinguishing between imitation and originality that relate to determining what is considered proprietary or common knowledge. The meaning of such terms may vary across cultures, although the student seems to argue that there are pedagogical differences in her previous university as well as the often discussed cultural ones.

Blogging in a Social Context

This chapter has explored blogging both as a heuristic for generating ideas and as a semi-public space for immersing students in institutional debates regarding plagiarism. Using blogging to create digital literacy spaces illustrates that how it is contextualized can impact student literacy. To satisfy course goals, the blogs were initially used as a heuristic for developing ideas later used in academic papers. However, as the course evolved, blogs were repositioned as texts that students could use in their writing. This shift reflects an evolution in our thinking about language. As new spaces were developed, such as by using multimodality, blogs could be used for other purposes, thereby demonstrating their high level of interoperability (Palfrey & Gasser, 2012) across various platforms.

However, students were also free to make the blogs their own. As seen in the examples, the students were free to write using their own voices without concern for correction, thus providing value not only to the form of their expression but also to the expression itself. Blogs' value as a form of literacy in the multimodal classroom will depend largely on how they become valued in the larger academic communities, particularly in how they can be cited in academic papers.

Consistent with Berkenkotter's (2012) argument, the blogging space was not considered a new genre but a bridge or a scaffold to the print genres. This relationship between the print and digital spaces will be explored further in Chapter 3 on multimodality. The issues involved in this discussion consider specific pedagogies and policies implemented in our institution but may still be generalizable to other programs. These issues are continually changing, particularly with the development of new technologies (Roll, 2017) and new values for blogging.

Blogs are not simply tools for helping students write academic papers but can also be part of the digital space, though not necessarily as an independent form of literacy. How they function can be greatly influenced by the design of the space. They can be either individually or group authored; each approach can foreground the type of authorship underlying the course. Blogs can be used for various pedagogical purposes. For example, they can exemplify the 'reading to write' approach as a means of helping students better understand what they read and then transfer it to other contexts. Other technologies such as Twitter, which has also increased in popularity in academic writing for short, immediate responses to ongoing controversies, provide different affordances for teachers to implement.

The design of the blogging space is still developing in importance in academic writing, although it may never replace formal research papers despite the testimonies of academic writers. In the class space, blogging can support the public voice of the students, allowing them to explore their ideas in whichever language they choose. Plagiarism was the topic chosen, but any topic related to public discourse can be selected. The power of students' voices can depend more on the architecture of the platform for reaching extended audiences. However, critics of these participatory literacies have raised concerns about the lack of traditional forms of filtering and verification on both authorship and the quality of the information that is found in blogs and similar forms of digital literacy (e.g. Carr, 2011; Foer, 2017).

These same features may also positively impact students in developing ideas and in reflecting on their writings. In the examples discussed in this chapter, blogging was judged to best fit the multiple goals for creating alternative literacy spaces to support new forms of literacy and extended audiences. These goals not only impact the types of writing in which students engage but also create different contexts for writing and reflecting. In these contexts, the blog can reveal the thinking pattern that the students are employing in developing their arguments as they explore ideas through their own levels of English language development.

The context of this digital space also illustrates the different affordances that different technologies bring to the design. Blogging was chosen because its affordances allowed for more spontaneous forms of writing, for some interactions with the audience and for designing texts that could contain images and links chosen for the needs of the audience. The designers of this space could then choose how to implement the blog and how to connect it to the course's other assignments. These blogs illustrate the complexity and originality of the students' voices on a topic that they are frequently excluded from discussing. Moreover, by providing a rhetorical space where students can mix various forms of academic and vernacular language, the classroom can become a space for authentic forms of code meshing that Canagarajah (2010) and others have promoted (e.g. Schreiber, 2015).

The main constraint was, nevertheless, the requirement to blog in English. However, not grading or correcting the blogs could allow for greater freedom in using whatever form of English they chose without concerns for grammatical correctness. Ultimately, as Feenberg's (1999) discussion of determinism predicts, the value of blogging is impacted by a combination of its evolving role as a form of academic literacy outside the classroom, how teachers value it inside the classroom and how students negotiate these relationships. Will blogs, for example, become as valued as citations to articles in peer-reviewed journals? Teachers can exploit this development but may not increase their value, as Canagarajah (2018) implies, which may be implemented at the institutional or disciplinary levels.

The design of the literacy space for blogging was equally important in impacting its usage. Blogging was implemented as a digital literacy because of its architecture, which is unlike that of other technologies such as Twitter or Facebook, promoting goals for literacy, particularly those related to developing and evaluating critical ideas. The affordances of this architecture supported sharing ideas through commenting on and even citing their classmates' blogs. Students themselves had a concern with the openness of these spaces. In one case, a student contacted me years after the course with a concern for displaying his language skills after finding his blog was open.

We wanted to encourage students to 'cut and paste' from their blogs with proper attribution to meet the course goals for evaluation. This approach was meant to remediate the problem we had with personal expression. How well the students addressed these pedagogical concerns could also affect how the literacy designs were implemented. The design presented here did not address the development of the students' repertoire of linguistic skills (c.f. Elgort, 2017). This design could explain the problems with language development that Casanave (2017) pointed out.

This design had several limitations. Unlike the students described by Crowther (2017), our students did not use their blogs beyond the class assignments. Despite the limitations, blogging has remained an important literacy space and an alternative form of literacy despite the popularity of new forms of technological literacies, such as Facebook and Instagram. Groom's 'a domain of one's own', as are blogs, is intended to represent the democratization of academic writing, and is cited as a warning that these other forms of social media are challenging blogging as a space for academic literacy. However, its future as a form of literacy is less certain. McKenzie (2018b) speculates about whether the closure of a popular academic blogging site at Harvard signals the decline of blogging as a voice in academic literacy.

There are still many unaddressed issues about using blogging in digital spaces. We do not know whether the students' concerns regarding plagiarism could have impacted the institutional debate since the 'public sphere' was not shared beyond the classroom, which is a limitation on the 'public sphere' that blogging can create. This lack of engagement with the institutional power structure resulted from another design decision to lock the blog to facilitate discussion within the group as well as a lack of political initiative to have the students engage with the institutional structure.

Another unanswered question concerned using blogs for transfer between the digital and the academic writing spaces. This question is complicated by the 'perpetual beta' nature of the blogging space, which has evolved with changes in the blogging technology. Our initial use of blogging primarily focused on its use as a heuristic, consistent with early work on heuristics in process (e.g. Flower & Hayes, 1980; Young, 1976). However, as the course developed and the design of the course changed, we saw more connections with other forms of academic literacy. We first tried to facilitate this transfer by asking students to 'cut and paste' from their blogs into their papers, particularly when they had used a stronger and more evaluative voice in their blogs. Later, prompts were added for reflecting on the connection between their choices of images and their narratives. However, we still have no evidence that blogging helped with other rhetorical issues in students' writing assignments (e.g. Yancey *et al.*, 2014). This evidence needs to focus on how they could transfer their blogging voices into more formal, and often more valued literacy spaces, such as an academic paper.

Finally, we could not answer the critical questions whether through this reflective analysis of their literacies, the students could avoid plagiarizing, which would necessitate a longitudinal study we could not undertake. Curry and Lillis (2019) call for more longitudinal studies to explore such questions; however, as Latour (1987) states, research can be expensive, requiring resources to which only a few elite researchers may have access. Despite these limitations, using blogging still provides valuable insights into what students are thinking about the plagiarism debate and how new forms of literacy can facilitate the construction of arguments in an academic writing course. More importantly, this discussion shows how using blogs as a digital literacy evolved with changes in how they were used across various assignments and literacy spaces, a concept in internet design known as interoperability (Palfrey & Gasser, 2010).

Notes

(1) To see a collection of articles from which those discussed here are drawn, see https://www.scoop.it/t/plagiarism.
(2) An interesting example of this can be seen in Bergen (Norway) University's video on plagiarism comparing a plagiarist to Ebenezer Scrooge (http://www.youtube.com/watch?v=Mwbw9KF-ACY). This theme is often found in videos designed to educate students about plagiarism (Bloch, 2012).

3 Multimodality as a Digital Space

Multimodal literacy spaces can take many shapes in their use as a form of literacy. Lim and Polio (2020) found that various forms of multimodal assignments and projects were assigned in university-level classes. Not only has multimodality been an important literacy skill that students bring to the classroom, but it is also one that has long existed outside traditional class spaces (e.g. Gere, 1994). The growing role of multimodality in the literacies such as Snapchat, Instagram and WeChat can make the mixing of images and texts, often a feature of multimodality, a common form of linguistic expression that can be found in many areas of writing pedagogies. Digital spaces have long been discussed in academic writing (e.g. Kress, 2003, 2005) and in writing courses (e.g. Palmeri, 2012; Selber, 2004).

Reid *et al.* (2016) observed that in undergraduate courses in their university, multimodal assignments were frequently found in writing across the discipline (WAC) courses. These multimodal literacy spaces have evolved along with changes in the technologies themselves and the backgrounds of the students using them (e.g. Gonzalez, 2015). Certain aspects, such as the use of narratives, have long been metaphors in academic writing (e.g. Medawar, 1984) as has the use of images and photos to provide alternative forms of expression (e.g. Kress, 2003, 2005). There has been a growing interest in using digital stories in undergraduate second language (L2) writing courses (e.g. Bloch, 2015; Hafner, 2015; Hafner *et al.*, 2015; Nelson, 2006) to meet various goals for personal expression. Gonzalez (2015) argued for connecting multimodality and genre studies as a means for students to explore their own forms of language, an approach to implementing translingualism in the classroom.

My interest in multimodal literacy spaces began many years ago when I was thinking about how to transform a rather pedestrian writing assignment into something more interesting. I had the idea that if the students added images and placed the assignment on a web page, the assignment would be more meaningful. Since then, digital literacies have grown in importance, particularly with the development of the World Wide Web (Berners-Lee, 1999) that has encouraged more creativity.

The introduction of multimodal literacies into the classroom further advances the importance of such discussions of narration, voice (e.g. Ivanič & Camps, 2001), intellectual property (Bloch, 2012), and alternative forms of literacy. As the space developed, it became clear that blogs were being used as an additional space for visual and musical texts that could be cited in arguments. Multimodal spaces have been important in our courses for exploring different aspects of the writing process from different perspectives.

Storytelling itself can be considered a threshold concept for academic writing that can be incorporated into the design of a multimodal literacy space. The implementation of digital storytelling in academic classrooms is supported by the research of Bruner (1994) and Medawar (1984) on storytelling in academic writing. Going back to Plato and Aristotle, there was a dichotomy between storytelling and argumentation; however, as academic discourse has become more argumentative in light of the 'paradigm shifts' (e.g. Kuhn, 1962) that described conflicting theories that had to be argued, some differences have melded together. Changes in discussions of voice have similarly impacted how students can approach academic writing from different perspectives.

The use of multimodality outside the classroom has demonstrated another key concept: the development of an authorial voice. As with blogs (Chapter 2), multimodality provides support for authorial voices in academic writing. Both Canagarajah (2015) and Tardy (2016) have examined how voice in academic writing has similarly provided a framework for how the more verbal technological spaces may help scaffold students in developing voices that can be transferred (e.g. Bloch, 2018). Using textual borrowing in academic writing can establish both the credibility of the claims and the ethos of the author (e.g. Latour, 1987). Plagiarism involves allegations of breaking the rules. These rules can vary greatly across genres as well as types of papers (Howard, 1999), which can be both a dilemma and an opportunity for composition pedagogy since there is a great deal of confusion about what constitutes plagiarism and how to respond to it.

While multimodality could be considered a new form of literacy, it was consistent with the goals for blogging. We had used blogging as a heuristic as found in process writing approaches (Flower & Hayes, 1980) and then later as a form of text production in the print texts. The introduction of multimodal literacies did not replace blogging but did provide alternative perspectives on addressing traditional classroom issues. Multimodal literacies provided similar opportunities for alternative approaches but with affordances for addressing these issues. Many challenges remain concerning the teaching of multimodal literacy. Belcher (2017) argued that the domination of print literacy has been changing. Even when successfully introduced into the classroom, however, there remains a pedagogical question of whether multimodal literacies should be considered alternative literacies or as bridges aiding the developing traditional print forms. As a result of these controversies, multimodal literacy has remained a contested space for multilingual writing (Casanave, 2017).

Belcher (2017) argues that multimodal composing offers an alternative to many of the constraints currently found in multilingual classrooms. She connects current interests in multimodality with many of the traditional pedagogical approaches used in the early days of the process approach. Belcher argues that these new approaches play important roles in the multilingual classroom since they have become important components of the literacy landscape. This role has been contentious. Casanave (2017), however, has questioned whether they address the issues that have traditionally been the concern of multilingual writing teachers who may question the authenticity of digital literacies.

Casanave's (2017) critique of digital literacy still highlights how spaces may be valuable for some aspects of teaching but not for others, including traditional approaches to teaching writing. Despite lacking the proof that students improved their writing ability in these spaces, they could offer useful alternatives to traditional writing spaces for various forms of writing. Belcher (2017) argued that they remain consistent with the goals of process-orientated pedagogies, such as 'voice'. Blogging, as discussed previously, can support students developing their own voices to express their ideas, which can be later used in their writing (Bloch, 2008b). As will be discussed here, multimodality can address these goals even further.

The Implementation of Digital Storytelling into a Multimodal Literacy Space

Despite their origins outside the classroom, integrating multimodal literacies with a traditional print literacy can depend on institutional goals for teaching literacy. As a newer form of academic literacy, the introduction of multimodality needs to be shown to have affordances that address pedagogical concerns for the linguistic and rhetorical aspects of the dominant form of literacy. Introducing multimodality as a form of academic literacy, for example, has been aided by new pedagogical approaches that can take advantage of the affordances of multimodality. Hessler and Lambert (2017) have used threshold concepts (Meyer & Land, 2003), a term discussed in academic writing (Adler-Kassner & Wardle, 2015), for digital storytelling. Hessler and Lambert found that both digital storytelling and academic writing share these concepts, meaning that digital storytelling can be used as both a bridge and an alternative form of literacy. However, Casanave (2017) still questions whether the affordances of these digital forms, such as using images and sounds, interfere with the acquisition of more traditional forms of writing rather than functioning as a bridge or alternative literacy.

Previous research in multilingual classrooms has focused on how multimodality can be used either as a bridge to traditional print forms (e.g. Hafner, 2015) or as a separate form of literacy (e.g. Palmeri, 2012). Despite this interest in creating multimodal spaces, there is concern among teachers about whether having to learn these new technologies increases time requirements as well as the requisite levels of technical skills (Reid *et al.*, 2016). Despite the pedagogical importance of multimodality, Belcher (2017) reported resistance to implementing multimodality from writing instructors who may reject multimodality as authentic forms of academic writing. After viewing a digital story, which was created in my course, Belcher cites one teacher saying, 'Don't you think this kind of thing in effect short circuits thinking?'.

Plagiarism, Voice and Textual Borrowing

The introduction of multimodality leads back to familiar questions regarding plagiarism, textual borrowing and voice previously discussed with blogging. However, since multimodality could be better used as an assignment, it was thought it could better address some problems. Researchers have identified various problems often experienced with voice and textual borrowing (e.g. Bazerman, 1988, 2013; Blum, 2009; Pecorari, 2008; Shi, 2010) that can lead to accusations of plagiarism. Bazerman (2013) has pointed out that the danger of textual borrowing can be in how the texts overpower the voice of the writer so that the writer can be 'written' by the texts they borrow. In discussing undergraduates' use of academic texts, research from The Citation Project (e.g. Howard *et al.*, 2010) showed that students often have problems knowing how to integrate borrowed texts into their papers.

Issues regarding plagiarism, particularly the attribution of texts, have often been linked with the authors' voices or lack of them. Blum (2009) found that students may simply 'regurgitate' texts, to demonstrate that they had read the texts as they felt their instructors wanted. These problems can be connected with the problems that students have with textual borrowing and voice. Plagiarism is not the only consequence of the breakdown of voice. I often tell my students about a chemistry postdoc in my class, for example, who was upset because his paper had been rejected by a journal since it did not contribute to the field, illustrating the dilemma of not using the appropriate voice in demonstrating the significance of research, an approach that had long been acceptable in academic writing but may have changed.

Multimodal literacy spaces can provide an alternative view of textual borrowing. Research has provided multiple motivations for valuing textual borrowing beyond simply avoiding plagiarism. These motivations reflect institutional demands, or as the foregoing anecdote shows, from the academic community. Threshold concepts in multimodal assignments may not have such institutionalized contexts that, in Adler-Kassner and Wardle's (2015) terms, need be uncovered and interrogated. What does it mean to express an identity or to borrow texts in a multimodal assignment? Providing an alternative form of literacy could provide a different way of seeing these connections. Blum found that students may not understand why they are borrowing the texts and Rose may not understand exactly what the texts mean, a problem often found among multilingual students, who may be trained in scientific writing in ways where deference to the borrowed texts can repress the evaluative power of their own voices.

The design of a multimodal literacy space to accommodate these different forms of literacy can affect our thinking about multimodality (e.g. Hessler & Lambert, 2017). The choice of which threshold concepts to implement in this digital space reflected the pedagogical goals of the course. Researchers have long attempted to categorize the rhetorical purposes for textual borrowing (e.g. Bazerman, 1988, 2013; Geisler, 2016; Latour, 1987). Karatsolis (2016) proposed four categories for classifying textual borrowing: reference citations pointing to the text; evaluative citations containing the creator's opinion; elaborative citations for developing specific claims; and citations commenting on the creator's project, often showing consistencies or sometimes differences with previous research. Latour (1987) introduced a more rhetorical framework for how authors use textual borrowing to support their claims as well as to show weaknesses or differences in contradictory citations to establish credibility or ethos as an author.

Connecting the multimodal spaces with the course goals could be manipulated with the choice of assignments. Once the space was created, the problem arose concerning scaffolding students for recognizing the possible connections to facilitate transfer. Because these assignments originate from different literacy spaces, the students may have different constraints on developing their voices. Vandergriff (2016) discusses using Web 2.0 tools, such as Chat, wikis or blogs, for developing literacy skills. However, their uses by students may be unpredictable since the students' familiarity with the tools may be unclear, echoing Canagarajah's (2018) use of the term 'rhizomatic' for describing the often chaotic nature of learning throughout the spaces.

The design of the space, however, may not determine which languages and literacies were used (Chapter 1), but their integration into the space could still be incorporated with the goals for learning. These digital literacies, much like traditional literacy genres, provide heuristics for creating knowledge and constraints on its creation. One of the differences with the traditional print spaces is that writers can use their chosen voices, so the design can be impacted by the affordances of the spaces for providing alternative literacy spaces.

Multimodal learning may free both teachers and students from concerns regarding grammatical correctness or linguistic development (cf.

Casanave, 2017), allowing them to use whatever form of English they so choose. In their book on voice and stance in academic writing, Guinda and Hyland (2012) reviewed research showing both the diachronic evolution of voice over time and the variations in voice both within individual writers and across genres, fields and texts. Their results show how varied and instable voices are. Discussions of plagiarism again show the great variance in both the rhetorical functions of textual borrowing and the penalties for violating its rules.

Thus, the question of voice can be of great importance in the design of all digital spaces. Hewings (2012: 188) found that voice was variously defined ranging from the individual expression and ethos to a dialogic interaction between writer and audience to a social context, making it an 'all-embracing' term. She then discussed the different manifestations of voice across several digital platforms, citing Warschauer (2002) on how different digital platforms can allow students different forms of expression. Such differences may have resulted from the 'outside' nature of these platforms and the resulting types of semiotic materials brought to the literacy space, although the exact relationship may never be clear.

Hewings did not directly address digital storytelling and voice, which did not have a strong pedagogical grounding as a digital space at the time the article was written, but she discussed earlier research on mobile learning platforms. Nor did she use the term affordances as is often used with discussions of technologies, but she drew a picture of how these different platforms allow for different forms of literacies. Digital storytelling, for example, may lack the affordances for interacting that chat rooms and tutorials do (e.g. Warschauer, 2002); however, it does offer the affordances for creating voice and repurposing texts, which can help in incorporating how such affordances may support different voices and different forms of textual borrowing.

The affordances of digital storytelling, for example, may not share all the linguistic resources that writers can use for textual borrowing in print texts, such as hedging (Hyland, 1998), stance (Hyland, 1999) and choice of reporting verb (Bloch, 2010). However, digital storytelling provides an alternative view of textual borrowing. The transformation of the voice and its transformative nature on the related images contradict the cliché 'a picture is worth a thousand words'. The words of the students recorded in their own voices both transform and are in turn transformed by the mixing process with the images. The process, however, is not the same as it is with print texts. Digital storytelling does not share the same resources for textual borrowing in print texts. Nor does it require the same necessary linguistic skills that paraphrasing print texts requires. Nevertheless, these affordances allow for different voices, contradicting the argument that voice in academic writing is monolithic (e.g. Matsuda, 2006).

The voices in both print and digital spaces also reflect the structure of the space. From a psychological perspective, the pedagogical question remains as to whether these digital spaces push the student further toward what Maslow (1962) called 'self-actualization' than traditional classroom-based spaces do. Many of the issues in Maslow's theory may motivate the writing process – creativity, ethics, problem-solving. Therefore, students may reveal more of themselves than they do in traditional classroom spaces, regardless of which tools they use, an idea Bergmann noted in his reference to 'Maslow before Bloom'. The introduction of other multimodal literacies, therefore, does not supplant blogs or any literacy, but provides a space for developing ideas without worrying about grammatical correctness (cf. Casanave, 2017).

The Use of Threshold Concepts for Discussing Voice and Textual Borrowing

Although discussions of threshold concepts are controversial (e.g. Rowbottom, 2007), these concepts can reflect complex ideas that are important in academic writing. Each concept includes several skills that are necessary in the development of academic writing. With textual borrowing are skills related to citation and attribution; with voice are skills related to evaluation and argumentation. The discussions of threshold concepts can demonstrate their value as well as connecting different literacies, regardless of how each is valued (Adler-Kassner & Wardle, 2015). Beyond using images for transforming texts, multimodal literacy may involve learning new skills for mixing texts and images, which can be problematic for international students as well as teachers. Implementing digital storytelling, in fact, reflected differences in the students' backgrounds and goals. However, as the students themselves sometimes noted, creating videos, such as in digital storytelling, was not perceived as preparing students for academic writing. Thus, the introduction of threshold concepts could facilitate at least their perception of transfer, if not transfer itself.

Similar threshold concepts can be identified in both digital and print forms, and students can then make the connections between those in digital and print texts, which can facilitate learning and transferability (e.g. Anson & Moore, 2017). In this discussion of multimodal spaces, we focus on two threshold concepts: textual borrowing (Shi, 2006, 2010) and voice (e.g. Canagarajah, 2015; Ivanič, 1998). The threshold concepts, for example, in textual borrowing in digital and print texts have been referred to as 'portals' that reveal the shared social values in both forms. By identifying these concepts in print and digital assignments, students could first develop them in different spaces and then connect them to develop their metacognitive awareness of these relationships between the forms of literacy. As previously discussed, this relationship is messy, often with contrasting learning objectives (Bloch, 2008b); however, their identification can support exploring the 'troublesome' concepts that can be transferred across literacy contexts (e.g. Perkins & Salomon, 1988).

Meyer and Land (2003) introduced several assumptions about using threshold concepts that can create a framework for discussing the connections between multimodal and print literacies: (1) Transformation: Students express their own voices and their relationships to the texts they borrow will be transformed. (2) Troublesomeness: These two concepts – voice and textual borrowing – have been difficult for multilingual students to understand, and when misunderstood, can lead to problems with attribution and resulting accusations of plagiarism (see Chapter 2) (e.g. Bloch, 2001, 2008b). (3) Liminality: These assumptions are neither clearly defined nor the same in different communities. (4) Discursiveness: From understanding these two concepts, students can become more effective creators in both print and multimodal domains. (5) Reconstitution: By understanding these concepts, students can become more aware of the constraints and values of print and digital literacies.

Adler-Kassner and Wardle (2015) called their book *Naming What We Know* to highlight how using the term 'threshold concepts' can help identify those concepts focused on in any classroom space. Yancey (2004) argues that the term 'threshold concepts' refers to shared concerns to identify the outcomes desired in different classroom spaces. These outcomes may be mediated by the nature or affordances of the available technologies. Threshold concepts associated with voice and textual borrowing exemplify areas of knowledge production that can be difficult for students to grasp but are still important within each community of practice. As Alexander (2017) points out, teachers have access to many technologies in these spaces. How teachers choose to develop these spaces can depend on their course goals. This awareness of concepts related to textual borrowing was important in our teaching about plagiarism by shifting the focus away from how many words were copied to the rhetorical purposes of textual borrowing.

This discussion examines how threshold concepts can be used to connect multimodal projects to traditional print projects. The discussion has focused mainly on the role of threshold concepts and the possibility for transfer in first language writing (e.g. Adler-Kassner & Wardle, 2015), but similar arguments often hold for multilingual writing where digital spaces may promote transfer, or what Nowacek (2011) calls repositioning or decontextualizing, between various language forms (e.g. Odlin, 2015) or across different literacies or languages (e.g. Canagarajah, 2018). Nowacek uses the term 'agents of integration' to describe how students can take agency in this process by remixing their literacies by developing their metacognitive understandings of the connections they are making.

Students moving between these different spaces and forms of literacy cannot clearly transfer a form between one literacy and another.

Threshold concepts can be used to connect print and multimodal assignments with textual borrowing and voice as a framework for comparing the types of literacy highlighting the social context each multimodality can support. The connection between the two literacies illustrated how the literacies connect to each other and provided an answer to the often-asked question: Is digital writing really writing? Context plays an important role in identifying the key threshold concepts across contexts. In our class, the context was a class that focused on various issues regarding plagiarism in the university. Thus, we chose to focus on those threshold concepts that could help with both goals. As Yancey (2004: xix) argues, identifying these concepts can help 'uncover and interrogate assumptions' in writing classrooms, particularly those related to the voice and textual borrowing.

Nevertheless, there may be confusion not only about the threshold concepts within each domain but also about how they compare across domains. Unlike the role of intellectual property in print assignments, for example, the legal issues regarding intellectual property borrowed from the internet may be more complex; however, these may provide a more complex view of textual borrowing, one of the pedagogical goals of the course.

The design problem for this space included incorporating the threshold concepts identified as troublesome, with both print and multimodal literacies. We chose digital storytelling as the primary assignment to introduce multimodality (Bloch, 2019). Digital storytelling could be used to combine the personal experiences of the student with their ability to reflect on these experiences. By moving it into the classroom, it could also exploit its multimodal affordances for reflecting on the content of the course, or in our case, the decisions made to cross borders to enter university. Hafner (2015) describes how digital storytelling could be used to explore both the content of the course and the literacies for reporting that content. Our primary goal for implementing digital storytelling was initially to provide this alternative perspective. A digital story mixes personal narrative with related images and music and can thus be particularly suitable for an academic writing course since it remixes a personal voice with supporting texts, usually images or sound, often borrowed from the internet or created by the storyteller (Lambert, 2020).

Digital storytelling can structure the relationship between personal agency and the needs of storytellers' audiences. Hull and Katz (2006) argue that storytellers position themselves in relationship to their audience, thus providing the storyteller with an agentive self, much like the author of an academic text. Citing Bakhtin, Nelson (2006: 57) argues that digital storytelling leads to rethinking authorship by allowing students to 'populate' the ideas of others with their own 'intentions'. Their approach builds on Jerome Bruner's (1994) research on narratives to argue that these personal moments in the narrative provide the storyteller with an opportunity to develop their perceptions of their lives. The centrality of this agentive self, along with the importance of an alternative approach to textual borrowing, makes digital storytelling a potentially useful literacy to be implemented with print assignments. Hull and Katz (2006) show how creators can mix these various texts with their narratives to transform both literacies, while learning to assemble texts as Canagarajah (2018) found with academic writers.

The designs of these spaces are never monolithic but vary with the differences in course goals. As Alexander (2017) points out, there are several forms of digital storytelling using different tools and media, depending on the goals. He describes how many of the social media tools – blogs, Twitter, wikis, Facebook – have been used as tools for storytelling. The story center offers various formats for using images, ranging from one to the multiple forms we used. Moreover, he suggests that approaches to digital storytelling are changing as technologies and uses for technologies develop.

New types of cameras, platforms for video production and means of distribution can impact how digital storytelling is used. Casanave discusses the different manifestations of voice across platforms, citing Warschauer (2002) on how these digital platforms allow students more freedom of expression than is often found in print contexts. For example, the stories in the blogs had first suggested to us the possibility of using digital storytelling (Bloch, 2015), although, as discussed here, adaptations, such as using blogs, were implemented along with moving this literacy into the classroom.

While multimodality has long been important in academic literacies (e.g. Kress, 2003), digital storytelling could connect an academic paper with a form of multimodality, encouraging the possibility for transfer (e.g. Perkins & Salomon, 1988). To facilitate transfer, the print and digital assignments were organized in parallel; a part of the week focused on the print spaces and a part on the digital space. This approach to developing multimodal literacy spaces could facilitate our goals as they evolved with the development of the relationship between the digital space and print spaces. It became more important 'to name what we know' as part of the transfer process. Yancey et al. (2014) argue that threshold concepts can be used as a heuristic to focus on the types of rhetorical skills needed across different literacies. Our classes focused on the rhetorical skills that may be useful across various literacy forms. However, the rhetorical skills across these literacies were not always similar. Across these contexts, there was a need for flexibility in using these concepts for addressing similar rhetorical issues.

The concepts focused on here, particularly voice and textual borrowing, illustrate the 'troublesome' concepts (e.g. Meyer & Land, 2003) students face in all forms of textual borrowing. No issue has been more controversial in multilingual writing than textual borrowing and voice. Simply identifying these concepts may not have the intended pedagogical effect. Drawing upon his background in anthropology and the work of Ruth Benedict, Maslow (1962) differentiates the function of the concept and the behavior itself. However, they still may have value in showing the connections between different literacy spaces. A similar distinction can be seen in the work of Levi-Strauss (1964), who differentiates between the concept of cooking as a cultural function and the literal behavior of cooking food. While discussing that the concepts have pedagogical value in helping students identify and reflect upon them, they can be a means for teachers to justify the use of digital spaces (c.f. Belcher, 2017; Casanave, 2017).

Digital Storytelling and Academic Writing

Lambert (2020) describes various modes of digital storytelling and types of digital stories. When digital storytelling moved into the college classroom, it was immediately situated in the writing classroom (Lambert, 2020). In our approach, digital storytelling focused primarily on individual stories, what Lambert called stories 'about me'. In the writing course, we primarily focused on the mode combining texts, images and possibly music. Digital storytelling was introduced to develop the multimodal literacy space (Bloch & Wilkinson, 2013). Lambert introduced a variety of tools that could be useful for digital storytelling. Our goal was to integrate the learning opportunities from providing alternative learning spaces with the ability to transform different forms of intellectual property by telling and sharing personal stories. The students could mix these forms and then decide on their licensing using Creative Commons. In addition to immersing them in a form of academic writing, the goal was to help them understand the use of intellectual property (e.g. Bloch, 2012).

The popularity of digital storytelling has developed with the importance in academic writing of constructing a discoursal voice and identity within the text (e.g. Guinda & Hyland, 2012; Ivanič, 1998). It supports various traditional pedagogical goals – such as developing voice, borrowing texts or responding to audience needs – that have troubled multilingual writers in traditional print assignments, providing a pedagogical advantage of foregrounding the narrative story over the borrowed texts that can support a stronger voice than is often found in student texts, which can be important for expressing identities in language learning (Vandergriff, 2016).

Digital storytelling has grown in importance outside the classroom with the workshops of Lambert (2020) and associates where individuals can find support for creating these stories. These workshops have focused on issues of social justice – immigration, poverty, globalization and spousal abuse. Hull and associates (e.g. Hull & Nelson, 2005; Hull & Katz, 2006) demonstrated their value as an alternative literacy form in after-school learning compared to assignments found inside the classroom. Multilingual writing teachers later began to implement digital stories in the classroom with students who struggled with traditional writing assignments (Bloch, 2015, 2019) or with problems with the assignments themselves. The multimodal space can therefore involve students in various print and technical activities related to writing stories, recording podcasts, mixing their stories with texts and creating movies.

Our digital story assignment focused on having students narrate a key moment in their lives and mix the story with images either downloaded from the internet or created by themselves. Compared to blogging, digital storytelling provided a literacy space where voice became the central focus (Lambert, 2020). Digital storytelling, for example, also provides opportunities for textual borrowing that call for analyzing the rhetorical impact of the choice of materials, the use of intellectual property (Bloch, 2012) and the role of attribution, all of which can provide alternative approaches to understanding how these concepts may be transferable into traditional print spaces (e.g. Anson & Moore, 2017; Nowacek, 2011; Perkins & Salomon, 1988) and then directly taught (e.g. Yancey et al., 2014). However, voice itself still plays an equally important role through the story. The idea that an academic writer is also a 'storyteller' is not a new one (Medawar, 1984), but this sense of authorship found in storytelling has been more problematic in developing a voice that requires extensive amounts of textual borrowing (e.g. Bazerman, 2013).

Digital storytelling, particularly with its roots in workshops and alternative schooling spaces, has challenged traditional approaches to using multimodality, more consistent with Canagarajah (2018) view of the shift away from traditional forms of multimodality, where information is discretely presented in different modes, as in charts or graphs, to remix or assemble, terms used to describe how new texts emerge and the boundaries between the original texts break down (e.g. Lessig, 1999). Mixing these texts has been pedagogically important for demonstrating how multimodal literacies can be considered academic literacies, which are, as Yancey (2015) argues, these new forms of literacy encourage participation and sharing, which illustrates how remixing texts in one literacy may differ from remixing in other literacies. Hessler and Lambert (2017) argue that digital storytelling can showcase how these threshold concepts can be similarly remixed. Hafner (2015) argues that digital storytelling is a form of remix where creators mix their own stories with images and music. Having the students remix and transform different modes of expression also had pedagogical importance for better understanding intellectual property law (e.g. Bloch, 2012).

The debate over the use of digital literacies focuses on the value of having students cross literacy boundaries according to institutional demands. Wilson and Soblo (2020) found evidence of the ability of multilingual writers to transfer their knowledge across genres. While Nowacek (2011) focuses on writing assignments in different courses, the relationship between the literacy demands within the same course is also important (e.g. Hafner, 2015). Voice is assumed important in academic writing contexts where voice may be repressed, often to the detriment of the paper. The anecdote about the post-doc having his chemistry paper rejected illustrates this problem. However, in a digital story, the students mixed their voices with images to create a personal, multimodal story that still explained their personal and public lives. This approach to textual borrowing is one of the threshold concepts that can be implemented in the multimodal space to connect visual and print assignments. Using images as texts contradicts the old cliché 'a picture is worth a thousand words' since they do not simply add information but can transform the meaning of the text.

Another example of a threshold concept is that the different literacies share a voice. It is the words of the students, recorded in their own voices, that both transform and in turn are transformed by the mixing process. Its affordances allow for multiple forms of voice, contradicting the assumption that voice was a unitary concept. Voice is not necessarily identical across these different literacies or even across literacy contexts. Hafner (2015) discusses the differences between voice in different texts, arguing how voice is constructed discursively when mixed with voices in other modes. Hull and Katz (2006: 44) called voice an 'agentive self', which can be used for expressing claims within the often complex requirements for textual borrowing. As Hafner argues, however, connecting voice and textual borrowing can be especially challenging for multilingual writers to meet those requirements. For some students, digital storytelling provides an alternative approach to expressing voice (Bloch, 2015, 2019). Digital storytelling, therefore, may be an integral part of teaching students to negotiate the constraints (e.g. Bazerman, 1988) traditionally found in academic writing. It remained our goal that expressing these identities could be made part of these multimodal texts. Lambert (2013) argues the importance of voicing one's own narratives. For our course goals, voicing narratives helped create an identity in the text. Lambert writes about voice in digital storytelling:

> This is why my first-person voice – the way I talk to myself about my own experience – is never far from the perspectives I am sharing. I realize that the story of ideas I am telling comes out of my own journey. They could not possibly fit any other human's story perfectly in alignment. (Lambert, 2013: 11)

Multimodal assignments have revived the interest in integrating orality with the other modes of expression (Selfe, 2009). Besides the voice of the narrator, music can be added. Music is somewhat more problematic both in intellectual property terms and in technical terms, although the biggest problem can be how its loudness can interfere with the narrative.

The implementation of digital storytelling assumes everybody has a story and by sharing that story, its creators can express their voices. As Lambert (2020) argues, creating the digital story itself requires the creator to self-reflect on their own experiences, much as they may do when they have to reflect on the significance of their own writing. Through this process of reflection, voice may be transferred to the academic writing assignments where the students had traditionally struggled with their voices. While this argument can be applied to any form of digital literacy, digital storytelling, particularly since it involved skills related to academic writing, was easier to justify. In an academic writing classroom, this appropriation process reflected the reasons for borrowing texts in an academic paper. Nelson (2006) argues that implementing multimodal assignments for multilingual students can increase their awareness of the purposes for textual borrowing. Exploiting these various motivations for textual borrowing can help students construct their selves as academic writers. Therefore, combining both in a graduate writing course can give students new perspectives on text creation.

To facilitate this goal, the students often told stories about the relationships between their majors and their personal lives. A Columbian student explored overcoming his fear of insects before embarking on his major (https://www.youtube.com/watch?v=_aTFfI05cJU&t=4s). In one case, a Korean graduate student had written a first draft on studying ichthyology that lacked any personal content. In his revision, he added a section on how he had worked in his family's fish market and had spent his free time fishing, which had led him to graduate school to study ichthyology. To elaborate on this theme, he chose photos to remix with his story. Other students focused on their personal experiences. In this example, a Taiwanese student told a story about having to break up with a boyfriend (https://www.youtube.com/watch?v=cD1pdzmG3BY). All these examples emphasize focusing on this appropriation process for borrowing texts in an academic paper.

Multimodality was used then to remediate a summary writing assignment that too easily lent itself to large amounts of copying (Bloch, 2019). One way of developing voice with this space was to focus on personal experiences, which in some cases could be attached to traditional academic concerns. The students created stories about the relationship between their major and their personal life without prompting from the instructors. The assignment was used in a chapter in Swales and Feak (2012). However, the use of digital storytelling to replace this assignment could shape this interaction between pedagogical goals and multimodal literacies to better explore the course goals, which in this case was plagiarism and intellectual property law (e.g. Bloch, 2012).

However, these goals could be changed by changing the texts used. To reduce the time necessary to search for texts, we encouraged students to use their own photos. By using their own photos for this project instead of downloading them from the internet, the students seemed to feel that they did not have enough content background to add anything to what was already published in Wikipedia. Therefore, by implementing digital storytelling, we could also explore alternative intellectual property laws that governed how images could be borrowed. This approach has complicated discussions of intellectual property with both print and visual texts and raises important questions of the legal constraints on textual borrowing (e.g. Aufderheide & Jaszi, 2012).

In all these cases, multimodal spaces could provide various voices for academic writing. Latour (1987), for example, focuses on the analytic voice that in the print assignment uses textual borrowing to support arguments, showing what Swales (1991) would call the gap between the current and previous research. Medawar (1984) discusses the narrative voice used in academic writing for describing the methodology and the data collection. Our focus on evaluation is similarly part of this narration. In her study of genres, Tardy (2016) identifies different types of voice that an academic writer may have, including what she calls 'a playful voice', often found in digital stories. Such connections could reduce the perceived distance between the concepts to better facilitate their transfer across assignments.

Early research into multimodal literacies (e.g. Knobel & Lankshear, 2007; Kress, 2003; New London Group, 1996) has supported this later implementation of how these literacies should be valued as alternatives literacies in the classroom. How multimodal spaces are implemented can impact their value in the classroom. Our primary goal for digital storytelling, for example, was to remediate problems with traditional literacy assignments. These considerations have motivated using threshold concepts for demonstrating the connections between the digital and print literacy spaces, which, in turn, can increase the value of these spaces.

The Potential Transfer of Threshold Concepts between Print and Digital Spaces

Defining a multimodal space for teaching academic writing inevitably raises the possibility of transfer between the print and multimodal modes. Using threshold concepts in multimodal spaces has provided a framework for discussing the transfer across literacies (e.g. Anson & Moore, 2017), but their roots in genre provide a structural framework for a deeper analysis. Nowacek (2011) uses genre to provide the context for identifying the threshold concepts to be taught. The threshold concepts discussed in this chapter, textual borrowing and voice, have been derived from the academic genres on which our courses focused. The design of these digital spaces to include different forms of texts that could be transferred can provide a new pedagogical direction for what Yancey *et al.* (2014) labeled 'teaching for transfer'.

Transfer has a long history in language learning, which also provides a framework for discussing the current issues in this context. As Odlin (2015) has argued, transfer has been important in language comparisons since the 19th century and has been a major component in multilingual writing since Kaplan's (1966) controversial article on comparative patterns of organization, which would be further developed in theories of contrastive and later intercultural rhetoric (e.g. Connor, 2011). Kaplan (1966) had shifted the focus to areas of organization where transfer was more difficult because the patterns of organization differed. Transfer was often seen as a negative interference.

In his concept of 'interlanguage', however, Selinker (1972) introduced a framework for describing how the transfer process can be both positive and negative, yielding a 'fossilized' state that can be pushed in the direction that both students and teachers prefer but without a clear end point. However, as new approaches to language learning developed, new approaches to transfer developed as well. Canagarajah (2018) argued that transfer may be viewed differently, less an 'arboreal' view of providing a rooting for future development and more a 'rhizomatic' pattern of potential connections for transforming expression.

In this discussion of print and multimodal literacies, transfer requires the ability to repurpose these concepts across disciplinary spaces (Adler-Kassner & Wardle, 2015; Anson & Moore, 2017; Nowacek, 2011; Yancey *et al.*, 2014). The ability to transfer can depend on recognizing the connection between the spaces, remembering the threshold concepts and persisting in repurposing it in another space. Nowacek's (2011) use of the term repositioning is useful here for pedagogically framing the transfer process with different concepts or measurable results. Transfer between print and digital literacies can be placed somewhere in the middle.

However, these alternative designs raise questions about the transfer process. As Nowacek (2011) argues, the transfer process involves an emotional level as students recognize the potential for transfer, which can be important in motivating using the space (e.g. Norman, 2013). When the concept of 'threshold concepts' is introduced into these digital spaces, the results can be as unstable as those found in any language learning space. Academic threshold concepts tend to be predefined by the constraints of the academy and the communities of practice within the academy where these concepts are often defined.

It was not simply the parallel relationships between the print and digital assignments that was a concern. Perkins and Salomon (1988) defined different possible relationships between the contexts for supporting transfer, using terms such as near and far transfer, which refers to the relationship between the contexts, or high and low transfer, which are used to indicate the similarity of these concepts. It is not clear, however, how deterministic these relationships are on the resulting literacies or how the outcomes can be manipulated through the course design or having the students reflect about relationships between the assignments. From their blogs, it appeared that the students' ideas of 'near' and 'far' transfer across the two domains do not seem absolute but are relative to the students and evolve as the students struggle with both. The relationship between print and digital spaces exemplifies 'far' transfer, an assumption that underlies the concern for the relevancy of multimodality in the academic writing classroom. When the print and digital assignments are parallel, students may connect the two assignments without necessarily an awareness of these connections.

Therefore, how students perceived these relationships became a critical factor in the design of these spaces. The potential for transferring these concepts can correspond to relationships between the locations of these spaces and the linkage between their roles in students' lives inside and outside the classroom, especially those 'participatory cultures' to which Jenkins (2006, 2009) referred. Belcher (2017) argued that the growing importance of digital literacy spaces has increased the responsibility of the writing teacher to bring these literacies into the classroom. Although the impact of connecting two modes of expression on literacy development is not clear, such connections demonstrate their value, not only because of the possibility of being detached from traditional academic spaces but also because of the amount of time and skills often needed for their implementation. For students concerned with preparing for writing in their academic classes, the role of multimodality may not always seem relevant to their goals.

New approaches to literacy have further strengthened this argument, as was the case with digital storytelling. Hessler and Lambert (2017) and Horner *et al.* (2014) focus on how multimodality is not simply a bridge between literacies but a literacy itself, consistent with the view advanced by the New London Group. In their manifesto on multimodality, Wysocki *et al.* (2019) argue for its centrality as a form of literacy, regardless of whether the transfer from one domain to another is positive, negative or both, arguing that

> scholars of rhetoric and composition must contend with and respect new forms of composing that integrate and hybridize computation, digital, and material processes. (Wysocki *et al.*, 2019: 20)

Even arguments that digital literacy can bridge traditional forms of print literacy question how writers cross back and forth.

Whether the transfer is positive, negative or both has been important for teaching these threshold concepts in the print and digital spaces (e.g. Nowacek, 2011). What is different between transfer today and in the past is that there are no clear answers to what is being transferred. Not only are the concepts discussed here, such as textual borrowing and voice, difficult to define, but the relationship between the contexts across the literacies is not clear. Thus, students often struggle with moving between these spaces, a concept that can be 'liminal' since they can be difficult to understand. The term 'liminality' can describe the disorientation that students may feel when trying to understand the often vague concepts they are working with, which has been especially true of textual borrowing and voice.

A breakdown in understanding these threshold concepts can undermine the potential for transfer but still create a space for teachers to provide 'scaffolding' (Vygotsky, 1934/1986) to help the student make the connection. What exactly does this scaffolding entail? Again, the answer is not clear. Our approach to transfer between the two spaces involved not only creating parallel print and digital writing assignments but also providing students with the tools, in this case blogs and storyboards, to help them recognize and remember the connections. The students' persistence in transfer, however, was up to them.

Designing Reflection into the Multimodal Space

Lambert (2020) describes storyboards for organizing the sequences of the narratives and for the interactions among the different modes of expression. In our course, the storyboards, along with the blogs, were repurposed to foster transfer by helping students develop the meta-awareness (Nowacek, 2011) for connecting the concepts across the assignments. Initially, these repurposings were not always successful since the students may not have been able to recognize those connections. Students blogged about their experiences with creating print and digital texts but often focused only on the content, not on the threshold concepts we hoped they were seeing.

Our initial implementation of blogging was not successful in supporting the transfer of the connections between the print and digital spaces, partly because of the prompt. As Nowacek (2011) argued, students do not always see the connections, resulting from apparent differences in the assignment context. This argument is consistent with the focus Odlin (2015) placed on memory since it was not apparent that the students remembered the threshold concepts from the previous context. Initially, the prompts did not clearly address transfer, but the students may still need more support in making these connections.

There have been various suggestions about the kinds of writing assignments for facilitating transfer. Taczak *et al.* (2020) suggest that students write a 'theory of writing' to explore the connections between their assignments. We modified the prompt for blogging so that students could explore the potential connections. To name the threshold concept (Adler-Kassner & Wardle, 2015), a column was added for the name of the threshold concept being considered. As was the case with the blogs, the goal was to develop the metacognitive awareness for connecting the texts (Adler-Kassner & Wardle, 2015; Perkins & Salomon, 1988). In these cases, a gap was created where students could build their own bridges between the two assignments.

Neither affordance, however, seemed to help students reflect on the possible connections. As Nowacek (2011) argued, students may not have seen the connections, often resulting from the apparent contexts for the different literacies. Our failure illustrates not only the importance of seeing these spaces as being in 'perpetual beta' that must be continually evaluated and remediated, but also the chaos that may result from constant changes, as illustrated by the confusion over intellectual property and openness that challenges how content can be used and who controls its use. There may not be a clear answer to how to foster transfer, but it may have been within the struggle with these 'liminal' spaces to support learning.

The potential for utilizing these freedoms in selecting materials is important for considering how the design may support but not determine the learning. Canagarajah (2016) uses the term 'co-constructs' to describe how English language learners appropriate the resources of a language to create their own meanings in their own language. Students may have broad freedoms in co-constructing meaning through using textual borrowing as well as their voices. These examples illustrate how students can create multimodal projects under the constraints of the assignments and their goals for using them force the students to 'turn', using Latour's (1987) words, the images to meet their rhetorical purposes. For instance, a student wants to represent her struggle in college.

In this example, each image at the beginning of her story reflects a different aspect of her struggle to find a major. She explores her current situation at the university and the difficulty of her decision. The images both depict who she is and her future life in the design classroom, assuming she overcomes the difficulties expressed in her narration. Taken together, they represent a more ambiguous picture of her position in the university. In some personal stories, the students explored their own relationships with the music they loved. The student adds a soundtrack with the refrain 'nobody knows me at all', which ironically encapsulates her purpose for creating and sharing her story.

The ability to move among these different modes, even without transfer, could have important consequences for literacy. Canagarajah (2013) described the process of moving strategically between languages as 'shuttling', which requires a more 'agile' framework where this process cannot be clearly defined. Story creators can 'shuttle' between different modes of expression (written, oral and image) as different forms of academic and non-academic textuality to better exploit the affordances of the outside-the-classroom origins of digital storytelling. Students seemed freer to explore the goals of their assignments compared with the print assignments.

Their reluctance in the print assignments was most apparent when making evaluations in their academic papers, perhaps reflecting a literacy tradition where the data should speak for itself or an insecurity with their ability to interact with the course readings. However, with the digital stories, this reluctance seemed to disappear as illustrated by her ability to transform meaning by 'shuttling' among the different modes of texts.

Blogging about Digital Stories to Support Reflection and Transferability

The expanded role of blogging as a space for reflection exemplifies how technological literacies can evolve as they are implemented into different contexts with new pedagogical goals. When creating a digital story was added to the curriculum, blogging evolved as a space for reflecting about these connections between the two discourses, although there is little evidence that transfer occurred. As discussed previously, the digital and print assignments ran parallel in the same course to foster this transfer. The assignments were structured to foreground possible connections. The blogs were expected to evolve to become a space to reflect on these literacy experiences. Students worked on their print assignments on Monday and Wednesday and their digital stories on Friday. Storyboards were similarly initially used for organizing the narrative (Bloch, 2018), but later both spaces were used for reflecting on the relationship between print and digital literacies.

The evidence from the blogs showed possible connections. While promoting the development of their ideas, this multimodal space did not promote connecting the assignments. However, there was evidence that the process helped. In this blog, the student discussed the social context of her revisions.

> After I finished my digital story, my classmates and I, we introduced and discussed each of our story by turns. After listening to my group member's stories, we exchanged suggestions about each other's stories and tried to make them to be better. One question that my classmate proposed to me is that some paragraphs are not connected to the previous paragraphs. To make a better digital story, I revised some paragraphs in my stories.

The oral narratives helped facilitate peer review by making the content more accessible in response to suggestions from her peer-review group. However, she still retained her sense of agency in the creative office. In her next blog, she reflects on the connections she made between the two assignments, primarily focusing on content issues rather than on the threshold concepts.

> In this semester, I have worked on my digital story and argument paper. At the first thought, the two works seem to be different issues, but are there any relationships between them? I am sure there is, the digital story and argument paper all come from the same writer; that is me. When I was making my digital story, I downloaded some images and music from the internet, which relate to some intellectual property issues. When I am writing an argument paper about Turnitin. com., it also involves a lot in intellectual issues. Thus, one relationship between the digital story and argument paper is the intellectual property issue.

The use of Turnitin, in fact, raises a host of issues regarding privacy and teacher–student relationships. In response to a more specific prompt about these connections, she again focuses on authorship; that is, she was the author of both forms. This connection did focus on her voice in both articles, which was an important observation related to the threshold concept for expressing her ideas in both assignments. As she develops her blog, the student connects the purposes of the two assignments.

> The other relationship between digital story and argument paper is that they all serve as the education purpose. My digital story is used for education but not for business. The argument paper also relates with the educational academy purpose. No matter we are doing digital story or argument paper, as a student, we should keep in mind to respect other's work and the importance of citation.

However, the student still struggled with connecting the two assignments, but the blog provided her with the space and motivation to work out this relationship.

> when start to consider the relationship between my digital story and the argument paper, I was all at sea. It seems there is no connection between these two articles: from the perspective of topic, the digital story is about my academic study, and the argument paper is about whether Turnitin can help stop plagiarism; from the perspective of writing format, the story is descriptive, while the argument paper is argumentative. But when think over, I am delighted. The digital story is about my personal understanding about my major based on my experience. The process of construct my understanding is similar with the way we argue and counterargue one's opinion.

The blog focuses on the connection between the argumentative nature of both assignments. However, she does discuss the 'struggle' she had with this 'troublesome' knowledge, which seems to help the writer connect the relationship between her argument about Turnitin and her understanding of how she chose her major.

The student goes on to reflect how she generated ideas for her two arguments.

> Understanding is one kind of knowledge, which is anything but objective. We generate one view at the first glimpse, which is like one opinion in the argument paper. Then with the increasing of our experience, the generated belief can be challenged, which is similar with we show disagreement in the argument paper. Next, we keep generating and construct new understanding, based on the former one and the latest experience, which is the same as we deliver our counterargument in the argument paper. For example, in my digital story, I delivered the change of my understanding about Educational psychology. At the beginning, I viewed this field as separated parts which are disconnected with each other. With the further exploration in my domain, this original understanding cannot have satisfied me anymore, since in practice, all these parts, such as educational philosophy, educational technic, education law, educational administration, educational psychology, curricular design, etc., are interacting with other. Thus, I constructed a new understanding that educational psychology is a perspective that can help view the whole picture of the field of education, as well as our life.

For teachers, blogs provide an insight into how their students constructed their arguments. For researchers, they offer additional possibilities for studying student writing. Perkins and Salomon (1988) see this struggle, as illustrated in this blog, to connect the two domains as important for the transfer process. This struggle does not automatically facilitate transfer, which can depend on discerning what should be transferred, selecting the relevant characteristics and remembering how the threshold concepts are related across contexts. As Perkins and Salomon argued, transfer can result from forming an abstraction in one context that guides using that concept in another context. Even though the blogger does not focus on the threshold concepts, she does focus on another connection she had made between her assignments.

Although we were interested in how the students used the two threshold concepts, the student connected the threshold concepts she saw as the most important. This strategy for blogging was commonly used by the students. In another blog, an Argentinian student identifies 'structure' as the key threshold concept he wanted to focus on in his digital story.

These two stories share the same writing's structure. Both start with an introduction of the theme. The argument paper starts with an introduction of the problem that professors and universities are having regarding the way to use Turnitin, while in my digital story start with an introduction of who I am, and what I am studying in graduate school. The second part discusses the different postures and opinions that professors and students have about Turnitin, mixed with my personal opinion of their opinions. This part talk about the problems the conflict of the story, where the events occur.

In my digital story (https://vimeo.com/99749936) the second part talk about the most important event in my life (motorbike's crash) that influenced me to take the decisions that guided me until The Ohio State University. Therefore, this part talks about the problem in the story. Same happen in the argument paper. Although, in the argument paper there are several opinions of different persons expressed in the second part, unlike my digital story that is just the relating of a fact that happened in my life.

Despite her concerns, the final part of both stories has more similarities in discussing their conclusions. Is summarizing the opinion of the author about the conflict in the story, in this case my opinion? In my digital story I finish it with a conclusion of how people act when they face problem in their life, and what they could do to handle bad moment better. In the argument paper I finish it given a conclusion about, in my opinion, which is the better way to more usefully and fairly use Turnitin. Therefore, both the argument paper and digital story share the same writing's structure.

There was a tension between our goals for blogging and the students' perceptions of these goals. The students seemed to perceive the connections between the two assignments differently from our goals, although in both examples they do focus on what they think are the important issues. By reflecting on these blogs, the impact of the prompt on the social context can be revealed, and thus by modifying the prompt, we could impact the design of the literacy space.

The blogs illustrate this liminality through how the students struggled to understand the connections. Again, the relationships between the assignments are malleable depending on the prompt. This use of blogs demonstrates what Yancey *et al.* (2014: 45) called the 'intersection of multiple sites of writing'. Our 'multiple sites', which were in the same course a chaotic interaction between the two modes of expression, illustrate what Yancey calls 'teaching to transfer'. Adjusting the prompt to better reflect our goals might facilitate different aspects of transfer, although the chaotic nature may be a part of the process. Here, the apparent vagueness of the prompt, and hence the more undefined the social context, allowed students to reflect on whatever threshold concepts they were most interested in. Our prompts did reveal more about what the students considered both important and, in some cases, frustrating about the multimodal assignment. Many of the blogs illustrated the value of reflecting on their experiences and decisions. How this agency was reflected in one assignment seemed clear; its transfer to the other assignments less so.

Using Storyboards for Facilitating Transfer of Threshold Concepts

The struggles discussed in the students' blogs required additional forms of scaffolding to support the students working through the liminality of the threshold concepts. With the print assignment, we provided students with a series of questions to help scaffold their understanding of the structure and content of their argumentative papers. Storyboards provided additional scaffolding in the digital story, focusing on the threshold concepts associated with mixing words and images. Storyboards were initially developed as were blogs as heuristics for connecting text and images (e.g. Lambert, 2020), but the assignment was later modified for 'teaching for transfer' by providing an additional space for reflection. Perkins and Salomon (1988) argue that teaching for transfer should directly focus on the connections between the assignments. Storyboards were modified to provide this additional scaffolding by adding a column for reflecting on their purposes for choosing the images. A fourth column was added to identify which concept this connection was designed to support. The goal was to modify the social context in the digital literacy space to achieve our specific goals.

Table 3.1 shows a model storyboard including all four categories. In this example, the connections between images and texts are plotted with reflections on utilizing these threshold concepts. Through this process, the writer could better 'remember' the concept although again we had no evidence that this occurred. Unlike in the blogs, the students were asked to 'name' what they knew (Adler-Kassner & Wardle, 2015). While the storyboard still provided a space for developing the structure of the digital story, the combination of the blogs and storyboards could help students with their struggle with the connections between the two assignments.

Multimodality and Threshold Concepts in Digital Literacy Spaces

This discussion of multimodal spaces illustrates how threshold concepts in a print context may differ from those in multimodal spaces. Therefore, while a multimodal space can incorporate both print and

Table 3.1 A shortened version of a model storyboard for the digital story 'Being a Muslim' (https://vimeo.com/manage/17709929/general), which was shown to the students to model the creation of their own storyboard

Story	Threshold concepts	Images	Purposes
I was blessed to get a scholarship to continue my graduate study	Defining voice	Map showing where student is from	Explain where she is coming from
But the question was where should I go? The USA? But I was a little worried	Defining voice – represents voice	Image of a question mark	Represent the question she has about coming to America
What happened on 9/11 focused the world on Islam	Problem – expands emotion of her problem	Image of World Trade Towers in flames	The cause of her problem
And judge Muslims. Instead of looking at the criminal as persons	Responds to problem	Images of remains of World Trade Towers	Concern with how the world sees Islam

digital literacies, their relationship must be thought out. This implementation is consistent with Hafner *et al.*'s (2015) argument for the importance of multimodality in creating personalized learning environments by providing alternative spaces for literacy where the students could explore meaningful experiences in their lives; however, this implementation neither produced clear-cut differences with previous courses nor fit with our original plans. As had often saw, Hafner (2015) found that L2 students may not respond to the assignment as their teachers expected, particularly with textual borrowing. Therefore, digital storytelling can provide them with a perspective on textual borrowing and how it can be mixed with written texts.

In a class context, the ambiguity of the multimodal assignments led to reconceptualizing the assessment to rely less on the outcome and more on the performance, as with the attribution of images, which did not depend on a single format. For using the intellectual property, the students were asked to attribute their images as they would in a reference list. The space could also be modified with the blogging assignment to emphasize reflections that revealed how the students were thinking about the connections between the multimodal and print literacies. As one Chinese student put it,

First, this assignment actually gives me a chance to look back and see what I did, why did I end up studying computer science and how did I get here. These are things that I don't give much thoughts before. And it is important because sometimes we just too busy with what we are doing but forget why we are doing it at the first place. Doing the digital story give me the chance to refresh the memory. Also, I learned how to use movie maker to make a small movie. That is something really useful. I can use it to create a story about my life here at the end of my time here. I believe that will be so interesting and so meaningful. And it will be much more interesting than me showing a bunch of pictures to my friends.

The blogs were important in understanding how the students could reflect on their lives and their literacy development. More important was developing an awareness of moving across these spaces. A similar reconceptualizing could be seen in the evolution of the technological tools and their usage. Blogging evolved from being a heuristic tool into a space for developing texts, and then for connecting the print and digital spaces, expanding the potential for transfer.

These evolutionary changes could also be seen in how the design of the space interacted with the context to better develop the students' 'agentive selves' for both assignments. As one blog indicates, these selves could be developed from classmates' peer reviews, highlighting the social context of these spaces. Another clear difference in reaching our rhetorical goals occurred at the end of the semester, when, instead of sending in a paper to their teacher, the students came together, often throwing a party to share stories and later, with permission, posting them on the internet, facilitating returning the literacy to outside the classroom where it originated.

Such constructions of self could also lead to resistance, which could have different consequences on literacy. The students' digital stories, as well as the students' reflections, demonstrated how the value of multimodal assignments often went beyond our goals. Canagarajah (2016) refers to this lack of control, or 'chaos', as reflective of the new classroom where assignments such as digital storytelling could provide more autonomy. Such 'chaos' can be a learning experience for students as it was in the early experiments of Papert (1980) to provide new teaching contexts where 'errors' can be turned into new directions for learning.

The affordances of these outside literacies could provide an incentive to replace the prevalent test-based assignments (Hull & Katz, 2006). Their work illustrates how learning can occur outside of school, so our goals were how to take advantage of this research for our in-school goals. Our goals for assessment were more modest, focusing on remediating weaknesses in previous assignments and providing alternative perspectives on critical literacy skills. We revised, for example, integrating the multimodal assignment into the other academic writing assignments by explaining our goals more explicitly.

As digital storytelling migrated from the workshop to the after-school program to the classroom, students produced texts that were full of the rhetorical expressions we wanted to see. Nevertheless, the goals for including this personalization necessitated adapting it to the goals for the spaces and the course. Despite the connections between digital storytelling and academic writing, our course pedagogy had its own unique goals to be accommodated. However, these examples do provide a 'yes' to whether digital literacy is writing. As with the design of other digital spaces, the context can be modified by the design of the assignments and their relationships with each other. Other issues can be addressed to achieve specific goals. Hafner (2015), for example, saw the value of addressing fair use issues of copyright that textual borrowing from the internet entails (e.g. Aufderheide & Jaszi, 2012). Introducing intellectual property law into the writing classroom, therefore, is important in explaining the possible constraints of textual borrowing on all texts.

Multimodality has continually challenged our conceptions of teaching, particularly in how students construct their stories (e.g. Bloch, 2015). In a fund-raising email, Lambert (2020) wrote that the goal of digital storytelling was 'helping people claim their storytelling power', reflecting what he had said to me that 'everyone has a story'. The same thing can be said about research papers. In designing a digital space with both print and digital texts, the goal was to implement both and show their connections. The result was often chaotic. One example of this chaos can be seen in the issue of downloading images from the internet, using only copyright-free images, or creating proprietary images. Some teachers may want their students to confront intellectual property issues by downloading images from the internet (e.g. Bloch, 2012); others may want to avoid the issues by having them use images with Creative Commons or in the public domain. These new, often transformative, ways of textual borrowing are important in understanding the purposes for remixing intellectual property, where such transformative uses can affect whether a usage is considered an acceptable instance of the fair use of intellectual property.

The problems with using intellectual property in the original print assignment could be remediated to make the assignments more interesting and relevant to the other academic assignments by emphasizing the relationship between author identity and textual borrowing. In creating this space, the teachers continually designed and redesigned the spaces, adding different contents and structures, to provide various forms of scaffolding. Clearly, they were not merely 'guides' but active designers of their teaching and learning spaces.

4 MOOCs as a Digital Literacy Space

The Background of MOOCs

This chapter examines the design of Massive Open Online Courses (MOOCs) as digital spaces for teaching and learning about writing. MOOCs were not designed as spaces for teaching writing; however, their potential for teaching literacy was soon recognized. Much of the research began in K-12 contexts but was soon extended to university settings (e.g. Lockwood, 2014; Roehling, 2018; Talbot, 2017). In the previous two spaces, new forms of literacy were discussed, but with MOOCs, new ways of teaching literacy would emerge. MOOCs were initially designed for exploring new ways of learning, in particular connectivism (Siemens, 2005). MOOCs became a paradigm for educational change, including literacy instruction. They could be considered as a step in the development of more openness for creating more connections among teachers and participants (see Chapter 6). The response to the posting of course materials by MIT gave an indication of the potential of openness for global learning. *Time Magazine* labeled 2012 as 'The Year of the MOOC'.

The term MOOC – Massive Open Online Courses – as coined by Cormier (2008a), would later be divided into the different approaches used in xMOOCs and cMOOCs. The origins of MOOCs were in Canada. The first MOOCs were motivated by two Canadians, George Siemens (2005) and Stephen Downes (2011), in which they took a small course taught in Alberta Canada and transformed it into a larger online course with over 2000 participants. As with multimodality and blogging literacies, MOOCs could be used to break down the artificial divide between inside and outside the classroom.

MOOCs were initially designed to extend the limited confines of the classroom but were popularized in Silicon Valley where the number of participants rose from a few thousand participants to hundreds of thousands from all over the world studying computer science. The space decentralized the roles of the teacher and centralized the roles of the participants, who could connect through various literacies such as blogs, tweets and discussion boards (e.g. Mackness & Bell, 2016). By expanding their capacities for more participants, more knowledge could be generated. However, from their beginnings, there was a decline in the number of participants posting, which dropped further as the course progressed (Swope, 2013).

The internet has long impacted literacy as had the printing press. Many forms of online communication, as well as assessments, were predominately written, which impacted both communications and audiences. However, soon teaching writing became a topic. The Stanford MOOC, which was primarily intended for medical students, mostly contained lectures and a few filmed discussions with well-known journal editors discussing publication. Although their 'openness' had the greatest impact on globalization, the presence of many multilingual writers who might struggle with these assignments was not always acknowledged. Part of the problem was the vagueness in which the first 'O' for openness was defined.

The design of this learning space, nevertheless, incorporated several new ideas about learning and knowledge creation in networks – the idea of generating knowledge from the 'wisdom of the crowds' (Surowiecki, 2004), for instance, which assumed that the more people involved, the more ideas could be shared, and connectivism, a more controversial form of decentralized learning that shared similar assumptions (e.g. Milligan et al., 2013). Participants could create their own nodes of learning, through blogs, (see Chapter 2) for example, and then connect them to the nodes of other learners. Participants could produce and distribute knowledge using any literacy form they preferred, such as blogs or tweets, that could be aggregated using various aggregation tools (e.g. Liferay Portal), so that the participants could connect with other nodes.

This connectionist approach to learning was incorporated into the cMOOCs. Siemens (2005: para. 27) defined connectivism as integrating 'chaos, network, and complexity' into an alternative approach to learning emphasizing the power of large networks. These features distinguish many of the approaches to teaching literacy. Kop (2011) argued that there would be changes in teaching and learning literacies, a factor seen in the MOOCs where participants sought more autonomy in their writing contexts. This approach differed from the traditional lecture approach, which would later dominate the xMOOCs, by emphasizing the distributed nature of learning among the participants rather than being centralized in the lecturer, the 'sage on the stage'. MOOCs could impact, along with other new forms of technologically enhanced spaces, how writing was taught and learned on a global basis (Czerniewicz et al., 2017). Unlike the xMOOCs where the content and learning were often dictated by the 'sage on the stage', learning in these cMOOCs would be dictated by the interaction between the design and the participants.

Unlike the more decentralized cMOOCs, the course content of xMOOCs emanated from the center. xMOOCs became more like cathedrals than the commons design preferred by cMOOCs. For composition teachers, this xMOOC format was problematic. A pre-taped lecture and a set of discussion forums for tens of thousands of students does not support individual student engagement or accommodation. Downes' recent cMOOC focuses on 'E-Learning 3.0' and contains discussions with key contributors to the topics he has chosen as well as his aggregation of the participants' blogs. Thus, while cMOOCs often looked more like spontaneous 'pop-ups', springing up on the internet and Facebook, the xMOOCs were more closely tied to institutions although sometimes still disruptive to their structure.

The goal of the first MOOCs was to create learning spaces where participants could feel 'comfortable, trusted, and valued and where people can interact with resources and each other' (Kop, 2011: 88). Following Herring's (1999) work on the factors influencing the use of asynchronous discourse, including the number of participants and their goals, these first MOOCs opened up the learning process to 'the crowd', who could create their own threads and post to or read whichever thread they found interesting. All aspects of the MOOC, particularly whether the assignments were completed, could be controlled by the participants, which followed the theory of connected learning.

Downes (2011) recognized an important aspect of MOOCs that would later appear in their designs: which tools would be implemented and how the participants used these tools impacted teaching and learning. This approach incorporating the affordances of the tools within each space is consistent with Norman's (2007, 2013) discussions of the affordances of such tools and designs.

There were also differences from the traditional classroom in the design of the lecture videos. The role of videos in capturing the lecture of the 'sage' can be replaced by shorter videos from different instructors or by group discussions involving both teachers and students. In one video discussing reporting verbs and arguing, each participant briefly explains how they balance the relationship and how their literature reviews reflect the development of their research questions. Occasionally, the voice of a faculty member is inserted into the video but with no special authority on how to write the reviews. There is no requirement to write a literature review, and the interaction consists only of questions and answers posted to a traditional discussion board.

There are other areas in the evolution of MOOCs, such as in defining what the 'C' (course) means. Courses imply having a beginning and an ending, but MOOCs disrupts that assumption by starting and ending when the participants decide to join and leave. However, MOOCs have often had completion rates, but what do these rates mean? This aspect of the MOOC changed how some teachers perceived a 'course'; instead, there was a space for learning as long as the participant wanted to learn. These courses changed as well. Courses have been revised into workshops emphasizing specific topics on publishing. Despite the early attempts to make MOOCs seem like writing courses, the focus shifted to videotaped lectures and discussions, such as in a MOOC distributed by FutureLearn from Wollongong University in Australia about how to write a literature review, which featured videos of lectures and discussions of the writing process.

EdX presented a six-week MOOC from the Technical University of Munich in Germany entitled 'Academic Writing Made Easy', whose website (https://www.edx.org/course/academic-writing-made-easy) promised to help writers 'from structuring and organizing an academic text to avoiding common pitfalls that can negatively affect your credibility'. They included lectures on various topics such as the writing process, cohesion, sentence structure and punctuation, but with no writing assignments. They employed the new business model that charged $49 for a certificate which included 'graded assignments' or a free version with no interaction.

The FutureLearn course focused primarily on writing academic literature reviews using a series of videos featuring both student and faculty discussing aspects of a literature review. Changing these spaces would not only reduce the clutter from so many posts but also the focus on where the responses could be made, which would no longer be limited to a single space, so additional technologies were needed for aggregating these different spaces. Their usage, however, was problematic, often depending on their design for balancing in-class and outside-class participation (Lieberman, 2018). In a MOOC, the problems with clutter were compounded by the number of participants and threads. Blogs had also been used as an alternative tool for student participation in MOOCs. Downes (2011) created new tools for aggregating responses and then emailed the aggregation as a daily newsletter that each participant could use to create their own learning spaces. In writing MOOCs, the participants created their own spaces. For example, a group created their own Facebook site to create concurrent discussions to those found within the MOOC (Bloch, 2018), which could also be an antidote to the social isolation in MOOCs (e.g. Watters, 2013a). Using Facebook allowed this group to create a smaller cluster of individuals connected with each other, undermining the hierarchical structure of the classroom as well as the MOOC.

The choice of tools has always been an integral part of the design of MOOCs for creating connections in these literacy spaces, but their use could be problematic. Therefore, social media sites, which often lack such controls, become popular in these spaces. Cormier (2008b) coined the term 'rhizomatic' in learning to describe a process where opportunities and content 'popped up' like the rhizomes of a plant. Cormier tried different platforms to achieve this, eventually choosing Facebook, where participants could post whatever they wanted whenever they wanted. Although the posting rate declined substantially, using Facebook allowed the MOOC to continue if the participants, not necessarily the designer, continued posting. MOOCs have long created spaces where participants could learn at their own rate. Materials could remain on the internet after the 'official' part of the course was over so that learning could continue.

There was always strong resistance to the idea that MOOCs could change teaching and learning literacy. MOOCs did change learning in several ways; however, in some ways, they look like the face-to-face courses they were meant to replace. The xMOOCs in particular began to resemble the traditional writing classroom. Its 'massiveness', its 'openness' and its 'courseness' became more like that found in traditional courses; its 'onlineness' seemed similar to any online course. Nevertheless, the new MOOC designs still maintained their original characteristics. As their initial hype subsided, MOOCs persisted in the third wave of the Gartner Hype Cycle as changes were made to their original design and purpose. Shah (2018), who created the website Class Central (https://www.classcentral.com/), argues that MOOCs have reached this third wave as providers create new forms of online degrees. They later reported that there were 12,500 Chinese language MOOCs, a testimony to their endurance and globalization. However, their role in teaching writing has been reduced to providing lectures on various aspects of the writing process.

More than any other form of digital space, MOOCs were subject to the economic concerns of the providers. As the MOOC providers began to show greater concern with their bottom lines, the commitments to openness decreased. The impact on teaching writing can be readily seen in their designs. Agarwal (2018), the founder of EdX, discussed the different levels of access in edX as well as different goals for what is called 'Open edX'. Along with issues regarding downloading lectures, their paywalls impacted the grading of assignments, which was only available to participants who paid for verification.

Access to these spaces has become an important factor in their use. Free access has often been replaced by subscription fees. Even their free trials may require presenting a credit card that will be automatically charged unless deactivated, much like Netflix and other subscription services. The Wollongong course had free openness but only for a limited amount of time. Nevertheless, MOOCs teaching writing have persisted even with these fees. Coursera offers a variety of writing workshops consisting primarily only of lectures.

The rise of for-profit and not-for-profit organizations to distribute these MOOCs popularized in particular the xMOOCs as important learning spaces although maintaining many classroom features. These organizations had business plans to monetize learning, as evidenced by FutureLearn's $199 price for taking as many courses as desired, so eventually the free MOOCs featured different pricing models, often depending on the types of certification that participants wanted. These new designs may have also resulted from a shift in sponsorship toward these corporations that saw MOOCs for training a potential workforce. Institutions still remained the primary developer of xMOOCs, but they were seen less as 'disrupters' to traditional educational approaches and more for reducing the costs of education. Their openness has been reduced, and unless the participants pay a fee, they may not have full access to the content. Networks were no longer simply sources of knowledge but functioned more like traditional online forums. Universities could leverage these MOOCs so that after the lectures were recorded, the 'sage' did not have to participate, and the MOOC could be run by lower-paid teaching assistants who responded to questions on the forums.

The Development of MOOCs as Writing Spaces

As will be discussed later, MOOCs attempted to explore the potential for writing instruction (e.g. Bloch, 2016; Halasek *et al.*, 2016; Krause & Lowe, 2014). Recent MOOC designs seem to assume that traditional writing courses cannot be replicated in MOOCs as the Gates Foundation believed. Peer review still plays a role, but less time is spent on training participants to be peer reviewers. In some cases, the participants were relegated to the discussion boards, as was the case in the first MOOCs. In other cases, MOOCs have been experimenting with formats involving individual instructors and groups of instructors and students. These approaches could be where MOOCs have been disruptive, although they are not necessarily alien to teaching writing, particularly in developing countries such as China and India where access to education may currently be more limited.

To understand MOOCs as a literacy space, it is important to understand their development as a general pedagogy that would often include writing. MOOCs were initially designed to provide greater autonomy to the participants to become more active in their learning. It was hoped that MOOCs would disrupt the traditional 'bricks-and-mortar' institution since now the lecturer as the dominant source of knowledge could be replaced by a network of learners, contributing to the popular, though somewhat problematic description, of teachers as 'guides on the side' rather than 'sages on the stage'. However, the 'sages' metaphor still dominated, but could later be usurped as illustrated by the designer metaphor used here.

The openness of the MOOCs has been the key factor in their role in literacy in global education. As discussed in Chapter 6, openness can refer to various aspects of education, but the popularity of the MOOCs is directly related to the ease with which participants can register regardless of their location. However, openness can also take on additional meanings. Levine (2014) discusses the openness of all aspects of the MOOC, a goal that has not always been achieved in the writing MOOCs. He gives the example of the ds106 MOOC designed by Jim Groom at the University of Mary Washington where Twitter replaced discussions, an approach that would be used in several MOOCs. As MOOCs developed, their openness became more problematic. Cormier (2008b) later designed a MOOC that solely utilized Facebook to support what he called 'rhizomatic' education where the discussion can incorporate multimodal posts that endure beyond the 'course'. However, for many of the MOOCs, their business plans limited their openness to those who could pay the fees.

However, there have been several disturbing trends in creating openness. This goal for open access would not be realized as the 'free' aspect of MOOCs gradually gave way to the financial concerns of the providers. The response to this issue of participation reflects how MOOCs have evolved as illustrated by The Gartner Hype Cycle: the initial period of excitement and then disillusionment was followed by a gradual period with new levels of acceptance as institutions began to implement feasible designs for teaching writing. Many designs were found to be economically efficient for designing multiple iterations of the course with little financial expenditure after the initial investment in their design. They also focused primarily on specific areas of content, such as writing a literature review, rather than on the writing process itself, as was found in the earlier MOOCs.

MOOCs development was consistent with what Vandergriff (2016) found using computer-mediated discourse (CMD): that using such tools was impacted by their implementation so that using the same tool could vary in different contexts and for different literacies. Thus, the tools could play different roles within and across the spaces, a view consistent with the discussions of technological determinism (e.g. Feenberg, 1999, which still influences developing open pedagogies (Weller, 2018b). However, there were negative developments as well. The chaotic nature of openness was an intrinsic feature of MOOCs, but later this openness was controlled by a 'publisher' who would fully admit only those willing to pay for continual access.

The institutional support for MOOCs often conflicted with the goals for teaching writing. The xMOOCs, which were primarily created by major universities and distributed by profit-seeking entities such as Coursera or FutureLearn, often reinstated the primacy of the 'sage on the stage' metaphor with the dominance of 'superstar' professors, such as Sebastian Thurin and Andrew Ng, who created xMOOCs attracting hundreds of thousands of participants. Head (2014), who was the leader of the Georgia Tech writing MOOC, argued that this design contradicted many of the traditional goals of the composition classroom. The design of these xMOOCs varied but generally centered on the instructor as 'sage', often designing a space around and adding discussion sections where the participants could still connect.

All of these factors would influence using these spaces for writing. Attempts to introduce writing into the MOOCs could be seen in the earliest MOOCs, although the direct teaching of writing started later. Although many of the engineering-related MOOCs contained little or no written work, some attempted to emulate the importance of writing in academic classrooms by adding writing requirements. The potential of the space to attract large numbers of multilingual students from different cultures seemed appealing, although the isolation of these students as well as potential problems especially with plagiarism and textual borrowing, were not always adequately anticipated.

Questions about the role of writing and concerns with plagiarism could be seen in some of the first xMOOCs. In an early xMOOC on the history of technology, Charles Severance, an enthusiastic proponent of MOOCs, attempted to recreate his classroom at the University of Michigan by including the same kinds of writing assignments given in the classroom. However, at the end of the MOOC, he issued a *mea culpa* that he did not realize how much plagiarism would result from those assignments and vowed not to give them in future iterations, an issue that would greatly expand in what Heilwell (2020) called 'paranoia' as many students and teachers moved to online and remote learning during the COVID-19 pandemic. In the literacy MOOCs, where writing was a primary factor, the plagiarism issues could never be completely addressed.

Despite the limitations, MOOCs as writing spaces received incentives from grants from the Bill and Melinda Gates Foundation, who hoped that MOOCs could help students better prepare for university writing courses (Bloch, 2018). The foundation issued four grants, three to universities and one to a community college, to create courses that could be repeated to help students prepare for their college writing courses. From their outset, however, course designers hoped that the MOOC space disrupted the traditional methods and narratives that had shaped their previous teaching. Halasek *et al.* (2016) found early on that the narratives about teachers and students that had shaped their classroom teaching simply would not work in a MOOC. Before the MOOCs were released, Head (2014) expressed concern about the influence of Coursera and the Gates Foundation on the MOOC design and on their ability to provide feedback and evaluation.

MOOCs, nevertheless, seemed poised to disrupt all levels of education, promising new approaches to learning that would provide more active and personalized learning. In her journal on teaching in her writing

MOOC from Duke University, Comer (2014), one of the first recipients of the Gates Foundation grant, describes her goals:

(1) to cultivate global conversations about writing so more people around the world can grow as writers and learn about writing from each other; and (2) to conduct research on how the MOOC impacts the teaching and learning of writing. (Comer, 2014: 131)

A problem emerged as to how instructors could respond to and assess the greater amount of writing created in the MOOCs. There was a general concern for the tools that Coursera supplied for automatic evaluation. Copy-detection programs were suggested for dealing with plagiarism and automatic essay assessors for evaluating papers. Their use in traditional composition courses was severely criticized, and their use and effectiveness were still suspected in digital spaces. Technological development responded to such suspicions with the development of new tools. As had been the case in the history of technological implementation, new technologies often incorporated both new and repurposed tools. As Norman (2013) showed, these tools had their own affordances, which could increase the ability of both teachers and partisans to negotiate the various constraints of the space.

The designers of the MOOCs often had to develop their own tools to solve pedagogical problems. A major concern was providing feedback since it was obvious that neither teachers nor their assistants could respond to every paper. Comer (2014) described how the Duke course used Google Hangouts, which could only include a few students, modeled the feedback process she hoped the participants would use in their peer reviews. Only a few participants could enter the Hangout at a time, so Comer invited them to submit papers to be discussed and then modeled the process. If the tools provided by Coursera did not meet the teachers' goals, some developed their own tools to meet their pedagogical goals. The Ohio State MOOC introduced WeX to help prepare participants for peer review (Halasek et al., 2016). Some students incorporated their own tools when they felt that they were not receiving sufficient feedback (Bloch, 2016).

As Severance had discovered earlier, the sometimes chaotic results illustrated how their design and technological structure could not always control the backgrounds of the participants or the types of learning. The large numbers of multilingual students greatly impacted the design of these literacy spaces, both in terms of logistics and the kinds of writing problems they would face. As Halasek et al. (2016) point out, the number of participants was larger than expected; in their course, they reported that over 32,000 participants signed up.

The high number of participants who did not complete all the requirements contradicted how many teachers defined the idea of a 'course'.

Krause (2014) raised this issue with the MOOC designers concerning the high dropout rate frequently reported in Coursera's MOOCs. Comer and White (2016) found that only around 2–3% of the enrolled participants received certificates for achieving a 'grade' of over 75%, an issue that would be central in the discussion of MOOCs as a learning space. It was not simply the completion rate but also how the participants worked at their own pace through the assignments.

However, if the word 'course' could be redefined in the MOOC, teachers found that the MOOCs could provide alternative learning spaces for teaching writing. Halasek *et al.* (2016) found that how their participants worked through the MOOC at varying rates was another way in which the design of the MOOC disrupted traditional classroom expectations. Better answers to the implications of this dropout rate for participant autonomy would come from those outside the literacy spaces, so participants could decide their level of participation and drop out whenever they so desired.

The limitations can be seen in the structure of some of the current MOOCs that address writing where traditional objectives are combined with greater accessibility. A course on academic writing from Garhwal University in India lists seven objectives, including lectures on plagiarism, digital writing and publication, and can address the specific backgrounds of the students. The University of Irvine, California, has a subscription-based course sequence on Coursera that charges $49 a month for students to progress through four levels of writing instruction that begins with grammar instruction and a capstone course requiring the completion of the previous four levels. According to the course's FAQs, by the end of the course, the participants should be able 'to write well-researched, structured, and effective college essays using proper English grammar'. Unlike earlier writing courses, the course was designed for participants with various linguistic and social backgrounds. According to the course's FAQs,

> Students who have not been exposed to rigorous English courses in high school, students whose native language is not English, and others interested in refining their written English communication skills are all welcome.

The course still relies on traditional lectures and readings, often more closely resembling traditional print literacy spaces. The lectures still use the dominant voice of the instructor as well as directly addressing plagiarism unlike the approach seen in the first MOOCs that included writing. For example, in the lecture on using sources, the instructor differentiates between what are acceptable sources and what are not, with a recognition that not all the participants have access to acceptable academic sources. None of the ambiguity, however, about the relative value of sources is discussed.

The MOOC design was always a controversial issue in these spaces, thus challenging attempts at imposing traditional classroom approaches. Writing pedagogies were still implementing the connectivist principles of the early cMOOCs, although the dominant voice of Comer as the lead instructor may contradict that approach. It is interesting to note how these issues could not be satisfied by either the xMOOC or cMOOC design. The challenge of mixing cMOOC and xMOOC designs shows how the design of a MOOC space can incorporate the complex pedagogies found in writing courses. While in one design, the voice of the instructor (Comer, 2014) dominated the delivery of information, other designs incorporated different ways of presenting knowledge, including group discussions and multiple presenters, which had previously been tried in another Coursera MOOC.

The Writing Process in the MOOC

Despite the dominance of the instructors' voices in these literacy spaces, students still control their own learning in different ways than may be possible in a face-to-face class. Comer and White (2016) argue that the greater importance given to assessment using peer review illustrates the integration of the cMOOC design and composition pedagogy in drawing upon the knowledge of the participants to provide feedback and assessment. They found that the participants could implement their own tools in addition to those supplied in the course. These design issues raised various pedagogical issues for discussion. Carbone (2014), for example, suggested using an online portfolio evaluation site such as LearningCounts.org (https://www.cael.org/higher-education/portfolio-assessment-with-learning-counts). Using such tools illustrates how the design of this MOOC literacy space could be impacted by the participants as the original designers had allowed the teachers to decentralize their roles and let the participants pursue their own goals.

This role in literacy pedagogy could be seen in the traditional participant forums for questions and concerns. In one thread, the participants reflected on the peer reviewing they both did and received. Without the instructor to provide feedback, the participants had to become peer reviewers for their classmates. Halasek *et al.* (2016: 160) cite a participant particularly ecstatic about her role:

> I am a happy reviewer! It is not so bad! I have done six now and will try to add some more. I am finding that it helps me to see my own writing better. I will now have to force myself to do the necessary editing of my own work!

Comer (2014) also had a participant who felt peer reviews were very helpful:

> I can see so much value in these peer reviews. I was thinking if we could form an online community, maybe a Google group, where we could continue submitting our future writing projects for peer review. My thanks to all my peers who reviewed my work over the last twelve weeks, and for all the reviews on the discussion forums, from which I learnt so much.

The participant's desire to continue the MOOC would be later manifested in her use of Facebook. Not everyone, however, found such value in their interactions. Many of the problems with the discussion boards that appeared in the first MOOCs remained, mainly the large and often unmanageable number of postings, although without the concern previously expressed. Halasek *et al.* (2016) report that the discussion boards were visited 116,845 times and 2,679 threads were created. There was little discussion on whether this number was manageable, but there were pedagogical issues that did raise concerns. Comer (2014: 144) cites one participant as being concerned with the reviews she was receiving:

> I've submitted 3 peer-feedbacks too, and also received 2 responses to my review. I understand the disappointment that some of you feel when having 3 proper feedbacks can mean so much to an aspiring writer.

As in other cMOOCs, the participants sometimes created their own interactions to remediate the limitations they found with the existing technologies (Bloch, 2016), for example, with the quality and quantity of the peer reviews. In one case, a participant used the space to ask for additional peer reviews when she found the reviews she received did not completely address her concerns. Another participant who was taking two writing MOOCs asked the participants in one course to review a paper from her other course. Woodworth (2014) also found that the Facebook group she joined seemed to provide an open space where participants could address their concerns. Such changes have often occurred in the history of technology, as the introduction of sound to the motion pictures illustrate, but these technologies were not created for the purpose by engineers but appropriated by the designers and participants to solve their own problems.

One of the major issues these MOOCs faced was the varied literacy backgrounds of the participants. Although these MOOCs were intended for first language (L1) students, the linguistic diversity of the participants could not be controlled. Such diversity could create spaces, unlike those usually found in classrooms, where the interactions among these participants could not be controlled, again leading to possible areas of chaos. However, the potential for exploiting the value of such chaos was never fully explored. Despite an awareness of the multilingual participants in the previous Coursera MOOCs, there was little consideration for them in the original design.

However, the dominance of non-native English speakers was eventually noticed. Comer and White (2016) reported that 77% of the participants in the Duke MOOC indicated that they were not native English speakers. To make these spaces more conducive to multilingual participants, some tweaks were made to their designs to include some, usually superficial, discussions of language issues relevant to multilingual composition. The Duke MOOC brought in a consultant to discuss language issues, although these issues were not fully addressed in the MOOC. Ohio State, for example, included discussions related to globalized English, although again their impact was not consistent.

However, the complexities of creating these MOOC designs for global participants resulted in changes in the goals for creating MOOCs, which seemed to lead to more simplified designs. The US State Department offered a MOOC through the University of California primarily addressed to multilingual students that had no formal assessment. Unlike the MOOCs supported by the Gates Foundation, this MOOC did not try to emulate a writing course but focused instead on grammar. Gilliland *et al.* (2018) critiqued the approach for using the affordances of the platform. In some cases, the discussion boards reverted to their traditional role of asking questions and making occasional comments.

The Limitations of the MOOC Design

Although the literacy MOOCs incorporated some aspects of the cMOOCs, they never focused entirely on learning to write. The more negative consequences were that the initial hope that the design of the MOOCs could alter the pedagogy for teaching writing never materialized. Except for their being online ('O'), the other aspects of the MOOC design were modified or disregarded. The idea of a 'course' (C) has evolved into a series of shorter workshops, mirroring how xMOOCs have been utilized for training purposes, relying more on recorded lectures by 'the sage on the stage'.

A more disturbing trend in MOOC design has been the diminution of MOOCs' 'openness' (O), particularly in light of the growing concerns for economic sustainability (see Chapter 6). Openness in the original MOOC design assumed that the MOOCs were open to all participants at no charge and, perhaps unintentionally, even to the researchers studying them. However, as with journals, a more difficult problem was the openness of the teaching materials. Even the initial openness was proscribed in the MOOC design: while some materials could be accessed openly, in other cases the materials could only be accessed by paying customers.

The idea of a paradigmatic shift in learning that Siemens (2005) and Downes (2011) argued for was largely predicated on the openness of the MOOC to expand the number participants and their knowledge. This potential for openness had an appeal to designers to reach out more to multilingual writers and teachers who lacked access to materials. This goal can be seen in how peer reviewing could be expanded in the MOOCs (Bloch, 2016). Clearly, learning has shifted both in terms of how the participants learn the content and what it means to be credentialed, whether that means a university or a corporation. This shift did not necessarily diminish the impact of MOOCs on digital literacy instruction, as they have retained their global nature, which has changed the potential of MOOCs in writing instruction.

MOOCs never had the impact on literacy that was expected, in part due to the required technological infrastructure. However, there were some positive consequences for literacy learning and teaching. MOOCs turned writing teachers into designers and the classroom into a digital space. Designers had to create sites where the participants could readily access different areas and materials on their own, whenever, wherever and how often they wanted to. However, their design is evolving outside of the platforms, as Coursera and EdX illustrate; they are becoming more flexible and expensive without the forms of peer review (BasuMallick, 2019) that have been exploited in the writing courses. Young (2019) reports on a project called LabXChange that allows mixing pieces of MOOCs to create a new MOOC, which opens new pedagogical possibilities.

However, other areas of MOOC design continue to develop. Downes has continued his designs, relying more on other digital literacies to support interactions. The sustainability of the original MOOC design has largely given way to the financial goals of the sponsors of MOOCs, particularly in the area of openness, which has limited the development of courses specific to teaching writing. There has also been the counter trend with MOOCs in different languages on different topics primarily for native speakers of these languages.

The Impact of MOOCs on Teaching Literacy

MOOCs never became the space for writing literacy that was initially hoped for. The various designs of MOOCs for teaching writing have illustrated attempts to scale pedagogies from a small classroom enrollment to an infinitely larger space with potentially tens of thousands of participants. The structures and affordances of the MOOCs, however, did not always support common writing practices. These spaces for teaching and learning about writing have often been detached from the university structure, allowing those who can access the internet learn about writing outside the traditional institutional structure without grades or the pressure to complete courses. Various economic forces from the institutions and the sponsoring corporations have impacted these spaces. The argument in the Gates Foundation grants that MOOCs could replace or bridge students into first- and second-year composition courses did not seem to work out.

What seems to have worked in MOOCs concerned with teaching writing, however, has been the ability of these spaces to support the participants to learn more about writing. As Carbone (2014: 198) argued, 'what fascinated me about the OSU [Ohio State] MOOC experience was the participation of students who were not in the course for credit; that's the shift that matters'. He does not dismiss the potential of MOOCs to teach credit courses in writing since these courses have not yet started, but he finds that their real potential lies in creating spaces for students with varying goals for learning to write.

One important consequence has been a recognition of the need for the continual revision of MOOCs. Halasek *et al.* (2016) saw the importance of revising their MOOC using data obtained from previous iterations. They found that MOOC instruction differed from classroom instruction. However, there were always critical differences. As Weller (2020) noted, collecting data was important in these distance contexts for replacing the information teachers could readily obtain in face-to-face contexts. These developments illustrate one of the most valuable contributions that these literacy spaces were in 'perpetual beta' where data could provide the basis for continual revision.

Despite the hype and the frustrations, Porter (2016) argues that MOOCs still present many opportunities for teaching writing. These opportunities can challenge traditional assumptions about teaching and learning literacy. As Halasek *et al.* (2016) argued, the MOOC design challenges traditional assumptions about the writing classroom, especially the roles that the teacher and the student play in the writing process. In describing their MOOC, they found that there may be an initial frustration from teachers with how the participants can control their learning, particularly those embracing the model where learning usually occurs in a lock-step fashion with deadlines creating constraints on when and how assignments are completed.

Clearly, the initial enthusiasm for MOOCs as a literacy space has given way to more directed and limited approaches, mostly in other fields with specific career paths or specific aspects of the writing process such as literature reviews. Since MOOCs can easily be iterated with much lower costs, their numbers have proliferated as new courses are added. For teaching literacy, however, they have become more like writing centers than classrooms, often addressing specific issues such as writing literature reviews.

Still, these opportunities have become more limited. The openness of MOOCs as a literacy space has dissipated as new, more narrowly defined goals for literacy have emerged, and fees have become more widespread. MOOCs disrupted and reshaped literacy education, particularly in creating digital literacy spaces. However, today they seem to focus on teaching specific skills, mostly for preparing participants for careers. When MOOCs do focus on teaching writing, as a FutureLearn MOOC illustrates, they can be used for learning writing skills such as a literature review. MOOCs can still serve a diverse group of participants as well as help familiarize them with the digital spaces and tools they may encounter in other spaces. As will be discussed in Chapter 5, flipped classrooms have taken over the roles of MOOCs in providing autonomous learning to students.

The economic trends of MOOCs have become more important in determining their roles. They often depend more on 'freemium' and 'subscriptions' that can limit their use. In this context, for example, Coursera is creating algorithms that can help students identify their skills and track their progress, a development that could help students with their literacy development although this approach does not seem to have been used. This trend illustrates that the money is going toward the business models that support training programs, micro credentials and certificates, but not writing courses as was true in the past. Writing courses or workshops could be a part of these programs, but there has been little indication that this direction has been taken. What is left are online lectures on various forms of writing with discussion boards for asking questions. Students who can pay for certification may, in some cases, receive some feedback on their writing, but clearly the 'massiveness' and the 'openness' have been limited. The legacy of MOOCs on the design of digital literacy spaces can be seen in discussions of assignments, peer review and assessment. How the teachers of literacy can utilize these changes in the design of MOOCs is a question for future discussion.

Given these constraints, how useful is the MOOC design for teaching literacy? While MOOCs could never provide the literacy spaces initially hoped for, they do provide concepts of autonomy, community, engagement, openness and flexibility that could be used in developing other literacy spaces. A comparison of the MOOC space with the traditional composition space is often problematic. An obvious difference is with the size of the courses. It is impossible for the classes to replicate all the pedagogical features, such as expanding the role of peer review or eliminating grading, prevalent in designing traditional classrooms. Woodworth (2014), for example, found her interaction with the Facebook 'tool' and her blogging experiences to be the most valuable for her own writing classroom. However, other participants noted problems with the lack of interaction found in the traditional classroom and the previously discussed concerns regarding responding to writing and the low completion rates.

5 Flipping the Multilingual Composition Classroom

Flipped Classes and Flipped Learning

This chapter will examine another form of digital literacy space called the flipped classroom, which has often developed as a blended literacy space, mixing classroom and outside activities. Flipped classrooms may not be appropriate for all pedagogical contexts, but the design of the flipped writing classroom has been adapted to promote flipped learning. Flipped spaces share some of the same values as Massive Open Online Courses (MOOCs), but flipped learning has largely replaced MOOCs as a space for teaching writing by extending the concept of space to take advantage of both the classroom space and the multiple spaces where students learn.

Unlike MOOCs, the flipped space can exist within a physical space, a blended space where students move between a classroom and an online space ('7 Things You Should Know About Flipped Classrooms', 2012), or a hyflex space ('7 Things You Should Know About the HyFlex Course Model', 2010; Malczyk, 2019) where the students can choose a space where they want to learn. As with MOOCs, the flipped classroom attempts to break down the walls or silos between inside and outside the classroom, so these different spaces can be blended or mixed. Especially consistent with the cMOOC, the flipped classroom challenges the domination of the teacher as sage, but similar to the xMOOC, its focus is more on emphasizing the content of the course rather than the networks through which the literacies are linked or how the information in these networks is distributed.

Many forms of flipped digital spaces can be designed, each with its own set of affordances that the designer wants to include. The flipped classroom can resemble the classroom form, whether restructuring large lecture classes or changing the pedagogical approaches of smaller classrooms, while still attempting to redistribute tasks for greater student autonomy. Unlike the MOOC, the flipped classroom is a hybrid space that includes a traditional classroom space that could be expanded to incorporate outside-of-class spaces such as libraries, homes and coffee shops.

The goal is to give learners more autonomy by providing more spaces for learning, using both digital and print. On the other hand, many issues incorporated in MOOCs have largely been ignored in designing flipped classrooms, most notably the networks of interconnected data, which, as will be discussed, can still be remediated particularly with videos. A single definition of the flipped classroom is not possible as it is often centered around the teacher's design of the classroom space rather than around a technologically designed platform, often found with MOOCs.

Flipped classrooms have developed in the long tradition of much hyped educational solutions going back to PLATO, TICCIT, One Laptop per Child and, today, MOOCs. As with MOOCs, the flipped space originated from the vision of a few individuals but has expanded its number of participants and its approaches. As with other digital spaces, the flipped classroom often relies on the use of various technological tools. These technological tools may also have costs regarding training as well as purchasing and designing learning materials. Technology vendors have seen business opportunities in all areas of design, whether recording lectures or purchasing furniture for new classroom layouts. Many of these programs still have free or low-cost versions. However, corporations such as Steelcase are looking at the potential for large amounts of furniture to support active learning (Talbert, 2019).

Moreover, designs can be easily affected by the economic goals of the companies designing the products. As I've learned when my favorite site for video creation went out of business, the failure of a vendor can force a teacher to change their approach. Surveys have shown a distrust of the vendors concerning the claims they make about the value of the technologies they are pushing (Jaschik & Lederman, 2018). As with other forms of technological commons, their openness can increase participation, which has contributed to the development of these spaces; therefore, as Zittrain (2009) has argued, restrictions on this openness can have detrimental effects on its development.

The main goal of the flipped classroom is to support flipped learning. Flipped learning is considered a form of hybrid learning where face-to-face class time is mixed with online materials (Bates, 2013) and can be adapted to other classroom designs. The challenge in designing such classes is the allocation of activities among the different possible learning spaces. Hybrid classrooms refer to any classroom where part of the learning space is outside the classroom, often online, in a cloud or wherever the student can access the material. The flipped classroom has become a popular pedagogical approach to dealing with the design of these hybrid spaces (Arfstom, 2013; Bergmann & Sams, 2012; Gerstein, 2011; Papadapoulos & Roman, 2010; Zappe et al., 2009).

Various attempts have been made to define the flipped learning class or space. The Academy of Active Learning Arts and Sciences (AALAS) defines flipped learning as

> a framework that enables educators to reach every student. The Flipped approach inverts the traditional classroom model by

introducing course concepts before class, allowing educators to use class time to guide each student through active, practical, innovative applications of the course principles. (http://aalasinternational.org/updated-definition-of-flipped-learning)

However, in a video released to the Global Flipped Initiative (http://community.flglobal.org/the-big-news), Jon Bergmann, a popularizer of flipped learning, called for teachers to explore this definition to consider ways to 'reach every child' (REC), which became a major goal for flipped learning. He discussed flipped learning as giving students more choices in the classroom reflecting the development of new teaching strategies, promoting active learning, reaching difficult-to-teach students, teaching troublesome and difficult concepts, making assignments social, using new tools for assessing students without providing grades and providing support for teachers. Although flipped learning is not a prerequisite for achieving these goals, many of which can be found in other digital or traditional classes, Bergmann, however, argues that the flipped classroom can best provide the necessary framework for these new approaches. Such new approaches required new forms of teaching training. The institute provided a website to familiarize practitioners with standards for flipped learning (http://aalasinternational.org/aalas-general-standards) and webinars, often with a subscription fee, aimed at developing new teachers.

Data has shown that interest in classroom flipping and learning is increasing. Yabro *et al.* (2014) found an increase in flipped classes although warning that there are areas where flipping may not be feasible. Setren *et al.*'s (2019) study also showed differences in where flipped learning was effective. Many studies have offered support for the implementation of flipped learning. In a 2015 survey of higher education faculties, 70% felt that flipping their classroom was beneficial for them and 65% felt that it was beneficial for their students ('Flipped Classroom Trends: A Survey of College Faculty', 2015). In a survey of flipped classrooms across the United Kingdom, Raine and Gretton (n.d.) found positive results including increased engagement in student learning. Dorman and Webb (2017) found an improved attitude among Chinese students toward language learning. Maycock *et al.* (2018) found evidence that student performance improved following several iterations of the course.

The Consequences of Flipped Learning on Student Engagement

Research on flipped classrooms often seems oriented to student and faculty motivation and their satisfaction with the results. These surveys, often conducted by established advocates of flipped classrooms, found high levels of engagement among students and high levels of satisfaction among instructors. Mediasite, a vendor of software for creating videos, found that over 80% of the faculty they interviewed thought that the flipped classroom provided a better learning environment for students and 57% of the faculty felt that their flipped classrooms were successful. These results offer some support for implementing flipped classrooms although without specific evidence for the flipped classroom in the multilingual classroom.

There are also reports suggesting that students have improved retention, greater mastery of information and more adaption to learner differences as well as, to a lesser extent, including learner interests and motivations. However, despite the potential of these goals for changing learning, challenges remain in teacher development: the lack of proven benefits and the difficulty in creating classrooms conducive to flipped learning. Much of this research has been anecdotal, but a few studies have attempted to evaluate their success across several disciplines such as design education (Senske, 2017) and calculus (Dove, 2018). The evidence for improved student performance has been patchy and not always generalizable to teaching writing. Evidence supporting flipped learning has been found in courses not related to writing. McLaughlin *et al.* (2014) flipped a pharmacy class after recognizing the difficulty the students had in processing long lectures. They found that the students preferred the shorter, prerecorded videos, as well as the additional time to participate in class activities.

Designing a Flipped Learning Space

The flipped classroom is not new, but its current popularity reflects what Reidsema *et al.* (2017) call a 'confluence' of social, economic and technological factors that dominate discussions of education. The flipped writing class challenges both the student and the teacher to rethink their traditional roles and approaches to learning, which, as is often the case, can produce both new learning experiences and pockets of resistance. For many students, learning in a flipped classroom can be a new experience, which may be resisted by both teachers and students and therefore requires some form of explanation to achieve the required levels of buy-in. Its goals have primarily been to have students work independently to gain an understanding of the discipline and to better understand themselves by working independently (Greenfield & Hibbert, 2017).

The goal of designing a flipped digital space was to change how and where content is learned, not the content itself, as was true in the cMOOC. Its importance in restructuring large classes did not change the content but how the content was taught. Its design incorporated what Bergmann and Sams (2012) describe as the four pillars of flipped learning: a flexible environment that creates various spaces to support different types of learning; a learning culture where both students and teachers can contribute to the learning environment; intentional content that fosters both procedural and conceptual learning; and an environment for creating professional educators who are reflective about their teaching ('A Review of Flipped Classroom Research, Practice, and Technologies', 2014; Arfstom *et al.*, 2013; Cheng *et al.*, 2018). Bergmann and St Clair (2017) divided the flipped classroom into two spaces: the group space (e.g. the classroom) and the individual space (e.g. outside the classroom), a design not required for flipped learning but one that is popular.

The design of this approach combines the classroom space with spaces outside the classroom. In the flipped classroom, assignments are often divided between these two spaces: students receive a higher percentage of the content outside the classroom, which they are expected to complete prior to entering the classroom space. Inside the classroom, they receive more interaction with the materials, the instructor and the other students. This design places more autonomy for learning on the student than found in the traditional classroom but less than what is often seen in a MOOC where the students may find more autonomy.

The design of the flipped classroom highlights the possibilities for different types of learning where students can, as in a MOOC, learn at their own rate and in their own spaces. In both areas of the flipped classroom, teachers can provide more opportunities for students to become active learners (Davidson, 2012). Lectures, which were once sites of passive learning, can be transformed, often using short, annotated videos, so students can interact with the content and better control when, where and how often the videos are watched. For some, this design provides more autonomy for student learning, although others have argued that it is simply a way to redistribute homework (e.g. Watters, 2019), reflecting what Ravitch (2019: para. 3) argues as 'the combination of unadulterated arrogance (i.e. chutzpah), coupled with repeated failures'.

In the flipped writing classroom, teachers can give the same writing assignments as before, but with flipped learning, these assignments can now be brought into social 'studios' where the writers can interact more with their teachers and classmates. Other factors can affect the structure not only of the space but also of the learning community. In the flipped classroom, teachers can create their materials that can be shared with other teachers and students outside the classroom, often in an open format (Wiley, 2007).

Despite the criticisms, flipped learning is in a continual state of development, referred to earlier as being in 'perpetual beta'. Initially, teachers focused on distributing skills, often using Bloom's taxonomy as a framework, in the different spaces or stations. Recently, the expression 'from Bloom to Maslow' has been adapted, reflecting a shift away from only focusing on Bloom's hierarchy of skills to integrating them with activities including Maslowian (1962, 1966, 1971) concerns with the personal, reflective, moral and emotional conditions of the students, all of which can be incorporated into the design of literacy spaces.

The flipped classroom was not designed as a replacement for existing learning spaces or as a modification of these spaces to better support flipped learning. It is not that the role of the teacher is reduced, but that these designs are another illustration of the changes in their roles as they become designers and possibly mentors. The flipped classroom may not be open in terms of either admission or material use; however, the constraints imposed on the participants may still be more flexible even when they are in a classroom on a certain day and time. Teachers may have to redesign their courses within the constraints of the institution in which they work. The flipped classroom has often been skeptically viewed as a 'technological solution' (Morozov, 2014) to pedagogical problems, sometimes by the corporations benefiting from its implementation and sometimes by teachers who see the flipped classroom as a panacea for some educational problems.

How much time is spent in class versus out of class on learning can vary. The flipped classroom design has redressed issues in using MOOCs for teaching writing. As MOOCs were analyzed with greater scrutiny, the flipped classroom emerged as an alternative approach to literacy learning design. Rather than using the massiveness of the MOOCs, for example, the flipped classroom returned the study of literacy to the classroom, where students, depending on how their classrooms are designed, could now interact with more personal interactions than found in the MOOC. This shift restored, however, the centrality of a 'course', which could have resulted in students having less autonomy in the flipped learning space than in the MOOC space.

This physical presence of classmates and teachers can differ from the social contexts in other digital spaces such as MOOCs. The discussion boards have largely reverted to a space for interpersonal interactions, sometime increasing the amount of interactions with a reduction in lecturing. While MOOCs have largely replaced teachers with videos, the flipped classroom has shifted some teacher-created content to videos while redefining the role of the teacher as an important factor in the classroom. Although the 'guide-on-the side' metaphor is still used, the role of the teacher is more active and dynamic in both the ongoing design and teaching practice.

While both MOOCs and flipped classrooms rely on videos that could be made interactive for more active learning, their designs differ, reflecting different approaches to learning. The long 'sage' video found in MOOCs was replaced by shorter videos, sometimes from 'sages', often focusing on specific issues and problems that students had experienced. Finally, the 'openness' that motivated the design of the early cMOOCs, and later lost their position as the financial value of this intellectual property became more apparent, could be partially reinstated in the flipped classroom, at least in terms of controlling how the videos could be shared. Other important differences have led practitioners to incorporate various approaches to teacher flexibility, which, in turn, support greater differentiation for student learning across these different learning spaces.

In the *Inside Higher Education*'s survey, a majority of faculty were influenced by how their peers were using the technology (Jaschik & Lederman, 2018). However, research is often not generalizable across classrooms and mediation is never static. The trends underlying the flipped classroom are in flux, reflecting what Bergmann (2017) calls 'Flipped Learning 3.0'. The '3.0' connects the current development of the flipped learning space to its previous iterations as the internet developed from 1.0 to 2.0 (O'Reilly, 2005).

The ability of Web 2.0 to encourage the participation and creativity of its users (e.g. Berners-Lee, 1999) has been extended in 3.0 to a more networked-based learning model where a piece of knowledge resides in everyone. For Bergman, that meant creating a global network of teachers contributing ideas about flipped learning even though the learners themselves largely remained in the classroom. Although the research as well as our own anecdotes show great potential for flipped learning as a digital literacy space, how multilingual writing teachers fit into this global network remains an important question.

Flipped Classrooms and Multilingual Writers

The development of flipped classrooms has continued the shift to making literacy instruction more interactive. Lage *et al.* (2000) used the term 'inverted classroom' to describe their redesigned medical school classroom before the term 'flipped' was popularized. However, their argument that teachers should employ different approaches exploiting the potential of the flipped classroom remains the basis of this space. The flipped classroom has required using new technologies to support its more personalized forms of learning that recognize differences in student learning.

Writing MOOCs started as near replications of the existing writing classes but gradually evolved in response to issues that arose in the digital space. Flipped classrooms had the same roots but viewed teaching literacy using different approaches. Flipped learning shared with MOOCs the attempt to incorporate the student voices so that they gained more control over their learning. In Downes' latest cMOOC, for example, participants can choose with whom they want to form communities and which tools they want to use. Flipped classroom teachers wrestle with the same issues. However, the content is still dictated by the designer, in most cases the classroom teacher.

Despite this attention, the design of the classroom remains vague and has raised many questions. Which activities are better suited for in class and which are better suited for out of class? How can both spaces be made more active? Are different activities, reflecting the hierarchy in

Bloom's taxonomy (e.g. Mehring & Leis, 2018), better suited for one space than the other? What are the differences in the roles of the instructors in these different spaces? The answers to these questions are problematic since there is no single classroom design; therefore, instructors who want to implement this design must continually modify the design to discover what works best for their students.

The design of the flipped classroom has encouraged teachers to develop various pedagogical approaches to its implementation, although it is less clear whether there has been any movement toward changing the content or how the content is assessed. As spaces for language learning, the courses never relied as much on a 'sage' as did the MOOCs. Depending on the content, one flipped classroom may be designed differently from another even though both may share the same learning approaches. A distinction, therefore, can be made between the forms of learning (flipped learning) and their instructional space (flipped classroom).

The design of flipped classrooms for teaching literacy (e.g. Lockwood, 2014), therefore, can also include learning experiences specifically designed for each student. Mehring and Leis (2018) argue that the flipped classroom can personalize learning experiences by including various forms of cognitive, scaffolding and social constructivism, a framework Weller (2020) traces back to the research on learning by Piaget, Vygotsky and Bruner, which would influence the development of technological literacy spaces that provide greater agency and autonomy to the students.

The main approach to increasing this engagement for students has been to increase in-class time, resulting from moving certain aspects of the course outside the classroom. Each learning space reflected can incorporate different approaches to openness in literacy education. Unlike the MOOC, the flipped classroom does not embrace openness although this is possible, especially for sharing course materials. While the flipped classroom was not initially designed for language learning, its focus on student-centered learning has made it a natural environment for all aspects of language learning including literacy, although the number of students in a flipped class is usually lower than found in traditional lecture classes.

The potential of these approaches for teaching writing has drawn the interest of second language (L2) researchers. Lockwood (2014), for example, argues that despite their own unique attributes, English as a second language (ESL) classrooms can also be flipped to make them more interactive, to better prepare students for these new approaches to learning and to rejuvenate one's own teaching practices. Kostka and Marshall (2018) argue that flipped learning addresses these challenges by providing more feedback to students and managing classes with diverse learners.

In cases where students may have limited access to the internet, the design can vary greatly in relation to the time spent outside the classroom. Teachers can spend more time on activities better suited to each space, such as student–teacher interactions or collaborative work. For example, in our writing class, students were given more time for in-class writing, which allowed them to ask questions the moment they encountered problems and for the responses to be shared immediately. In the flipped model, the teacher, who may have a reduced role as a 'sage', can now respond to individual questions.

Eliminating lectures has been another approach to increasing student engagement. Bergmann has proposed redesigning the flipped classroom to incorporate these new approaches, which could be adapted to teaching literacy. However, there has never been overwhelming evidence of higher levels of engagement. In a study of Norwegian students, Steen-Utheim (2017) found that students reported higher levels of engagement, including increased interactions with peers, than in conventional classrooms. Another early approach has relied heavily on using peer mentors in the learning process (e.g. Mazur, 2009), an approach used in MOOCs and other online learning spaces. Such spaces have not always delivered what they promised. Davidson (2012), however, critiqued an early version of flipped learning, focusing on the ability of the flipped classroom to produce critically engaged learning.

The writing classroom could be readily redesigned for flipped learning, which is especially true for student–teacher interactions. If a question were relevant to the other students, the teacher could interrupt the writing time and discuss the question with the entire class. Class time was also allocated to answering questions about the homework, which was connected to the class videos. As will be discussed, homework assignments were connected to each lecture as a way of motivating the students to watch the videos (Bergmann & Sams, 2012). This homework assignment was later discussed during class time. Other blocks of time were given to special projects, oral presentations and group work. Teachers could implement mini tutorials inside the classroom by allowing students to share their work to receive immediate feedback.

Questions of interest to the entire class could be instantly raised. Bergmann and Sams (2012) found that the flipped classroom increased not only teacher–student interaction but also student–student interaction. Leis et al. (2015) argued that flipped learning could improve the writing proficiency of their students, although it was not clear exactly what proficiency included. Many students may find it difficult to participate in a flipped classroom. While there is no comparable research on multilingual writing, these students may follow a similar pattern. Despite the difficulty in defining a ratio between in-class and outside learning, Bates (2016) argues that the amount of online learning in the flipped classroom can easily be increased; therefore, a key question is what ratios better foster good or bad learning.

As with MOOCs, assessment issues affect both how students are evaluated and the kinds of proof necessary to motivate other teachers to adopt this approach. Assessment may serve the purpose of convincing other teachers to adapt the method or any possible revisions to pedagogical practices, which has been the primary focus here. Assessment has been especially problematic with multilingual writers. There is a lack of evidence specifically supporting using the flipped classroom with multilingual writers (c.f. Lockwood, 2014). While research on flipped learning and flipped classrooms has often focused on where there are clear objectives (e.g. grades or test scores), less is known about subjects such as language learning where these objectives are not as clear-cut. Sun *et al.* (2018), for example, found problems in researching flipped classrooms with their variability in design and implementation. Questions about classroom interaction are issues that multilingual writing teachers often address. The often contradictory findings can provide writing teachers with a framework for thinking about their students and learning within the digital space.

Such research or 'proof' can be important for convincing teachers or administrators to change the pedagogies of their courses. However, research has often found only small differences between flipped and traditional classes. Sun *et al.* (2018) found individual variations depending on student confidence areas. Clark *et al.* (2018b) compared flipped and blended learning in engineering classes and found similar levels of increased learning. They implemented a series of pre-class activities that improved the results of the flipped classrooms. Setren *et al.* (2019) also found differences in achievement depending on the course. While this research may not be directly applicable to digital writing spaces, it illustrates how flipped classrooms are in 'perpetual beta' in response to their assessments.

Technology in Flipped Writing Classes

Although flipped classes are not dependent on implementing various technologies, certain technologies can be useful for achieving pedagogical goals. The Flipped Global Network (https://flglobal.org/) adopted the motto 'Pedagogy first, technology second' to highlight this aspect. To support this initiative, the network collected materials from those teachers who had been certified by the network and made them available either openly or for a fee. Such initiatives help provide teachers with greater access to a repertoire of technologies, many of them free or at a low cost, much as other technologically enhanced spaces have accomplished by integrating other technologies (e.g. Wu, 2010). For teachers, these technological tools require greater reflection on the affordances each tool brings to the learning experience, as is true for their use in every digital space.

New designs often require new tools for changing pedagogical goals, as moving classes online has shown. Increased discussion time, for example, may help the instructor in discovering problems as the students are addressing them. However, depending on how the instructor organizes this space, the responsibility for discussing these issues shifts to the students who may be reticent to speak. In response, multiple technologies have been designed to address these concerns. Socrative (https://www.socrative.com), Menti (https://www.mentimeter.com) and Top Hat can be used to facilitate such discussions by having students respond anonymously to questions before the class.

For students who may be shy to ask questions outside class, tools such as Piazza (https://piazza.com) can also facilitate classroom interactions with or without the instructor. Each of these technologies can impact student–teacher and student–student relationships, sometimes in subtle ways. As with all forms of cloud-based software, however, issues regarding privacy also need to be considered. The employment of these tools, and the affordances they include, illustrate how these literacy spaces can evolve as new tools are developed. Using these tools reflects on the goals for changes in the learning experience.

Creating a Flipped Classroom as a Multilingual Composition Space

Writing classes pose unique problems for flipping since they may contain elements that can be enhanced or diminished through flipping, again requiring extensive reflection by teachers on their designs. The problems surrounding the design of flipped classrooms illustrate a fundamental principle of digital literacy spaces: they are always in flux as new theories of learning and new tools with new affordances are introduced. Flipped learning can be relevant for multilingual composition students who may find it difficult to follow classroom lectures and can therefore benefit from listening to them at their own pace. In a recent survey of multilingual students in universities in the United States, a frequent request was for materials to be made available outside the classroom (Redden, 2017a), so teachers are often interested in finding suitable materials without copyright constraints.

Utilizing various technologies to redesign flipped learning spaces to impact learning has long been a goal for every form of technological implementation. The flipped classroom is a recent stage in the evolution of using technology in writing pedagogy. Studying this approach can help us rethink both the design of our composition classrooms, regardless of whether they are 'flipped', as well as the evolution of the role that technology can play in teaching writing.

By providing greater agency to the students, the videos do not simply encompass the lower levels of Bloom's taxonomy. There are several ways in which the flexibility of the videos can be increased to give greater agency to the students. The videos can be captioned, using tools from YouTube, which can further help with understanding the topics to better motivate the students (Ozdemir *et al.*, 2016). Lockwood (2014) argues that such videos are particularly important for multilingual learners since they can take as much time as they desire to view the video or they can review the materials as often as they wish, which she finds allows students to feel more comfortable and therefore less stressed.

Flipped spaces raise similar design questions as do all technologically enhanced learning spaces. The reduction in lecture time through using videos was intended to provide more opportunities for creating connections among the students and between the students and teacher, thus shifting more of the responsibility for learning to the students. Unlike in the MOOCs, students had more opportunities in the classroom for interaction. In another model, the teacher could roam around, looking at the students' writing and commenting or asking questions. The focus of classroom design issues reflects decisions on how much time should be allotted to classroom writing, other classroom activities or formal tutorials, as the classroom would become a 'studio' (Sutton & Chandler, 2018) where the students could focus on their projects, ask questions or interact with their classmates.

For English language learners, the videos can provide more time for writing as well as greater control over learning, particularly the ability to stop and rewind, which can help them compensate for difficulties in language processing.

Short, interactive videos replacing longer lectures are being used to increase student engagement in the flipped space (e.g. Eddy & Hogan, 2014). Although flipped classrooms borrowed this use of videos from MOOCs, these videos more often address specific content, such as syntactic or rhetoric issues, that could reflect specific issues from the classroom and could be arranged exactly when needed. In this way, the content of the videos can be more accessible, as well as being shorter, which can make the digital space more conducive to differentialized learning.

Our approach did not invert these existing pedagogies for flipped learning, focusing more on modularization by recording lectures on the linguistic and rhetorical topics that had previously been discussed in class and then posting them online for either the students or a larger audience. Much of the educational content of the course was contained in the videos. Since the students can work out of class, what then can motivate the students 'to take the bus' to the face-to-face classroom (Bates, 2016)? To receive a course 'grade', the student showed a physical presence by completing all the assignments as was the case in the traditional classroom. Bergmann and Sams (2012) found this approach not only increased teacher–student interaction but also student–student interaction, although our observations could not verify the latter. This shift in responsibility did not always result in improved student performance or course satisfaction.

Redesigning and Remediating the Flipped Classroom for Teaching Literacy

The design of every aspect of the flipped classroom has been challenged since creating digital literacy spaces involves almost every aspect of the class, from the choice of furniture to the syllabus of each course. While the learning processes do not completely depend on changes in the design, some problems with learning can be remediated by changes in classroom design. Implementing the flipped classroom can involve considering what has already occurred in the classroom and a continual evaluation of how the implementation is working. One instructor posted in his blog:

> Friday's class was a bit of a stumble. it lacked long term planning concerning timing when the revisions would be sent back. As a result, some of the students had something to work on and some didn't. However, I was able to improvise by having them read the next article. From this chaos, one of the better classes emerged. On Monday, everyone had something to do: some people worked on their revisions and others on their first drafts of the second article.

For many instructors, the flipped classroom reflects this chaotic, disruptive learning environment often associated with online learning spaces. Teachers, for example, would have to learn to give up some control over their classrooms to foster more student autonomy. In our class, for example, teachers sometimes lost control when the textbooks they often relied on were eliminated, although some teachers still depend on them.

Replacing textbooks with open access materials can change the copyright status of the materials available to the students. While textbooks often had the usual copyright restrictions, the videos could be open access. Although such open educational resources (OER) have been important in the flipped classroom (e.g. Downes, 2011; Wiley, 2007; Willinsky, 2006), teachers do not always feel comfortable sharing their own materials, so they lock down their own materials either in a cloud space that is restricted to the other teachers or in the university's learning management system (LMS) that is restricted to registered students.

The assessment of flipped learning spaces has required redesigning these literacy spaces using what has been found from various forms of assessment, often focusing on how students required greater interaction to support and motivate them. Lieberman (2017) reported on a professor in Australia who found many problems with his flipped classroom and had to make changes to his course design. It would be a major challenge in future iterations of the course to remediate this lack of interaction. Yong *et al.* (2015) likewise find that research in flipped learning has raised questions concerning the conditions in which it will be successful. This post suggests that implementation, particularly using group work, was a key factor in the design of our flipped classroom. As Bergmann and St Clair (2017) argue, the goal is no longer to prove flipped learning works, but how to improve its implementation.

Increasing student motivation was often the key factor in revising the course. Strayer (2012) reported that in an introductory statistics course where the students may not have been strongly motivated, the flipped model resulted in lower performance. He argues that such findings do not invalidate the significance of the flipped classroom but require the teacher to continually adjust the learning approaches to support the students.

The Design of the Short Lecture Videos for the L2 Composition Classroom

One area of technology that has greatly impacted flipped spaces has been the use of videos for expanding the space for learning and for providing greater autonomy to how course content can be learned. Videos are often delivered asynchronously, which can reduce the amount of interaction and engagement in comparison with synchronic delivery. On the other hand, they can provide more flexibility in how the information is viewed and accessed. In some ways, these videos are vestiges of the earlier interest in learning objects (e.g. Downes, 2001) since they cannot be easily copyrighted using Creative Commons and then reused. However, such usage was not always the case. As they were used in the MOOCs or flipped classrooms, videos could be used to create multiple spaces for student learning outside the classroom. Of course, these videos could only be viewed by students who had stable access.

Videos have become increasingly important throughout education as the technologies for creating and distributing information. The Khan Academy model (https://www.khanacademy.org), a collection of videos located on YouTube, has been designed to connect individual exercises to each video as a motivation for viewing them (Tasi, 2013). The videoed lectures can be viewed through different mobile devices, such as laptops, smartphones and tablets. Such flexibility has been incorporated to promote different types and levels of students, flexibility in the design of the space and different learning processes, all of which are intended to foster effective learning (Boelens *et al.*, 2017).

Videos can be designed using the voices of a single instructor, a group of instructors or the students, or they can be curated from existing videos, depending on their intellectual property status. Videos can be designed using various formats, so their aesthetics can vary depending on the time and the resources available to their creators. Although videos can be time-consuming to create and may not provide the active learning desired, their advantage is that they can be customized to the specific goals of the class. Designers can use animations, short lectures or diagrams, employing various pieces of equipment, depending on the resources available. Therefore, many predesigned videos may not be appropriate for the course goals. Designers must decide what resources they have, how to deploy these resources, how many videos to create and how granular the videos need to be for addressing course goals.

By increasing access to classroom knowledge anytime and anywhere, the teacher can increase the agency of the student to decide how the video content can be learned by providing more opportunities to reflect on the ideas of the lecturer (2020 Educause Horizon Report™ | Teaching and Learning Edition, 2020). As with many approaches using technology to view content, this approach attempts to improve upon traditional learning practices by providing more flexibility (e.g. Bensen & Voller, 2014) in how students choose to view the lectures. The videos allow the students to, as Bergmann and Sams (2012: 24) put it, 'pause and rewind their teacher'. Speaking of mathematics classes, Lo *et al.* (2017) found that the two key design factors are duration and style.

The design of videos can focus on whichever rhetorical or grammatical issues are most relevant to the pedagogical goals, thus adapting the space to be more responsive to the students' needs. How many and how long the videos should be are further questions that course designers must address. The creation of videos raises many questions about evaluating the affordances of the tools used to design the videos. Videos designed with cartoon figures may have a different impact on learning than videos designed with lecture tools (e.g. https://www.youtube.com/watch?v=D1Fh5FS9eGU&t=97s). These differences are important in understanding how the choice of tools is not neutral (c.f. Canagarajah, 2018) but can impact the artifacts for which they are used. We chose to develop many short videos addressing these issues. While many flipped courses have long lectures chunked into shorter segments, the specificity of our topics could limit each video from 2 to 12 minutes, averaging around 6 minutes.

The development of MOOCs demonstrated the potential for implementing these videos in the writing classroom. There have also been various technologies for designing the videos depending on their specifications. Flipgrid (https://flipgrid.com) can be used to create threaded video discussion boards. YouTube can store videos created for the classroom; its media studio can produce captions for aiding user understanding. Software such as Subtitle Workshop (http://subworkshop.sourceforge.net/) can translate captions for multilingual students, providing an additional mode for learning. Teachers can make the videos more interactive by stopping them to ask questions or attaching assignments that can be discussed later in the classroom. However, in many of these cases, the architecture of such platforms as YouTube may sacrifice the privacy of the students in achieving the course goals. This dichotomy between the goals of the course and the realities of using technology exemplifies the dilemma that both teachers and students may always face when implementing technologies.

Since writing classrooms rarely contain long lectures, the videos are often similar in content to their role in the traditional classroom. In our classroom, the videos focused on topics such as plagiarism and intellectual property (https://www.youtube.com/watch?v=8mrmyYmbeX0&t=189s), discussions of class assignments (https://www.youtube.com/watch?v=QzYANkg1mso) and, in particular, rhetorical and grammatical issues (https://www.youtube.com/watch?v=W_g2HxC2mUg&t=2s). Participants can rewatch them if a question arises or if they want to review them at another time, although such decisions are beyond the control of the teacher. Teachers may be required to add subtitles for hearing-challenged students, which can provide an alternative learning channel for multilingual participants.

Although YouTube may not be accessed in every country, it provides a valuable space for hosting videos. For some teachers, videos can be used to dump information from the classroom to create more class time for what are considered more interesting activities. For many teachers, creating videos is a means of moving 'less important' information out of the classroom so 'more important' learning can take place. Underlying this use of videos is an assumption that there are aspects of a course that may be transferred from one space to another (Bates, 2013). However, the assumptions regarding using technologies have not been fully explored since their value has remained ambivalent. Bergmann (2018) argued that teachers may feel that posting videos was the major strategy for flipping a classroom, that they could move the lower-level skills on Bloom's taxonomy into videos to focus only on the higher-level skills inside the classroom. However, the goal for the videos was only to promote the lower-level skills of learning the basics of the subject.

Whether these videos better promote higher- or lower-level skills can depend on what affordances they bring, as well as the attitudes of the users and how they are contextualized in the classroom. The design criteria that Norman (2007) proposes can be applied equally well to the design of these videos: their design can both support and constrain their usage; their behavioral design must incorporate their usability; and their visceral design must make them pleasant to view and use. Although videos are not a requirement of the flipped classroom, they can require much time and resources to create. However, this could be a positive feature in adding creativity to make the videos more accessible. In our videos on intellectual property, for example, various animations and dialogues were used to incorporate Norman's psychological principles to make the topic more appealing (e.g. https://www.youtube.com/watch?v=8mrmyYmbeX0&t=204s).

There are clear parallels even with older technically enhanced spaces, such as the 'talking pictures', where new tools, such as recording devices or focusing, can change their design and usage. In the flipped classroom, these new tools have made it easier for teachers to design their videos to meet course goals. As with the digital stories, more freely available tools could be used for designing the videos. Apple and Windows operating systems, for example, provide free moviemaking software that could be supplemented by free or inexpensive programs such as Screencast-O-Matic to record these videos.

Posting the videos online can impact multiple levels of student learning from just learning the facts to incorporating the videos in classroom discussions. Platforms such as YouTube, Vimeo and Tumblr provide inexpensive ways to distribute these videos, highlighting how information previously locked in the classroom could be opened to anyone with internet access. YouTube has also developed tools that could help in making video design more interactive and for providing captions that could be important for scaffolding the information for multilingual students as well as to fulfill certain legal requirements in the United States.

The implementation of these videos can impact the relationship between teacher and student This change is not absolute but incremental since there is no single approach to video design or the design of the literacy space. Bergmann (2018) uses the 'operating system' metaphor to describe how the flipped classroom is not a predefined set of approaches but a space where the teacher's goals can be more readily implemented. As with any operating system, this space is another example of being in 'perpetual beta', which needs to be continually evaluated and 'upgraded'. The designer can add, within certain parameters, whatever pedagogies, technologies or content are desired.

However, to be used effectively, their interactivity is also important. Watters (2013a) complained about the loneliness of watching videos, a factor that must be considered in their design. Miller (2014) finds that effectiveness is related to length, with shorter, more focused videos often containing low-stakes, multiple-choice exercises highly motivating. She also argues that integrating videos with exercises can provide alternative educational approaches that each student can utilize. Individual videos can be modified to add interactivity. EdPuzzle (https://edpuzzle.com), as with YouTube's media studio, can be used to add questions to the video as can blogs (see Chapter 2) for assessment or to help students focus on key aspects of the video. Other programs, such as Top Hat or Poll Everywhere, can be used to create questions outside the videos but can serve similar purposes.

While primarily designed for individual learning, videos can influence a more collaborative design of flipped classrooms (e.g. Straumsheim, 2013) by allowing students to view them together. They can also be created to quickly respond to problems that either students or course instructors might encounter, allowing the information to be shared in every section of the classroom. Coupled with short, 'low-stakes' exercises often found in online courses, these videos can motivate students by providing more rapid feedback than they would normally receive (Mazur, 2009; Miller, 2014). One goal of reducing the costs is to provide more videos on more topics but with lower production costs, which not only allow more student control over their learning but also disrupt traditional approaches to classroom learning (Greenfield & Hibbert, 2017).

Another factor that could burden teachers has been understanding the different uses of tools. The design of videos utilizes various tools, requiring their creators to have a certain familiarity with technological tools, which, of course, could be worked around using pre-existing videos, such as found in the Khan Academy, or through the sharing process discussed above. Our videos were either animated or contained recordings of the instructor hosting a PowerPoint or Word document. For example, grammar or rhetorical issues can be explained using apps (Explain Everything, bPocket), lectures using lecture- and screen-capture tools (Tegrity, Screencast-O-Matic) and animations can be created for discussing issues on course assignments or key controversies using Xtranormal (now defunct), Adobe Character Creator or Plotagon[1] or by making the videos more interactive using tools such as EdPuzzle. Each tool has its own unique features, for example having one or more voices, that need to be considered.

The role of videos in the flipped classroom has also been a source of controversy for the same reasons they have been praised – their design, their function in the classroom and their means of distribution. Videos have been called a 'crutch' for learning that teachers rely on and that students may only use for memorizing information (Barba, cited in Johnson, 2018: para. 4). Bergmann, too, seems to recognize their limitations, arguing that new directions are necessary for what he calls 'reaching every child', which could critique the focus on Bloom's lower-level skills in the videos as seen in the quote from Barba.

Designers must understand the implications of each tool used. All the videos were hosted on a cloud-based space so that all the teachers could share them and assign or post them in easily accessible open spaces (e.g. YouTube and iTunes). The complexity of the video design exemplifies how the space makes teachers neither 'sages' nor 'guides', but 'designers' whose main pedagogical problem is often apportioning materials into the different activities to engage students in the classroom tasks differently than they could in the classroom. The design of these short videos emphasizes this role even more than found in the longer videos often utilized in MOOCs that highlight the voice of the 'sage on stage', which can deemphasize the teacher's voice as is consistent with the design of the flipped classroom.

The Controversies over Using Videos in Flipped Literacy Spaces

The design and use of videos is only one of many controversies teachers face with flipped learning. Teachers have also struggled with various design issues regarding the length of the videos and their relationship to the content of the course, and how they motivate students to view them. Limitations on access can affect both teacher and student roles in these spaces. Bergmann (2019) suggests not to worry about perfection and use the minimum number of production tools. Nevertheless, some teachers feel that issues, particularly regarding access, could be eliminated by replacing the traditional flipped class with in-class flips where stations can provide different learning experiences.

There have been other questions about how to motivate students to watch the videos. We, for example, required students to blog about the videos. Other teachers ask the students to discuss the video content during class time, pressuring them to watch them before the class starts. Some teachers have responded to the design problems by using lecture-capture software (e.g. Mediasite, Tegrity) to record lectures and post them online, sometimes breaking them into more manageable pieces as is often found in MOOCs.

The xMOOCs that relied on the lecture format often tried to make the videos more interactive by interjecting questions and discussion points in each video, perhaps because without such interactivity, these lectures were mimicking the delivery of information found in the class-room space. However, the question remained whether these videos simply moved 'lower-level' activities out of the classroom space or whether active learning could be equally implemented in both spaces.

Lecture capture software also raises questions about the passivity of the students when listening to lectures. Smithers (2011: para. 1) called lecture capture 'the single worst example of poor educational technology use in higher education' because it did not address the passivity of students, which could be addressed using programs such as EdPuzzle to insert questions and quizzes. However, new issues related to technology have also developed. Some lecture capture programs can track the usage by the students, which exemplifies Stephens' (2018) concern over how technological designs affect privacy. This controversy over 'data analytics' and privacy is currently found in many controversies about the internet, in particular in Facebook, Snapchat and Google. The 2020 Educause Horizon Report™ | Teaching and Learning Edition (2020) warns about the possible consequences of the increased use of data on privacy. Some programs can monitor how much of the video the students watched or where they paused the video, which could provide teachers with information on student performance but at the price of increased monitoring of student behavior.

There have been other designs concerns regarding how students use videos. Should videos be scripted or improvised? How can they be integrated with other course assignments? How can they be captioned for non-native English speakers so that they have another channel for understanding? How can they be made interactive to promote active learning? How do students use the videos? How do they learn from the different modalities incorporated in the videos? How videos are created often reflect questions about how they are to be used: whether to use university resources to create fewer but more professional-looking videos or to create more videos using relatively inexpensive programs such as Screencast-O-Matic.

One of the critical factors that flipped classrooms raise about digital spaces is the relationship between the apparent dichotomy between personal and technologically enhanced learning. Many students still want lectures, and many teachers still feel that lectures are important (Talbert, 2014). Malan (cited in Jaschik, 2017), however, found that regardless of the effectiveness of the videos, students often missed the face-to-face interactions in the classroom space.

Another controversy in the design of digital literacy spaces is their implementation in the class. How can students be motivated to watch the videos? Students may see the value of the outside materials although sometimes the motivation is external, often from assigning credit or from integrating outside materials with classroom discussions. Assessments can also be integrated in the video. Many of the MOOCs, which similarly rely on short videos, allow for some form of assessment. We did not initially have this capability, but later homework or blogging assignments could be integrated with the videos. This approach did not guarantee that the student would watch the videos but might still motivate them to do so.

Unlike their use in large lecture courses, the videos in the writing classroom only replace a small portion of the class time. However, they only offer the potential to transform the traditional role of the lecture as a means of dispensing knowledge into a more active form of learning. As the recent move to more online education has shown, students may still value class time and do not necessarily want to replace it with online interactions. Nevertheless, as has often been the case, many of these problems can be remediated using more interactive activities sometimes embedded in the videos.

Teachers can ensure that students watch the videos by connecting them to learning in the classroom spaces or by exploiting the affordances of blogging to create more active learning spaces. Our course assessments have shown that the value of videos was in their flexibility, although it was less clear whether the students preferred them over in-class discussions. One objection was their lack of interaction, which could be remediated with additional tools. On the other hand, Veletsianos (2020) reported on a student who felt isolated, that watching videos cut her off from instructors and classmates, which is an issue that can be remediated in the video design. Although their usage raises similar issues as open access materials (see Chapter 6) regarding copyright and the relationship between teachers and students, the question remains as to whether the content contained in the videos is learned differently than in the lecture format (e.g. Cunningham, 2016).

Assessment and Remediation of Digital Spaces

As with questions regarding completion rates in MOOCs, attempting to assess the effectiveness of the flipped classroom has been plagued by problems with measurement (Levy & Yong, 2014) and the generalizability of the results (Setren *et al.*, 2019). Simply moving assignments from a physical space into a digital one has proved problematic (e.g. Flaherty, 2020). Often exam scores and enrollment numbers carried over from traditional approaches to assessment. In a meta-analysis of research on flipped classes, Cheng *et al.* (2020) found small differences in the outcomes and question whether these results justify the resources required for flipping. This research utilized clear-cut methods of assessment: standardized testing or pass/fail rates, which may not exist in the more chaotic nature of the writing classroom.

Moreover, since the design of the flipped class may be incomplete, assessments need to incorporate changes in class design. It is not simply the assessment that is at issue; there is also confusion among students over the goals of the flipped classroom. Therefore, teachers need to be more explicit in explaining their rationale for flipping, its benefits and challenges, the differences in syllabus design and the specific tasks expected of the students (Lo *et al.*, 2017). Such approaches can be important for instruction in any form of digital literacy space.

Mixing literacies can also be important in designing the flipped spaces, as has been true with other spaces. As is true with other approaches to blogging (see Chapter 2), its usage was another attempt to implement technological tools for students and teachers to reflect on the course. Blogs were important in the assessment process for revealing how students and teachers were negotiating these new spaces. One teacher commented in his blog on feeling frustrated by the lack of engagement among students.

> I still haven't been able to figure out how much interaction there is. The layout of the class is still a problem. It's hard for me to get around and even harder to see their screens. Maybe five or six students asked questions; the rest worked quietly. I was hoping for more interaction since we hadn't gone over the revision strategies, so I expected there would be a lot of problems, but there were still very few questions.

Therefore, after our initial implementation raised such concerns, we surveyed each class to better help us understand how both teachers and students perceived our initial implementation, and in the case of the students, how they used the materials posted online. The results could then be incorporated into redesigning the space.

Frequently redesigning the spaces, as Casanave (2017) argued, can place additional burdens on teachers and on institutional resources as well as on the expectations of the students. Teachers often report initial frustrations with the designs of flipped classroom spaces (e.g. Talbert, 2014, 2017). Such courses frequently require much revision, so both teacher and student feedback was used to guide future implementations. Teachers often do not share the same attitude to learning processes as do their students. The assessment of flipped classroom spaces has focused on whether students had higher grades or did better on tests, factors that may not be as relevant in writing classes.

Therefore, flipping may not be suitable for remediating all the limitations of these literacy spaces since there is not one way for their creation. Each instructor used the flipped framework for implementing changes, but again, they could implement the changes differently or not at all. Some teachers, for example, wanted to continue formal tutorials while others set aside time for each student to ask a question. In this approach, the teacher could call on each student to ask a question, allowing instructors to address questions as the students were asking them (7 Things You Should Know About Flipped Classrooms, 2012). Student questions could also be crowd-sourced using platforms such as Piazza or Top Hat and later used for classroom discussion.

The assessments could not necessarily prove or disprove the effectiveness of the flipped classrooms or provide a superior learning environment but could explore how the students negotiated their experiences so that changes could be made in future iterations. These variations allow multilingual composition teachers to choose which design to implement. In contemporary technological environments, optimization of these choices may never be the case. As more autonomy is provided, there is a greater obligation to redesign the learning spaces. Such objectives could not, if ever, be measured until the design of the optimal classroom is reached.

Another problem in designing these spaces was accessing the technologies. As mentioned earlier, a key constraint on technology has been its accessibility. In technologically enhanced environments, student access is usually assumed, but for many, such access is not available. Integrating accessibility is another factor that can lead to resistance. Faculty, for example, has expressed concern at the reduced amounts of interaction with students in these technological spaces (Jaschik & Lederman, 2018). Even changes in engagement may not result in changes in student performance. Smallhorn (2017) found increases in student attendance and video watching, which, however, did not result in gains in academic performance, a finding that may hinder the adoption of flipped learning by some teachers.

It is important, therefore, not to simply accept technological changes. Gonzalez (2014) discussed the in-class flip as an alternative when accessibility is an issue. With the greater autonomy afforded students, their reflections on their learning may become more important in remediating the weaknesses of technological implementations. The same issue of assessment can apply to evaluating videos. If much of the educational content was contained in videos, there were additional questions about what could motivate the students 'to take the bus' to the face-to-face classroom (Bates, 2013).

Open Access in Flipped Literacy Spaces

Flipped learning can incorporate many of the same issues found in other spaces. The design of activities for flipped learning can incorporate various open access resources. As with MOOCs, the role of openness (see Chapter 6) can be important in designing the space, especially with developing videos that can also be shared, depending on how they are copyrighted (Bloch, 2012), internally among a teaching group or with any other teachers and students (see Chapter 8). Thus, videos can be open educational materials (OER) for teachers and students to use whenever desired (e.g. Chae & Jenkins, 2015; Farrow, 2014; Willinsky, 2006). Farrow (2014: 2) argued that there are two key elements of OER: (a) OER improve student performance/satisfaction and (b) learners use OER differently from other materials. These same concerns can impact the implementation of flipped learning by providing individualized learning to support greater autonomy for the students.

Flipped learning also has the potential not only to create more active learning spaces but also to create more open access resources (Colvard et al., 2018). Open access can reduce the cost of educational materials, which can narrow the gap between developed and developing countries in the availability of information. This reduction can be especially important in the global use of flipped learning, although it is not a requirement. Depending on personal factors such as age and position, teachers can decide whether their materials can be shared, how they can be shared and for what purposes. Each set of materials comes with their own affordances, which help the teacher define their pedagogical frameworks and the student control their learning.

Designers can choose how their videos are to be distributed, which can be facilitated by copyright laws (e.g. Bloch, 2012). All videos are considered intellectual property and therefore are treated the same as any copyrighted materials. However, the creator has the option of making them open by using Creative Commons to determine how they can be distributed, whether they can be revised or repurposed or whether they can used for commercial purposes. Moving course materials online facilitates freely sharing their content with other teachers and students, thus increasing their potential audience, consistent with all open access materials.

As has been true with all uses of technology, sharing in flipped learning depends on how copyright laws are applied. Flipped learning supports teachers sharing resources (Wiley & Green, 2012), as operating systems support or constrain computer applications. Although creating and/or using OER in the flipped classroom space is not mandatory, videotaped lectures could be copyrighted using Creative Commons to be shared through platforms such as YouTube. This openness could make the flipped classrooms much different from the xMOOCs where materials were often locked down by copyright laws.

However, copyright use has been more complex. A report on the status of recorded lectures in the United Kingdom, for example, showed that may institutions were still grappling with using copyrighted materials, particularly when the lectures contained third-party materials that may not have been openly sourced (Amaya-Rios *et al.*, 2016). Therefore, the designer of the videos must consider their copyright status when planning how and with whom they can be used.

The Flipped Classroom as a Technologically Enhanced Literacy Space

Flipped classrooms raise important pedagogical and technological questions regarding the role of digital spaces for increasing student autonomy and alternative forms of active learning. Such autonomy has already developed as students can increase their mobility with laptops, iPads and phones to further explore the content of the course in whatever ways they want, or they can become distracted and go in a different direction out of the control of their teachers.

As new technological tools are found useful for the composition classroom, new spaces, such as the flipped classroom and MOOC, for teaching composition have developed alongside the traditional classrooms. As with the introduction of many new technologies, the students and teachers often resisted and reconstructed the classroom, so that it best served their goals. Examining these spaces illustrates that technology does not determine learning but does shape the teaching and learning process in new ways.

A controversy over the perceived reduction in teacher–student interaction in 'blended' classes highlighted the gap that may exist between the goals of administrators and the attitudes of students (Lieberman, 2018). In defending these new designs, the administration responded that a period of adjustment should be expected and that there was no indication of lower test scores or enrollments. The resistance to flipped learning, as well as to other forms of new literacies, highlights the importance of the teacher. Reduced in-class time is a possible model of flipped classrooms, but the controversy illustrates the problem of implementing, or perhaps imposing, new digital learning spaces. By providing more autonomy to the students, the designs may invite more controversy as well. The development of flipped classrooms, and other forms of blended and online classrooms, reflects new developments in the role of technology in the composition classroom. There still may be a heightened consciousness, as Krause suggested, of the relationships between design, teaching and learning to write.

The extra costs that occur, however, may be why there has been resistance from more tuition-sensitive students who want more interaction and teachers who are concerned with lacking resources. There is also a lack of convincing evidence that in practice the flipped classroom is effective (Cunningham, 2016), which can reduce the number of teachers willing to experiment with it. While the flipped approach may require additional costs for hardware, including desks and chairs, and internet access, this approach may also draw on the infrastructure of the institutional or learning communities, which can also be addressed by the availability of open resources, so teachers do not have to continually reinvent the wheel.

The often chaotic nature of flipped learning, as teachers attempt to reach every student, can become the pedagogical instantiation of a quandary reminiscent of Papert's (1980) argument that even mistakes can lead to new types of learning. Moreover, with multilingual students, such changes can be even more unpredictable. Littlewood (1999), for example, warns about generalizing the attitudes of East Asian students toward autonomy since there can be wide variations in their attitudes. The flipped approach, therefore, may not work as desired for every student, although it may be more conducive for some students than the traditional classroom, forcing the teacher to become even more agile in their designs for flipped learning.

Every aspect raises questions for designers, including discussing the effective use of materials, particularly those developed for outside-of-class activities. Flipped learning in the writing classroom, however, has not changed the literacy, but how the literacy is learned. Its main contribution to the design of digital spaces for teaching literacy has been to reallocate resources and activities as well as allowing teachers to add new dimensions for learning literacy to the original course design. However, most importantly, flipped learning, like MOOCs, has impacted the 'sage on the stage' and the 'guide on the side' metaphors, which have become more problematized since the flipped classroom may require more detailed changes for individual learners or for learners from different cultures and language backgrounds (King, 1993).

The impact of flipped learning on the design of literacy spaces can be best seen in the proliferation of different activities to support literacy pedagogy. The freeing up of class time in the group space can allow teachers to experiment with different activities – more tutorials, gamification, interactive software (e.g. Socrative; Poll Everywhere) – as well as the more traditional approaches. The flipped digital space, however, may be difficult to scale, an issue central to the MOOC spaces, to include more teachers and classes. Such scaling can build upon blending the existing materials to create new approaches, which can help teachers become more confident in their implementations.

The goal of increasing student engagement illustrates how technologies are subservient to the goals of the course. For example, our use of blogging has evolved to meet the goals of the digital space. The variations in the designs of literacy spaces challenge teachers to personalize instruction to the needs for different forms of student engagement. Many questions, however, remain as to which types of students, particularly with their background knowledge and levels of self-efficacy (e.g. Sun et al., 2018), may benefit from or may struggle with flipped learning. Questions remain as to the impact of flipping on improving student writing and learning. Creating digital spaces requires much reflection on remediating both the traditional and the new approaches for teaching. Much remains unknown about how students learn literacy in these spaces, for example how they learn from the videos and how students use them differently.

The Potential of the Flipped Classroom and Flipped Learning

As has been true with all forms of technologically enhanced digital spaces, the flipped classroom is evolving with the development of new research about teaching methods, new forms of learning, especially those involving student collaboration, new forms of student–teacher interactions and new technologies to support course goals. Bergmann's attitude toward 'reaching every child' has reflected a shift from thinking about flipped learning as a set of skills (Bloom et al., 1956) to include emotional development (Maslow, 1971). By providing students with more support from their teachers and classmates, the flipped classroom can provide a digital learning space where the students can receive more emotional support.

Such research, nevertheless, can help sustain new learning environments by continually providing new pedagogical approaches while eliminating those that do not work. The potential for chaos in this approach inevitably leads to resistance among both teachers and students. While this research did not 'prove' the value of these pedagogies, it illustrated how designing flipped writing courses forces teachers to rethink their pedagogies. Currently, the flipped classroom is in a state of 'perpetual beta'. As Bergmann (2017) has argued throughout his videos on the Flipped Global Network, new forms of flipped learning have evolved with the development of new technologies, illustrating again the potential for at least a limited amount of determinism from implementing technologies. The 'agile' metaphor for software design is useful to support how training must be evaluated and revised. As McLaughlin *et al.* (2014) found in their student surveys, addressing such problems helped them design new strategies for implementing their course. These solutions had an impact, though perhaps not as great as their early advocates had hoped. To expand the number of potential contributors to address the problems, Bergmann has developed a large network of teachers (e.g. The Flipped Learning Network), many of whom have paid for training or attending workshops that can address their isolation.

As we have seen with the introduction of many technologies, flipped learning has encountered resistance among teachers that can result from the increased number of participants and students. The final stage of the Gartner Hype Cycle illustrates a slower acceptance but perhaps with wider adoption. This scaling has been slow because all these changes can be applied in a slow and detailed manner, class by class, with much support for both teacher and student. Several networks have developed supporting teachers to become more involved with flipped learning.

As with all technologies, the design of flipped learning has changed as the technologies have changed. The greater speed and accessibility of the internet can increase both the number of participants and their learning experiences. The growing number of participants has resulted in a growing number of ideas and concerns with flipped learning being discussed. Thus, the future of flipped learning will depend on the direction of this type of scaling to include more and more practitioners and learners.

Note

(1) See https://www.youtube.com/watch?v=GjZeJ4oQJVE for an example of using Plotagon to introduce a flipped class.

6 The Promise of Open Access Journals for L2 Publishing

> On the one hand information wants to be expensive, because it's so valuable. The right information in the right place just changes your life. On the other hand, information wants to be free, because the cost of getting it out is getting lower and lower all the time. So, you have these two fighting against each other.
>
> Stewart Brand, 1985, *Whole Earth Review*

The Meaning of Open Access

Although its original intent was not to define open access resources, this quote from Stewart Brand has been adapted as an important component of multilingual learning. Openness has long been a force in the design of computer tools. The loss of tools such as Xtranormal when its owner decided to shut illustrates the dilemma of the cathedral-like approach to design. Brand's aphorism that 'information wants to be free' underlies the battle over the creation, distribution and repurposing and sharing of information, all of which are important for writing teachers. Throughout this book, openness in these literacy spaces has been important both inside and outside the classroom. Each of the spaces discussed so far has a component of openness, often depending on the personal situation of the creator. Open access journals have made important contribution to the development of publication practices (Harnad, 2014). Openness, however, does not always mean 'free'; journals may assess article processing charges (APCs) that may be in lieu of or in addition to subscription fees. The so-called 'gold' standard that some journals from major publishers employ can run into thousands of dollars, which are expected to be folded into grant applications. Other journals, often from more obscure publishers, may charge lower fees and attempt to differentiate between charges for 'high-income' countries and 'low-income' countries. Often the processing fees can be difficult to discern. Springer-Nature, however, have promised more transparency in their fees in their new 'transformative' journals that provide a hybrid approach to open access.

Nowhere has this move toward openness been more controversial than in discussions of journals as literacy spaces for both publishing, reading and archiving information. The role of these APCs may seem to contradict the meaning of open access. The definition of open content (http://opencontent.org/definition/) has incorporated Wiley's (2007) five factors, all of which depend on flexibility in intellectual property law:

Retain – make, own and control a copy of the resource (e.g. download and keep your own copy).

Revise – edit, adapt and modify your copy of the resource (e.g. translate into another language).

Remix – combine your original or revised copy of the resource with other existing material to create something new (e.g. make a mashup).

Reuse – use your original, revised or remixed copy of the resource publicly (e.g. on a website, in a presentation, in a class).

Redistribute – share copies of your original, revised or remixed copy of the resource with others (e.g. post a copy online or give one to a friend).

Early examples of open access can be found in how software code was shared (e.g. the Free Software Group). The concept has spread to cover various locations for curating texts. The current interest in open-sourced educational materials was greatly enhanced by MIT's (https://ocw.mit.edu/index.htm) and Carnegie Mellon's Open Learning initiatives (https://oli.cmu.edu/). From its modern inception with the posting of course materials from MIT, there has been a movement to open information that was previously only available to a small number of readers. For example, MIT Press in conjunction with the MIT Media Lab created the Knowledge Futures Group (https://mitpress.mit.edu/blog/mit-press-and-mit-media-lab-launch-knowledge-futures-group), whose goal is to

> develop and deploy technologies that form part of a new open knowledge ecosystem, one that fully exploits the capabilities of the Web to accelerate discovery and the transmission of knowledge. (para. 2)

In fact, there have been several definitions of open access for educational materials. The Budapest group proposed one definition that has been widely used:

> free availability on the public internet, permitting any users to read, download, copy, distribute, print, search, or link to the full texts of these articles, crawl them for indexing, pass them as data to software, or use them for any other lawful purpose. (Cited in Weller *et al.*, 2014: 47)

The Budapest definition emphasizes the role that technology plays in the spread of open access by lowering the barriers for the 'public good'.

> An old tradition and a new technology have converged to make possible an unprecedented public good. The old tradition is the willingness of

scientists and scholars to publish the fruits of their research in scholarly journals without payment, for the sake of inquiry and knowledge. The new technology is the internet. The public good they make possible is the world-wide electronic distribution of the peer-reviewed journal literature and completely free and unrestricted access to it by all. (Budapest Open Access Initiative, 2012 para. 1)

This definition emphasizes the removal of many of the constraints attached to copyrighted materials, often through licensing using Creative Commons to provide different levels of distribution. Open access information may no longer be considered 'stolen' as are copyrighted materials but can be freely distributed under these licensing agreements. Openness, however, does not necessarily mean that research is without costs, as Brand's metaphor implies, since there can be hidden costs to openness.

This chapter will examine open access as spaces for disrupting literacy. Open access has disrupted the relationships between publishers and their customers as well as between authors and readers. Their openness has become a battleground over what is considered openness and what are the consequences of that openness. In Bloch (2010), I attempted to first explore the development of an open access learning object (e.g. Downes, 2001) for use in choosing reporting verbs in academic writing. Today, open access is thought to include teaching materials and publications. Open access can affect many of the literacy spaces that students enter into, including dissertation publication, research sharing and textual borrowing, as will be discussed in Chapter 6. Therefore, understanding the consequences of openness is an important consideration in designing digital literacy spaces.

In multilingual literacy spaces, open access can foster global engagement among authors ('Action Agenda for the Future of the TESOL Profession', 2017), for, as Hegarty (2015: 3) argues, an increase in learning through greater 'openness, connectedness, trust, and innovation'. Although sometimes limited by the 'digital divide' across regions, these models still have the potential to disrupt these barriers. Open educational resource (OER) Africa argues for creating sustainable models that balance the creation and use of open materials ('Understanding the Impact of OER Achievements and Challenges', 2019). This increase in the use of OER reflects the desire for creating networks where many participants can contribute their knowledge. Today, terms such as Ed 3.0 reflect a change in the role of the internet from distributing photos of 'cute cats' to a wider distribution of information, where users can build connections among creators, users and researchers.

The concept, however, is not new. One of the foremost progenitors of today's open access movement was the creation of the Royal Society in the 17th century. Although not necessarily open by today's standards, Willinsky (2017) argues that its goal was to make public much of the scientific information of the day and that its journal *Transactions* utilized the printing press in the same way that the internet is used today, making this knowledge more open to a wider public. Its motto *nullius in verba* (take no one's word for it) set the standard for modern concepts of peer review.

Open access materials have been popular for over 25 years (Suber, 2012), although faculty are still hesitant about using them because of questions about their value (Blankstein & Wolff-Eisenberg, 2019) or publishing in OER journals because of how they are valued. However, in fields such as multilingual composition, they are still relatively new. As seen in the discussions of Massive Open Online Courses (MOOCs) (see Chapter 4) and flipped classrooms (see Chapter 5), open access materials have been a part of these new spaces for publishing and distributing information. Controversial sites such as GitHub, as is ResearchGate and Academia.edu, provide spaces for uploading data, algorithms and texts, which may be in violation of copyright law, and are later incorporated in various other forms of expression. The use of OER in both textbooks and publishing spaces has responded to access issues for all students but especially for multilingual students who may face unique challenges in accessing current research.

The growth of open access has been paralleled in intellectual property law. *Transactions*, according to Willinsky (2017), developed an open model with new intellectual property laws that were passed to restrict the openness of distribution resulting from the introduction of the printing press. He concludes his argument with a discussion of how the work of Locke was influential in creating the tension between the rights of the author and the use of intellectual property for learning. There is the same tension in this space as there has been in the ongoing battle between the ownership of and the access to intellectual property that has long been debated. Conflicts between journal publishers and universities, such as the one at the University of California (e.g. Anderson, 2017a), have been predicated on the availability of open access materials as alternatives to traditional gated ones.

Willinsky (2017) traces the debate over openness and intellectual property from its beginnings in the 4th-century monasteries through the philosophy of John Locke and the contributions of scholars from the Jewish and Islamic traditions. He argues that open access can trace its roots to the same arguments over intellectual property law that have long existed. It is the hope that the diverse locations of researchers in multilingual writing can benefit from having access to not only the open resources (MIT Opencourseware, 2013; 'Open educational resources why they have yet to reach their full potential', 2018) but also the questions and problems to which all researchers have access. Today, changes have continued to appear in the evolution of open access journals as new models for publication and distribution appear.

In the United States, open access has primarily been a response to the costs of both journals and textbooks. These changes in access have been facilitated by the debate over intellectual property and the internet, and its implications for multilingual pedagogies (e.g. Bloch, 2012). Taken in conjunction with copyright changes, pedagogical changes have allowed for more ways of mixing and repurposing materials, as discussed with multimodal literacy spaces (see Chapter 3).

Some journals have evolved from being gated to being open, one model of which is called the 'read and publish' model (Wilson, 2018), which can use technology for more access by charging lower fees to institutions that subscribe to the mode. In comparison to the breakdown in the negotiations between the University of California and Elsevier Publishers, Carnegie Mellon implemented a read and publish model with Elsevier that shifted payment of open access charges to the university (McKenzie, 2019a, 2019b). Other approaches, such as 'Subscribe to Open' (Hinchliffe, 2020a) or 'The Big Deal' (Clarke, 2018; McKenzie, 2019) add additional dimensions to in research distribution. These changes in access may not completely address the problems of accessing, but they may contribute to increasing access for multilingual writing spaces at least for writers who are members of the community paying for it. However, when they leave the institution, they may lose the access that will help them with their publishing, which is where open access comes into play.

The Value of Open Access for Publishing

The value of open access journals primarily lies in providing accessibility to researchers who may not have the financial resources to access the traditional gated journals. Such an approach, as will be shown here, does not disrupt education but rather addresses problems with accessibility. Accessibility controversies can be traced back to the ideas of Bush (1945), who argued for greater accessibility to scientific knowledge. Harnad (1995) presented what he called the 'Subversive Proposal' in which he argued that certain research should always be open. In the information age, the key question has been how the proliferation of information can be accessed and distributed. Websites such as Written Commons (https://writingcommons.org) offer an alternative to textbooks for writing teachers as well as an open access journal on writing analytics.

The role of open access can be found in its knowledge production and the resulting opportunities for publication today. Its roots can be seen in the controversies over whether the open commons was detrimental (Hardin, 1968) or beneficial (Ostrum, 2015) to the preservation of its contents, which could be fish, cattle or information. This question was extended to discussions over whether the abundance of information on the internet was detrimental to its production. Lessig (1999) identified the open metaphor for the conflict over intellectual property laws that erupted with the creation of the internet. With the internet, copies could be created without the concern that the author or creator did not possess the original copy. This metaphor could impact how intellectual property was viewed. The open commons, however, was not free of laws and rules, often governed, as Lessig pointed out, by its own architecture, its need for sustainability, and external laws. Lessig identified the rock group The Grateful Dead as one of the first to embrace the potential of openness by allowing their fans to freely record their concerts while still charging for tickets, albums and merchandise. However, it was the internet that most facilitated openness.

Gated journals have attempted to charge often large fees for open publishing while the development of open access predatory journals (see Chapter 7) has made journal choice more complicated ('Predatory Publishing: Red Flags', 2020). Existing sites for sharing research often conflict with intellectual property laws and thus raise ethical questions regarding sharing. The most important challenges have been to the digital publishing process. In an open environment, researchers often publish without many of the copyright restrictions on how their papers are used, which can provide other researchers with greater access to relevant questions and problems.[1] The possibility of an expanded audience can mean a greater number of citations for the author, still an important measure of an article's value and the status of the author (Wiley, 2007).

Today, new technologies have impacted the open access spaces as they have every other literacy space. Open access has been most disruptive to the publishing process. Preprint servers (Davis, 2018) and blockchain (Rosenthal, 2018) have disrupted the distribution and evaluation of research. Preprint servers could be important for multilingual writers by providing feedback before submitting a paper. Blockchain has been associated with distributing alternative currencies, but its ability to create networks for sharing has challenged the licensing agreements as Creative Commons had challenged the legal constraints on information distribution.

Other new technologies have similarly challenged existing practices. Johnson and Chiarelli (2019) found that preprint servers, which are utilized for peer review, have dramatically increased downloading as well as how the discipline is perceived. As has been the tradition of these new technologies, their introduction can alter the current processes of traditional approaches. Davis (2018) discusses how technologies have changed citation practices in both positive and negative ways by making research more accessible before being submitted for publication, which is an important goal in multilingual research where English is taught all over the world. Without traditional peer review (2018 Global State of Peer Review, 2018), the quality of articles can vary, which may limit their rhetorical importance in some literacy contexts.

Sage Publishing has recently posted its guidelines for Advance, a preprint server for the social sciences and humanities (https://advance.

sagepub.com/f/submission-guidelines), which allows registered readers to respond to posted articles, providing feedback before an article is submitted. *The Journal of Writing Research* now has a preprint server that allows papers to be viewed before being submitted for peer review (see Chapter 7), although the server may be used for either reviewing or archiving papers. These preprint servers have already raised questions about the future directions for publishing. A controversy over the new developments in publishing spaces concerns a paper rejected by a sociology journal because it had already been pre-published by ArXiv has raised questions about the relationship between prepublication and publication and the future of double-blind reviewing, since reviewing could easily find the name of the author by searching the prepublication server (Flaherty, 2019a). Nevertheless, such preprint servers provide a faster and more widespread means of publication, but one that may impact the publication process.

However, in some situations, particularly when speed is important, preprint servers can play a valuable role in quickly disseminating information, although sometimes without the authentication of peer review to establish its credibility (Kupferschmidt, 2020). A statement from the Wellcome Trust, in response to the spread of the COVID-19 virus, urged researchers to share their data and publish rapidly on preprint servers, assuring them that such publication would not jeopardize further chances of publication (https://wellcome.ac.uk/press-release/ sharing-research-data-and-findings-relevant-novel-coronavirus-covid-19-outbreak). Other publishers, such as Springer-Nature, followed suit in releasing content openly. These assurances concerning the role of technology in distributing information, particularly in a crisis situation, raise questions about the future relationship between prepublication and publication in less urgent contexts. The pledge to open and share resources was taken up by groups of educators and students, with the recognition that not everything could be opened.

Open Access and the Design of Literacy Spaces

Contemporary open access journals have developed in different ways, often responding to both pedagogical and institutional goals: the 'flipped' type in which the journal is converted or more often extended from a gated type into one with multiple forms of access, and the 'born-open' type which begins as an open access journal. One early impetus to creating open access materials was MIT openly distributing their course materials, which allowed access to those who could not attend the university. A second impetus has been mandates from governments in North America and Europe and from many funding agencies requiring the research they fund to be published as open access.

Open access spaces have not developed as have MOOCs or flipped classrooms but as a part of an open network with multiple nodes that authors can connect to in their research. Various approaches to openness have affected how different literacy spaces are viewed. In previous discussions of MOOCs and flipped learning, the critical factor has been which aspects of these courses are open and which are locked down. The development of the internet and the World Wide Web (Berners-Lee, 1999) has facilitated these changes in distributing academic content, which, in turn, has addressed problems with the isolation many multilingual researchers may feel from the central discussions of their fields.

All of these principles depend on the use of various technologies, such as the Web; therefore, these spaces can be considered technologically enhanced. With open access, authors can still control how their research is distributed over the Web using Creative Commons to constrain their uses; however, the costs for such distribution are lowered. The distribution of knowledge over the Web has supported the more theoretical goals for open access. The Budapest group focused on open access journals as a key element in the new approach to distributing knowledge. Their declaration for the need for open access journals stated that

> scholars need the means to launch a new generation of journals committed to open access, and to help existing journals that elect to make the transition to open access. Because journal articles should be disseminated as widely as possible, these new journals will no longer invoke copyright to restrict access to and use of the material they publish. Instead they will use copyright and other tools to ensure permanent open access to all the articles they publish. (Budapest Open Access Initiative, 2012: para. 5)

The development of technologies has supported the increase in open access journals, while simultaneously frightening away some potential contributors. Estimates of open access sites vary greatly across disciplines. Laakso et al. (2011) found that the number of open access articles increased from zero in 1993 to almost 20,000 in 2009 (cited in Weller et al., 2014). As of October 2015, the Directory of Open Access Journals (www.doaj.org) has listed 10,623 open access journals from 135 countries, a statistic to support the goal of multilingual research for global distribution. As of May 1, 2019, the number had increased to 3,939,109 articles from 13,113 journals.

The assessment of the value of these open access spaces for increased research has been one of its most controversial aspects. Can open access publications be evaluated as are other forms of publications? The impact of metrics on measuring academic literacies is broad, although the value of each individual metric may be questionable particularly when comparing disciplines. Newer metrics such as the H-factor, which tries to measure the most-cited papers from an individual or journal, can still vary a great deal across disciplines, at least in part from the number of papers cited. Newer models of assessment, such as provided in Altmetrics (https://www.altmetric.com/), attempt to measure the impact of publications across different literacies and for different stakeholders. Even variations in traditional measures of journal importance, such as impact factors (Garfield, 2005) and downloads, can be affected by both practices and higher accessibility, making comparisons more problematic. In *The Metric Tide*, Wilsdon *et al.* (2015) critiques the use of metrics:

> Too often, poorly designed evaluation criteria are 'dominating minds, distorting behaviour and determining careers'. (Wilsdon *et al.*, 2015: iii)

The issue concerning the comparative values of different literacies can change with the development of literacy spaces supporting open access journals, which have evolved in different ways: the 'flipped' type in which the journal is converted from gated to open access, and the 'born-open' type which begins as an open access journal. These journals are not isolated from other forms of open materials but exist within a constellation of open access materials. These new models for open access publishing have increased the number of such journals, as well as ways in which publishers have attempted to respond with their own forms of openness.

The resulting openness therefore provides more information to researchers, teachers and students, which has been an idealistic response to the challenges of publishing for those living outside of the dominant publishing spheres. Hook *et al.* (2019) argue that using open access ensures the greatest number of people can access published materials, which can lead to increased citation and collaboration and an awareness of the rhetoric and language of academic writing. Free open access has meant that academic materials or 'artifacts' used throughout the writing processes can overcome the limits of the scarcity resulting from copyright restrictions and traditional publishing practices.

Some view the results as profound. Willinsky and Moorhead (2014) have argued that these open journals can facilitate increased information distribution, provide more freedom for creating new journals and facilitate research from outside the traditional academic centers by giving greater control of the distribution to the authors, which can extend what they consider the fundamental 'right to know' to a greater number of people (Willinsky, 2006: 154). Open access can therefore provide a more level relationship between researchers in developed and developing countries (Tennant *et al.*, 2016), which can help researchers formulate relevant problems and find supporting evidence for creating future research.

In these ways, open access journals have expanded the larger publishing ecology by including publishing research and peer review while opening up new possibilities in areas such as pre- and post-peer review (Ross-Hellauer, 2017) and new social media sites (e.g. Academic. edu, MLA Commons, ResearchGate) used for crowd-sourcing the distribution of unpublished and already-published academic research

(Gardner & Gardner, 2016) as well as providing spaces to pre-publish and possibly receive feedback, interact with each other and ask questions. Data networks, both open and gated, also allow researchers to access data sets for their own research (Schonfield, 2019b).

Along with many other social media platforms, these sites, which often contain 'author-originated sharing of work' (Fitzpatrick, 2016: para. 2), can bypass the constraints and metrics of the publication process, although they are still constrained by the potential for intellectual property violations (e.g. McKenzie, 2018c). ResearchGate, for example, provides additional services such as tracking citations and creating discussions that do not involve copyright. These connections can foster 'loose ties' among researchers that can help in developing their work and careers. The business model of ResearchGate, as is the case with many 'free' sites, is to collect data they can sell while the publishers can charge fees without having to pay authors. Such sites can provide authors with more autonomy for distributing their research but leave them caught between competing forces in meeting their goals for publishing, which can make the publishing space even more complicated for multilingual writers to negotiate.

Nevertheless, the potential for disrupting traditional publishing spaces remains controversial, not only because of the possible increased charges for publishing and the concurrent rise of the 'predatory' journals (e.g. Beall, 2012), but also because of a lack of data on whether the goals of open access have been met. With literacy spaces such as MOOCs, there has already been a pivot away from their original goals as new questions arise. Does open access reduce costs or simply shift costs from one stakeholder to another? Will these journals increase access to knowledge, or will they be appropriated for knowledge control today? Will this increased access change the roles of research in the developing world?

Open Access and Intellectual Property Law

Open access has often served as one more complication to the publishing space. One of the limitations of open access is how these new publishing approaches will affect the copyright status of the research, and thus the ability to later publish a work. Papers may have to be released early, sometimes depending on the funding sources. Such requirements can impact publishing at a later date. This impact can vary across disciplines and countries. Publishing in open access can greatly impact multilingual writers as graduate students or junior researchers who want to publish their dissertations or research from them. As has been mentioned, copyright law has been one of the critical factors in the creation and distribution of all forms of intellectual property, and therefore changes in how the law is viewed can greatly impact the distribution of intellectual property.

One of the final steps of the publishing process has been the transfer of some degree of copyright from the author to the publisher, a process that has grown more complex and confusing as laws and attitudes toward copyright law have changed. Authors and creators enter into larger controversy over intellectual property when they must sign over their copyright. Open access represents one of the latest challenges to the domination of copyright law over the distribution of research. While this process may sound simple, it involves a variety of factors in determining which version of a paper is copyrighted, what is considered non-commercial and whether the journal has an embargo over sharing published articles.

The growth of an 'abundance' of articles and their various versions has complicated this procedure. The growing 'bazaar' of open materials has been facilitated by changing attitudes toward the copyright of intellectual property (e.g. Lessig, 2002). The initial development of open access materials has often conflicted with the international rules of copyright. The debate over intellectual property law has raised important questions about how research is accepted for publication. One example is in the status of preprints, which can spread new research more quickly and more cheaply but may be considered by some journals as prior publication, thereby disqualifying it for consideration for future publication.

Open access digital spaces have been impacted both positively and negatively by changes in how intellectual property law is applied in digital literacy spaces. New perspectives on controlling intellectual property distribution and its role in these open spaces have given greater prominence to Creative Commons for freely sharing ideas. One of the motivations for developing Creative Commons was in response to the growing litigation over copyright. The growing availability of open access materials, including course articles, texts, books, images, movies, academic articles, as well as academic journals, has had a major impact on research, teaching and learning (e.g. Downes, 2011; Weller et al., 2014; Wiley, 2007).

Copyright remains an important concern in publishing spaces, involving multiple issues, sometimes with the use of texts and images in a research paper or with the transfer of copyright from a university to an author and then to a publisher. Under United States law, the copyright of academic articles belongs to the universities where they are written, under what is referred to as the 'work for hire' provision – that if the employer provides services, the employer controls the copyright. However, universities rarely exercise that right, especially for faculty, so the copyright usually reverts to the author.

Intellectual property law in publishing spaces has evolved with the development of new forms of publishing. Willinsky (2006) argues that copyright has been crucial in the development of open access resources. Traditionally, the transfer of copyright, as inherited in the 18th century from British law, primarily benefited the publishers. In an open access journal, the copyright often remains with the author. Although transfer may also indirectly benefit authors by sustaining the publishing industry, authors receive little financial benefit since they rarely receive compensation beyond the value of their publications for their careers and status. While many journals have modified these transfer rules, such changes have not been consistently practiced.

The role of intellectual property in publishing has evolved along with the models in other fields of distribution, resulting in services such as Spotify and Apple Music, that charge users in exchange for reducing the restrictions. With book publishing, the WAC Clearinghouse at Colorado State University, for example, has established itself as a major contributor to the open access space, publishing an open access journal, *Writing across Disciplines*, as well as new and previously published books and other resources. The challenges to existing restrictions may result in additional fees or raise ethical questions about using intellectual property (McKenzie, 2018d). However, as in music publishing, these spaces have caused traditional journal publishers to lose some control over what they publish. Interestingly, the conflict has not been between the young and old, as it was with Napster and other peer-to-peer services (Lessig, 1999), but between researchers, libraries and the gated journals.

Various Approaches to Creating Open Access

The varying definitions of openness in digital literacy spaces has resulted in further complications for students with the term 'open'. Such complications can confuse the authenticity and reliability of open information. The debate over openness has greatly affected how traditional journals are published and distributed (e.g. Schonfield, 2019a). Conflicts between universities and even nations with publishers have been fought over how these journals will be financed and the price that authors will have to pay to publish. The recent example of the conflict between Elsevier and the University of California libraries illustrates the battle over paywalls, who pays for journals and how these conflicts impact research (Anderson, 2019c). Their impact on content in the digital publication space can have long-term ramifications.

Some journals sustain their openness from grants, institutional support or author publishing fees. Pressure for open access has come from funders of research, particularly governments that feel research funded by taxpayer money should be freely available. Although open access may receive more downloads, major authors do not feel they are as highly rated (Davis, 2010). As the demise of *Dialogues* shows, journals must attract quality research often before obtaining the supposed credibility of impact factors that appeal to hiring and tenure committees, although Garfield (2005), its creator, warned about its use in evaluating journals. This relationship provides a useful example of how digital spaces can be constrained by their institutional contexts, so unless the institutional constraints change, the space's usefulness will be limited.

Traditional journals have responded to these open access spaces in various ways. Some publishers require an APC to obtain open access. Piwowar *et al.* (2018) identified various forms of open access, ranging from completely free open access to 'pirated' publications that intentionally mimic more established traditional gated journals that charge large fees to publish articles as open. There have been proposals for creating more open access, ranging from 'flipping' gated journals to ones always open (Solomon *et al.*, 2016) to charging APCs to open gated articles.

The Gold approach requires an upfront processing fee, sometime $2000–$3000, while the Green approach (Page, 2015) allows for distribution after varying embargo periods, giving journals the rights to archive research that can later be freely accessed (Harnad, 2011). Even a 'Platinum' approach has been designated for journals where open access is funded from outside sources. Gated publishers have often responded to these approaches by differentiating their requirements for open access. These responses have led to the creation of different approaches to open access, sometimes referred to as 'hybrid open access', which combines open access and traditional publishing methods, and the 'Gold' and 'Green' approaches (Weller *et al.*, 2014). A newer approach, labeled 'Bronze', has become a growing space where articles can be openly read but not distributed (Crotty, 2017).

The growth of Gold open access is one factor that differentiates publishing in multilingual research journals from publishing in science and technology, where authors may already have the funding to pay the authors' fees to publish openly. Publishing fees are often prohibitive without grants, although, regardless of the fees, authors may still archive a draft for sharing, which, in turn, can raise additional copyright issues over the ownership of different drafts. The Green approach gives more flexibility to the author in controlling their research but still limits how data can be accessed. The result is sometimes a reluctance to use these approaches. For example, it has raised often confusing differentiations among what copyright means – what version of a paper is copyrighted and how long do these copyrights last.

Recent legislation in Europe, known as Plan S (https://www.scienceeurope.org/policy/policy-areas/open-access-to-scientific-publications), has attempted to apply the goals of OER to academic publications in a more systematic, but more confusing, way that can further complicate OER. Funded by the Wellcome Trust and the Gates Foundation, this approach has not been universally adopted even in Europe and has created much controversy over its implementation, particularly over the retention of copyright and its elimination of journals that publish both open and gated research. The goal of Plan S has been to push open access onto reluctant publishers (Dodds, 2019). The implementation of Plan S has been controversial in terms of the costs for authors to publish versus its support of open access (Mudditt, 2019). As with *PLOS* and PubMed Central, questions about sustainability have arisen.

In fact, Plan S is one of multiple approaches to open access, with various forms of support. As is the case in North America, authors themselves are divided as to its merits (Dodds, 2019). Plan S has raised questions about sustainability that can vary across disciplines. In conjunction with Plan S, for example, a group of universities in Europe have formed a consortium for publishing called 'University Journals', which utilizes alternative and sometimes controversial ways of responding to traditional approaches to funding, copyright and peer review (Esposito, 2019b). The result has potentially further complicated the understanding of publishing for junior authors with, as to be expected, much variation across disciplines.

However, opponents to open access, often the publishers themselves, have argued that open access has created an equally controversial set of new rules for publishing, publishing fees, distributing information and judging appropriate intellectual property use (R. Anderson, 2018b, 2019a), which could increase the costs of publishing, which is important for small publishers (Cochran, 2018). Hinchliffe (2019) found that publishers expressed great concern for the future of their models of open access with its often expensive processing charges. For many authors, paying for publication and access but receiving no compensation is problematic.

However, there have been areas of compromise. Some publishers, usually for a fee, have allowed libraries to make their publications open, which may have unintended consequences depending on the size and prestige of the university (Esposito, 2018b). While these approaches may be steps to sustainable open access, the fees have been a barrier to publishing for many researchers. Such sustainability goes beyond monetary concerns to include their status in publishing, which then could be important for decisions regarding publishing and data sharing (e.g. Schonfield, 2019b).

The move toward open access has been slow across many disciplines often because of questions about its impact; therefore, it may be difficult for students to understand the implications of these designations on their publishing. One of the factors that can confuse novices in publishing has been the frequent similarities between open and gated journals. Many open access journals have retained the trappings of gated journals except for the subscription costs. While increasing the distribution of articles, particularly in an international context (Hook *et al.*, 2019), these journals still retain some form of peer review for providing support to its authors and the evaluation of their work. Often, journals retain the same criteria for publishing while others have opened the process so that more articles can be published. *PLOS*, for example, has changed its approach to publishing so that more evaluation can occur after the article has been published, but it still charges authors a fee, which can shift the burden of sustainability from the institution to the author, who can build the fees into their grants (Fitzpatrick, 2011).

Sustainability has been a major argument for charging fees. *PLOS*, which has endured financial problems because of a decline in publishing articles (Davis, 2019), has created an open access peer review system to eliminate the blind- and double-blind processes (Weller *et al.*, 2014), which has resulted in increasing the number of articles published. Established journals could also provide authentication through an extended peer review system for papers that have already been circulated (Hook *et al.*, 2019).

These platforms have supported open access publication in the sciences, although compared with gated publications, they remain a 'niche' operation (Esposito, 2019b). Open access has also emulated the archiving role that traditional journals have played. ArXiv was developed to share preprints, particularly in those areas of science where speed of publication is highly valued. These open publications provide an alternative literacy space, again open to some authors but not all, but do they respond to the problems that multilingual writers still have with publishing? For multilingual writers who may feel that traditional publishing outlets are prejudiced against them (c.f. Hyland, 2015, 2016a), open access journals, even predatory ones, may be an alternative space. While there may be more alternatives, multilingual writers are still under greater pressure to write standard English. These predatory journals have caused problems for multilingual researchers in making more nuanced judgments since they may be more attracted to publish in them because of the language issues.

The Contribution of Open Access to the Production of Knowledge

The goal here is to propose two important observations for students to understand about publishing: that it is evolving, often unequally, and that this evolution has created a chaotic publishing space. Open access has disrupted the evaluation process of the digital space in deciding what articles to publish. The growth of predatory journals, for example, has led to greater scrutiny of the digital publishing space. The space for publishing multilingual research has expanded but not as widely as has the space for writers in other disciplines. The question is whether these journals should be a model for publishing multilingual research or should the journals go in their own direction. Many of the models for open access have not developed in the multilingual research space. Journals such as *PLOS*, which can publish thousands of articles, has increased its space for publishing by reviewing, primarily focusing on the soundness of the argument rather than on the quality of the results, thus somewhat relieving researchers of the need to find new results and providing more autonomy to the readers for evaluating the significance of the article (Mudditt, 2018). *PLOS* has also allowed researchers to publish their peer reviews and revisions along with their research.

There are other factors that open journals for multilingual research have not fully exploited. The open space has incorporated new, often controversial, directions in sharing data to make the peer review process more transparent (Crystal, 2019; Vines, 2018), but these have not been adopted in the multilingual literacy space. These new spaces have changed the roles of editors and peer reviewers from being gatekeepers to being evaluators of the appropriateness of the research. These so-called 'mega journals' (Mudditt, 2018) have yet to develop in the writing field. These mega-journals are less selective and publish more articles with the majority from the medical, engineering and biology fields, leaving more of the evaluation process to the readers (Petrou, 2020). Petrou reports that as new mega-journals, often supported by commercial publishers, enter the field, the publication rates of the original journals decline, which can affect their citation rates. However, authors in the composition field must go through the traditional peer review process to be published, but those articles chosen for publication are then open to anyone with access to the internet.

The development of open access journals has not been consistent across disciplines. While some areas of open access may challenge conventional assumptions about language appropriateness, other forms of academic writing have been more resistant. Judgments about language appropriateness, which is important in discussions of translingualism in multilingual composition (e.g. Atkinson *et al.*, 2015; Hall, 2018; Matsuda, 2014), and its impact on publishing have not been well studied. Some open access journals may not have the same concern with linguistic correctness, at least when articles are submitted, and therefore are more welcoming to researchers whose first language (L1) is not English. The growing costs of materials for both universities, faculty and students have greatly contributed to this acceptance.

However, open access journals still face skepticism as to their value in what is published. There has been controversy over the quality of open access materials and their impact on the publishing industry (e.g. Wiley, 2007). Taylor & Francis (2014), a leading publisher of academic journals, found that its authors viewed open access favorably for providing wider circulation and higher visibility but were still concerned for research quality and the production values of the journals, which can explain that while traditional forms of peer review have been disrupted, some form of peer review has remained to guarantee that the research follows the guidelines of the journal and its academic community, even though those guidelines may not be explicitly stated. These guidelines can include length and type of article, its format, the intellectual property rules for transferring copyright, communication with the editor and the role of peer reviewers; however, other rhetorical concerns such as the goal of the research or the type of problems addressed may not be as explicitly discussed.

The development of open access has met with strong resistance from both publishers and teachers. Research by Desire to Learn ('Flipped Classroom Market to 2023 with Key Players like Cisco, Dell, Adobe, Desire2Learn, Echo360, Panopto, OpenEye, Saba Software', 2018), a creator of learning management systems, found that despite increasing usage, there is still resistance among faculty to using open access materials and publishing in open access journals. Kahle (2010) argued that open access materials have always been subject to the 'get what you pay for' assessment, which can be especially problematic for researchers on the periphery of their communities to judge. Wakeling *et al.* (2017) found that authors expect the same levels of technological sophistication in open access journals as found in traditional journals. However, the need to limit the purchase of journals because of budget constraints, as Wakeling *et al.* found, has also limited their use of these technologies. Thus, the goal of open access to spread more content into the publishing space has never been achieved as had been originally hoped.

The Impact of Predatory Journals on the Open Access Literacy Space

One of the controversies that multilingual students face is judging between 'authentic' and 'predatory' journals, a distinction that is not always clearly defined. While some factors, such as the falsification of editorial boards and even authors seems obvious, other factors, such as requiring payments, the 'pay-to-publish' model, are more problematic in disciplines where author charges are rare. Even quality peer review may be difficult to quantify. A recent query on the myTESOL Lounge from a potential author in Algeria was regarding the possibility of fees for publication since, she later explained, such a publication would not be considered for tenure; this illustrates the growing sensitivity that writers have toward paying to publish. While paying to publish may be common in some disciplines, it is unknown in others.

These 'predatory' journals (e.g. Beall, 2013) that charge fees have been criticized not only for their fees but for the quality of such factors as peer review, the authenticity of impact factors and the quality of the editors and the editorial boards. While many emphasize their peer reviews, these reviews are often promised in a much shorter time period and they may not be of the same quality as those in more traditional journals. There are also questionable standards for recruiting editors, editorial board members and potential authors. In some cases, individuals listed on an editorial board never gave permission for their names to be used (Pettit, 2018). Teachers and researchers may be inundated by requests to publish their research and editorial board membership by journals that may sound reasonable but may still be 'predatory'.

The issues surrounding open access and predatory journals have forced all journals to reevaluate their publishing practices. SAGE, a publisher of many traditional journals, has guidelines for their own open access submissions. However, SAGE charges a fee of $395 for publishing an article as open, comparable to the charges in the so-called predatory journals but lower than the $2000–$3000 charged by other publishers. *Written Communication*, another journal published by SAGE, charges individuals $155 for print subscriptions, which increases to $1076 for institutions, with a $108 discount for electronic subscriptions. Even the newest journals can charge fees. *PLOS* charges fees, ranging from $1500 to around $3000. *PeerJ*, a medical and biology journal, charges $1095 for publishing an article. It boasts having editors and advisors from leading universities, charges membership fees, so authors can publish as much as they like while still promising peer review.

The rise of these predatory journals has complicated the evaluation of open access journals for all potential authors (Pyne, 2017). Skepticism over the value of a journal can affect the willingness of researchers to publish in open access journals. Articles submitted to these journals may not always be well reviewed, and thus may not be considered a reliable source, which can negatively impact the goals for publication. Especially for multilingual students, the proliferation of these journals necessitates that greater care must be taken in searching for and evaluating publishing spaces (e.g. *Think. Check. Submit.*).

The relationship between predatory and open access journals has itself been controversial. Beall (2013), who is often credited with publicizing the problem of predatory journals until he 'disappeared' from the discussion, argued that the distinction between these predatory journals and open access ones is smaller than may appear because of the growing development of open marketplaces that the predatory journals can exploit. The growing problem of journal sustainability, for example, has led some journals that might not be considered 'predatory' to imposing APCs. Beall blamed their spread on the anti-corporate bias of open access journals, arguing that open access journals reflect a 'negative movement' designed to destroy the creativity of the traditional publishers. He writes:

> The open access movement isn't really about open access. Instead, it is about collectivizing production and denying the freedom of the press from those who prefer the subscription model of scholarly publishing. (Cited in Esposito, 2013)

The relationship between predatory and open access journals remains highly controversial. As a result, literacy spaces may appear confusing to emerging scholars. Anderson (2018c) argues that the connections have too often been dismissed, but studies from India, Germany and Canada have taken a more critical view of judging the authenticity of publications. In some cases, these practices have increased because of the scrutiny by government agencies in the United States (Anderson, 2017a).

The Federal Trade Commission (FTC), for example, has created criteria that can be useful in developing a pedagogy for developing courses on publishing spaces (see Chapter 7). It lists the following issues related to predatory journals: falsely advertising rigorous peer review; lacking reputable editors and credible impact factors; making unethical solicitations for articles; deceptive naming practices that may plagiarize the titles of more reputable journals; and a lack transparency in fees (cited in Anderson, 2017c). Often, they seem located in unreliable or out-of-the-way places such as deserts or garages that are not normally places of academic publishing. Many predatory journals rely on deceptive practices that can jeopardize the ethos of the publication and the authors published in them. Fasel and Hartse (2018) attempted to categorize predatory journals by counting the 'red flags' that differentiated the practices of these journals from traditional practices, providing a useful pedagogy for understanding these different journals.

The controversies over predatory journals, such as accusations of mislabeling their titles (Basken, 2017a, 2017b), eventually resulted in Beall's controversial blog being shut down due to what his supporters called 'threats and politics' (Straumsheim, 2017), although Cabell (https://www2.cabells.com/about-blacklist) later started their own 'blacklist' of predatory journals (Anderson, 2017b), for which they charge a fee to access. Cabell's website lists a group of criteria used in judging predatory journals: integrity, peer review, fees, access and copyright, publication processes and business practices; and then categorizes violations from minor to severe (https://blog.cabells.com/2019/03/20/blacklist-criteria-v1-1/). Anderson (2019b) argues that since Cabell may not share the antipathy to open access that Beall expressed, their list may be more objective and acceptable, although he later questioned the clarity of the definitions of these terms. One of the most controversial areas has been in the area of peer review.

Shen and Bjork (2015) found that these journals had increased ninefold from 2010 to 2014. This increase may have some positive implications for expanding the publishing space, but the problems associated with them often outweigh their advantages. These journals may appear to emulate the dedication to high standards for peer review, but often speed up the process by claiming it can be accomplished in a week. In some cases, peer review was outsourced to the lowest bidder using an Uber-like platform for matching papers with reviewers, so potential peer reviewers could bid for the job, although only a small amount was paid to the reviewers. Such a model may appeal to emerging authors frustrated with the slowness and the sometimes aggressiveness of the peer reviews.

The impact of predatory journals on the publishing space has been widespread. Harvey and Weinstein (2017) blame predatory journals for increasing retractions and publishing unreliable research that can distract readers from more authentic research. Some opponents to predatory journals have tried, often successfully, to trick predatory publishers by submitting 'fake' articles, which can reveal some factors in deciding where to publish. A group of researchers from Poland submitted the name of a made-up professor to the journals to be an editor and found a third of journals accepted her and only 13% rejected her (Sorokowski *et al.*, 2017). Crotty (2018) has called on all stakeholders to act against these predatory journals, although he admits he is not clear what actions are appropriate and effective. However, even reputable publishers have published predatory journals, so their location may not always be a red flag.

The Pedagogical Implications of Predatory Journals

This development of varying types of openness and open access journals has placed greater importance on evaluating open material (Ray, 2016). As a pedagogical issue, evaluating predatory journals can provide many teachable moments in designing a digital space for publishing. As with the other literacy spaces discussed here, its complex nature, which has resulted from the increase in predatory journals, has important pedagogical implications for understanding their distinctions for publishing. What constitutes a 'predatory' journal can be highly contested, reflecting the difficulty in judging fraudulent practices. Shamseer *et al.* (2017) found 13 factors in biomedical journals that could be used to distinguish a predatory journal.

There are other strategies for evaluating a journal, often involving examining the same factors found in every journal. Deceptive practices can sometimes be revealed by Googling the names listed on the editorial page. For example, one of my students found the website of an editor listed on a journal who denied she was ever the editor and warned potential authors of submitting articles or sending money for publishing fees. The quality of the impact factors can be another red flag in deciding about publishing. Impact factors can influence prospective authors on deciding where to publish. Although the values of impact factors are themselves controversial, citations are still expected to come only from reputable sources, so potential authors may have to judge their validity.

It has often been difficult to determine what constitutes fraud in these journals. The Himmelfarb Health Sciences ('Predatory Publishing: Red Flags', 2020) published a list of factors to consider in judging whether a journal is 'predatory', which the Committee on Publication Ethics argues places more responsibility on open access journals to demonstrate their transparency ('Promoting Integrity in Research and Its Publication',

2017). Whether the growth of these predatory journals has had any effect on expanding publishing for multilingual students, they have certainly made the publishing process more difficult and the design of pedagogical spaces more complicated.

Overly high impact factors or those supplied by less reputable sources can indicate that the journal may be considered 'predatory'. Similar ethical concerns with citing articles from these journals (Anderson, 2019b) have spawned several sites, such as *Think. Check. Submit.*, which can help potential authors decide on the validity of these publishing spaces. *Think. Check. Submit.* offers a video and a checklist in different languages for potential authors to consider before submission. This confusion from these different approaches to creating open access literacy spaces, however, has not necessarily refuted the value of open access but has sometimes resulted from pay-to-publish journals obscuring the distinction between the various types of literacy spaces. Several attempts have been made to at least educate potential authors about the possible dangers in the publishing space.

The current controversy over openness has its roots in the previous controversies over Napster and the sharing of music online, which itself reflects another controversy over using intellectual property that has carried over from research-sharing sites such as ResearchGate and Academia.edu. ResearchGate, for example, has been under attack from the Coalition for Responsible Sharing (CRS), primarily publishers, for uploading copyrighted articles (Dodds, 2019), although earlier versions of papers may still be shared. Regardless of the legal issues, the conflict illustrates the constraints on potential education uses that copyright imposes. The growing commercialization of publishing has been further complicated by established, gated journals that may charge much greater fees to have an article published as open access.

The conservative nature of many open access journals can be seen in the constraints on the lengths of submitted articles similar to those found in print journals even though the article length has little effect on the cost of production. Many authors from developing countries, who may doubt their ability to publish in more traditional journals, are preyed upon.

The Development of Openness in Academic Journals for Multilingual Writers

The science fiction citation by Gibson that the future is already here but not equally distributed applies even more to researchers in developing countries. Open access has not developed equally across all disciplines. Salager-Meyer (2012) found that the preponderance of open access journals was in the hard sciences but that this situation was beginning to change in second language (L2) learning communities. The field of multilingual writing research has been affected by this development in open access journals, although not necessarily as in other fields since its growth has not been equally distributed, often within small niche areas but sometimes in competition with other forms of distribution (Davis, 2018).

While open access can benefit multilingual students, they may have their own challenges in entering these spaces, which in some cases have been addressed by technologies. Understanding the often complicated rules for copyright has been a problem for multilingual students from cultures with different rules. There has been a growing interest in the potential for publishing in periphery and non-English journals (e.g. Curry & Lillis, 2004, 2018; Salager-Meyer, 2014) as well as growing controversy over 'linguistic injustice' (c.f. Hanauer & Englander, 2011; Hanauer et al., 2019; Hyland, 2016a; Politzer-Ahlesa et al., 2016) toward multilingual or so-called 'periphery' writers wanting to publish, who are discriminated against. However, as Irfanunallah (2019) argues, many journals in countries such as Bangladesh do not have the same standards as journals in the Global North.

Research on the perceptions of multilingual writers (e.g. Hanauer & Englander, 2011; Hanauer et al., 2019) can be balanced against the number of multilingual writers being published and the continuing importance of English language journals. Curry and Lillis (2019) have identified publishing as having been shaped by the 'lore' of the field. Perhaps more important has been whether the changes in publishing have impacted problems with publishing. Open access journals are seen to be one answer to Curry and Lillis' question of how multilingual writers can participate more equitably in the global production of knowledge. These issues may include not only grammatical issues but also issues related to how research integrity is defined in their countries.

One of the critical aspects of pedagogy for multilingual students is the role of textual borrowing and its impact on the arguments that the writers are trying to develop. The changes in these digital spaces can respond to the high costs of purchasing gated journals where these texts are archived. The impact of this increased access to these texts attempts to address this pedagogical problem. Lacking access can pose problems for potential authors wanting to publish. Minai (2018) argued that researchers and teachers in developing countries may lack access to the journals that address the 'conversations' in their disciplines that help shape their research and teaching, particularly in the social sciences and humanities. Lacking research accessibility can limit the publishing of multilingual research since the researchers are often unfamiliar with the most recent issues in their fields. Therefore, researchers who do not have such access may not create the arguments often required for publishing.

This increased accessibility can be helpful in developing their papers, particularly those working in developing countries who face problems with accessing gated journals, which can be more expensive than their institutions can afford. Therefore, a major factor in providing accessibility has been the copyright restrictions placed on the distribution of research. Copyright served to create securities by limiting the free distribution of research. Before the development of the internet and using PDF files in journals, gated journals often gave the authors only a limited number of copies of their articles to distribute. However, the development of the internet addressed this scarcity issue by making information easily reproducible, which has threatened publication in gated journals (Suber, 2012) and has created a complicated context for potential authors.

The changes in how open access has affected multilingual research can be seen when comparing it to research in other fields. The questions raised by Lillis and Curry (2006) concerning publishing by multilingual authors incorporated the values by which academic writing is evaluated. Some open journals (e.g. *PLOS* and *Sci-Hub*) already address how the 'bazaar' metaphor conflicts with the 'cathedral metaphor' as represented by traditional publishers and paywalls, in that almost anyone can both publish and access information. *Sci-Hub*, in particularly, has often been labeled as a 'pirate' by publishers, although some publishers have attempted to participate in this process, leaving the publishing space as contested as ever.

Multilingual research has largely avoided the kinds of copyright conflicts found in journals such as *Sci-Hub*. As the controversies over intellectual property at ResearchGate and other such sites have shown, these journals have been immersed in controversies regarding intellectual property law (Pitts, 2018) and the limitations it causes to the abundance of research. Open access journals in multilingual research have largely avoided these controversies while gated journals are often in the middle of the controversy, thus often leaving researchers confused about what rights they possess.

Fees can place another limitation on accessibility. Some open access journals cannot sustain operations and may rely on authors' fees. *The Asian ESP Journal*, which had been open, only recently announced fees for both submission (US$20) and publication (US$300) as a means of achieving sustainability. Open access journals in science fields may also charge fees to publish, which can filter out many articles that might be of interest to their readers. These limitations have also been the case in open access journals in multilingual research. Gatekeeping in open journals can be similar to that in gated journals: first establish the guidelines for expressing the values of the publishing spaces and then limit the research made available to the public. While peer-to-peer networks such as ResearchGate can redress the issues regarding distributing information, researchers who need the validation of journals for their careers cannot necessarily rely on these networks.

Some factors have been more resistant to change. Journals have evolved as their sponsoring disciplines have evolved, and the technologies for publication and distribution have often reflected changes in the academic communities in which they are published (Bazerman, 1988). No issue is more ready for disruption than peer review. With the tremendous growth in the number of authors wanting to enter the publishing space, there has been a corresponding increase in the need for peer reviewers, which cannot always be matched. No process has been more obscured, especially from the early career researcher who may not have had experience with the process. Friend (2020) argues that journals like *Hybrid Pedagogy* allow readers to look behind the curtain at the publishing process, to see how the peer review works.

As with some open access journals, the peer review process has been changed with the elimination of the blind review; new relationships between reviewer, author and editor; and the extension of the review beyond the publication date. Its impact on other journals, both open and gated, remains to be seen. The rise of peer review as a means of legitimizing knowledge itself was a response to changes in publication (Baldwin, 2018). Changes in peer review today have been a part of the continuing evolution in how the quality of the research space has been designed.

In many journals, peer reviewing has remained as it has been in gated journals. While peer review has retained its role in the evaluation of research, it has also been criticized for lacking transparency, meaning that readers often rely on the journal quality or the reputation of the space for determining the value of the research (Krumholz, 2015). Various practices, such as review sharing (Squazzoni *et al.*, 2017) and tools have been proposed to support the traditional peer review system. Smith (1999) had argued that such transparency is valuable since the main contribution of peer review has been to improve a text, not judge it. Krumholtz also argues that the process can be too slow, creating bottlenecks that may be addressable. Wulf (2017) argues that open access could increase the speed of publication, although she warns this could negatively impact some journals. However, such increases have become more important during the COVID-19 pandemic.

Other issues, such as the speed of publication and the diversity of the reviewers, often interest multilingual researchers since the authors and readers may be from different cultural and linguistic backgrounds to those of the editors and reviewers. *The British Medical Journal*, for example, has attempted to open the process by inviting patients to contribute to the reviews of medical submissions (Anderson, 2018b). Other journals have implemented 'open peer review' where reviews may be published so that the publication process (Rittman, 2018) and the peer review process (Almquist *et al.*, 2017) become more transparent. Bravo *et al.* (2019) found that such open peer review does not compromise the integrity of the publishing process. Such changes if implemented in multilingual research could have important consequences for the publication and accessibility of research, again with the caveats regarding the value of such research still in question.

The Role of Open Access Journals in Multilingual Research

The growth of APCs for open access has shut out many potential authors who do not have the funding. For many authors, the result has been the simultaneous rise of predatory journals and sustainable open access journals as potential publishing sites. Therefore, multilingual writers may find open access publishing even murkier since there is great variability in its approaches to these issues. Many gated journals in multilingual research have created levels of open access for a relatively large fee, although few researchers can afford it. The *Journal of Second Language Writing*, for example, requires a $1800 per APC for Gold access. *The Journal of English for Academic Purposes*, which is also published by Elsevier, charges $1100. These approaches remain controversial since the consequences of implementing the Gold standard has been the devaluation of editorial standards since more publications can mean more profits (Esposito, 2017).

One of our graduate students from Indonesia, for example, was forced to publish in an English language journal to receive his degree. His paper was accepted for publication almost immediately in a pay-to-publish journal if he could pay $400. While the $400 fee to receive his degree may seem outrageous, for many students, this is a small price. These problems contribute to the chaotic nature of the publishing space.

Open access, therefore, contributes to the development of academic communities throughout the world by reducing the constraints on both reading and publishing. Curry and Lillis (2010) argue that open access allows for more locally generated journals that can increase the opportunity for help for multilingual writers. This opportunity is a product of the technologically enhanced power of 'the long tail' (Anderson, 2006), which privileges abundance over scarcity and a social context that encourages what Lillis and Curry refer to as the gift economy, which better facilitates all aspects of the publishing process by reducing the costs of knowledge production.

While not a journal, YouTube exemplifies the extension of digital spaces where such technological affordances can support openness, as illustrated in the discussion of multimodality (Chapter 3) and the creation of videos for flipped learning (Chapter 5). Anyone can share anything of any quality and, depending on the type of copyright chosen, it can be readily shared. There are few gatekeepers – either reviewers or editors – to prejudge the quality of the materials. Judgment is by the audience who through their viewing of each video will determine which goes viral.

The goal of openness has been to increase the abundance of space, including publishing spaces, to access information. However, despite such an expansion, many of these changes have not reached multilingual research. Open digital literacy spaces have not always addressed many of the issues related to the academic writing of non-native English speakers but have increased access to the latest research by writers in developing countries, where the abundance of intellectual property has traditionally not always been evenly distributed and where predatory publishing has had its biggest impact (Manca *et al.*, 2017).

As previously pointed out, multilingual researchers may enter a biased process (e.g. Hanauer *et al.*, 2019). Wellmon and Piper (2017) argue that publishing has been contaminated, which may impact multilingual research. Although such biases may predominate in publishing, the conservative open access in multilingual composition publishing has limited implementing the developments found in other disciplines. Open access journals may not completely address these problems but may still contribute to a solution to the problems.

Despite these concerns about open access, there are several important open access journals for multilingual researchers. The number of open access journals has increased (e.g. *Asian EFL Journal*, *TESL-EJ*). Along with the newer open access journals such as *Journal of Writing Research*, *Writing and Pedagogy*, *Language Learning and Technology* and *The Journal of Academic Writing* in multilingual writing, these journals are part of the trend of freely accessible research that can be made available to L2 teachers and researchers. These journals do not charge readers or writers but may have issues with sustainability and scalability.

Speaking about publishing in the humanities, Salager-Meyer (2014), however, addresses the problems that non-native English speakers can face in the publication space. The barriers to publication may not only be linguistic deviations from standard English but also rhetorical concerns in judging the problems researchers address and the arguments used to support their claims. Since publishing for multilingual researchers involves more than simply mastering writing skills but includes accessing complex information networks (e.g. Hyland, 2016a, 2016b; Lillis & Curry, 2014), providing open access research cannot alone address the factors that cause this inequality but may at least detail the current issues and controversies to support their current approaches. The expansion of preprint services could also help multilingual writers by providing feedback before the research is published.

The growing importance of open journals may be more suitable for multilingual writers (e.g. Curry and Lillis). Potential authors must address the problem of accessing social networks related to publishing, which may be more important than issues related to language or rhetorical skills (c.f. Hyland, 2016b; Politzer-Ahlesa *et al.*, 2016). New design features, as is true with the development of affordances with other technological spaces, may confuse those wanting to enter the publishing space. The problem for publication spaces can be seen in the vagueness of the guidelines. Often, journals try to be more explicit. For example, in this email soliciting submissions, the goals are not clearly stated. '*The Asian Online Journals* are fully committed to the *Open Access Initiative* and all articles will be available freely as soon as they are published. Please visit journal's webpage at http://www.ajouronline.net for more details'. Although this policy may be a response to the criticisms discussed here, such as the $100 fee for publishing only 10 pages, the controversies surrounding predatory journals need to be included in discussions on publishing spaces (see Chapter 7).

These digital spaces have been augmented by developments in the controversial area of networking. One recent email received from ResearchGate noted that my research was published in open access and had been cited by writers from Ethiopia, Poland, Indonesia and Iran, illustrating the value of open access in the globalization of research in multilingual writing. However, Minai (2018) argues that open access journals may not directly address this problem, particularly concerning the power differentiations in academic publishing. As will be discussed, open access journals in the field of multilingual composition research have not addressed the problem of publishing in their new digital spaces, often opting instead to mimic the publication processes of traditional journals. Journals where open access can be purchased at usually high fees, which include most of the main journals in multilingual research, seem to have had little impact on the publishing process.

The critique that Curry and Lillis (2019) have made concerning the need for alternative publishing spaces reflects the problematic nature of the domination of 'English' in the publishing world. While the spaces for publication may have expanded outside of English-speaking contexts, their primary use of English has reinforced standard English as a dominant form of communication. The growth of predatory journals in the open access space may provide an alternative to the English language journals that can be much more difficult to publish in.

Open access journals have not always provided a suitable alternative to gated journals in responding to the problems that Curry and Lillis have identified with traditional publishing approaches. As Salager-Meyer (2018) points out, open access in the humanities and social sciences has lagged growth in the sciences. Nevertheless, the development of open access in multilingual composition was accelerated by the growing cost of journals, the growing sensitivity to problems with access, particularly among scholars outside of the traditional Western universities, and an interest in providing authors with more opportunities to publish both internationally and locally (e.g. *The Journal of Writing Research* does not mention in its guidelines a specific maximum paper length although it suggests authors write 'as clearly and concisely as possible').

Other types of journals that publish alternative forms of academic writing may also have limits because of the sustainability issue. As mentioned above (Salager-Meyer, 2018) open access in the humanities and social sciences has lagged the sciences and their extraneous factors, such as funding, have accelerated this development. However, the recent growth in the digital humanities has narrowed the gap. There are other areas where open access journals have potentially greater differences, particularly as a result of the lower cost factors. While the costs of inserting color photographs or videos can be expensive in print journals, they may cost little or nothing in online journals.

The design of many open access journals, however, has increased the opportunities for publication (see Table 6.1) even though the individual journals have not increased the number of articles they publish per issue. The result has been more room in the publishing space for alternative literacies. L1 writing journals have led in incorporating these new literacies. *Kairos*, for example, encourages the submission of multimodal presentations. *Hybrid Pedagogy* (http://hybridpedagogy.org) and *The Journal of Interactive Technology and Pedagogy* (https://jitp.commons. gc.cuny.edu) have expanded the type of articles that they publish. *Hybrid Pedagogy* is an open access journal resembling a group blog, which has tried to challenge the traditional views of publishing and peer review (Morris & Stommel, 2018).

In other cases, there have been attempts to further expand the journal content. The *Community Literacy Journal* (CLJ) and the *Journal of Response to Writing* illustrate how open access allows for the publication of journals on narrower topics than usually found in more established writing journals. Some journals may support the use of different modes of expression or author voices, often from outside the traditional research paper. These spaces, such as *myTESOL Lounge*, have become more important for communicating globally. These journals vary in how they incorporate the features of an online community – networking, social media, collaboration – to extend the discussion and, as a result, the traditional state of the publication process has been disrupted but not overthrown. These journals have provided the possibility for increased citation rates (e.g. Niyazov *et al.*, 2016), meaning that once the article is published, its rhetorical power may increase. However, some of these changes have necessitated new skills for communicating.

Lacking understanding of key research questions may negatively impact researchers from developing countries participating in these social networks. Social networks support sharing questions and experiences about the publishing process and serve as a space for connecting to other researchers. The development of these networks has been facilitated by using Creative Commons rather than relying on the traditional copyright laws often imposed by established publishers. Questions about the role of language and rhetoric remain paramount in the choice of journals. However, an indirect benefit has been a possible aid to multilingual researchers who find it difficult to keep abreast of current issues and controversies. Research on publication among L2 writers was constrained not merely by their writing skills but more importantly by their understanding of the social network in which research is published (c.f. Hyland, 2016b; Politzer-Ahlesa *et al.*, 2016).

The open access publishing spaces are not always different from the traditional ones. Many open access journals are fairly conservative in their standards for publication. These journals *have* exemplified how open access journals can obtain the same quality and recognition as the gated journals. Besides maintaining traditional approaches to peer reviewing and the role of the impact factor, another similarity has been the requirements for standard language use.

Despite the controversies over translingualism and other approaches to non-traditional forms of English (Atkinson *et al.*, 2015), there is little indication that there have been changes in how acceptable language is viewed in these open access journals (cf. Flowerdew & Wang, 2016; Rozycki & Johnson, 2013). Flowerdew and Wang found that multilingual writers still had to undergo intense periods of negotiation with editors over grammatical issues. Most open journals specify either British or American English or 'high standards', which, however, is usually not defined. Gated journal publishers may suggest using editing services that charge $300–$400 with no guarantee of publication or ask authors to have a 'native speaker' proofread their papers before submission.

The possible disruptions to the dominance of standardized English in publications have occasionally been found in multilingual, open access journals. Rozycki and Johnson (2013) found a limited number of examples of journals that accepted alternative forms of English. Baker (2014) points to *The Asian EFL Journal*'s statement in their submission guidelines that they 'welcome submissions written in different versions of world Englishes as well as non-standard forms of rhetoric' (https://www.asian-efl-journal.com/guidelines).

However, such guidelines rarely exist outside of applied linguistic journals. My students found one journal where writers were told not to worry about their writing ability. As a homework assignment on examining academic guidelines for my publishing course (see Chapter 8), a student found an engineering journal published by *IEEE* that encouraged these kinds of submissions but promised to clean them up themselves. Authors may face a similar dilemma with the rhetorical standards for publication. Despite its flexibility with linguistic standards, *The Asian EFL Journal* requires authors to also show what is 'new about your study' and to address a similar 'broad international audience', two factors with which multilingual writers often struggle.

The disruption resulting from the openness of the publishing space has also had consequences for the decisions that writers must make about where to publish. For all early-career writers, the value of these spaces must be considered, but the decision has been complicated, especially for multilingual writers who may not feel secure about their English language writing ability so have been publishing in 'predatory journals'.

The proliferation of these so-called 'predatory' journals has resulted in part from the lower costs for publishers to enter the space. Open access journals, including those considered 'predatory', have challenged the constraints that can limit their possible audiences.

To gain a perspective on open access in multilingual education, I compared open access journals with examples of the more respected journals in writing research. Table 6.1 shows some similarities and differences between gated journals and open access journals in both first and multilingual composition. In Table 6.1, the open access journals in disciplines related to L2 writing have all been of the 'born-open' type. The traditional journals have adapted some features of open access, but the main differences have been copyright and of course, cost to access. Gated journals can play various roles in establishing the authenticity of a space for publishing (Anderson, 2018a).

Table 6.1 illustrates the extent that the growth of open access journals has impacted the digital publishing space. How has this development of open access impacted researchers in developing countries? While the importance of open access seems clear, the evidence from practice is less so. However, supporting evidence still exists, although it may be limited to 'lore' (Curry & Lillis, 2019). Many of the questions and requests for articles posted on these network sites seem to come from researchers in developing countries, but which still raise questions about intellectual property laws, highlighting the need for new ways of sharing, reusing and repurposing information that neither violate copyright laws nor become the profit-oriented publication platforms they are trying to replace. Questions about practices will, therefore, be better answered by the writers themselves from their choice of which space to publish in.

The Design of Open Access Spaces in Multilingual Research

The length of articles, which can vary greatly given that there are no additional costs to publishing longer articles, is similar, usually around 8500 words, but this number may have changed. This similarity indicates that despite the difference in costs, most editors seem to feel that this length is 'ideal' for an academic article.[2] There is also a similarity in impact factors among the journals that had one, the most recent numbers ranging from 1.019 to 1.773, which can vary over time with some journals having a higher factor since they may have larger audiences although no evidence for that is presented here.

The criteria for evaluating digital spaces as places to publish can be similar to those found in traditional journals. The factors that affect where writers choose to enter the publishing space can vary. Traditional factors, such as impact factors or time to publication, can lead authors to favor one journal over another for publication (Davis, 2016). Peer

Table 6.1   A comparison between some characteristics of gated and open access journals

	Journal of Second Language Writing (gated)	Journal of English for Academic Purposes (gated)	Language, Learning and Technology (open)	Asian EFL Journal (partially open*)	Kairos (open)	Written Communication (gated)	Journal of Writing Research (open)	Journal of Responding to Research (open)
Recommend article length	8500	8000	8500	None	None	9000	None	7500–8000
Recent impact factor	1.773	1.629	1.13	Not given	Not given	1.219	Not given	
Focus of articles	Applied linguistics, especially teachers of L2 writing	Teachers of EAP	Issues related to language learning and language teaching, and how they are affected or enhanced by the use of technologies	Issues within the Asian EFL linguistic scene	Variety of digitally enhanced web texts	Research in the study of writing	Theoretical, empirical, review	Research
Number of research articles in last five issues	27	27	30	33	31	18	3 (one issue)	
Copyright	Transfer but retain personal rights	Transfer but retain personal rights	Authors retain rights	Transfer but author retains rights to share	Authors retain their copyright interest in their work	The author retains copyright of the work but grants SAGE the sole and exclusive right and license to publish for the full legal term of copyright	Retain	Retain – cc
Open access	Gold – $1800 green – 48-month embargo	Gold – $1100 green	N/A	After one year	Open	Green – by depositing the version of the article accepted for publication (version 2) in their institutions' repositories	N/A	
Language requirements	British or American English	British or American English	N/A	Expect a high level of academic and written competence in whatever variety of English is used by the author		High standards	High standards	

*Requires registration and embargos articles for one year.

reviewing, which is still important for establishing the credibility of research, has not changed much in the gated/open spaces.

However, one factor that has changed in journals such as *PLOS* (Weller *et al.*, 2014) or *Hybrid Pedagogy* (Morris & Stommel, 2018) has been their approaches to peer review for opening the publishing process. Peer reviewing is not only important for maintaining academic rigor but also for providing researchers with potentially valuable feedback, which can be especially important for those multilingual researchers who lack strong networks or collaborators with which to work. Mega-journals, such as *PLOS One* and *PeerJ*, which are both peer reviewed, may publish thousands of articles online, often on broad topics such as the biosciences, based primarily on the soundness of the research.

These journals have greatly increased the distribution of research while encouraging the research community to decide for itself on the value of the research after its publication (Binfield, 2013). By changing the criteria for peer review, these journals could make a broader array of topics available for potential researchers to consider, thus responding to the challenge of making research more widely available. However, the hoped-for increase in interaction between authors and readers has not necessarily materialized. Although *PLOS* states that it encourages commenting from its academic communities, very little commenting has been found (Wakeling *et al.*, 2019). The situation, in areas such as peer review, has been even slower to develop in areas such as the humanities (Denbo, 2020), which highlights many of the controversies over the role of open access (Fitzpatrick, 2011) that still exist today.

As previously mentioned, open access journals for research on multilingual writing have largely rejected this model, choosing instead to attempt to be similar to their gated counterparts. By mimicking traditional journals, perhaps to gain acceptability, open access journals have achieved this status often without necessarily receiving impact factors or other such rankings. In a recent talk at the 2018 SIG writing conference in Antwerp, Luuk van Waes (2018), the editor of *The Journal of Writing Research*, reported how the journal had achieved a 90% rejection rate, comparable to what is often found in traditional journals. Such comparisons are inevitable since open access journals may provide the same forms of rewards – job offers, tenure or promotion – as found in traditional journals. Graduate students may need to publish to receive their degrees or sometimes to find a job. Faculty may have to publish to receive tenure and promotion, all of which can influence decisions regarding where to publish.

A Discussion with Three Editors of Open Access Journals

In this section, I explore with the editors of three open access journals in applied linguistics and multilingual writing how they, as both teachers and designers of these open access spaces, have negotiated some of the constraints discussed above. I sent a nine-item questionnaire to the three founding editors: Dorothy Chun (*Language, Learning, and Technology*), Luuk van Waes (*Journal of Writing Research*) and Grant Eckstein (*Journal of Written Response*). Their answers illustrated a different perspective on how these digital spaces have been designed and maintained.

Question 1: What was the motivation for creating an open access, online journal?

There was a general agreement that providing free and easier access was a major purpose for creating an open access journal. However, there was also a personal interest in gaining more control over the publishing process. Van Waes felt that open access publishing gave the journal more 'autonomy' than working with a traditional publisher. He also echoed an issue often found in the research community – that research supported by public institutions, such as universities, should be freely available. This approach is controversial by forcing the author to continue to publish without receiving compensation. There were also some controversies in using open access to extend the focus of these journals, particularly by creating more opportunities for interdisciplinary research (see Graff, 2015). Eckstein, the editor of the newer *Journal of Response to Writing*, reported that the founding editors had a concern for creating an online journal that could break down the silos separating different fields of writing by crossing over L1, L2 and foreign language (FL) writing communities. This ability to experiment to create connections among these communities may be an important development if proven to be accepted.

Question 2: How did you find support for the creation of the journal?

The controversies over fees has highlighted the importance of finding sustainable funding sources. Open access journals rarely have the funding provided by large publishers to build many of the technological tools that try to keep competition out. There have been many suggestions, as well as options, for matching funding levels. The result has been complicated for journals wanting to remain open but still have the appropriate levels of funding. Willinsky (2017) suggests that libraries should learn from the history of the Bodleian Library at Oxford University and use their subscription fees to support opening gated journals, an issue that resurfaced when the University of California stopped purchasing journal subscriptions from Elsevier (Anderson, 2017a), highlighting shifts in both how readers are accessing these spaces and the shift in power from the publisher to the author.

While many of the gated journals have the support of large publishers or teaching organizations such as Teachers of English to Speakers of

Other Languages (TESOL) or the National Center for Technology in Education (NCTE), the development of open access journals has often relied on institutions or foundations for support. Wakeling *et al.* (2017) found that open access journals rarely had a firm sense of their costs and lacked consistent funding to scale their journal, which led some open access journals, such as *The Asian EFL Journal*, to employ a 'freemium' model where articles were opened after a one-year embargo, which could provide some support for maintaining their open access.

As has been discussed, sustainability has remained an important concern for all journals, gated and open. Funding has been an issue since these journals do not charge subscription fees. None charged potential authors, so they did not receive the income that may come from Gold approaches. All three editors reported that they had obtained alternative funding, sometimes relying on grants from universities and academic societies as well as from the affordances of the 'the gift society' for volunteer help for peer reviewing and serving on editorial boards. These journals are all independent of consortia or learned societies, so their sustainability depends on individual efforts, often the institution where they are published. *LLT*, for example, is funded by the University of Hawaii while the *Journal of Writing Research* receives support from Antwerp University and other sources in Belgium, which may not be sustainable.

Question 3: Besides the openness of your journals, how did you conceive your journal as being similar or different from traditional journals?

This question examined how these digital spaces compared to their traditional counterparts. Potential authors have expressed concerns over the quality of research, the production standards and the benefits of open access journals (Taylor & Francis, 2014). These journals have responded to the issues regarding increased access, but not to the increased opportunities for publishing (e.g. Salager-Meyer, 2014). Some similarities between the open and gated journals could be seen in the author guidelines. Chun stated that their decision about guidelines reflected what was found in other journals.[3] These open access spaces for multilingual writing have largely copied the guidelines of gated journals, which could make these journals more acceptable to both the authors and the funders.

Open access journals have the technological potential to differ from the gated, print journals but mimic many of their features. One case is the value of peer review for establishing credibility, which is usually comparable to the process in the traditional spaces. There were also similarities in areas such as page length and articles per issue. While peer review has long been the primary method of providing both evaluation and credibility to research, the similarity of the latter two factors is less clear. Both Chun and van Waes stated that their goals compared to those found in print journals, to establish their journal's credibility. Van Waes reported that the *Journal of Writing Research* was designed to resemble traditional publishing spaces with peer reviews, regular publishing schedules and 'academic rigour'. Eckstein stated that he wanted to better exploit the technologies for greater interaction between readers and authors, although this goal may not have been implemented at least in the first issues.

Question 4: Specifically, how did you consider such factors as the number of articles per issue, the length of each article and your publication schedule?

While some open access journals publish a large percentage of articles that had been rejected (Wakeling *et al.*, 2017), this may not be the case in these journals. Although Table 6.1 shows that the open access journals did not necessarily increase their amount of publishing beyond what any new journal could, the motivations of the editors for maintaining these guidelines were consistent with their views of the digital publishing space. For example, some of the guidelines, such as article length, did not depend on the costs of production or distribution. Moreover, while gated journals were limited in the number of publishable articles by their costs, Wakeling *et al.* (2017) found few open access journals were equipped to publish many articles, regardless of their goals.

The limitations on the number and length of published articles have often been intended to ensure credibility. One of Beall's (2013) critiques of open access was that the cost factors associated with gated journals have ensured that only the best research is published. Beall argues that the Gold track encourages publishers to print more articles to make more money; however, none of these journals charged to publish, so increasing the number of articles had little monetary benefit. However, achieving credibility was still the main issue. Open access journals have had to face these credibility concerns as part of the design process (Wakeling *et al.*, 2017). These editors were concerned with how the research community would view their journal and what was feasible given the resources. When the open access journal *Dialogues* announced it was folding, the editor expressed concern with whether a newer journal such as *Dialogues* could attract more quality submissions, which reflects the same concerns authors may have with the status of their publications (Schonfield, 2019a).

Potential authors are usually more concerned with how published articles are judged. Therefore, costs may not have been the only factor, at least initially, in limiting how many articles could be published. As the status of the journal increases, submissions could increase as well. Chun mentioned that *LLT* began with two issues per year but increased to three when more articles were submitted. Eckstein explained that his concern for providing quality peer reviewing had also limited the number of articles published but that longer articles could place a greater burden on reviewers and editors. Production costs were also not mentioned in determining the number of issues published, but having the resources to initially publish more than twice a year was also mentioned by Eckstein, although he felt that the schedule may expand in the future.

Question 5: Has your journal changed the peer review process?

The peer review process has been used by most open access journals for establishing their credibility (Marcus & Oransky, 2011). Peer review has long helped differentiate academic writing from other literacy forms, a role that persists with the journals discussed here. Perhaps, more importantly, peer review provides feedback for writers from members of their community, which can replace the feedback writers used to receive in school. Other journals such as *Hybrid Pedagogy* have implemented alternative forms of interaction and mentorship to help authors improve their writing, although they reject the traditional role of peer review for evaluating research (Morris & Stommel, 2018).

The quality of peer review has been of great concern in both open and gated journals as well as the proliferation of predatory journals. Traditional forms of peer review have been criticized for the often nasty tone of the language of anonymous reviews, the length of time reviewing takes, the diversity of the reviewers and the possible conservative bias to the admittance of new ideas, which have all contributed to calls for either reforming or eliminating these biases. Editors of print journals have become more sensitive to these issues, particularly the languages used, but peer reviewing has remained crucial for ensuring academic rigor.

The editors stressed that they have all used traditional peer review methods, often sharing the same problems with finding reviewers. Thus, the problems with peer review that have long persisted remain. Some open access journals have adopted 'crowd-sourced' reviews, where articles are published online, sometimes as preprints, and then anyone can unofficially review them before they are submitted if desired for formal peer review. The editors of *Sage*, as mentioned above, have implemented this type of reviewing as part of their digital publishing space. The editors of *Hybrid Pedagogy* argue that they have found their approach to peer reviewing focuses more on helping authors than evaluating them (Morris & Stommel, 2018). However, none mentioned the possibility of using these approaches, which have shown limited promise in open access journals. Thus, peer review has remained largely the same in these spaces as it has been in the gated journals.

Question 6: How much has not being able to control the copyright of intellectual property affected how your journal has developed?

Open access materials have increased with the changes in how intellectual property is viewed in the age of the internet (Lessig, 1999, 2002, 2004, 2009). Differences in the application of copyright law has been a major difference between open and gated journals, although pressure from journals and external forces have even changed how gated journals treat copyright. As discussed earlier, copyright transfer is still a major difference between open and gated journals. The three editors stated that their authors all retained their copyright, which is possible but rare in gated journals. Van Waes mentioned that their articles were published with Creative Commons licenses to allow the author to control how articles can be distributed, shared, used and attributed. Conflicts between publishers and libraries also illustrate how technologies such as the internet impact the distribution of knowledge (McKenzie, 2019a, 2019b).

Question 7: What do you feel has been the greatest effects on making your journal open?

The editors confirmed many of the arguments raised by proponents of open access. Chun mentioned 'the sheer number of readers' and citations, which she feels has positively affected their impact factor, which Suber (2016) had also found with other open access journals. As shown in Table 6.1, impact factors are comparable across gated and open journals. Van Waes felt that the most important consequence of open access has been for the journals to publish high-quality writing research and an increased number of downloads, an average of 3,000 per article with some receiving as many as 10,000. Eckstein pointed out that their journal has played an important role in the new information age as well as the teaching of multilingual composition, particularly its narrower focus on responding to writing.

Question 8: What contributions have your journal made to our field (multilingual composition)?

The similarities between open access and gated journals assume they share similar goals for providing new and important research. Chun argued that the goal of *LLT*, for example, was to provide 'cutting edge research in the field of CALL (computer-aided language learning)', comparable to the value of newness found in all journals. Its website supported this claim, boasting that its impact factor is ranked near the top in linguistics (14 out of 179) and education (30 out of 230).

Eckstein added a goal that more reflected the potential of the technologies for creating digital spaces. He felt that his journal will contribute to 'the conversation of response to writing', which resulted from being able to provide narrower focuses. He also discussed the larger issues that open access has raised for publishing: 'We are... part of a larger trend which, in aggregate, will shape our field and the landscape of publishing in general, as our collective experiences become contextualized historically'.

Question 9: What future developments do you see for your journal? How do you plan to keep your journal going? What resistance to your goals have you had to overcome?

Sustaining a journal requires several factors ranging from funding to motivating authors to publish. In interviews with open access journal publishers, Wakeling *et al.* (2017: 314) found that publishers saw that sustainability was related to researchers' perceptions of the 'brand and prestige' of the journal. Such growth has been magnified by the role of the internet in distributing research papers to anyone who has access.

Financial sustainability is another consideration in designing open spaces. These technological spaces require some form of financial support to sustain them (Chesbrough, 2006); therefore, these editors recognized the need for financial resources to support their activities (e.g. Esposito, 2018a, 2018c, 2019a). *The Journal of Writing Research*, for example, receives some support from related scholarly organizations and is connected to a biennial conference held in different European cities. Van Waes reported that such increased funding has coincided with the journal becoming more accepted. Increased acceptance can also lead to increased submissions and downloads, which can result in increased funding. Thus, the future of these journals as alternative publishing spaces may rest with their continued ability to obtain this funding to attract the research for increasing their credibility.

Funding remains a concern in all areas of open access, since open access journals do not receive the profits that gated journals receive because of their paywalls. Chun mentioned the problem of finding more stable sources of funding, perhaps from a university press. Sustainability also referred to having similar metrics used by gated journals to attract authors to publish (e.g. Hinchliffe, 2020b). In his talk at SIG 2018, van Waes focused on the importance of obtaining an impact factor as a means of attracting quality research as well as more funding. Since there is no charge for subscriptions, editors do not worry about the costs for libraries, which are therefore not a funding source for these journals. van Waes also mentioned the need for promoting the journal using the free potential of social media, a source that may not require any funding, again reflecting the concern for keeping the journal going.

The Promise and Limitations of the Open Access Literacy Spaces for Publishing

These journals show various approaches to the implementation of open access while competing with the traditional gated journals for acceptance as well as quality submissions. This chapter has discussed how the development of open access journals, particularly in multilingual research, has created a digital literacy space for writers wishing to publish, primarily for distributing research but which could have a direct response on pedagogy. The journals discussed here differ from their counterparts, both open and gated, in how they are funded, reflecting differences in the communities in which they exist.

There are also pedagogical differences. These technologically enhanced literacy spaces differ from the spaces previously discussed since they are not teacher designed, but teachers must understand them to prepare their students to become participants. The value of open access in the digital literacy ecology, as is true for all these literacies, will depend on new technologies for developing the space as well as changes in how new literacies are valued in the institution and across disciplines. These digital spaces play an increasingly important role in spreading information globally, and thus can be dependent on copyright, but how well they perform this role has raised questions about the importance of openness and what information should be open.

Since open access focuses primarily on content distribution, the use of open content may depend entirely on the users. Do they respond to the concerns of Curry and Lillis (2006) about the problems that multilingual writers from developing countries have with publishing in journals published in developed countries? It will be difficult to judge the consequences of openness. Nevertheless, open access materials can be critical in developing pedagogical spaces for publishing (see Chapter 7).

The apparent dichotomy in Brand's quote on 'free' or 'open' has taken a new direction in academic publishing. The term 'open' has gradually replaced 'free' as the primary focus of these spaces, but many of the factors, such as the number of published articles, particularly in scientific fields (Bornmann & Mutz, 2015), have grown exponentially. Open access journals have not always solved the problems related to indexing research so that researchers can find what has been published. Publishers have attempted to create moats to protect their position by increasing resources to make their journals more attractive to potential writers. Therefore, encouraging authors to contribute to open access is of utmost importance for open access journals in countering the resources made available by the established journals.

One of the consequences is that the open spaces for both publishing and pedagogy are no longer monolithic but have branched off in multiple directions. Clearly, there are still gated and open spaces for publishing, paid and free or low-cost texts, as well as variations in all such cases. There have been limitations to how these spaces disrupt previous practices. While providing more openness, these journals have not 'decolonized' the relationships between authors in developing countries and publication spaces in developed countries, which can be especially important where investments in technological infrastructure are necessary. As the UNESCO ('The Impact of OER: Achievements and Challenges', 2019) report shows, case studies in developed and developing countries show that the adaption of OER has been limited, although its production has been diversified across different languages. Moreover, while open access journals may provide literacy spaces for publishing alternative voices, they may not provide spaces for these writers to explore their own problems and cultures.

Nevertheless, these journals are gaining in popularity at a time not only when multilingual students are coming under greater pressure to publish but also when more concern given to whether so-called 'linguistic injustice' is hindering their ability to publish. These spaces have often been limited by the decisions of the editors in their design of these spaces. While the Institute of Educational Technology at The Open University (Ferguson *et al.*, 2019) called for a 'decolonising' of teaching pedagogies by incorporating the views of all participants, these journals have taken a different approach to open the publication space on a global level while maintaining the standards that have existed in the publishing space.

Willinsky and Moorhead (2014) argue that open access journals, therefore, reflect the values of openness in academic communities. The growth of open access spaces has reflected trends in technology and copyright law that have largely emerged with the development of the internet and the World Wide Web while maintaining the approaches for sharing scholarship that have existed since the creation of the first journal by the Royal Society of London (Willinsky, 2006) and the initiation of peer review for establishing the acceptability of a claim (Biagioli, 2003).

The designs of open access spaces often retain the traditional values of the publishing and practices of the communities in which they develop, sometimes mimicking the form and practices of traditional journals and sometimes exploring new possibilities in the publishing process and peer reviewing. Often, open access for both journal articles and monographs or books has been facilitated by new technologies, although the results of these changes in publishing spaces have been incomplete. The development of open access itself has been highly contested. Fund (2018) criticizes how the various ideas toward creating open access have been implemented and advocates a greater focus on consumers, such as libraries, as being the primary force behind the implementation of open access rather than the publishers. His organization – Knowledge Unlatched (https://knowledgeunlatched.org) – has created a platform for publishers, authors and libraries to distribute various forms of intellectual property.

The growth of these spaces supporting open access journals has even impacted many of the traditional 'gated' journals which have created 'open' alternatives where they can charge authors sometimes up to $4000 to publish. As has occurred in these digital spaces, the evolution of the publication process in both gated and open journals has been augmented by the addition of new technologies. The push for open access has not always been as smooth, as illustrated by the dispute between Elsevier and the University of California libraries (Anderson, 2017a, 2019c).

Open access, like other literacy spaces, has spurned many conflicts, such as the economic ones between Elsevier and the University of California libraries discussed above, whether open access has changed teaching practices, how teachers can design open access materials and how students access and share research. Not every issue has changed with the advent of open access: authors and peer reviewers still do not receive financial compensation for their work. This issue has been contended since the gated journals can charge large fees for others to read them.

Since the inception of journals in the 18th century, authors and reviewers have not been paid for their contributions; however, all journals need some form of financial support to sustain them. The UNESCO ('The Impact of OER: Achievements and Challenges', 2019) report warns that outside financial support can leave the recipients vulnerable, raising questions about paying for these journals: readers, authors, institutions or scholarly societies. For the authors and reviewers, however, receiving no payment may be more acceptable in an open space than in a gated one. Open access, therefore, is often sustained as much by this 'culture of sharing' as outside financial support.

Regardless of these controversies, the ongoing conflicts have changed the publishing space, again in some fields more than others. These open journals have developed as publishing spaces alongside the traditional gated journals, as have changes in the publishing process, not so much to disrupt the publishing space as to extend its access. Open access journals often rely on the same metrics – impact factors, downloads, rejection rates – as gated journals. The growth of openness has caused gated journals to evolve as well, often in response to the challenges of open access, by providing their own forms of openness, often at high costs to the authors (Anderson, 2018a).

Despite their limitations, the development of open journals has had a major impact on writing. Compared to gated journals, the open access spaces have attempted to better balance increased access and potential citation rates with the concern for whether their authors would receive the usual academic capital in terms of tenure and promotion. The development of open access journals has occurred when there has been a greater concern with the ability of multilingual researchers to publish in their home languages (e.g. Lillis & Curry, 2014). While open access can increase the research outlets in different languages, this change has not manifested itself evenly. Journal output has not changed greatly; open access journals have greatly increased the number of articles published in English language journals and rely on English-speaking reviewers.

By remaining both free and open, however, these journals attempt to balance the different approaches to open access in the gated journals and the pay-to-publish journals. As with gated journals, the power to publish remains with the editors and peer reviewers. As van Waes stated, the *Journal of Writing Research*, although not yet receiving an impact factor, still had a rejection rate of 90%, comparable to gated journals and with a similar rhetorical impact on the credibility of the journal and thus could be considered comparable to its gated counterparts. The downside of this number is what happens to all the rejected ideas – do they appear in the predatory journals where the standards for publishing are lower?

While these journals may reflect new trends in academic publishing spaces, they are only a sample of the growing amount of open knowledge available to researchers. Their impact derives from a growing network with which researchers can connect. As Latour (1987) argued before the internet had gained this power, these connections can benefit authors in developing the textuality of their research by accessing the latest research to support their claims and address the most important questions in the field, thus responding to the questions peer reviewers are asked about the significance of the research. While openness is not always universal, these journals are part of an expansion of these networks to connect with other researchers without the concern for costs or the intellectual property constraints found in traditional journals.

While many of the decisions regarding the distribution of gated and open journals remain at the institutional level, teachers must prepare writers to understand the implications of both using and publishing in all such forms. Open access is one aspect of the networks that Lillis and Curry (2014) argue multilingual writers must build as part of their development as published authors. Open access can vary both across disciplines and in how information is published and distributed. Many of these changes have resulted from how information is created and distributed. As costs to publish have increased and become more globalized, and as the spread of new technologies has accelerated, open access has evolved to address these issues. Gated journals have been affected, as illustrated by their responses to open access, from the competition of open access journals.

The journals provide the authors with the opportunity to share their research without costs either to themselves or their readers. Their articles can be shared without the concern for possible copyright violations. Peer-reviewed journals are still considered reliable sources for credible information for research purposes. Their development, nevertheless, does not answer all the questions concerning globalization and research, particularly where sources of open resources are blocked. However, the proliferation of open access opportunities from commercial publishers that charge for reading and sometimes publishing, as well as the explosive growth in predatory journals and sharing sites that may be in violation of certain copyright laws, can further confuse potential authors and researchers.

The development of open access literacy spaces has not always resolved this quandary. These journals present only a limited view of the possibilities for open spaces. Many researchers still must publish only in English to grain credibility, and even these open spaces mostly hold researchers to the same standards of content and language as do their gated counterparts. The production of research similarly resembles the process in the gated journals. Submitted articles are often reviewed by unpaid labor. Although their importance may still be measured by the impact factor of the journal, the authors may have more autonomy than provided in gated journals.

These journals are also conservative in upholding rhetorical standards for developing knowledge. Students and researchers are often disconnected from the latest research necessary for publishing. Journals can help authors incorporate the 'newness' of recent research and controversies in their work without having to beg more copies of articles or move to institutions with more resources to spend on better access to traditional journals. Literacy practices in these spaces reinforce traditional methods of knowledge creation, such as through expanded citations, which have increased in importance since these journals can be freely accessed and their research archived. This research can later be remixed and cited in new research, thus further developing the academic network.

The role of open access itself warranted new research on two critical issues: the quality of the research and the sustainability and scalability of the sites for publishing and distributing the research. Both issues require an increase in the ethos of the research and the writers creating it. Tenured faculty have greater respect for research published in gated journals (Jaschik & Lederman, 2016). In response to these issues, some journals have attempted to replicate more traditional journals in terms of reviews, regular publication and even article length while others provide more radical guidelines that encourage new forms of literacy and new approaches to publishing.

Open access literacy spaces are part of the network for the evolution of knowledge creation and distribution, as well as how knowledge is governed, created and accessed. Various policies, platforms and apps have been developed for sharing and distributing information. Unlike platforms such as ResearchGate, these journals have remained within the global constraints of intellectual property laws, and unlike the predatory journals in disciplines where author charges are rare (e.g. Beall, 2013), they have resisted charging the authors to publish.

Despite the threats from established publishers that open access may reduce the opportunities for publishing, open access journals have not replaced gated journals (Suber, 2012), but have, in a few cases, increased opportunities for publishing in non-dominant areas and languages. Not all research needs to be open or open in the same way, any more than all open access journals need to be technologically enhanced. The publishers of gated journals often provide greater support for authors, peer reviewers and editors than the open access journals can. Boyle (2010) argues that openness in publishing spaces often needs to be balanced with traditionally published research. Not everyone wants to share their work, sometimes because of the fear of losing the benefits of closed publishing and/or because of the privacy issues pervading all uses of technology.

Nevertheless, open access has made major contributions to the development of the publishing space, although sometimes bringing chaos to this space. Sharing information and connecting with others in online learning spaces using open materials can create spaces where both teachers and students can more actively participate in the research process. Open access journals have challenged the dominance of the assumptions of traditional journals about their definitions of intellectual property as well as still being gatekeepers and reviewers. Some traditional journals have also embraced the goals of open access. For example, a rebellion over charging subscription fees for access to the linguistics journal *Lingua* led their editors and editorial board to leave and create a new open access journal (Jaschik, 2015).

There have been other limitations as well. Open access has not addressed all the issues that Lillis and Curry (2014) have raised about publishing for multilingual writers, but it has provided more access to the current issues in the community that can be used for publishing, sometimes in different languages for different regions. Open access journals have not yet disrupted the traditional publishing models in the communities for multilingual research as they have in other disciplines (cf. Schimmer *et al.*, 2015). Often, the concern is money since many gated journals have implemented open access with the funds from charges to authors, which multilingual researchers may not be able to pay, so the open access journals in multilingual writing have had to search for funding on their own.

Many questions remain regarding the role of open access journals in this networked ecology. Cronin (2017), for example, questioned whether open education is applied similarly in open access journals:

How can we minimize the cost of textbooks? How can we help students to build, own, and manage their digital content? How might we support and empower learners in making informed choices about their digital identities and digital engagement? How might we build knowledge as a collective endeavor? And, how can we broaden access to education, particularly in ways that do not reinforce existing inequalities? (Cronin, 2017: para. 1)

The cost of textbooks that Cronin mentions is largely a North American problem; however, other issues related to collaboration and access are more global. These open access journals have contributed to the answers to these questions, which will continue to evolve as the spaces evolve with new technologies and pedagogies. New technologies have impacted these issues in the publishing spaces as they have for all forms of open access (Michael, 2018), as have changes in pedagogy.

The economic concerns illustrate that publishing is often a profit-seeking business. As the Elsevier example illustrates, publishers may respond to potential competitors by creating 'moats' that often incorporate new technologies to differentiate them from other publishers. Many of these publishers are buying up smaller companies to create new platforms for submitting, reviewing and distributing information, what has been called 'workplace flow', which has often been accomplished by acquiring small technologies developed by other companies, all of which responds to the changing economics of publishing (Esposito, 2018b).

Often, open access journals cannot afford these technologies. Smaller journals, such as those published by academic societies, may incorporate similar technologies in order to compete. Schonfield (2017, 2018a, 2018b) has suggested various ways in which smaller publishers can collaborate by using technological tools to compete with the larger publishers. These technologies can change how research is shared both before and after publication, how research is assessed and how it is passed through the publication process.

Despite the limitations, open publishing has long been a means of addressing the inequalities that exist in academic communities (Wellmon & Piper, 2017), a process especially important to multilingual research. Open access journals related to multilingual research are helping expand the spaces for publishing but not necessarily changing the function of the journals. These journals can help create these academic networks and communities of practice that are more open to writers and readers from outside traditional centers of research. However, these journals have not always addressed the issues of openness that might result from supporting a more diverse set of authors and reviewers who might bring new voices and perspectives to the publishing space. Still, gated journals often have more resources than their open counterparts. Elsevier, for example, has the resources to provide access to networks such as Scopus and to purchase new technological tools that both researchers and reviewers can use.

The main question is how will these developments in the design of publishing spaces affect the publication and distribution of research and then its pedagogy? The changes are mostly, but not always, technological, but they can also involve changes in the transparency of journals as expressed in their guidelines to authors, as well as new definitions of prior publication, rules for intellectual property and the peer review process (Edington, 2018). Open journals have addressed some of these issues, particularly the rights of authors to control the distribution of their research. Other issues, such as peer review, have often remained unchanged.

The interaction between open access spaces and the writing process is important for developing and contextualizing writing pedagogies and their social spaces, as is true with all the literacy spaces discussed in this book. As Wiley (2019) argues, open access materials can change the teaching practices that still date to the creation of the printing press. The journals discussed here have largely existed outside the traditional library system as sources of information. Their impact on the research and publishing process thus remains inconclusive The chapter title 'The Promise of Open Access' implies that while the promise for change exists, we still do not know all the consequences of open access, either for teaching or publishing. As Downes (2019) has argued, open access involves being able to work openly, a feature that both teachers and students may fear. As discussed in the following chapter, these changes have greatly impacted the design of a teaching space to help students understand the issues that open access has raised.

Notes

(1) For an animated introduction to open access, see https://www.youtube.com/watch?v=L5rVH1KGBCY.
(2) This assumption was based on informal discussions with the editors.
(3) It should be noted that *LLT* has recently added a section addressed to teachers who may not be as interested in the formal research articles they mainly publish. Gated journals, such as the *Journal of Second Language Writing*, have also on occasion added additional sections, often a forum, so this flexibility is not necessarily the sole purview of the open access journals.

7 Teaching Writing in the Publishing Space

> The future is already here; it's just not very evenly distributed.
> William Gibson

Graduate students are under growing pressure to publish, which impacts them both as writers and readers. The publishing process is a system where today neither authors nor peer reviewers are financially compensated but for whom publication can positively impact their careers. As discussed in Chapter 6, journals can be supported by traditional publishers, scholarly societies (e.g. Teachers of English to Speakers of Other Languages [TESOL], The European Association for the Teaching of Academic Writing [EATAW]) or independent funding. The changing nature of the publishing space has further impacted its design by adding new dimensions of publishing and ethical concerns that are changing the publication process.

Students are often asked to create multiple publishable texts for their thesis, referred to as a publication-based thesis (Cayley, 2020), a practice that has been growing globally (Guerin, 2016). While not always the same as individually written publishable articles (e.g. Cayley, 2020), the goals for these papers can motivate students to enter the publication space. Multilingual writing teachers whose students come from various disciplines are faced with creating spaces for students with differing opportunities for publishing, some of which have already been decided at the institutional level (e.g. Clarke, 2018). Perhaps the most complicating factor in of all is that all these changes are not occurring uniformly across disciplines.

The quote from William Gibson, the science fiction writer best known for coining the word 'cyberspace', about the unequal distribution of the future clearly applies to publishing and distributing information across disciplines, particularly in the area of open access. Almost every aspect of the publishing process ranging from the process itself to individual decisions about where to publish or which language to publish in has become disrupted, although to different extents in different fields. Open access has been dramatically changing due to policy changes in

North America and Europe, which has meant that the choice of journal can greatly impact job prospects due to the continuing importance of publishing in journals with the highest impact factors. These changes have raised many pedagogical problems related to the ability to connect to more research that have only recently been addressed. These changes in the publishing process have also impacted teaching about publication, particularly because of the chaotic nature that the technological changes have brought to the publishing space.

A few textbooks have appeared for helping students transition into the publishing space (e.g. Belcher, 2009; Paltridge & Starfield, 2016). Differences in literacies have long been identified in the publishing process. Research by Curry and Lillis (2016) and pedagogical approaches (e.g. Cargill & O'Connor; Casanave & Vandrick, 2003; Paltridge & Starfield, 2016; Simpson *et al.*, 2016) have explored the various literacies and other forms of communication that graduate multilingual students face. This research has shown that the design of publishing spaces entails a shifting relationship between the student and the social context of the publication process. Curry and Lillis (2016) found issues with publishing in English language journals that further complicate the design of these spaces. These issues range from changing student identities, the relationships among native-English speaking and multilingual students to the changing nature of advisor–student interactions. Rhetorical problems such as the role of evaluation in the academic genre or the role of the student in collaborative writing experiences may change as these contexts change.

Students may feel confused and frustrated by these changes, which is often compounded by their perceptions of their levels of English. The importance of 'linguistic injustices' in the publishing world, despite the claims of Hanauer *et al.* (2019), remains controversial. The importance of publishing in non-English language journals may not address the issues regarding the distribution of information or the status of the authors that are entailed in English language publication. Curry and Lillis (2019) have questioned how well the issues regarding publishing have been assessed, ranging from the problems multilingual students have with publishing to pedagogical attempts to remediate these problems.

The often chaotic nature of changes within the publishing space has necessitated the creation of new literacy spaces where multilingual students can study the publishing process to understand these changes and make informed decisions about how to respond to their constraints. The 'quandaries' that multilingual students face when crossing boundaries into the English language publishing space have necessitated creating new literacy spaces for teaching about publishing. There has been a tremendous growth in the number of articles coming from outside traditional English-speaking countries where most journals are published, without a comparable increase in available reviewers with the same language backgrounds as the authors.

Despite the increased opportunities for publication, the competition for publication has remained intense, often resulting in higher levels of rejections for which students may not be prepared. Van Waes' (see Chapter 6) announcement at the 2018 SIG Writing Conference in Antwerp that the rejection rate of the *Journal of Writing Research* had reached 90% is a similar indicator. For multilingual authors, who are under more pressure to publish to receive advanced degrees and find and hold academic positions, open access journals may provide not only more opportunities to publish but also more competition. Flowerdew (2000, 2015) shows that language problems can negatively impact the acceptance of a paper from a multilingual writer.

This research, in fact, points to the importance of developing pedagogical spaces. Harwood and Hadley (2004) argue that teacher perceptions of student learning call for a more pragmatic approach to teaching academic writing that stresses the forms of English that would most help multilingual writers to publish. While such perceptions, on the other hand, may indicate systemic issues in the evaluation process, they can also provide an argument for the importance of developing new pedagogies and new approaches to preparing students to enter the publishing space. Changes in the publishing spaces, often resulting from the implementation of new technologies discussed in Chapter 6, have disrupted traditional approaches to learning literacies, which had largely relied on the osmosis of information from advisor to advisee.

The controversies over open access and predatory journals discussed in Chapter 6 have resulted in more pedagogical problems that are addressed in the design of a literacy space. Entering the publishing space reflects a shift away from having relationships with people whom the students are familiar with and may understand their work to relationships with often unknown editors and reviewers who will evaluate the research without necessarily understanding or agreeing with it. The growing importance of publishing for graduate students has necessitated the creation of new spaces for supporting students entering the publishing world. Lappalainen (2016), for example, reports that in Finland, government funding has indirectly placed greater pressure on graduate students to publish.

Often, the growth of networks has created their own spaces for learning about publication literacy. Some literacy spaces simply allow for sharing research or asking questions about the publishing process. ResearchGate or myTESOL Lounge provide forums where participants can ask questions without the constraints of either digital or print spaces. Questions such as 'Which software is used to check for plagiarism in journal publishing?' or 'Can you please recommend a journal which publishes quotations and sayings?' illustrate the kinds of problems that authors, often isolated from each other, can crowd-source for understanding publishing.

Changes in the publishing space have necessitated changes in the metaphors used to describe the writing process. Canagarajah also borrows the 'rhizomatic' metaphor, popularized in the discussion of Massive Open Online Courses (MOOCs) (Cormier, 2008b), to describe how the learning process is non-linear but like rhizomes, spreading out in all directions. While his metaphor was not directly aimed at publishing, observations about the process fit the publishing context, just as Latour's (1987) actor/network theory previously did. As the example of ResearchGate and myTESOL illustrates, these 'rhizomes' in a network can include both technological features and traditional friends, mentors and brokers. Each 'node' can contribute specific types of information, such as the audience, that the author must 'assemble' into their research even when such information may be contradictory.

The design of a publication space incorporates many of the values of the communities of practice, so learning to become an author also involves learning to become a member of these communities. The publishing space embodies the linguistic, rhetorical and ethical values of the communities of practice that often control the publication, so to become published writers it is important to understand the constraints and opportunities the publishing spaces provide. Canagarajah (2018) borrows the 'assemblage' metaphor to describe how authors remix their own research, borrowed texts, first and second languages, comments from other authors, friends and mentors, and other semiotic materials in creating academic papers that 'transform' not only the text itself but the rhetoric and language of the creation process.

This social context then needs to be incorporated in the design of the space consistent with the desired learning. Some design factors include issues regarding genre and voice with variations that may reflect differences in the communities of practice. Bazerman (1988) noted how changes in genre often reflect changes in the practices of each academic community, an argument that frames much of the discussion in this book. In preparing to enter the publishing space, students can understand these changes when they are occurring. Chapter 6 discusses how open access publishing can address concerns for both the publishing and distribution of research, which can help unravel the publishing process, even for sophisticated writers with access to the most recent research.

The Teacher's Role in Designing a Literacy Space for Publishing

Unlike other literacy spaces that rely on the need for developing a community (Veletsianos, 2020), the students entering the publishing space may bring their own sense of community consisting of advisors and fellow students, although Veletsianos argues that this is not always the case. The roles of a teacher/broker/sponsor in publishing spaces have had to be flexible to accommodate these different social relationships among students from different disciplines. As in the flipped classrooms, even questions about grammar could be turned into lessons for all the students. These problems with preparing students for publishing can be further complicated by changes in the publishing space, in areas such as peer review and intellectual property, that can pose new challenges for novice writers. Salager-Meyer (2014) argues that writers in developing countries face additional issues ranging from lacking academic infrastructure to problems with electricity that can limit the amount of time spent online. Countries must often pay large amounts of their education budgets to access research that their students can develop.

Teachers must decide what aspects of the publishing process to include, while students must also decide about what and where to publish. Thus, teachers and students must share in the design of these spaces, often having to provide more personalized and personal spaces for learning. In her keynote speech at the 2019 EATAW conference, Castelló Badia (2019), for example, describes a workshop meeting every other week at Barcelona University to prepare doctoral students for the university's publishing requirements. Freeman (2016) describes a program at the University of Toronto that provides a variety of short-term programs in both oral and written communication that seeks to integrate multilingual and native-English speakers. Cargill and O'Connor (2006) proposed a series of workshops to help multilingual students overcome their anxieties and prepare for publishing. Chalmers University in Sweden has two courses on publication, separating the publishing process and the writing process (Gustafsson *et al.*, 2016).

Developing a pedagogy for publishing spaces can involve integrating many pedagogies and literacies. Pedagogies for scaffolding multilingual students in these publication spaces vary within and across institutions and social contexts. Preparing students to negotiate these challenges is the goal for designing a literacy space where they can better understand the process as well as prepare submissions. Pedagogical issues surrounding publication and the related aspects of academic writing are more frequently addressed in pamphlets, such as those by Swales and Feak (2012), or in textbooks designed for the publication class (e.g. Paltridge & Starfield, 2016).

Latour's (1987) research on actor/network theory considers the publishing space as a network of multiple spaces that the actor or author must navigate to be successful and, in Lave and Wenger's (1991) terms, move toward the center of their communities of practices. In addition to writing research papers, the network includes related literacies for finding money for research (grants), sharing and discussing research (conferences), communicating with others (abstracts, letters of inquiry, responses to peer reviewer) and searching for jobs (resumes, CVs and cover letters).

Additionally, language needs to be part of the publishing space. Lappalainen (2016) argued that publishing courses require specific grammatical forms. As has often been the case, designers can draw upon alternative sources of research for their ideas. The growing importance of blogging for academic voices (see Chapter 2) is another source of information on specific issues related to publishing. For example, Retraction Watch is an important blog for discussing ethical issues in publishing; Scholarly Kitchen is similarly important for discussions of the changing publishing space.

Genre analysis, textual borrowing, voice, and lexical and syntactic choices are part of the publishing process. Therefore, understanding literacy in the publishing space can also help students address the many demands of academic literacy spaces. One approach to the design of publication spaces has been to discuss the specific roles for language in publication. This pedagogy has been labeled English for research publication purposes (ERPP), attempting to place it in the constellation of various types of English already taught. Publication spaces, therefore, may present teachers and writers with different challenges than they have previously encountered, often less concerned with technical competency for uncovering publishing's hidden values. Swales related that his goal for the design of publication spaces has been to

> take them [students] behind the scenes into the hidden world of recommendations, applications and evaluations. (Cited in Hyland, 2012: 162)

At the macro level, there are also questions about creating networks that are more unique to the publishing process. As Latour (1987) describes, these spaces often contain technological artifacts whose roles in publishing are connected to the writing process. Teachers can embrace these attributes, some of which allow students to bring their research and related social contexts into the literacy space. The connections between the publishing space and other literacy spaces give greater importance to issues of transfer. In the next section, I discuss the issues that novice researchers need to understand about the publishing process. Many of these issues are never directly taught but have been learned in different ways, sometimes by osmosis through interactions with mentors and their academic communities.

Publishing spaces, like flipped learning spaces, may alleviate the consequences of perceptions of unfairness, but the research on their effectiveness is even thinner than found with flipped learning. With the absence of solid research, teachers must often rely more on the 'lore' of their fields in designing these spaces. In an important, but problematic article, Curry and Lillis (2019) argue that there has been too much focus on lore instead of research in teaching about publishing. They argue for the necessity for longitudinal studies on the rate of publishing; however, such studies are expensive and difficult to carry out. North (1987) argued that focusing on lore gave primacy to teacher experiences over researchers, thus elevating the role of teaching in the design of literacy spaces. Curry and Lillis, on the other hand, feel that the pendulum has swung too far, so teachers may ignore research that contradicts the lore from individual or shared experiences.

Both research and lore provide teachers with information related to assessing the design of the space, although data creation, evaluation and distribution may vary (e.g. Cochran & Wulf, 2019; Schonfield, 2019b). This information can reside in many sources, so the technological framework can provide a means for connecting this data in personal networks, regardless of its origins. Neither research nor lore may be enough to help teachers deal with the problems in the design of their literacy spaces. As has always been the case across these spaces, research is not always generalizable to the unique problems teachers face and thus may not be usable in all the designs of these spaces.

As discussions of networks illustrate, teachers can draw upon both pedagogical research and lore in their design of literacy spaces. These pedagogical spaces rely heavily on what students bring to the classroom. The students bring different language and writing abilities, disciplinary memberships, interpersonal relationships and motivations to the publishing space, reflecting all the reasons researchers have for publishing – a job, personal satisfaction or prestige, institutional requirements for publishing or simply the desire to share knowledge – so a publishing space may accommodate these various incentives, which can impact on motivations and decisions for publishing. For example, deciding whether to publish in an open or gated journal, or in a journal with traditional or more radical publishing values, may depend on the students' goals and values.

Technological changes have impacted all aspects of the publishing spaces, from how papers are submitted to how journals are evaluated. Research has shown potential sources of confusion in these changing spaces, ranging from micro-level controversies over the language of publishing (Hyland, 2012, 2015) to macro-level discussions of where multilingual students should publish (Curry & Lillis, 2018). Hanauer and Englander (2011) attempted to quantify whether the concerns of Spanish-dominant scientists were more related to linguistic or disciplinary problems, with the former outweighing the latter. How can publishing spaces adapt to the concerns expressed here?

However, such research on multilingual authors in publication spaces can be equally problematic because of problems with overreliance on their perceptions, differences in participants and the limited generalizability of their research. How do these concerns shape the publishing spaces? Such research does not always provide answers to designing literacy spaces. Relationships with mentors, one of the most common ways of learning to publish, may fray or break down or, in some cases, never exist, limiting students in deciding when and where to publish. In response, there have been various approaches – workshops, bootcamps, writing groups and courses – for supporting students entering the publishing community. While the choice of spaces is often determined by institutional concerns, such as a course versus a workshop, the role of teachers in designing these spaces can vary.

In our design of a pedagogical space for publishing, for example, a full-term course is divided into two strands: one dealing with issues related to the social context of publishing and the other to the specific linguistic and rhetorical issues the students have faced. Curry and Lillis (2019) argue that there has been little research on their effectiveness; therefore, teachers must obtain feedback usually from students for redesigning their spaces. The students may enter the publishing space with their own collaborative groups or mentors. With students from multiple disciplines, instructors may not have the topic knowledge in every field, so they can become 'literacy brokers' (Brandt, 2001; Curry & Lillis, 2006), whose role is to support students and develop their confidence with these literacies. Brandt used the term 'sponsors' to illustrate how this mentorship occurs in various literacy spaces. Mentorship may not necessarily be a factor in student development. As Brandt has argued, mentorship can play a conservative role in modeling traditional ways of publishing.

Literacy brokers can play many roles in the publishing space. Curry and Lillis (2006) found literacy brokers may help potential authors negotiate this publishing process. In our tutorial sessions, the broker can raise questions that the student can later discuss or sometimes argue about with advisors or other members of their groups. Publishing pedagogies require more personal learning to deal with more personal issues, such as isolation or the lack of motivation, which can further decenter the role of the teacher. Thus, the design of publishing spaces includes issues that multilingual students may face in the publishing space. Students may not feel the kind of 'respect' they had previously received. There are also issues that student may have never faced. What, for example, does 'revise and resubmit' or 'reject but resubmit' mean? Writers may be criticized in ways with which they are not familiar. Their relationship with reviewers may differ from their relationship with professors. Perhaps because of the anonymity of the peer reviewers, the type and tone of these letters from journal editors can challenge writers in ways that may differ from the feedback they have received from their teachers.

As the publishing spaces become more complicated with additional challenges for negotiation, preparing students has become more challenging. Help with negotiation can also be found in other spaces, often located outside the classroom. In some cases, crowd-sourced sites such as ResearchGate, have provided forums for discussing writing and publication. A writer from Ghana recently asked about academic writing: 'I will need a bit of education on what exactly makes an academic writing different from an article writing, especially the introduction?'. Whether this site was the best space to find answers to help her publish can ultimately determine the value of such sites. Nevertheless, her interactions illustrate how the development of networked spaces can substitute for or at least augment traditional mentorships. Criticisms about my lacking background knowledge may have resulted from the greater pressure these students were under but also point to the greater importance of creating networks to support publishing.

However, language is still a major concern for multilingual writers in publishing spaces (e.g. Hanauer & Englander, 2011; Hanauer *et al.*, 2019). Guidelines reminding writers of the need for grammatical correctness or publisher suggestions that prospective authors pay a service to have their papers checked before submission may be a warning about language demands. Canagarajah posits a literacy space where authors can mix their languages. As with MOOCs (Chapter 4) and flipped classes (Chapter 5), teaching in these spaces often requires letting go of previous approaches to student–teacher relationships. Curry and Lillis (2004, 2010) found that a tension can exist between the writer and the broker over suggestions, which may be amplified by the degree, or lack, of content knowledge the broker possesses.

However, students may resist the decentering of a broker/sponsor. The tension also serves to decenter the role of the broker/teacher in the publishing space, so they are neither guides nor sages but must function more as a designer to set up the network. Brokers may lack the academic background to make definitive statements about research papers, which is why students need to become their own researchers in discovering many of the questions they raise. To compensate for this problem, I used sample articles from the journals to help students understand the local discourses of their own publishing spaces. Technological tools, such as Hypothesis, can be used as an alternative to discussion boards to collaboratively annotate texts and then share their responses, either with classmates or future classmates, so learning cultures can be established to better understand the rhetorical, syntactical and lexical features in published articles.

Tutorials in a Publishing Course

Traditional approaches to genre (e.g. Swales, 1991; Tardy, 2016) are still useful for designing publishing spaces, but they do not always incorporate the variations that exist both across disciplines and even across journals within a discipline. For example, one student reported that in the journal he had chosen, the guidelines warned him not to report on collective summaries (e.g. 'research has shown') but go through the significance of each study. In response to a concern expressed by Curry and Lillis (2019), the tutorials for the publishing space were designed to allow students to discuss what aspects of the writing process they were interested in. These examples can be brought back into the classroom and sometimes augmented through implementing tools. For example, the results of a question posted in Poll Everywhere were used to demonstrate how contradictory data results could be dealt with, which was a question raised in a tutorial. In such discussions, the concept of a 'growth' mindset (Dweck, 2007) was important in having the students find themselves and develop their own voices and sense of autonomy when shifting from being a student to being a published author.

Although the one goal of the tutorials in the publishing course was to respond to the 'felt' need of the students regarding their feelings about their language ability (e.g. Hanauer *et al.*, 2019), the broker might not be able to respond to disciplinary goals. The tutorials, therefore, addressed whatever problems the students brought and offered possible solutions that may or may not be enacted on. For example, I had a mathematics student whose research consisted mostly of formulae I did not understand. I would later ask him if he had received value from our tutorials, which he had faithfully attended. He replied that it was useful for him to discuss his formulae before going to see his advisor. Here, my role as a literacy broker differed from that of an advisor, who may better understand the content. In other cases, I had the necessary topic knowledge, so I functioned more as a co-author or mentor. As is often the case in these literacy spaces, teachers may have to give up their preconceived ideas of what their relationships with their students may be.

The Social Context of the Publishing Space

Along with the personal goals for the individual student, the role of academic publishing is to serve the communities of practice, which is becoming more complex as costs rise and open access expands. The social context of these communities is one component to be designed into the space. This context has been described as an 'ecosystem' connecting various shareholders – authors, readers, publishers and librarians – who may have conflicting values and goals (Wulf & Meadows, 2016). The process itself can vary a great deal across disciplines and even journals, and, like the other spaces discussed here, can reflect the values of the journals, and therefore the publishers, editors and reviewers of the journals. Sometimes these values are expressed in their 'Guide to Authors', which should, but often does not, make these values more transparent to potential contributors. Therefore, it is important to include the guidelines in the design process, but they must be supplemented.

One important value in designing spaces for all forms of academic writing is appropriate textual borrowing. As Fitzpatrick (2011) argues, alternative types of literacies, such as blogging, that are not part of this hierarchy in the academic community of practice, are often excluded from the publishing process. However, this practice may be changing (see Chapter 2). Although, as Canagarajah (2018) argues using the term 'bricoleur', such 'found' sources may becoming more prevalent. Understanding how such issues are evaluated within the publishing network can help create the social context for designing a pedagogical space. Latour's work contextualizes the earlier discussion by Crane (1972) on what she called the 'invisible college' by connecting all the literacies, as well as various tools and artifacts, included in the publication process. Students may need to improve their English or learn new forms of English, sometimes referred to as English for research purposes (Curry & Lillis, 2016), where a deficiency may impede the ability to publish. Therefore, the design of a publishing space has included both aspects of publishing.

These networks or invisible colleges extend the social concept of writing beyond that of the classroom or even interactions with mentors. The influence of this approach on designing the space focuses on connecting the research paper with the auxiliary forms of writing, such as obtaining money through grants; sharing information both formally in conferences and informally through sometimes impromptu discussions in hallways; and creating CVs, resumes and cover letters for jobs. Each form includes specific rhetorical practices, often for responding to the needs of the audience. Unlike the classroom paper where the demands of the audience may be vague or reflect the values of the teacher, these demands may be more complex or reflect different values than found in the writing classrooms.

The ethical rules that constrain the digital space can also differ from what is experienced in the writing classroom, where often the focus is primarily on copying or plagiarizing (e.g. Lederman, 2006). Ethics in publishing can cover various topics, sometimes extending the writing process far beyond the publication of a paper. Retraction Watch published a number of stories that led to retractions, including problems regarding multiple authors, the failure to reproduce results and the falsification of data. They also published a story about the unethical behavior of an editor who added references from his own journal to boost its impact factor.

The *TESOL International Journal* requires potential authors to include the following guideline: 'Authors shall make reference to at least two (2) references from the *TESOL International Journal*'. Traditional concerns, such as plagiarism, may be defined differently in different publishing spaces. Even what is meant by plagiarism may differ from what is usually taught in writing classrooms. Journals may be concerned not only with copying from other texts but also with submitting a paper already submitted to another journal. The guidelines for plagiarism published by the Committee on Publication Ethics (COPE) can vary depending on the different motivations for copying in different parts of a paper, which might not be considered by institutional academic misconduct commit-tees (Text Recycling Guidelines, 2018).

On the other hand, what may be considered a major concern in one space may be thought trivial in another space. Copyright is one example of such a difference, which may vary across journals. Traditionally, authors sign over their copyright to the publisher once their paper has been accepted. Today, however, as copyright laws change and various forms of open access are implemented, the copyright process has become more complicated. Such complications make understanding copyright and intellectual property law a more important part of the publishing space.

The guidelines for the publication process – the limitations on the number and length of articles – and the peer review process have changed at different rates. Such guidelines are often specified in the journal although the details are not always clear. Sometimes, the guidelines may indicate what the authors must first communicate with the editor: that the paper had not been previously published or submitted to another journal; that the additional authors accept responsibility for whatever has been published; or that there are no conflicts of interest. The com-munications between the authors and the editor, however, are a literacy form that Swales (1996, 2009) refers to as an 'occluded' genre, which may be neglected in understanding the process but still may have important consequences for publishing. As authors transition from being students to published authors, they themselves and the texts they produce may change.

Teachers need to be agile to adapt publishing spaces to different student goals. Students at this level may face various literacy challenges (e.g. Freeman, 2016). However, here we are focusing on publishing, which could encompass many of these other literacy forms. For students, becoming published can mean deciding what to do with the research they may have already completed. This decision could reflect the quality of the data already collected, without which one might collaborate with others or, because of new open access sources, use data already deposited. It is common for students to try to transform their dissertations into one or more publishable articles, which may have previously been incorporated into the dissertation writing process. One reason for the difficulty of this process is the problem of transforming a dissertation written in one space into publishable papers for another space with different guidelines and different audiences. Thus, the goal of the publishing course is to help stu-dents cross the boundaries between being a student and being a published author. However, there are other areas, such as grant writing and confer-ence proposal writing, that may also reflect student goals for publication.

The publishing space often incorporates personal aspects of the writ-ing process that may not be considered in traditional writing courses. Authors must connect to different audiences, sometimes by clearly expressing why their research is new and exciting. Writing about how her paper on the history of the University of Utah was rejected, Mower (cited in Anderson, 2018a) expresses her own concerns about how these values may affect the review:

> I can imagine an editor asking herself, 'This author probably won't continue to research within the discipline so is the topic interesting and substantial enough for me to introduce my journal's readers to an unknown author?'

Journal Choice

One of the most important aspects of this space is choosing an appropriate journal from the proliferation of gated and open journals and the different methods of publication they encompass. The choice of journal can be an important, though often confusing, factor in how the research is viewed and how the authors are judged for future employment. Here again, there is great variation across and within disciplines. Some factors such as the length of an article can be discerned from the journal guidelines; other factors such as the organization or the multiple factors involved in textual borrowing, must be deduced from analyzing the journal itself.

The native open access journals discussed in Chapter 6 are all attempting to find ways of establishing themselves as spaces in which potential authors, and readers, would want to participate. Often students bring papers they have already started or where their advisors have already selected a journal for submission; however, it is still important that they understand the journals' audiences and values before proceeding in the writing process.

Journals are not simply spaces for publications but, both overtly and covertly, also provide the affordances that students need to demystify the publication process. Since their inception a few hundred years ago, journals have played various roles in the publishing process: registering, archiving, disseminating, filtering and verifying research. Students, therefore, can access the journals they are interested in publishing in to better understand these goals. Tools such as Hypothesis can be useful in annotating the journals to help understand these issues.

While journals are no longer the only means for these processes, they still play an important role for students; therefore, they remain an important starting point in the demystification of the publishing process. For multilingual students, the opportunity to publish in their own language raises another factor to be considered (e.g. Lillis & Curry, 2014), although, as part of the graduate writing program, the students in this course chose to publish in English language journals. Through the guidelines most journals publish along with an analysis of the linguistic and rhetorical choices published authors make, the space can provide a myriad of clues for discerning how submitted papers are to be judged.

Although not as systematic as the corpus-based approach suggested by Harwood and Hadley (2004), designing a publishing space is consistent with questions raised about teaching academic writing (e.g. Elbow, 1991). Questions about academic writing remain relevant although the specific issues found in the publishing space are continually changing. One such issue is the choice of an audience as reflected in the choice of a journal. Since their inception, journals have played four roles in the publishing process: registering, archiving, disseminating and verifying the research of a discipline. The selection of a journal can reflect the author's understanding of how their research is to be valued. Authors can choose from ranked journals often using comparative impact factors or whether they are open or gated (see Chapter 6).

Decisions about journal selection reflect potential authors' own reflections on themselves and their disciplines. Choosing an open journal over a gated one, for example, can reflect the authors' reflections on their position in the field and their political views toward openness. The process itself includes a complex series of steps that reflect the social conditions of the community space; however, there are also constraints reflecting the values of the community for authors to consider. Thus, multilingual writers must incorporate this ability to reflect on these factors in deciding where to publish.

Once a journal is chosen, potential authors can examine the author guidelines that specify the constraints on publication. Demonstrating familiarization with the guidelines can have a positive impact on the relationship between the author and the editor and reviewers. Guidelines can reveal the constraints on publication: the definition of academic authorship, the publishing process and the rules of the field regarding plagiarism, intellectual property laws and prior publication. However, there are other factors that may not be clearly specified, such as the evaluation of citations – their number per article or their recency of publication – that are never clearly defined and therefore must be uncovered by potential authors. Even discussions of the authenticity of impact factors in predatory journals can be important for reflecting on their value even in reputable journals.

Choosing a journal is an opportunity for the student to consider not only the quality of the journal but their own roles in publishing. These choices can be influenced by the values institutions place not only on publishing, but also on the journal itself and on the language in which the journal is published. The choice between gated and open journals may reflect how writers want to see themselves in the community, how they wish their research to be acknowledged, their choice of topics or their understanding of their potential audiences.

Writers may rely on impact factors that, in sometimes controversial ways, attempt to measure the importance of impact factors, which may affect how the publication is viewed for jobs and tenure and the type and quality of peer review. For multilingual writers, the choice of which language to publish in can also be of critical importance for choosing an appropriate journal (e.g. Gentil & Séror, 2014). Salager-Meyer (2014) suggests that authors may consider smaller, regional journals as alternatives to the Anglo-centric journals many younger researchers choose (Curry & Lillis, 2010). Even the so-called 'predatory journals' can provide alternative spaces for some multilingual writers (Fasel & Hartse, 2018).

Thus, the space can include the criteria, whether the impact factors or journal language or the language it is written in. Students must understand the types of articles each journal publishes and their values for evaluating them. *TESOL Journal* (TJ), for example, states in its guidelines: 'The manuscript appeals to the interests of *TJ*'s readership'; thus, a potential author must demonstrate this interest, often at the beginning of the article as well as make appeals to this distant and anonymous readership. The problem of finding the appropriate journal becomes a central focus of this space, so in our classes, we ask students early in the course to decide on a journal. Making such choices can require a relationship between the author and a mentor, including the teacher. Later, their values can constrain the students' writing processes.

Moreover, the rhetorical form of the article needs to be understood, from either the guidelines or an analysis of journal articles. Despite changes in how research articles are published and distributed, their forms have changed little. However, other aspects of an article, including the length of the introduction or where the significance of the research is discussed, do vary, so information about these variations need to be discovered and then integrated into the publishing space. This publishing space incorporates both the overt features of the publishing process often detailed in the journal guidelines and the covert features that can be understood from a textual analysis of the articles found in the journal.

The covert aspects of journals can be more difficult to discern. Since students may choose different journals, each student can decide for themselves. Questions that potential authors must answer about what makes an interesting article, what contribution does it make to the discipline, what proofs will convince the readership, how should writers express the significance of their research and what evidence is needed to support a claim, reflect their contexts and the values used to make judgments. Some principles, such as how often to cite the journal, how to find acceptable topics and even how to use certain rhetorical and lexical issues may be discovered through careful rhetorical readings of the journals, which could be a major focus of the publishing space. Questions related to the writers' voices can vary greatly both within and across different publishing spaces. Thus, students may need to understand such factors as rhetorical choices, paper organizations and even verb form choices through these rhetorical readings of the articles (e.g. Haas & Flower, 1988). In their study of an engineering student, they found a 'multidimensional representation' of the text that included both the content and structure, which can be valuable for students wanting to publish in journals with which they may not be completely familiar.

The choice of journal has been further complicated by the growth of predatory journals (Salager-Meyer, 2014), which forces students to distinguish between a fraudulent journal, a poor-quality journal and a reputable one since often the criteria for distinguishing differences are unclear. Predatory journals usually charge fees for publishing, which is rare for journals in multilingual research but more common in other fields. These journals may often create a false front – publicizing editors who do not know they are editors, having locations in odd places such as deserts and garages, hijacking titles of established journals to trick authors to publish in them or promoting fake impact factors. Despite these issues, they may still have an allure to authors, particularly those on the fringes of their communities of practice, who may submit articles hoping to at least establish a publication record.

Predatory journals have had consequences for multilingual writers, who may be under pressure to publish in English language journals (Fasel & Hartse, 2018); therefore, evaluating the quality of the journal provides an important opportunity for obtaining a deeper understanding of these spaces. Tao (2020) discussed the problem of predatory journals in India, where many originate and have had their greatest impact on publishing, and the steps that have been taken to respond to their proliferation. Evaluating these predatory journals can itself be controversial since the definitions are unclear. Deciding whether a journal is predatory is not simply a problem for early-stage writers but can challenge experienced writers as well. Thus, designing a pedagogical space requires discussion of the criteria for evaluating journals. There have been many attempts to expose such journals, which often emphasize their important factors, some of which may be fraudulent, such as fast turn-around times. In one case, a writer falsified research and used a phony name from a television show to submit a paper. Within three days, his paper had been peer-reviewed and accepted for publication (McCool, 2017). These concerns can provide valuable frameworks for discussing publishing spaces.

The Evaluation Process through Peer Review

What often differentiates academic publishing from other forms of publishing is the role that peer review plays in evaluating research, making judgments about a publication and confirming an authority on published articles. In a recent controversy over using a gene-editing technology called CRISPR, one of the criticisms leveled against the researcher who had made claims about its use in editing human cells was that he had not submitted a paper on this research for peer review. Monteiro and

Hirano (2020) found that Brazilian students reported problems with content and methodology in the comments from reviewers, which can result from a lack of funding and English language proficiency. Bocanegra-Valle (2014) suggests that the pressure to publish in English can negatively impact the ability of students to publish. Standards for publication are often inherent in peer review although these standards are not always clearly defined (Edington, 2018). For novice researchers, entering the publishing space requires understanding how to discern these values even when they are not clearly defined.

All of these factors make peer reviewing a critical factor in whether multilingual writers can publish, which, in turn, makes it an important component for multilingual writers to understand in the publishing process. While peer review has long been the means for evaluating claims, its future remains unclear. This evaluation process has been consistent over its relatively short but controversial history. Even its origins are controversial (e.g. Fitzpatrick, 2011). The history of peer review as part of the publication space has been greatly contested: whether it began in the 18th century along with the publication of *Philosophical Transactions* or later in the 19th and 20th centuries. Fitzpatrick argues that the term itself was not consistently used until the second half of the 20th century but that scandals and controversies, as well as the political concerns of funding agencies, have led to a greater emphasis on peer review.

The peer review process itself is not monolithic. Edington (2018) lists four types of peer review: single blind where the reviewer knows the name of the author but the author may not know the name of the reviewer; double blind where neither the author nor the reviewer knows each other's names; peer review where both know each other's name; and open review where papers are made available for comment. However, these factors have been evolving at different rates across different disciplines. How these factors will evolve may not change the role that peer review plays even if the process itself changes.

The peer review process not only concerns evaluation but also conveys the values of the organization or field the novice researcher must consider during revision. Peer reviewers often receive a series of questions to consider in the review process, all of which can be used by the researcher for revision. For example, one of the fundamental questions that all reviews ask is what is the 'novelty', 'appropriateness', 'clarity' or 'importance' of the research. Such questions can provide heuristics for revision although their expression can vary across disciplines. Even titles and abstracts are often evaluated for their demonstration of audience awareness.

Another goal for peer review is to ensure that the community trusts the research and the researcher, in terms of the problem being addressed, the methodology being used and the integrity of the results and discussions being presented. The writer's role then is to understand how these values are expressed in the journal in which they want to publish. The peer reviewer's role then is to convey to the writer those aspects of ethics, transparency and integrity that the community expects. In a video on the value of peer review made for *National Peer Review Week*, Hall (2018) argues that high-quality peer review in the health fields must be understandable to all readers, credible to the readers and relevant to addressing key problems.

These goals for review can be incorporated into the rhetoric of the paper. Questions such as whether the paper is appropriate for the journal's audience or its significance illustrate key rhetorical goals that writers address. How they address these issues may vary across journals and disciplines, but the questions are often universal. Demystifying the peer review process (e.g. Tardy, 2019) has revealed questions that can only be answered by analyzing journals: how writers make their research relevant for their audiences or how they demonstrate the value of their research are examples of the questions that form the basis for peer review.

The number of reviewers can vary according to the goals of the editors and their ability to find unpaid volunteers to review. The editor will later summarize the reviews and communicate them to the authors. However, it may be unclear whether it is the editors or the reviewers who decide about publication. Who then are the real gatekeepers in the publishing space? Starfield and Paltridge (2019), who were editors of *TESOL Quarterly*, argue the peer reviewers are the gatekeepers, not the editors since they have more 'topic-specific' knowledge to evaluate the claims as well as to provide feedback. However, the editors may still be the final arbitrators in judging the value of the research.

The publishing process includes establishing relationships with the journal editors, as well as the reviewers. Editors can be both gatekeepers and mentors to help researchers enter into their new communities of practice. Writers may try to communicate with editors about the possibility of publishing or why they think their article should be published specifically for the audience of the journal, as well as the concerns that editors may have about prior publication, authorship or conflicts of interest. Therefore, appropriate email writing can be included. They may also need to use their writing to demonstrate their acknowledgement of the guidelines in terms of recognizing the rules regarding publication, possible conflicts with their co-authors and the originality of their research. Editors can choose reviewers to evaluate the research and provide feedback.

The peer review process remains a unique aspect in confirming credibility on the publication of research as well as a process through which authors can understand the goals and values of publishing. Even rejections can reveal important factors in publishing. Marcus (2018: para. 2) reports that he tried to publish but was rejected 'because of ethical and scientific shortcomings'. This controversy illustrates both the role of publishing in establishing the value of a paper and the covert values, relating to the ethical concerns, that are not always clearly expressed.

The pedagogical space, therefore, can help students understand the various factors in publishing. Table 7.1, published by COPE, illustrates the factors considered during their institutional review process. Design needs to account for the variations both across and within different communities, being double blind, blind or open, depending on whether the researchers know who the reviewers are and whether the reviewers know who the authors are. In most journals in multilingual research, peer reviewing is usually double blinded, where the authors do not choose or know who their reviewers are.

Peer reviews can reveal the key threshold concepts in the discipline the journal wants to promote. Peer review provides an opportunity for early-stage researchers to learn about these concepts. One such concept is the value of citing research. One way of learning how to write literature reviews, which was the subject of a MOOC as discussed above, can also be understood through the criticisms of reviewers. Authors may be criticized for not building arguments supporting their research questions rather than simply reviewing current research. Reviewers are often asked specific questions from the editors about the significance of the article or whether the claims and conclusions are appropriately hedged. In their own networks, authors can ask about the writing of a paper or definitions of 'self-plagiarism', which could then be incorporated into the design of the space as part of the curriculum. These terms can be important for understanding what is meant by 'prior publication', but even such definitions can vary greatly.

The same concerns about understanding the structure of academic writing can arise with the rhetorical impact of a 'problem statement'. Students, for example, may use lexical bundles (Biber & Barbieri, 2007) such as 'there is no (or little) research on this topic', sometimes without understanding the threshold concept of making the paper interesting to

Table 7.1 Factors considered in peer review

Timing	Preprints	Pre-publication	Post-Publication
Identifiability	Double blind	Single blind	Open
Mediation	Editors mediate all interactions between reviews and authors	Reviewers interact with one another openly	Reviewers and authors all interact with one another openly
Publication	Peer reviews are not published	Peer reviews are published but not signed	Peer reviews are published and signed
Facilitation	Review facilitated by a journal	Review facilitated by a third party	Review facilitated by authors

Source: Committee on Publication Ethics; https://publicationethics.org/files/Ethical_Guidelines_For_Peer_Reviewers_2.pdf.

the readership rather than justifying the need for research, as is often the goal. Another bundle – 'little or no research' – may indicate that there is little necessity for more research. It is not necessarily a question of whether these writing strategies are 'correct', but whether they are 'appropriate' for the values of the journal for expressing novelty or importance.

Peer reviews gain some of their ethos from the knowledge of the reviewers. As mentioned before, the value of peer reviews can result from the topic-specific backgrounds of the reviewers. However, the increase in the number of published articles and journals, both gated and open access, has strained the capacity for finding reviewers with the appropriate backgrounds, since reviewers are seldom paid or receive recognition. There has been a growing specialization in research, which has meant that fewer reviewers share the same specialty as authors.

The increase in the need for reviews has not necessarily been matched with an increase in the number of reviewers. Publons (https://publons.com/home), a website for tracking peer reviews, estimates that in 2016 there were 13.7 million peer reviews. However, there may be a mismatch with the number of available reviewers, which could prolong the length of time or even reduce their value for revision. Without compensation, reviewers may be hard to find. Publons found that around half of the requests for reviews are rejected by potential reviewers, which has resulted in an increased need. All editors face the problem of finding suitable reviewers. As Crotty (2018) argues, the value of sites such as Publons is their ability to help editors find suitable reviewers. New approaches to reviewing and mentorship, as suggested in *Hybrid Pedagogy*, may be valuable for changing the status of peer reviewing.

Despite these limitations, peer review can reveal the potentially troublesome threshold concepts (Meyer & Land, 2003), such as 'significance of research' or 'relevance to audience', along with more general concepts such as which articles to cite, how papers are organized, how claims are hedged, the importance of the research problem or the topic or the limitations of the research. Many, if not all, of these topics can be addressed during the revision process if the author understands the comments or has the persistence to accept rejection, make the revisions and, if necessary, look elsewhere for guidance.

The Current Context of Peer Reviewing

Today, the publishing process is under pressure from all sides regarding the diversity of the reviewers, their quality, the time it takes for evaluation and the transparency of the process. During times of increased research, such as with the COVID-19 pandemic, not only does the pressure on reviewers increase, but peer review also plays a greater role in validating research. Nevertheless, problems still remain. As Meadows

(2019) argue, diversity in the context of journals, editors and reviewers can encourage more research across different topics. They list five aspects of peer review to be considered in this revision process: respect for the authors, thoughtfulness of the review, expertise from diverse perspectives, efficiency in responding and transparency of the journal guidelines. However, reviewers receive little if any feedback about the quality of their reviews or financial compensation.

The complexity of peer review can be illustrated in Myers' (1990) study of the revising processes of a scientist crossing into different research communities. Myers recounts that the scientist reported that he revised the comments differently depending on his position in the different communities. In the periphery position where he was not well known, he responded to the reviewers by revising everything asked for. Such complexity could make peer reviewing more complex for students or any early-career researchers to understand and negotiate. Therefore, students entering the publication space understand the problems areas of the process: the large variations in reviewing time are important for understanding what happens after a paper is submitted. Predatory journals have sometimes exploited these weaknesses to gain potential authors who can be lured by the promise of speedy reviews, which may not have the quality found in more traditional reviews. Most problems found can be remediated in the revision process. The issues regarding peer review – who performs them and what are the imitations or the idiosyncratic nature of the reviews, as well as their interactions (Fitzpatrick, 2011) – mean that peer review is an important, though often paradoxical, space for obtaining feedback.

There is also a chaotic aspect to the publishing space, possibly resulting from the reviews lacking transparency. Often, there is little communication between the author and the reviewer. As with many of the research values found in publishing, this may be difficult to discern simply by reading the journal guidelines. Tardy (2019) refers to the peer review as a 'secret world', where the standards or values for evaluating research are not always clearly defined. Edington (2018) suggests some form of accreditation to ensure that standards are met. Smith (1999), a former editor of the *British Medical Journal*, goes further in arguing against blind reviews as being inevitably biased.

Receiving peer reviews can be a painful experience for which students need to be prepared. Hyland and Jian (in press) found evidence of highly critical reviews, which can have a deleterious effect on multilingual writers who may already be concerned with their writing ability. However, as Tardy (2019) argues, the alternatives to traditional reviewing may not be better or effective. Therefore, peer review may continue, although with a variety of possible changes. If the goal is to make the publication space more transparent, then peer review, with its double-blind format, may change.

As discussed previously, preprints have been one suggestion for making peer review more transparent by providing informal reviews before formal submission. Using both old and new technological tools, such as discussion boards, preprints and post-print comments, would allow the readership to take greater control of validating research. These tools can also provide more opportunity for negotiations for illustrating a deeper understanding of what may not be clearly explained. Journal guidelines do not always clearly reveal this process. Such approaches have been limited by the lack of reviewers willing to participate as well as a general lack of consensus over whether these papers will be considered as 'published'. Therefore, there is little indication that preprints provide such opportunities for more revision or that they provide a viable alternative, although again differences across disciplines is one of a number of factors further complicating the publishing space.

Negotiating the Peer Review Process

One of the most difficult aspects of the publishing space is facing inevitable rejections, often after spending many hours writing and revising a paper. Often, students and junior researchers can only be comforted by telling them to try again. Trying again often involves negotiating with the comments in the peer review process, sometimes immediately if the author has been invited to 'revise and resubmit' or perhaps in the future if the paper is rejected. In all cases, the integrity of the peer review process is a key factor, as illustrated by the report that Springer Publishing retracted 64 journal articles because it could not verify the integrity of the review (Kulkarni, 2015). One of the important goals in designing the publishing space is to provide writers with the opportunity to negotiate the feedback from the reviewers.

The quality and consistency of peer reviews have meant that authors have a wide space to enter into negotiation even when the reviews are blind. Publons found that there were wide variations in the quality of reviews, although they did find that journals with higher impact factors received longer and more detailed reviews. Quality problems may result from the reviewers' lack of knowledge or from not taking reviewing seriously. This concern for quality has often limited the value of preprints, for example, where the reviews are sometimes not substantive as in formal reviews. The depth of these reviews may not be important to established reviewers, but for some writers, they are the primary source of feedback.

Regardless of possible changes to the process itself, the problematic nature of peer reviewing can provide a space for negotiating responses to the reviews. As the balance between authors and publishers shifts in favor of the authors, it becomes more important for learning how to negotiate this space. Although journals sometimes supply questions for the reviewers to consider, reviews often contain the personal views of the reviewer. The often idiosyncratic nature of comments can make the inter-action between author and reviewers' criticisms problematic. However, even such reviews may be seen as a heuristic for generating responses in the negotiation process over the criticisms the author cannot or does not wish to revise . The sometimes paradoxical nature of peer reviewing makes it an ideal space for negotiation by responding to, or sometimes ignoring, the suggestions or criticisms from the reviewers.

As students move into the publication space, the opportunities for negotiation become more prominent. In an analysis of their own letters as editors, Flowerdew and Dudley-Evans (2002) found ambiguity in how they communicated with the authors of submissions, thus opening up more areas for negotiation. Such ambiguity in reviews can be frustrating. Curry and Lillis (2006) cited writers complaining about their frustrations with receiving comments from different reviewers that seemed contradic-tory. As Canagarajah (cited in Flowerdew, 2015) pointed out, the word-ing of a review can be so ambiguous that novice researchers have trouble recognizing the editor's intent. This negotiation process is not unique, however, to the publishing space. As Belcher (2017) argued, the graduate student can always negotiate with their teachers or advisors, which may prepare them for peer review, although the consequences and personal relationships may differ greatly.

Although peer review can be a form of governance over what is to be published, the lack of clarity around such governance may make negoti-ating a potentially useful though frustrating experience. One of the most ambiguous outcomes to peer review can be the 'revise and resubmit' recommendation, where a paper is initially rejected but which the author can resubmit after revision. However, it may not always be clear what is being asked for, especially with the often contradictory responses of the reviewers. Moreover, many of the comments can be responded to. The forms of such responses have also been standardized. Most journals require writers to document their revisions, which can provide an oppor-tunity to respond not only to the comments they agree with but especially those with which they do not agree.

Multilingual writers, who may find themselves in that periphery posi-tion, may not have the rhetorical skills for responding to the criticisms. In his lecture for the *2019 Peer Review Week*, Rowe (2019), a language editor and peer reviewer, distinguishes between grammatical correctness and rhetorical effectiveness, the latter often more important than the for-mer since it refers to how clearly the meaning of the research is expressed. How should the writer respond to criticisms of their English language writing? One researcher asked about this on a forum on ResearchGate.

My question is – do the reviewers some time give biased statement on English grammar, for an author from a non-English speaking country? Though, the affiliation of an author is not shared to the reviewer by the journal, but he can know the country from the material method of acknowledgement section. How I can handle this reviewer's comment?

Using technology to deal with grammatical questions has long been a goal. Websites such as Capterra (https://www.capterra.com/proofreading-software/) provide information about various tools for proofreading. The questioner's concern with correctness reflects these changes in English as a global language in the publication spaces. In another question, a researcher asked about the length of his manuscript, a question that may reflect their vagueness.

Learning to respond or negotiate with reviewers' comments is an important part of the publishing process. In their responses to reviewers' comments associated with the 'revise and resubmit' evaluation, there are numerous tropes the author can use. In teaching negotiation, I often use my own experiences as a writer and a reviewer to discuss different responses. For example, in response to a comment about including research that I had left out, I decided the value and viability of including such research. I acknowledged that I had omitted a reference because it did not seem relevant to my argument.

Another situation is when I was once critiqued for leaving out references to what, unbeknownst to the reviewer, was my own work. In the final draft to the editor, I did put the references into my book. Negotiation can often involve demonstrating an understanding of the sometimes conflicting guidelines writers may face. Writers have responded to my criticisms by arguing that a complete response would put them over the word limit, which itself was arbitrary. Here, it became the role of the editor to decide if this response was warranted. For me, the publishing space entailed much greater personal involvement to satisfy my role as a literacy broker, whether as a reviewer or a teacher.

Authors can reveal various emotions in their response letters to peer reviews. As the editor of *TESOL Quarterly*, Canagarajah (2010) recalls an author who was so angry when asked for a second round of reviews that he pulled his paper from consideration. However, mostly authors do attempt to respond. Canagarajah recounted sympathetically how in response to receiving multiple reviews, another author responded more positively, sending a preliminary letter highlighting the intended changes to head off receiving additional comments. Writing these responses to comments is an important part of uncovering this 'secret place' in the publishing space. These responses not only recognize that the space is highly contested but also that the author can understand the values expressed in the reviewer's comments and is prepared to respond to them, even when ignoring them, which may apply to other aspects of the publishing process, even for copyrights constraints.

Auxiliary Forms of Writing in the Publishing Process

The publishing space itself is not a unified literacy but includes auxiliary forms of writing to form the networked ecology. Crane (1972) highlighted various auxiliary literacy spaces, including grant spaces for securing money to support research. Latour and Woolgar (1979) discussed the different forms of language that may be found in these different spaces. Latour's actor/network theory illustrates how publishing networks are constructed not simply by publishing a paper but through various auxiliary literacies and social interactions connected to publication. These auxiliary spaces can also provide alternative heuristics for writers to respond to different types of audiences and thus serve valuable pedagogical purposes for introducing various forms of literacy and social contexts.

Grant Writing

Grants not only support research and publication but also guide what is being researched and how it is being published. As mentioned previously, open access is often more available to authors who receive grants that can fund making a paper 'Gold'. Grant writing is one form of literacy that supports publishing by providing funding, but it requires a different relationship between the author and the audience. Latour (1987) observed that the publishing space requires money to conduct research: 'Build a lab, and they will come'. Money is important for buying equipment, attending conferences, hiring support and paying for subjects. It is acknowledged that a grant in a paper can have a strong rhetorical effect on how a paper is received.

However, grant writing is not simply about applying for money but also about demonstrating an understanding of the values of the community. Including grant writing has several purposes: it focuses literacy on the specific values of the audience, more specifically the funders of the grant, but grant writing can also make students aware of the constraints of money on the research process, whether it means funding research, paying for technologies, traveling to conferences or, in some cases, paying to publish. Although Johns (2017) found that grant writing was the primary literacy experience in some fields, the design of this space followed the work of Latour (1987) that grants provide the funding that makes research and consequently publishable papers possible.

As with other forms of academic writing, grant writing incorporates responding to the values of the audience, most often the financial provider, thereby preparing novice writers for addressing wider audiences than simply their instructors or mentors. As mentioned earlier, these values are changing as new approaches to openness are being implemented. The explicit goals in the grant guidelines can reflect the macro-level political concerns of the grantor. Grants can shape both research and how papers are distributed. An interesting example has been how the grants from the US government have required authors to publish their results openly because they were supported by taxpayer money (see Chapter 6), although what 'open' means is not always clear. Perhaps what is most important about these guidelines is how they support new ways to share data and provide directions from the publishers on how authors can control the distribution of their research.

The guidelines can provide heuristics and constraints for generating ideas related to the goals of the grant. These goals are often explicitly stated in the guidelines for authors, unlike in an academic paper where the goals may not be as explicit. For example, the requirement for expressing the significance of the research or in Bazerman's (1988) example of writing a methodology section, may be deduced from a rhetorical reading of the journal. Although not necessarily with the same funding, grants issued by institutions similarly reflect institutional goals. The Ohio State University, for example, offers a grant to satisfy their goals for advancing research in the field of energy. The personal statement required is worded in the following way:

> Be sure to discuss (a) your interest in energy, the environment, and sustainability; (b) your academic background and career goals; (c) your level of involvement in this event; (d) how your participation in this event advances your work in energy, the environment, and sustainability; and (e) your plans or contributions to lasting changes in energy, environment, and sustainability.

This goal statement reflects both the heuristics and constraints for responding to the grant guidelines. The four distinct points can be a heuristic for organizing a grant. The requirements for this grant reflect the university's commitment to advancing research by having the applicants argue for their 'involvement' in this research, to reward relevant interest in the field, how the grant will satisfy the goal of the university for completing their research for their degrees and how applicants will participate to support the goals of the university. The applicants can learn what these goals mean and how to adapt their writing to these goals. In writing the grant application, the applicant must respond to the values of their audiences, in this case the university, as they would for any form of writing.

Conference Proposals and Presentations

Preparing and presenting at conferences can be an important support for a writer prior to publishing. Writers can receive feedback on their research as well as learn the important issues and possible controversies in their field. Attending conferences can help writers in identifying new and interesting issues that may reflect the goals of the journals where they hope to publish. Conference spaces have both social and literacy components where students can engage in several forms of literacy – proposal writing, presentation, creating and responding to criticisms, as well as creating social networks for interactions. Therefore, they provide an opportunity for various oral, written and visual voices in presentations and discussions. However, as in the case of predatory journals, conferences have to be carefully evaluated as to their authenticity, value and costs (e.g. Asadi *et al.*, 2018).

Some aspects of conferences that require written literacies, such as proposals, reflect the values of the sponsors of the conference. A conference may want proposals that will attract a wide audience or reflect the current state of research. They can provide a forum to participate in various forms of face-to-face interactions. Therefore, they function as a space for sharing research, interacting with practitioners and researchers, and discussing research problems that can later be addressed in the publishing process.

The types of literacy represented at a conference can expand as the types of sessions are expanded, which may increase the opportunities for connecting and for using different voices with different audiences. A potential author may need only an informal voice to ask questions or discuss a topic or a multimodal voice to present a research topic using either PowerPoint or Prezi, whose design can be an important pedagogical goal. Across different conferences, these different voices can be valued differently. Presenting a poster, for example, can result in interactions between an author and an audience, although how they are valued in an academic community can vary. Posters may be more highly valued in some conferences than in others where poster presentations are relegated to those whose conference proposals were rejected.

For the participants, conferences can provide a space for discussing what the organizers may feel important. These values may be expressed in the call for papers itself or in the requested presentations. For example, the call for papers for the 2019 Conference on Communication and Composition attempted to mix both the vernacular and rhetoric of African Americans, which included themes. Conference presentations may also address key research areas on which young or novice researchers can focus. Proposals may attempt to incorporate the conference themes as a means of demonstrating an awareness of the values of the sponsors as well as a heuristic for the conference topics.

The social contexts of conferences reflect the same social connections found in other digital learning spaces, particularly in combining oral, written and multimodal literacies. In his early MOOC on technology, Severance mentioned that he liked to travel and would try to schedule meetups during these trips. In other MOOCs, meetups were similarly attempted although they often failed to endure. Digital spaces have grown in importance as conferences become more expensive. Social media could replace in-person meetups as alternative ways for the participants to interact. Conferences have remained the best opportunity for participants in a community to interact face to face. However, they have become increasingly expensive and are usually held at fixed times in difficult-to-reach places.

In response to these concerns, some conferences have attempted to create a digital space where these limitations can be remediated by using recorded sessions, which allow presentations to be watched or rewatched at the convenience of the viewer. However, recordings are not consistently made, highlighting the fundamental social nature of conferences, and therefore viewers often lose the opportunity to connect and interact. Although open access (see Chapter 6) cannot deal with the latter problem of the need for face-to-face interactions, it has attempted to provide digital spaces where the same issues addressed by conferences can be discussed online.

Conferences can raise several questions regarding evaluating the value of different publishing processes. There may be a clear connection between the publishing space and the conference space. Conferences often promise participants the opportunity to publish in journals, proceedings or edited books. The potential to publish presentations might seem attractive but requires close attention to the quality of the publication, since any such publication may bar further publishing in more reputable spaces. Conferences are subject to the same issues that predatory journals have raised and therefore are judged with the same critical perspective as are journals.

The conference space can be judged as is a journal, thus providing important pedagogical concerns for discussing issues regarding evaluation. Conferences are springing up everywhere in often expensive places to visit, so it is important for potential participants to judge the validity of a conference. Conferences can lure participants with the same factors that are found in all conferences: location, potential participants, keynote speakers and topics. Each of these factors, however, can be evaluated with their counterparts in the conference spaces where the participants may feel more comfortable. These conferences at worst may be fictitious or charge exorbitant fees and have a less specialized audience who may not provide relevant feedback. Often, there are numerous presentations from many unrelated fields designed to maximize the collection of fees, but there may be too many to attract a group of disciplinary experts.

A critical factor is the costs in comparison to what other comparable conferences cost. Costs can be high for a conference that may last only one or two days. Also, there may be pressure to register so there may be little time between submission, notification of acceptance and registration deadlines to carry out a more thorough review. A new wrinkle is to email an already accepted proposal title that only requires the participant to send in the fees. Even keynote speakers, who often seem to be chosen for their fame, may no longer be on the cutting edge of their fields. Therefore, participants must become reflective on whether the conference meets their goals before committing to spending the resources to participate.

The future of conferences as places for meeting in person remains unclear as technological changes allow for new forms of interaction that can replace the traditional need for interaction (Benchekroun & Knepper, 2020). These technology changes can provide important spaces for professional development while lacking the personal quality of face-to-face interactions. Conferences can have important financial consequences as well as support for their communities (Cochran, 2020). They provide a deeper understanding of the networked approaches to publishing as well as opportunities to use the various literacies that are used in how research is proposed and discussed. Therefore, conferences will probably remain an important part of the publishing space, regardless of how they are impacted by technological changes.

Ethical Considerations in the Publishing Process

One aspect of the publishing process often neglected in designing publishing spaces are the ethical concerns, which are often more complex than the concerns for plagiarism encountered in the writing classrooms (see Chapter 2). Ferric *et al.* (2013) has found that academic misconduct is growing, perhaps resulting from increased competition and the growing need to publish. Ethical considerations are not only moral concerns but also illustrate many important aspects of the publishing process, especially how the publishing space can extend far beyond the publication of an article. Blogs, such as Retraction Watch, provide weekly examples of ethical issues, demonstrating how ethics in publishing can incorporate issues involving authorship and proper research methodology, as well as copying different forms of expression. Since many accusations of misconduct are made after publication, they are much broader than the often narrow focus on plagiarism found in graduate writing classes. Moreover, it illustrates how the publishing process can be extended.

As the publishing space changes, concerns related to ethical consideration are also changing, often in ways that may be very different than previously confronted in writing courses. Authors may have to rewrite their papers when they discover their own errors ('"I was shocked. I felt physically ill". And Still, She Corrected the Record', 2020). Controversies between journals and authors over the extent that copyright governs post-publishing distribution illustrate the complex legal issues authors take on when they sign the agreement to transfer copyright when publishing (e.g. Flaherty, 2019b). Journals in fields where there is a great deal of money at stake, such as medical research, may assert more stringent conflict of interest rules for editors and reviewers than do journals in other fields. One journal 'expressed concern' over its publishing an article on a controversial treatment for the COVID-19 virus ('Hydroxychloroquine-COVID-19 Study Did Not Meet Publishing Society's "Expected Standard"', 2020).

Discussions of ethics may also raise issues connected to other discussions of open access. Research, for example, sponsored by corporations may be embargoed so that only the corporations benefit from the results, which may negatively impact student control over their research. However, as previously mentioned, even journals where financial reward is not a concern, have adopted these embargo strategies to control distribution. In all these contexts, the ethical concerns of these spaces can impact authors, editors, reviewers and conference organizers.

Authorship in the Publishing Process

Concerns over the ownership of a piece of property have pervaded many of the discussions on ethics. They have long reflected changes in the technology of distribution (e.g. Lessig, 1999). Because of controversies, especially with ethical issues, one question often asked by editors when submitting a paper is who the author or authors of the paper are and do all of them share the responsibility for the research. In one case, Retraction Watch ('A Mystery: "None of the Authors Listed had Any Involvement With or Knowledge of the Article"', 2020) reported that none of the authors had submitted the paper. However, many of the controversies reflect conflicts among the authors. Senior researchers blame their junior researchers when ethical or methodological questions arise. Since often these concerns are only discussed after the paper is flagged, more questions arise as to who really is the author of the paper. In a traditional writing classroom, student relationships are often clear-cut, both individually and in groups. The growing importance of collaboration has complicated definitions of literacy. Defining authorship can vary greatly across publishing spaces and therefore must be clearly defined in preparing students for participation. Academic papers in some disciplines have listed over 2000 authors, which makes traditional discussions of authorship moot.

Due to the frequent scandals over responsibility for what has been published, journals are more concerned about definitions of authorship. Editors are more cautious of controversies over whether multiple authors are aware of ethical violations. Along with acknowledging the publishing history of the article, the editor must be reassured that all the authors who have contributed to the research are aware of the contributions of the other writers. Often, the negotiating process regarding authorship as well as prepublication occurs during another auxiliary form of writing – the cover letter to the editor – which at the minimum can respond to the concerns about prior publication and authorship. This anecdote illustrates how definitions can be contested and fluid.

Relationships among authors in the publishing space can be more complicated, especially when defining who is an author. When I was a graduate student, I was going to publish a short paper on using a platform a professor in the computer science department had developed for teaching English. I went to see him to ask about the specifications of the platform, when he informed me that in computer science, it was necessary to make him a co-author since I would be using his platform. This acknowledgement does not completely solve the problem since there have been many controversies over who was responsible for what problem. Investigations into publication violations often center on whether the faculty in charge of the research or the other authors were responsible. Nevertheless, the submitting author must recognize the role of co-authors in the production of the research paper.

In response to the growing concern about authorship in publishing spaces, COPE has suggested another set of guidelines for determining authorship:

(1) substantial contributions to conception and design, or acquisition of data, or analysis and interpretation of data; (2) drafting the article or revising it critically for important intellectual content; and (3) final approval of the version to be published.

Guideline (1) may be difficult to interpret, which may explain why editors often request the submitting authors to define their contributions. Such confirmation is intended for all authors to take responsibility for what is published, although in practice, authors, particularly faculty, may still deny responsibility for problems and blame their students or post-docs. At a time when there are increasing numbers of collaborations, such conflicts are inevitable. What further complicates this guideline is what 'substantial' refers to in designating authorship.

Intellectual Property in the Publishing Space

Graduate students may face many issues regarding intellectual property in both teaching and writing, both the requirements for publishing and even the requirements for sharing their data. One student asked about the intellectual property status of an algorithm he planned to upload to Git Hub, a controversial site for archiving data. Publishing, however, forces writers to understand copyright and intellectual property law and therefore is an important component of the publishing space. Copyright is automatically given to any form of expression placed in a fixed format, regardless of what that format is. Unlike other forms of property, certain rights allow for the use of intellectual property. This use is why property can be 'borrowed' for use in other texts without having to ask for permission, which is sometimes referred to as 'fair use'. At least for a limited time, traditional copyright, as does Creative Commons to differing extents, allows the holder to control how the work is used.

Copyright, therefore, can be involved in various aspects of the writing process. One of the final steps in the publishing process is signing over intellectual property rights to the publisher. Using copyrighted material is one of the most complicated and least understood areas of textual borrowing, and therefore its understanding is important for all potential authors. Lessig's (1999) observation that intellectual property law can constrain the affordances of technologies has become an important issue in discussing ethics. Intellectual property refers to legal ways in which content placed in a fixed medium is protected and used, particularly in the educational contexts in which the property is used.

Publishers traditionally wanted to control both the ownership and distribution of the research they published, so they required copyright to be transferred to the journal. Journals would offer authors a few reprints to distribute as they pleased, but after distributing the journal, further distribution could only come from the publishers, who argued that this transfer enabled them not only to control the reproduction of articles but also to represent the authors after their articles had been published. Changes in attitudes toward intellectual property law have changed how publishers grant rights to authors. Publishers may still ask for the traditional transfer of rights or they may ask for a license that gives them certain rights but allows the author to retain their own rights. The result has been that writers must understand various options for controlling their work once it is published.

Understanding the copyright process is therefore important for understanding the constraints on the ownership and distribution of content. The implications of signing a copyright transfer agreement at the end of the publishing process can be confusing because of the unclear and sometimes contradictory nature of the agreement (Herrington, 2020). Potential authors must understand whether they control the copyright as well as the implications of assigning it either as a transfer or a license. In countries that have fair use provisions, using copyrighted materials may be protected although how they are protected and to what extent they can be used vary according to the different interpretations of fair use.[1] Using images in a publication can be more complicated since authors may be forced to black them out after the article is published.

Therefore, by signing a release form, the author may 'give' their rights to the publisher. What rights the journal will give to the author and what will be retained by the author are often described in the author guidelines. However, these guidelines are frequently underspecified, so the designers of teaching spaces must explain how intellectual property law can affect publication. Although there is usually little an author can do to alter the intellectual property restrictions, understanding these laws can help writers better understand the implications for how research is conducted and shared, both their own and the research of others. Rules regarding publishing may contradict intellectual property law, such as how journals can restrict authors from submitting their paper to another journal until at least they have rejected the paper.

The growth of open access (see Chapter 6) along with changes in attitudes toward intellectual property (e.g. Lessig, 2002) have sometimes changed how publishers use copyright transfer to control distribution. Changes have also been spurred by the development of new social contexts in the United States and Europe for publishing. New regulations concerning how government-sponsored research must be open has led to various interpretations of which version of an article can be copyrighted and which must remain open. The rise of Open access journals may provide authors some rights while retaining other rights, so that some journals have modified their copyright rules allowing the author more control over distribution while retaining some aspects under their control. Open access journals may provide authors some rights while retaining other rights to allow for later distribution.

Changes in publishing have been important in changing policies toward intellectual property. In open access journals, authors can control the ownership and distribution of their research. However, in gated journals, these rights can be more complicated. For example, there is the question of which version of the paper is copyrighted since authors may write multiple drafts. Under traditional copyright law, all versions have the same copyright restrictions, but under some publishing rules, the author may share an earlier version but not the final version.

One of the most highly contested areas of intellectual property law has been sharing research using platforms such as ResearchGate or Academia.edu. As with Git Hub for data, these sites have become controversial for archiving and distributing information. After publication, authors may want to increase the visibility of their research through these networks (see Chapter 6), particularly as an alternative to the traditional metrics that can vary greatly across disciplines; however, they may be restricted from contributing to this network by the intellectual property waiver they signed.

These platforms have shifted the control of metrics from the publisher to the networks, giving authors a greater profile in determining their value as creators of information. Increasing visibility, by self-citation or by uploading papers to networks, is important for textual borrowing but may still be restricted by intellectual property law. Journals can have rules restricting authors from submitting papers to one journal while being considered by another journal. As with most of these rules, they reflect the social context in which journals are published, perhaps because of the difficulty in finding reviewers, although these restrictions are often unclear and can vary, depending on the different values of each context.

New approaches to copyright, as exemplified by Creative Commons, provide alternative approaches to the one-size-fits-all approach of traditional copyright law, including how research is attributed, shared and repurposed. Open access journals frequently use these agreements to substitute for traditional copyright laws. Green and Gold approaches, on the other hand, have been constrained by copyright laws. The global nature of research can also challenge dominant intellectual property laws, which can vary across disciplines and cultures. All copyright laws reflect the social or community values to be incorporated in the design of the spaces. Writers may have to consider an increased number of copyright considerations, for example the meaning of 'informed consent' or 'prior publication', which illustrates concerns regarding intellectual property law on the creation and distribution of research. Many authors may be ready to celebrate when they learn their paper has been accepted for publication, but not understand the implications of signing the intellectual property release. For many writers, the rewards of publishing make this step perfunctory but not understanding the constraints on their distribution rights may have serious repercussions.

Plagiarism in Academic Publishing

Plagiarism issues have dogged multilingual writers for many years and has remained an important issue in academic writing. An early case reported in China, for example, concerned two researchers who were caught copying large parts of a literature review in a paper submitted for publication to a European journal. When accused, they responded that they were not native speakers and that what they had copied was not as important as the significance of their results. Their case, although it happened over 20 years ago, reflects many of the concerns that teachers and editors have today. A recent headline from an Indian university asked, 'Publish or perish: Driving scholars to cheat?'. There is often confusion about what needs to be cited and what does not. A common misassumption about citing is that what is known as 'common knowledge' may still need to be cited as proprietary knowledge in order to demonstrate awareness of the research, to show the research influential for the authors, or to provide additional resources for the readers.

Plagiarism is the one issue regarding textual borrowing that is most often discussed in writing courses but takes on additional dimensions in the publishing space. However, it is only one of a number of concerns regarding textual borrowing in a publishing space. These include establishing the ethos of the writer; demonstrating supporting and critical claims; demonstrating whose 'shoulders' one stands on; and providing information for other researchers. Textual borrowing is a complex issue since acknowledging authorship is one way not only to avoid accusations of plagiarism but also to demonstrate a familiarity with prior research, build stronger arguments or create networks upon which the current research is built (e.g. Latour, 1987). Peer reviewers often critique the lack of citations, which is often connected to the writer's ethos. However, overzealous citations may increase the impact factor, an issue that may pose contradictory views for authors on deciding whether to cite.

The publication space contains many issues as well as some new rules for textual borrowing. Organizations like COPE have created guidelines indicating how the rules for 'text recycling' may differ from those in classrooms. The COPE guidelines contradict the traditional guidelines of some journals and popular pedagogies in writing classes but still create what Howard and Robillard (2008) referred to as 'pluralizing plagiarisms', where there can be many definitions of inappropriate textual borrowing. Because of this complexity, researchers may find themselves caught between conflicting goals in negotiating the ethical complexity of textual borrowing with the desire to publish. Again, COPE has attempted to create guidelines that can help understand the problem, here by criticizing editors requiring authors to cite certain texts that may increase the reputation of the editor (https://publicationethics.org/case/ editor-and-reviewers-requiring-authors-cite-their-own-work).

Of all the issues regarding textual borrowing, plagiarism is still a reminder that textual borrowing, whether print or multimodal, can still be highly contested. Plagiarism issues have long dogged multilingual writers. Even today there is often a confusion about what needs to be cited.

Moving into the publishing space, however, can entail new ethical issues regarding textual borrowing not encountered in the classroom. Textual borrowing is a complex issue since the acknowledge of authorship is one way to avoid accusations of plagiarism but also to meet to demonstrate a familiarity with prior research, build stronger arguments, or create networks upon which the current research is built (e.g. Latour, 1987). Peer reviewers often comment on the lack of citations, which may reflect concerns with the *ethos* of the authors. However, overzealous citation may lead to accusations of attempts to curry favor with the editor or manipulate the impact factor of the journal.

There are also issues with plagiarism or prior publication that the editors may try to discover prior to acceptance. Therefore, journals often employ various copy-detection tools to discover violations. Such tools, however, may not reflect the local criteria of a discipline. The guidelines of organizations like COPE for recognizing plagiarism or 'text recycling' may differ from those found in writing classrooms or in universities (https://publicationethics.org/files/Web_A29298_COPE_ Text_Recycling.pdf):

How much text is recycled? Where in the article does the text recycling occur? Whether the source of the recycled text has been acknowledged. Whether the article is a research or non-research article. Whether there is a breach of copyright. In some circumstances, cultural norms at the time and place of publication. (para. 5)

These criteria for judging textual borrowing indicate how plagiarism can be considered a 'local' phenomenon, whose rules reflect the specific community values for constraining how much and what can be copied (e.g. Howard, 1999).

Technology plays a critical role in these aspects of ethics. The goals for the use of technological tools by journals for copy-detection illustrate how textual borrowing may differ in different classroom spaces. Copy-detection programs are used to check not only for possible plagiarism but also for redundant publications, an issue that can contradict intellectual property law regarding the ownership of property. As discussed above, these issues are often unique to the publishing spaces confronted in the classroom. Plagiarism is still a concern for multilingual writers, regardless of how writing teachers may feel about these issues.

Publication spaces often contain many additional ethical issues that can lead to retractions or criticisms before, during or after publication. One approach for introducing these concerns is to present students with cases discussed in blogs such as Retraction Watch, which discusses various ethical issues. Accusations of academic misconduct can occur any time after publication. The penalties are often not as clearly defined as they might be for classroom writing. For example, we had a classroom discussion with a student whose advisor had been accused of duplicating a control image in a cancer-research paper primarily authored by a post-doc in the department. The student felt there was 'no harm, no foul' in publishing the image.

There have been many controversies over copying images. In one example, a well-known chair at The Ohio State University was removed after numerous violations over copying images from one article to another ('Probe into Carlo Croce', n.d.). However, an inquiry to the Retraction Watch blog expressed a much greater concern with the ethical conduct of the author than did the student. The fact that the issue was raised by another scientist who had read the article and then reported his concerns illustrates how ethical concerns can be raised long after an article has been published. Such queries illustrate how questions regarding plagiarism are being 'crowd-sourced', which can be complicated because these issues are more than 'rules' but can also inform the rhetorical and ethical understandings of the publishing space.

Prior Publication of Research

One of the most common ethical issues for the publishing space has been that papers can only be submitted to one journal at a time, a rule that reflects the pro bono nature of much of the publishing process. While the tools for detecting prior publication may themselves be controversial, its nature may be even more so. Concerns over prior publication differ from those over intellectual property, which would allow authors to do what they want with their research but reflect the social contexts of the publishing space. Often these concerns reflect other aspects of the publishing space. Controversies over preprints as well as rules regarding paper submission often arise from questions concerning what publication means in different contexts and why there is this concern. Students frequently ask whether a paper or even a dissertation is published if posted on preprint services, conference collections or even online in general. A researcher from Ghana posted a question on this topic to ResearchGate: 'What do you reply when journals ask if your manuscript has been previously considered by another journal?'.

This question illustrates the difficulties in understanding the ethical aspects of the publication space. These technological developments have increased opportunities for publishing before publication. The role of preprints raises issues regarding not only prior publications but also citations, the role of peer review and general ethical considerations. How they are defined as 'published' articles can impact whether writers can later submit them to journals. The answers are often unique to this community, may vary and sometimes contradict existing intellectual property law. Most journals will not accept papers previously published. However, what does 'previously published' mean on the internet, which provides many ways to publish different versions of a paper. Technological developments such as preprint servers and peer–peer networks have increased opportunities for publishing and reviewing, which can also complicate the publishing space.

Prepublication can complicate the roles of the author and peer reviewers, as well as the definitions of publication and authorship. In some communities of practice, prepublication is a requirement that may not affect whether the paper is published while in others it can be detrimental to future publication. The availability of papers for publication on personal and institutional websites, as well as peer–peer networks and preprint services, has muddled what prior publication means across different disciplines. These spaces all have rules used by the community, including what prior publication might mean; therefore, understanding these rules can help students utilize the constraints imposed by the community.

What then does publication mean? Students frequently ask whether a paper or even a dissertation is published if the paper had been previously published on preprint services, conference collections, and even online dissertations. The role of preprints raises issues regarding prior publications, citation, the role of peer review, and general ethical consideration comparable to traditionally published articles (COPE, 2018). Whether research is considered 'published' can impact whether writers can later submit them to other journals. While such practices may provide more autonomy and flexibility, they also leave students in more vulnerable positions.

The Pedagogy of Academic Misconduct in the Publishing Space

The pedagogy for teaching about ethics can help students understand the values of the publishing space (e.g. Crotty, 2016). The importance of teaching about ethics is two-fold. First it helps students understand that the publication process does not end but continues in two possible directions – a positive one in which papers are cited and discussed and a negative one in which papers can be retracted for ethical violations often from tips from whistleblowers. The second reason is that publication space brings together many of the issues addressed in other literacy spaces with the specific values from their academic communities. Publishing is not simply having a research article accepted but the creation of a new node in a network for sharing information.

The ethical standards of journals has frequently been challenged (e.g. Davis, 2009; Koebler, 2020). Students in publishing spaces may need to understand these additional ethical issues. In some institutions, ethical violations are considered differently from classroom violations. Institutions often have an integrity and compliance office that could level penalties much different from those levied by the publications but often invisible to the authors until problems with their research arise. In an attempt to increase this transparency, Ohio State University's office, for example, created a series of short videos on reporting violations (https://youtu.be/fPYkzZmM1X0), conflicts of issues (https://youtu.be/h-fZn8uYT4Y) and using public records (https://youtu.be/EPTxxxb8Rd4). Understanding these concerns are important in helping students understand not only how the process extends beyond publication but also the constraints of the discipline. Many problems result from the differences between the social context of the classroom space and the publishing space, which places writers in contexts they may not have previously encountered.

Newcomers may feel that the publication process is over once an article is published; however, many of the criticisms of ethical violations are found after publication. Many accusations do not come from the journal but from an outside 'whistleblower' who may have noticed an issue with the research long after the article was published. Problems with the knowledge creation process are often blamed on failures in the peer review process and are not discovered until sometime after publication. Many of the retractions found in the Retraction Watch blog occur long after publication. Ethical concerns are dealt with by using technological tools. Turnitin.com, for example, is used to check for plagiarism and for prior publication (cf. Twomey, 2009).

The proliferation of these accusations has made it important for the community to create ways of notifying editors and authors if some ethical violation occurs. Many of these articles have already been verified through peer review, and therefore its failure to uncover these violations highlights the limitations of the peer review process, which has resulted in calls for new approaches. The concern with the citation of retracted papers has been complicated by the spread of open access (see Chapter 6) where articles can still be downloaded even after they have been retracted (Bar-Ilan & Halevi, 2018). Concerns about citing retracted articles raise questions about how the social concerns of a community of practice, for example, are manifested in important rhetorical issues specific to the discipline, such as the rules for textual borrowing.

Even common rhetorical strategies can have ethical considerations. Wilhite and Fong (2012) distinguished between suggestions on textual borrowing made to improve the paper and what they call 'coercive' suggestions designed to increase the impact factor. Because of their peripheral position, multilingual students are often most vulnerable to such coercion. Therefore, for students, the sometimes conflicting rhetorical and ethical demands on textual borrowing can confuse even the most experienced author.

The Future of Digital Pedagogical Spaces for Publishing

Changes in access to intellectual property have been strongly supported by new interpretations of the laws constraining their use. New technologies in these publishing spaces have changed not only the role of intellectual property law in the publishing space (e.g. Lessig, 2002) but also the understanding that multilingual writers need about its constraints on these new literacies and their connections. These technologies have changed other aspects of the writing process. New tools for distributing research illustrate the complex and continually changing relationship between academic goals and intellectual property. One way to counter the open access movement has been to acquire new tools that might appeal to potential authors. The acquisition of Mendeley by an academic publisher, for example, exemplifies how journals try to create wider moats to protect their distribution by acquiring a technology competing with ResearchGate and Academia.edu (Hinchliffe, 2019). Recent conflicts between publishers and libraries over the costs of publishing and reading research illustrate the contentiousness of these relationships.

New attitudes toward publishing are also changing the publishing space. New attitudes to teaching genre (e.g. Tardy, 2016) have focused on the variations in genre that can frustrate teachers with traditional attitudes toward genre. Such variations can again mean that teachers must cede authority to their students in understanding the variations in the genres they are encountering. Traditional attitudes toward peer review and its role in gatekeeping research have been challenged with alternative approaches to evaluation. Traditional views, for example, toward the 'reject' or 'revise and resubmit' evaluations may not be efficient for receiving feedback and could be detrimental for readers who may never see the research (Vines, 2019).

High rejection rates, which can give a journal a better reputation, can mean that many ideas never reach the readers. How this system will work and its impact on the publishing process remain unclear. Vines questions whether authors will update their research once it has been published. Will changes in peer review, such as their publication, be accepted in the research community? Can every paper be reviewed and published with the review, so the readers can decide on its value? How will these changes impact the choices authors make on where to publish? Vines questions whether every issue – sustainability, anonymity and the quality of the review process – will be accepted by readers.

For students wishing to publish, the increasing complexity needs to be addressed even as traditional issues persist. The growth of open access has created new opportunities as well as greater pressure to publish early and often. Designs can address, although not necessarily resolve, both the pedagogical and ethical problems faced by multilingual writers by raising the curtain, to borrow a metaphor from *The Wizard of Oz*, on the publishing process. Therefore, the publication space has become an important area for helping novice researchers understand the ethical constraints of their academic communities.

Making the spaces more equitable has been addressed from different perspectives. Besides the highly contested argument over gated versus open access publication, there have been discussions on what form of English is more acceptable in the publication space. There are important issues around what is considered acceptable language and rhetoric in these spaces (e.g. Kuteeva & Mauranen, 2014). These concerns in the publishing space may not be transparent, which provides areas for teachers to further their designs. For example, I use postings from Retraction Watch to acquaint students with the myriad reasons for retraction. Besides understanding these constraints, students can learn the underlying values of their academic communities.

One of the issues is how the publishing space has become more contentious as the need to publish has increased. With continual changes resulting from the growth of open access and the shifting role of the author (Dodds, 2019), the development of publishing spaces has become more problematic and more subject to shifts in technology and the institutional concerns of research universities. Therefore, their design can directly address issues with global publication, particularly the role of other languages and other forms of English in the publishing process (e.g.

Corcoran *et al.*, 2019; Curry & Lillis, 2010). The design of these spaces does not necessarily reflect the decisions about publishing. Therefore, students must still decide on the language they prefer to publish in and the role of the first language in addressing the audience concerns in an English language context. Beyond the changes in the publishing process, there have also been changes in how writing is viewed that may affect publishing, often manifesting differently in different journals and different fields. Particularly with the new technologies being incorporated into the spaces, pedagogies must be flexible enough to accommodate the varying and evolving process.

Note

(1)   For a humorous view of fair use, see 'A Fair(y) Use Tale at https://www.youtube.com/ watch?v=CJn_jC4FNDo&t=12s.

8 What We Talk about When We Talk about Digital Literacy Spaces

New Contexts for Digital Literacy Spaces

When Raymond Carver popularized the oft-repeated expression, 'What We Talk about When We Talk about Love', which was modified in the title of this chapter, he was speaking about the struggles of love, both its passion and its violence. Love in the era of dating apps may not be the same as it was in the past and it may be even more different in the future. Similarly, literacy in the era of technology has also changed in ways that make it difficult to predict. When we speak of the design of digital spaces, we are similarly speaking of contested and often creative spaces where there is little governance or agreement over their appropriateness or quality. Publication, for example, in the era of changes in requirements for distribution, has been changing in ways not fully understood. Lacking such constraints can provide greater creative as well as pedagogical potential for implementing these digital literacy spaces. This book has attempted to discuss the design of such spaces, how they are connected and how they may provide new challenges and opportunities for both teachers and students.

Discussions about technologies used in teaching writing can incorporate discussions about pedagogies and learning theories that are relevant not only to technology but also to literacy as well. These spaces are designed to increase the learning experiences of students by using the affordances of various technologies that can help address both new and traditional problems in the writing classroom. They do not simply incorporate these technologies but also address the same learning and teaching issues that are discussed throughout the multilingual writing community. These spaces have developed from the interaction between the participants – teachers and students – and the affordances of the spaces and the tools incorporated into them. By providing alternative spaces for student autonomy, these new spaces have sometimes increased the value of the different forms of languages used in the classroom, the audiences that the students address and the types of learning in which the students engage.

The design is important in every digital space, and like love, is often chaotic, unstable and continually changing, requiring an 'agility' of the participants to negotiate these factors. No design is complete and therefore necessitates feedback from both teachers and students as to their experiences in the same. Their implementation often depends on sometimes uncontrollable factors such as the backgrounds of the students and the availability of the technologies. The designs of these spaces, and their corresponding literacies, have been highly contested. The proliferation of openness, for example, is indicative of the potential of these digital open spaces but is an issue that has not been generally accepted. These spaces have affected their literacies so as not to privilege one over another. Although the goal is to empower the teacher in their design, such empowerment is not always the result, as Casanave (2017) has forcefully argued. Thus, the ambivalence of these spaces in the writing process reflects the problem with literacies throughout the writing process.

More importantly, these spaces are not separate but often connected, allowing teachers and students to cross from one space to another. Therefore, what can happen in one space can impact what happens in the other spaces, again reflecting the interoperability of these spaces (e.g. Palfrey & Gasser, 2012). Such crossings can support student literacy development, provide alternative perspectives or reflect multiple literacies.

One of the arguments for the value of Massive Open Online Courses (MOOCs), for example, has been in how they have influenced teaching in traditional classrooms, particularly the reliance on peer review and collaboration among teachers (e.g. Halasek *et al.*, 2016). I have adapted a MOOC practice in assigning multiple readings for students to decide on. Openness in publishing can affect openness in pedagogy. In the publishing class, I have collected and annotated these readings in an open textbook (https://issuu.com/joelbloch9/docs/6912ebook), which contains information related to some of the topics discussed in this book. Designs can also share the same concerns as considered in society. As Stephens (2018) argues, design decisions can impact how technology is used for protecting privacy or, in some cases, for addressing concerns, for example, the privacy of the students. On the other hand, some technologies provide data that purposely excludes some participants, thus depriving these participants of some degree of autonomy. Therefore, understanding the implications on pedagogy in designing a literacy space has become important for being a teacher as well as a citizen in the digital world.

Although these designs can impact the role of literacy inside the classroom, they should never be considered deterministic in their impact on either literacy or pedagogy. In some spaces, students can experiment with different forms of languages while in others, standard English may still be required. In other cases, these spaces provide access to open teaching materials that were formerly unavailable. However, the spaces allow students to continually cross boundaries across different spaces and different kinds of texts. Some spaces have been designed to facilitate these crossings. While the trajectory of this book begins with blogging and multimodality and progresses through MOOCs and flipped classrooms to open publishing, these spaces are not linear, all originating in the instantiations of technology in the classroom as well as in different spaces outside the classroom.

The book focuses on only a few of the issues that pervade technology use in society, although the limitations in these digital spaces could be changing as new technologies are introduced. Many of the digital spaces – blogs, digital stories, MOOCs, open access – were primarily developed outside the classroom while other spaces were designed to incorporate the tools used outside the classroom to support the institutional literacies valued in the classroom. The tools used in one space could be used in the others and the methodologies developed in one space can be used in another. The goal of this interoperability of these spaces by how they can be aggregated into a 'commons' (Raymond, 1999) where the writers can move through these spaces with greater choices in the language and content of their work while still being supported and constrained by their design.

The 'commons' metaphor was initially compared to 'the tragedy of the commons' (Hardin, 1968) to describe how the openness of spaces, such as fish beds, could be exploited to the extent that their value was greatly diminished. Later research, on the other hand, by Ostrum (2015) showed that this openness could be beneficial to the development of the commons. The internet created abundant spaces that encouraged more and more participants to create shareable materials (Lessig, 2002). Such spaces can include the new digital voices found in blogs and multimodality, as well as in other literacies as found in Twitter and Instagram, and the openness of interactions and new learning environments in flipped classes and MOOCs. As Vandergriff (2016) points out, regardless of the terms used, these spaces are always fluid and changing in terms of how both languages and rhetorics are valued, creating unique challenges for multilingual students wanting to become members of a community of practice and their teachers who want to design spaces to support these students.

The complexity of these literacy spaces illustrates the trajectory of the development of technology on literacy, beginning with Plato's often cited dictum in *Phaedrus* that literacy would degrade memorization to the later effect of the printing press on the Protestant Reformation and then the creation of the personal computer, the internet and the World Wide Web. For example, open access journals (see Chapter 6) reflect a development in the history of the effect of technology on spreading literacy and publishing, as exemplified by Eisenstein's (1980) research on the relationship between the technological developments surrounding the printing press and the increased circulation of the Bible and its resulting impact on the social conditions of literacy and the Protestant Reformation. This development was not necessarily Gutenberg's plan but exemplifies how the consequences went beyond the initial goals of the innovation.

This brief historical discussion illustrates how the internet and the World Wide Web could not determine the development of literacy any more than the printing press could. Each technology can impact literacy development in its own ways. As Olson (1994) argued, the printing press supported literate readers to learn from the meaning of the texts rather than from the precedent of dogma. The argument of this book is that there are multiple technologies that can affect literacies differently. As Weller (2018a, 2018b) points out, there have been technological advancements related to the internet, all of which have affected teaching and learning in the multilingual writing classroom.

These approaches to discussing literacy spaces and tools are a subset of both the historical and current theories about technologies and their relationships with their users. The spaces mix the chosen technologies with the theories and pedagogical goals of academic writing. There are design spaces for incorporating every tool and classroom. The research of Gibson (1977) and Norman (2013) on the affordances of design has provided a framework not simply for using the technological tools but also as input for determining how design can support and guide writing. How these technologies impact literacy can depend on the choices that teachers and students make in their usage. Greeno (1994) argues that affordances are interactive and non-deterministic in that the user can choose among the elements of the design. These choices can impact how such affordances affect the literacies used in them.

The book is not designed to be an evangelistic tract of the value of technology but to provide a perspective to reflect on these digital spaces in student literacy. These spaces were not isolated from other developments in other technology usages, both today and in the past. Wu (2010) describes how the development of the telephone evolved from having decentralized control; digital spaces, on the other hand, often evolved from having centralized to decentralized controls found today, though often with intermittent attempts to centralize.

Without centralized control, the introduction of new technologies has always affected the creative process. The introduction of sound into movies was rapidly followed by the development of new technologies for recording sound and speech as the actors move across spaces. These technologies were supplemented by newer camera technologies for deeper focus, faster film stock for night shooting, gyroscopes for cameras to swing around without wires and, eventually, the digital distribution of film for changing projection. Wu (2010) describes how other technologies used today, such as the telephone, the radio and the television, have similarly developed.

The development of these literacies spaces has followed a similar trajectory as have other technologies, which have been both constrained and expanded by related economic factors. Open access has been boosted by economic concerns with the costs of publishing and distributing materials, as MOOCs were by the increasing costs of education. New spaces can involve a greater need for new resources, both human and financial, that cost money. Flipped classrooms have required both tools and training as well as new furniture for the classroom design. Many of the tools that teachers use have been constrained by the need for new revenue sources and the addition of more affordances to protect the products from competition.

These spaces have extended the places for learning and the abundance of available information, what Ostrum (2015) called 'growing the commons'. These developments can support more personal learning, which may be further extended by introducing new technologies. Each space can contribute to the writer's development of both their language skills and their identities as writers. Each has its own affordances that both help and constrain questions related to both the rhetorical and linguistic aspects of writing. They all have the possibility of supporting new pedagogical developments, for incorporating pedagogies for using different languages and genres with different values and learning approaches as well as different literacies.

The Disruption of Academic Writing

Disruption is an often controversial and overused term to describe how one technology can replace another (e.g. Christensen, 1997). As the example from Plato shows, new technologies can disrupt existing forms, which, in turn, can impact how literacy is taught. The New London Group (1996) saw that these new forms of literacy, often dominant outside the classroom, could disrupt traditional classroom forms and consequently the enculturation of students into the dominant academic norms of the university. The New London Group shared a more relativistic view that rejected the dichotomy between literate and non-literate students as well as between different values attached to literacy and orality. This view allowed for new forms of literacy – blogs (Powers & Doctorow, 2002), gaming (Gee, 2003), social media (boyd, 2014), multimodality (Hull & Katz, 2006) – almost all of which developed outside the classroom and often in opposition to the 'essayist' (Farr, 1993) tradition favored in the classroom. Even issues such as 'pandemics', which are completely outside of the control of writing teachers, have forced them to consider technological alternatives to traditional classrooms.

Today, these digital literacies have been discussed in terms of their academic value. Stewart (2015), for example, discusses how Twitter posts from academic writers can be evaluated according to the logic used in their arguments as if they were traditional rhetorical forms. Their value, as is true for every other form of literacy, could change as the values of the contexts in which they are implemented change. As Resnick (1990) pointed out long before there were digital literacies, what it meant to be literate was always evolving. Today, these new forms of digital literacy contribute to this evolution. The result is often a more chaotic classroom that lacks the traditional constraints on how different literacies are valued.

As Weller (2018a, 2018b) has argued, disruption has been a slow process, what Watters (2013b) tried to capture in her 'zombie' metaphor where the same problems and solutions with teaching keep returning. In other cases, students have used technologies to respond to their problems with their courses, for example apps used to find support from their classmates in answering questions in the same way social media and other networks can be used. In other cases, there have been technologies for transforming large lecture classes into smaller, more collaborative learning spaces. New multimodal literacies, such as blogging and digital storytelling, have disrupted the dominance of the traditional print literacies. Use of these literacies has evolved as well. Yancey (2019) describes how her use of blogging evolved to include new assignments and more collaborative relationships among the students. Similarly, new designs in publishing have disrupted traditional publishing models and how students are being prepared to become authors in these spaces.

Despite the controversies, the impact of these spaces on academic writing cannot be underestimated. The introduction of new forms of multimodality have changed textuality in the classroom, introducing visual images to the same level of importance as the traditional print texts. These digital spaces have provided new voices and identities for their participants, consistent with the argument for multiple voices in academic literacies (Matsuda, 2006). The introduction of these new technologies has increased the role of these alternative voices in the academic writing classroom.

None of the spaces described supports a monolithic academic voice, so throughout these spaces, the writer emerges with multiple English language voices along with the voices the students bring from their home languages, incorporating these voices within multiple contexts for addressing writing problems. Therefore, they may have multiple opportunities to use the threshold concepts in one genre in other genres, often reflecting the contexts in which they are taught. Some students who may have difficulty with a print literacy may feel more comfortable with a multimodal one (Bloch, 2015).

Digital Spaces and Learning

The term 'disruption' has been frequently used and misused; however, it has impacted the often chaotic nature of the design of these digital spaces. These designs have a long history in the development of digital spaces for language learning. The development of technological spaces for teaching writing can parallel the development of technology and language teaching (Vandergriff, 2016), by mixing theories of technology with theories on literacy, learning and pedagogies. These spaces have always been controversial.

Vandergriff discusses many of the controversies of digital language learning spaces, comparing Lave and Wenger's (1991) use of the term 'community of practice' and Gee's (2004) use of the term 'affinity spaces', but favoring the latter for designing spaces where participants are connected to participants. 'Communities of practice' have been a very important concept in the discussion of publication spaces, as part of the social context for students moving toward the centers of their disciplines. The approach discussed here combines 'communities of practice' for influencing the design of the spaces and the 'affinity groups' for connecting participants, affecting the relationships among the participants, a principal that has guided designing the role for participants in all these spaces.

These ideas have been discussed in all areas of the internet. Weinberger (2002) used the term 'loosely joined' to define spaces where individuals can easily move in and out without the stigma of dropping their membership. These new spaces both inside and outside the classroom require new perspectives on how they coexist. Raymond's (1999) 'commons' can be an equally useful metaphor for capturing the various literacies, learning activities and languages found in these spaces.

Digital spaces have had a major impact on the use of language from the earliest designs for email and discussion boards where written language often replaced oral forms. Some spaces allow for various languages and rhetorics while other spaces, particularly publishing, may be more restrictive. As Vandergriff (2016) pointed out, spaces for blogs and multimodality encourage students to draw on their native forms of language, which as Canagarajah (2018) argued, could be mixed with other languages. Certain spaces may be more restrictive than others. Publishing may be more restrictive as to which voice can be used, although multilingual writers still have some choice in what language to publish in (Lillis & Curry, 2006). However, if they choose to publish in English, they may have to conform to the demands of the publishers for standard forms of English or have sometimes to correct their 'errors'. So far, open access journals have had only a limited impact on the dominance of English, although, perhaps ironically, predatory journals may provide greater flexibility in the varieties of English accepted.

The design of these spaces is never stable, often evolving with changing approaches to learning or from remediating designs by incorporating student feedback. Our concern with blogs, for instance, initially focused on their roles as heuristics but evolved as the goals of the course evolved. Our use of multimodality followed a similar trajectory as the relationship between the goals of the multimodal and text assignments became more connected, which raised new perspectives on old topics, such as transfer. One consequence of how spaces can be connected is their potential for transferring rhetorical knowledge. Transfer focuses more on just skill transfer as has often been seen in language studies. While not dependent on these spaces, their design has been seen as facilitating transfer. In their review of the literature on transfer, Gardner and Barefoot (2017) find that transfer can depend on the ability of students to reflect on their experiences and be willing to cross boundaries between the spaces in which they write.

Often, the impetus for change came from organizations supporting the design of the space. In this way, the new mantra of the 'Flipped Classroom 3.0' is an evolution from Bloom *et al.* (1956) to Maslow (1962, 1966), which incorporates a growing concern with the development of the student as well as developing learning strategies best suited to the different styles and abilities. In his discussion on creativity Maslow discusses creating an environment where the individual can continually experience the 'now', a framework supportive of the design of these learning spaces. The goals of the flipped classroom, for example, no longer focus only on distributing the skills in Bloom's taxonomy (Bloom *et al.*, 1956) in different spaces, but also on providing students with greater autonomy and more personalized learning spaces.

This focus on transfer epitomizes how the design of the space can connect the technology, the teacher and the students. The role of transfer on the threshold concepts can be facilitated by the design of the space, but its execution is primarily up to the students to connect the common threshold concepts across literacies and apply them in new contexts. The affordances of the different technologies can support seeing these concepts from different perspectives, and the teacher can then scaffold how the assignments and concepts can be connected, providing both with greater autonomy along with the chaos that may accompany it.

Often, the design of these classroom spaces incorporated the learning approaches of the spaces where these new forms of literacy originated. Digital storytelling, for example, initially brought social issues into the storytelling space. As with this original purpose, they supported the personal voices of the creators. When we brought these spaces into our writing classroom, we designed them to allow the students to develop their own topics, with certain constraints. Differences between those topics and the ones found in groups organized by StoryCenter (www. storycenter.org) illustrate how political differences can affect the development of stories. These new spaces allowed writers to reflect in blogs and for teachers to provide scaffolding for moving between multimodal and print spaces, often depending on the resources the students brought to the classroom. Teachers could shape these voices in how they chose the assignments for these spaces, as Yancey (2019) did with blogs and collaboration, or as we did with blogs and reflection.

Publishing, particularly for students, involves crossing spaces from being a student to being a professional. The commons metaphor can still apply to such crossings by allowing authors to develop their own ideas with their own voices appropriate for each space, although such autonomy has been applied differently in different communities of practice. Spaces for teaching about publication allow for students to reflect on their own issues they are experiencing with publication, and often provide brokers to support literacy development prior to formal submissions.

The Development of Literacy in Digital Spaces

Nowhere is the passion and chaos that Carver alluded to in his discussions about love more evident than in discussions of what it means to be literate and what forms of literacy are more valued inside and outside the classroom. Answers to these questions can motivate these new designs for literacy spaces. Canagarajah (2018) links these approaches to literacy with his argument about translingualism by borrowing several terms from digital spaces in explaining new directions in translingual literacy. Concepts such as 'bricolage', 'rhizomatic' and 'assemblage', all extensively used in these spaces, can describe new approaches to changes in both how texts are created and how writers can connect themselves. Changes in these values can be especially seen in using textual borrowing (Shi, 2004, 2006, 2010) to create digital forms of narrative and argumentative literacies. This book frequently cites blogs in part because in a rapidly changing field such as the role of technology, blogs often provide the most up-to-date information for writers to draw upon.

Again, these are not new developments. Bazerman (1988) saw the same concerns with the sharing of new information in the history of science when the distribution of research in physics was accelerated with a new platform for the faster publishing of letters in physics. The design of cMOOCs introduced the concept of rhizomatic learning (Cormier, 2008b), which Canagarajah (2018) later borrowed for his discussion of translingualism. Digital storytelling emphasizes 'assemblage', although alternative terms are sometimes used, as one of its key threshold concepts. The introduction of these forms has not only affected what it means to be literate but also how such literacies are incorporated into these designs. Both Plato's argument about whether literacy destroys memory and Carr's (2011) 'Google makes us stupid', reflect the intense discussions about what is literacy and what forms of literacy are most valued. Canagarajah's uses of terms borrowed from digital literacy offer a much different role for defining literacy and valuing its varying forms.

The design of digital spaces has been affected by the Plato/Carr framework for critically examining digital literacies, as seen with Casanave (2017). Both print and digital spaces have often posited an extremely deterministic view of literacy on the users' views of the world, which would lead to a division referred to as the literacy divide.

Olson (1994: 262), using a theoretical framework borrowed from Russian psychologists, argued that the acquisition of literacy led individuals to see the world in more complex, often more abstract ways of thinking, derived from the affordances of print text. He argued that the invention of the alphabet provided 'an altered perception of language and an altered conception of rational man'. Rhetoricians also saw literate cultures as different from oral ones. Ong (1982) summarized several ways that oral and literate cultures differed, arguing that the acquisition of literacy changes how individuals perceive the world. Goody (1977), for example, argues that lists and indices belong to the literate way and provide a means of organizing information not found in the oral world, which often relies on memorization.

As is also seen in the discussion of literacy spaces, this debate incorporated questions of the determinism entailed in these literacies. This 'literacy divide' incorporated a strongly deterministic view of the impact of literacy on those who use it. Opposing this divide had been the center of the work of the anthropologist Franz Boas and his two most famous students, Edward Sapir and Benjamin Whorf, whose work on the linguistic complexity of non-literate languages not only attempted to counter the argument that oral cultures had less complex world views but also laid out the argument for cultural determinism (Freeman, 1983). What role then do these spaces play in the development of student literacy? Carr (2011) has been outspoken in his criticism of these literacies being detrimental to the development of literacy. The inverse of this strongly deterministic view is that digital literacies would have a positive effect, perhaps on the impact of visual elements in literacy development. The non-deterministic approach focused on the relative values of different literacies.

Different literacies may enable different world views, in which one may not be more complex than another but may have greater value in the institution or culture. Scribner and Cole's (1981) research on the multiple literacies of the Vai people would similarly argue that the acquisition of literacy may not determine how the world is perceived since it is not literacy itself but the contextualization of the roles for literacy that can impact these world views. They distinguished between school- and non-school-based literacies, which still play an important role in this discussion of how school affects literacies developed outside the classroom. Heath's (1983) research on literacies in different racial and economic contexts provided an expanded discussion for valuing the different forms of literacy, including those developed outside of school. She used the term 'literacy events' to describe the different types of literacies found in different contexts, arguing that school-based literacy valued some events more than others. Street (1984) likewise attacked the literacy divide, arguing that such a divide assumes the existence of autonomous forms of literacy that ignore the effects of their social contexts on the writers. As seen in all forms of literacies discussed here, there are, in fact, multiple forms that have to be accounted for.

These digital literacy spaces developed in the context of this controversy, particularly supported by Heath (1983) and Street (1984) on the value of different literacy events. The New London Group (1996) is often credited with valuing the inclusion of digital literacies in the writing curriculum by critiquing the enculturation process through which the dominant print literacies are learned in the classroom. Digital literacies combine literacies first developed outside of academic institutions and those developed primarily inside them. In many cases, the dominance of the printed word has been disrupted by the increase in multiple modalities or the value of multiple literacy contexts, as Heath (1983) argued.

Digital literacy spaces extend this connection between in-school and outside-school forms of literacy, which accounts for the differences in the types of literacies these spaces support. The difference between these approaches to literacies can be observed in how digital storytelling could be used outside the classroom and inside the classroom. For Hull and associates (e.g. Hull & Nelson, 2005; Hull & Katz, 2006), using digital storytelling as an after-school literacy was often antithetical to traditional classroom literacy assignments. By bringing digital storytelling into the classroom, the social context for literacy could be affected by the assignments and how they were aligned in the classroom (e.g. Yancey, 2019), which could equalize the value of multimodal assignments to those of the print assignments. However, these assignments were not deterministic of the changes they could bring. By bringing these literacies inside the classroom, their nature could change as well. By connecting the multimodal assignment to the print assignment, digital storytelling, for example, no longer played the role it played outside the classroom, as it did in the StoryCenter, but could be connected to the pre-existing goals for the course and possibly change the literacy value of both literacies.

Flipped spaces have impacted how literacy is learned but not the literacy itself. The flipped classroom challenges how literacy is learned but not necessarily the literacy used in the course. MOOCs similarly focused on existing forms of literacy, but the problems with completion rates, for example, also challenged what the term 'course' meant in teaching literacy. Multimodality, the form which had its roots outside the classroom, could be incorporated into the classroom as a form of academic literacy, making its relevance for disrupting traditional forms of literacy dependent on its implementation in relation to other forms of literacy.

Regardless of this relationship between the print and digital literacies, these digital spaces have incorporated the same technological source – the design of the World Wide Web – as well as the associated technologies later developed. The Web created a platform for creating literacy spaces and the latter provided a framework for integrating them into traditional writing curricula. Before the development of the Web, the primary purpose of the internet was for discussing and sharing information. In what would become known as Web 2.0 (O'Reilly, 2005), the Web became the center for creating and sharing literacies. Berners-Lee (1999) was clear that what he wanted was for everybody to have the ability to create for the Web. Berners-Lee's most recent work on 'social linked data' (SOLID) is an attempt to connect decentralized applications (https://solid.mit.edu) that may impact teaching literacy in the same way in future iterations.

Therefore, new literacies may better support at least some of these traditional literate concepts. Hull and associates' work with digital storytelling demonstrated the expressive power of literacies developed outside of school classrooms (e.g. Hull & Nelson, 2005; Hull & Katz, 2006). MOOCs and open access journals, as well as open educational materials in general, have shown the potential for using digital literacies in global education. Once the technical and economic issues of accessibility are solved, these new approaches to distributing knowledge could provide a deeper understanding of the communities of practice students were trying to enter but did not necessarily increase their support for their moving from the periphery to the center.

The connection between literacy and technology has always been important and has raised a variety of questions to be considered and reconsidered: Is digital literacy a part of being literate? While it has been argued that these 'literacy events' (Heath, 1983) be included in pedagogical approaches, their value has been with their assumptions about literacies that can be imported into the classroom. Graff (1991) popularized the term 'the legacies of literacy' to argue that becoming literate did not necessarily bring the social and economic rewards often associated with literacy more correlated with economic and racial status. Whether these new forms of digital spaces impact that relationship remains to be seen. New technologies, some of which are just coming online, may not yet be ready to be used for effective pedagogies but could develop in ways that will make them more compatible with the current teaching practices.

This discussion has shown that becoming literate involves acquiring multiple literacies, which exist on a continuum of what Graff (1991: 390) calls the 'literate bias', the potential of which has excited many teachers in part because these literacies have disrupted classroom practices, although some teachers may still feel uncomfortable with this disruption. Their impact on literacy practices remains unclear, although they provide a framework for how technologies are discussed here. Even literacies developed specifically for the classroom, such as the publication and flipped learning classes, were designed to disrupt traditional classroom practices, whether they are the domination of the lecture or the traditional role of mentorship.

Even open access journals, which may simultaneously be traditional and disruptive, have adapted their design to respond to concerns over how their literacies would be valued for jobs, tenure and promotion, a question that Heath (1983) originally raised in her discussion of valuing literacies and was then expanded by the New London Group. The flipped classroom similarly attempted to adapt the traditional classroom spaces to incorporate new approaches to learning about literacy. MOOCs have moved in a similar direction but greatly increased the number of potential learners. Technological changes have extensively affected publishing spaces, requiring, in turn, new spaces for teaching writing.

How these spaces impact literacy from both a social and a cognitive perspective remains an important research question. Validating these new literacies often depended on how well they helped students and teachers reach traditional goals, whether that meant writing an academic paper or using publications to support job searches. How then are these literacies and the values inherent in them transferred to the multilingual classroom? What then are the 'legacies' that these literacies will bestow on the teachers and students? How will teachers and students be rewarded by adapting these new approaches?

Multilingual Teachers and Students in Digitally Enhanced Literacy Spaces

It is the fundamental premise of this book that teachers and students, not inventors or administrators, play the primary roles in designing these new pedagogical approaches. As Casanave (2017) has argued, the role of the teacher in these new spaces may be their most controversial aspect. The flaw in the 'digital immigrant/digital native' metaphor (Prensky, 2001, 2011) has been undervaluing the contribution of the 'native' in this discussion, the teacher. Both students and teachers, in fact, may bring different skill levels regarding using the various tools. How well students understand these literacy practices can impact their classroom performance.

While each space has its own qualities, the students are bringing their linguistic and digital knowledge, both from their own literacy backgrounds and from their encounters with the newer spaces. Their impact on literacy development, and the connections that students can make among each other, has been influenced by accessing student learning, incorporating their problems and how their teachers design curricula reflecting these changes. The goal here was primarily to show the relationships among the different literacies to provide insights into the genres that were being introduced as well as to provide alternative perspectives on key threshold concepts shared among the different literacies. While each form of literacy has its own affordances, students better develop their literacy skills by shuttling across the boundaries between them.

Contrary to the arguments about how technology may replace teachers, these new technologies have enhanced the importance of teachers in designing these spaces by integrating new and traditional technologies and literacy practices. How well the teachers are prepared to move among these spaces is not simply through learning how to use these technologies but how to conceptualize their use to incorporate issues including plagiarism, genre analysis, translingualism and rhetorical transfer. Accommodating, even encouraging, the multiple languages used in these digital spaces remains one of the central pedagogical concerns, focusing on the roles of new forms of language and rhetoric. The language in many of these spaces is a convergence between the traditional languages of the classroom and the new languages of the digital world, found in the blogs, digital stories and other forms of discourse brought to the classroom.

Integrating multiple languages may be the greatest challenge teachers need face. Multimodality is considered here an alternative language as well as a digital learning space, so that teachers can understand its usage in ways that may be more suitable to 'digital natives'. Multimodal spaces, for example, have challenged existing forms of literacy, but that challenge has been more controversial in publishing spaces. Multimodal literacy spaces provide a perspective on the various debates over issues such as translingualism in multilingual writing spaces. Canagarajah (2013) has criticized traditional uses of the term multilingual as being additive. Multilingual students may have more than two languages. Instead, he prefers the term 'translingual' to refer to mixing literacies from which new forms of literacy emerge. Languages in the age of the internet may include multimodality or other forms developed outside both the classroom and the home. Regardless of what materials are considered, his argument moves away from the more deterministic view on linguistic imperialism advanced by researchers such as Phillipson (1992) by providing greater agency to the writer in developing and using their preferential forms of language despite the domination of English.

The goal for designing these spaces has been to create different learning experiences, including new ways to think about language, literacy and rhetoric. These experiences result from the combination of the literacy and the teacher's approach to implementation. This goal may be in line with the goals that teachers have always had. These new spaces have meant the spread of new metaphors to describe their contexts. In all these spaces, teachers function neither as 'sages' nor 'guides', but 'designers' who play a more active role in the learning process. Bergmann (2018) has informally introduced various metaphors for teachers in discussing flipped learning, which may resonate throughout all these spaces.

The idea of the flipped classroom as an 'operating system', a metaphor sometimes credited to Robert Talbert, (2017) illustrated how the design of the flipped classroom, as well as any learning space, was not limited to activities predetermined by the choices of technologies, but the spaces could be modified to shape activities for supporting classroom goals. Blogging, for example, brings its own characteristics, but when integrated into a course, is shaped by the goals for which it is used, while as Lessig (1999) has argued, the use of these technologies can be constrained by the underlying architecture of the design of the spaces.

Another Bergmann metaphor, 'from Bloom to Maslow', illustrates the goal of 'reaching every child', which pervades every digital space. There has been a shift in the concern for the experiences of the student in these digital spaces, as Bergmann expresses in his discussion of flipped learning 3.0, from thinking about Bloom's (Bloom *et al.*, 1956) hierarchy of skills to Maslow's (1966, 1971: 180) goals to integrate individual instincts with the broader 'speciehood' of the individual student shaped by the values of the community of practice, institution or discipline in which the student is located. As more courses moved online, the greater focus on the learner necessitated creating more social contexts and what can be called 'a pedagogy of care' for students who had their own unique spaces for learning.

It is interesting to note how Maslow's terms such as actualization, creativeness, motivation and reflection have been integrated into discussions of teaching in these digital spaces. Maslow (1966) explains self-actualization as having a 'more efficient perception of reality and more comfortable relations with it' (cited in Lowry, 1973: xi). This perception focuses more on a macro-level view of student self-actualization than on the specific skills. Maslow explains that 'the consequence is that they [self-actualized individuals] live more in the real world of nature than in the man-made mass of concepts, abstractions, expectations, beliefs, and stereotypes that most people confuse with the real world' (cited in Lowry, 1973: xi–xii). This discussion of self-actualization reflects a greater concern with the development of the student in the digital space by connecting the real-world views of language and cultures that students bring to the space, creating an often chaotic context where both teachers and students may reach greater levels of understanding but also simultaneously allow for more negotiation.

When Yancey (2019) discusses implementing collaboration in blogging, there is a recognition of the social context of learning rather than focusing only on the skills needed to become literate. This same context appears in Hafner's (2015) implementation of digital storytelling. These pedagogies are designed to provide more autonomy by providing more awareness of their literacy communities. In flipped learning, the 'reach every child' metaphor illustrates how teachers could reflect less on which aspects of Bloom's taxonomy are connected to which space and more on how digital spaces could address the development of each student, much as Maslow's approach was orientated to the individual needs of each patient. While the ideas of Bloom and Maslow can be simultaneously integrated in the spaces, Maslow's research has been receiving greater attention in examining the impact of digital literacy.

Many of these spaces were designed to integrate Maslow's concerns by countering the isolation of students with spaces that potentially can be connected. In the anthropological films of Michael Wesch, the traditional classroom is depicted as a cold, alienating space where students have negative interactions with their teacher or their classmates. In his movie on classroom practices, Wesch has students sitting silently in a lecture hall holding up signs reflecting about their classroom experiences. These films have been used to critique the alienation of the lecture space and its 'sage on the stage' approach to teaching. Several attempts have been made to break down this alienation by using technologies, such as illustrated in the earlier discussions on using note-taking apps or open access textbooks, that leave the structure of the classroom intact.

The dilemma that all digital spaces face is integrating more personalized forms of learning, which has meant designing the type of digital space where each student learns best. The large MOOC platforms claim that they are designing new approaches to personalization. At the individual level, technologies, such as machine learning, can address this issue but without necessarily creating the intended space for such personalization. The goals for the digital story are for the students to share their own personal experiences using whatever language or form of English they choose.

Introducing alternative literacies can help teachers meet their goals. Blogging, for instance, could be shaped by its implementation to serve different pedagogical goals. It similarly allows students to express their ideas using various forms of Englishes that can be valued as texts by their classmates. Open access materials similarly provide information that can be used in the 'real world' of publishing. Open access does not simply provide information, it can also serve to redesign the publishing experience, expanding how new information is created and distributed, which, in turn, requires new pedagogical approaches to prepare the participants in these spaces.

The publishing space can connect these developments in how knowledge is created and distributed with the design of a pedagogy for helping students negotiate the goals and constraints of the space. The design of a publishing space combines a pedagogy for teaching with support for the psychology of a student moving into a new and perhaps more hostile space. As with other spaces, it has its own unique requirements, such as choosing a journal or judging authentic from predatory journals. Its design, particularly in the context of the growth of open resources, provides a different role for the teacher. The space, which combines what is learned inside the classroom and the evaluation process from the journal, requires more than simply learning skills but also a psychological framework for the writer to respond to the range of emotional issues connected to publishing.

As with the development of literacy in other spaces, the goal is to create self-actualized students who can work independently to share their expressions of self with a potentially far greater and more complex audience than just the teacher. However, as Fitzpatrick (2011) argues, the highly controversial nature of current approaches to double-blind peer review contradicts the trends toward openness and the growth of the commons, as discussed in Chapter 1. Therefore, the peer review system often supplies contradictory evaluations from reviewers unknown to the author. Unlike the open 'wisdom of the crowds' approach found in MOOCs, the author does not know the reputation or source of the criticism, so that peer review, as Fitzpatrick argues, continues to be a 'gatekeeper' rather than a 'filterer', which Fitzpatrick feels is more compatible with contemporary forms of openness.

However, these spaces have not always been well modified. For example, until these limitations on peer review are addressed, authors still face the problem of negotiating these sometimes contradictory and usually anonymous criticisms. Therefore, an understanding of the publishing process and the roles of each participant becomes more important. The same approach to integrating the goals for publishing with the development of the self in academic writing has meant that understanding the publishing process and negotiating with reviewers may be more important than producing a publishable research paper. As Maslow argues, the process of individual creativity is not the product but the main goal, which in our case, refers to the development of literacy spaces for developing writers.

Maslow provides a framework for the role of the teacher, not as someone who is either a 'sage' or a 'guide', but as a designer scaffolding the writing process differently for each student. Maslow (1971) compares the role of the teacher to that of a boxing manager who needs to draw on the styles that everyone brings to the training space. Designing digital spaces, therefore, is about relationships between teacher, student and literacy and how these relationships can be mediated through the design of technological spaces. Teachers, of course, must 'train' every student, regardless of the cultures and languages students bring to the classroom; however, as Vandergriff (2016) argues, teachers can draw upon the various rhetorical and linguistic 'styles' that students bring to the spaces. Such is the basis for teaching in these spaces, from the flipped classroom to the publishing space. Students are not 'deficient' (e.g. Shapiro, 2014) either in their abilities or in their technological sophistication but bring their own 'content' to use within the constraints on the teacher/designer.

Different spaces supported different relationships among teachers and students. The digital story space allowed for different roles for the teacher, depending on their goals for using multimodality, particularly in their choices of technological tools for the classroom. The publishing space similarly has different roles as exemplified using the term 'broker' or 'sponsor' (Curry & Lillis, 2010). Brandt (2001) illustrates these variations in teachers' roles, which can depend on the backgrounds of the instructors or the assets and needs of the students. In some cases, the teacher may have 'expert' knowledge on the topic the student is researching, but in other cases, the teacher may know little or nothing about the content. I had a mathematics doctoral student who came to tutorials each week with a series of formulae on which he was working. Since I knew little about mathematics, I felt I was giving him little help. After the course, I asked him whether he benefited from the course, and he explained that it was useful to explain the formulae to me before explaining them to his advisor.

As a broker, I could play a much different role with a student who was writing about technology and language learning than one who was writing about mathematics. In the multimodal assignment, teachers could also relinquish some control in terms of which images the students chose and how they mixed them with their own stories. Maslow (1971) argues that it is the goal of creative individuals to integrate contrasting ideas for both teaching and learning. Implementing such goals often meant disrupting the traditional design for writing classrooms. For teachers, there was the goal of negotiating the disruption of the traditional writing classroom with these new technologies.

For the students, there was the disruption of their relationships with the instructors and with classmates, as well as the design of the assignments that enhanced the disruption. The idea that blogs could be used as texts could change how the students valued each other as classmates. These disruptions are also not clear, so the result is often a chaotic classroom beyond the control of either the teacher or the student. With the digital story, for example, it was the connections between the narratives, the images and even the music of the story with the words and texts designed to challenge or disrupt their understanding of literacy.

The openness of these spaces provided various modes of feedback from teachers, classmates, fellow participants and even anonymous reviewers who can help writers develop their research, perhaps utilizing these new resources that open access publication makes available. As shown in Lessig's (1999) discussion of the architecture of the internet, the designs of these spaces could still impact the acquisition of literacies, although still limited by the students and teachers who participated in them. In publishing, the writer might receive negative comments but could negotiate the comments during the revision process. Comer (2014) discusses her frustrations with the amount of criticism she was receiving from the participants.

Negative feedback is coming from many directions: some learners in the course who post complaints on forums; writing program administrators around the country posting to the Writing Program Administrators Listserv (WPA-L); commentators and pundits posting online and in publications. Some of the negative feedback from students involves confusion with the course site or critiques about course design. (Comer, 2014: 140)

Comer's concern with her own writing process reflects what Maslow (1962) called the final stage of the creative process as 'the comparisons, the judgments, the evaluations, the cold-calculating morning-after thoughts, the selections, the rejections'. It may be difficult to find a better explanation for the publishing process, but it is also appropriate for responding throughout these spaces.

This disruption of the teaching process is at the heart of the debate over digital literacies. Casanave (2017) criticized the number of digital resources necessary to create these spaces, although the tools necessary for designing these spaces can vary according to the backgrounds and abilities of the designers. Teaching digital storytelling requires both teachers and students to have certain skills and some visual literacy. The potential for lacking this technological knowledge can decenter the role of the teacher, as it might in other digital spaces. Then, there is simply the amount of time that teachers must spend on class design. Comer (2014) discusses the tremendous amount of time necessary, for example, to create the videos for her MOOC. Flipped classes also require more upfront time in designing videos and alternative classroom spaces. The idea that such objects could be shared and reused, thus saving much of the preparation time, has been one of the most fundamental principles of designing these spaces.

Coursera, the provider of these MOOCs, made available tools to help teachers standardize their teaching, although sometimes too restrictively (Comer, 2014). There is still a tremendous interest in digital literacies. Comer (2014) admits that she still wanted to teach her MOOC. Her more positive reflections of these new spaces were echoed by other MOOC teachers. Perhaps, the most important contribution of MOOCs, for example, has been the transfer of teaching approaches to the writing classroom. Halasek et al. (2016) found that many aspects of the MOOC, such as peer review, could be ported into their face-to-face classrooms. Comer similarly found aspects of how she connected the assignments so that the goals of the course could be transferred into her face-to-face course. Halasek et al. (cited in Krause, 2014) also acknowledge how their MOOC experiences have shaped how they respond to grading (or not grading) student papers in their face-to-face courses. I also felt the freedom shared by MOOC instructors over not having to give grades. Such examples highlight the connection between issues in technological spaces with issues throughout every writing pedagogy.

These examples illustrate how the role of the teacher is changing when new forms of digital literacy are introduced, sometimes with changes in the context of the literacy and sometimes with the literacy itself. We have seen how the implementation of digital literacies challenges the 'sage'–'guide' dichotomy as teachers emerge as the designers of the digital spaces. Comer (2014) describes herself as a 'facilitator', but her role during the MOOC was one of an instructor as well. If she added her work in designing the preliminary stages of the MOOC, her role would also be more consistent with that of a 'designer'. Having to play these multiple roles is the challenge all teachers creating digital spaces will encounter.

The Problems with Designing Digital Spaces

While the challenges in the design of digital spaces are continually addressed, one enduring issue has been the pockets of resistance to their implementation. In every space, there has been resistance by teachers and students to its implementation. There have been attempts to counter this resistance both through argumentation and research. Casanave (2017) has been cited throughout this book on the problems of digital writing. Belcher (2017) addressed some of Casanave's concerns by arguing that teachers have the responsibility for using the literacies with which their students may be familiar. This argument regarding technological literacies is consistent with previous arguments about print literacies. Resnick (1990) discussed the expectations and limitations of being literate. Literacy has become more an issue of exploring new ways of thinking rather than demonstrating familiarity with a set of rules. As found in the 19th and early 20th centuries, new ideas about literacy brought about new approaches to teaching, as has been seen in these digital spaces, which is not the only reason for implementing these spaces.

Plato's warning about the downsides of technology have become even more important as more technologies develop. The Web has fostered more and more technologies that challenge the values and norms related to literacy. Phones, social media and YouTube have raised issues ranging from privacy to the value of new literacies that teachers may find difficult to understand since they may contradict traditional values. As argued before, the role of teachers must become more flexible in these spaces. Nowhere has flexibility been more important than in assessment where questions are raised concerning the relevancy of applying traditional approaches to assessment in digital literacies.

The assessment of these digital spaces can have different goals: to assess its design for future remediation or to assess student performance in the space. The results of both goals may be limited or even impacted by the methodology of the assessment. As Curry and Lillis (2019) argue, much to its detriment, assessment has often resulted more from lore than research. Nevertheless, assessment can include such metrics as student evaluations, which cost much less and are more easily obtained than more formal evaluations. Some of the metrics are controversial. Arizona

State University, for example, recently cancelled its MOOC with EdX because of low completion rates and even lower rates on credit and subsequent enrollment than it had hoped for (McKenzie, 2019). The metrics regarding course completion or the number of participants might not indicate their value for learning to write. Clearly, traditional assessment values may fail to justify the courses, regardless of their quality. Many of the arguments for the value of these spaces has centered on theoretical discussions on the backgrounds of the students and the future directions for literacy. Therefore, Belcher's (2017) concern regarding the assessment of digital literacies remains as problematic as ever.

The Economic Constraints of Using Digital Spaces

The design of these spaces has often been constrained by their economics. As Graff (1991) has shown, there has long been a connection between literacy and economics. Such funding is usually beyond the reach of teachers and thus must be provided for the development of such spaces. That connection has been increased with the technological development of new digital spaces and practicing literacy. Each literacy space has been impacted by such economic constraints, from the costs of blogging to those for sustaining open access and the economics of publishing. The UNESCO ('The Impact of OER: Achievements and Challenges', 2019) report on open educational resources showed the deployment of OER to be overly constrained without government and institutional support. Issues regarding openness and copyright have furthered the controversy, often pitting creators against distributors.

Each new space has its own cost factors to be addressed if the space is to be sustained. Of primary interest has been access to the internet, which can vary both in cost and availability across and within different countries and regions. Even in wealthy countries, accessibility has been an ongoing political issue. While the costs for technology may be dropping, there are still costs necessary for developing and using these technologies. While some spaces, such as open access, have been designed to reduce costs, in some areas they have increased them.

Costs have often affected both the MOOC and flipped classroom spaces. Many of the companies distributing the xMOOCs have created business models involving charging participants for access, using a 'freemium' model where some access levels are free and some cost. The idea of pure 'openness' has faded as new business models often limit free access, although some MOOCs have remained open.

Similarly, MOOCs have reduced costs in some areas but have increased them in others, particularly for access. Flipped learning spaces can be designed using existing resources but may be improved with additional expenditure on accessibility, tools and even new furniture.

Often, practitioners have attempted to address these cost factors. Open access has been at the center of these highly contested areas of publishing costs, although the growth of open access has been constrained by the processing charges (Michael, 2019), which can affect some disciplines more than others. Publishers may have 'Gold' standards, where the charges can be folded into grants or hybrid journals, where some articles may be open and some not. *The Asian EFL Journal* charges $800, which it claims gives the author 'priority in the preliminary editorial review'. One goal for open access has been making research more available by creating free, online journals with changes in the intellectual property approaches through using Creative Commons. These changes in copyright allow authors to better retain control over how their research is distributed so that research articles can be read without charge and distributed over sites such as ResearchGate. However, users, such as those in the production of digital stories, may be constrained depending upon their interpretation of intellectual property laws.

Copyright is an important factor in determining costs and revenues. These spaces can still raise concerns about copyright as well as about providing information on who is reading a paper or watching a video. Issues such as linking, which has been an important part of intellectual property law controversies since the internet was first developed, have a new dimension with the expanded role of making connections. What Canagarajah (2018) refers to as 'rhizomatic' shifts in translingual learning may require new approaches to sharing intellectual property, which have been promoted by Creative Commons. Copyright can serve to raise the costs of both publishing and distribution. The current practices of publishers charging for Gold open access has made it almost impossible for many researchers, across both disciplines and regions, to participate. Open access journals must have sustainable funding to continue publishing but may not even be able to compete in providing these tools. Initial funding is also required for the initial production of learning objects such as the videos in flipped classrooms although in the long run these costs can be absorbed into their expanded usage.

Even open access sites require funding and sustainable business models. Gated journals, for example, have created several approaches to open access, often charging authors $2000–$3000 for providing open access. New publishers, many of which have been classified as 'predatory,' have sprung up, asking authors to support the open access of their research. Many publishers have also been investing in tools for archiving and distributing information, and even smaller companies with niche products, used for submitting, researching and distributing their work, sometimes bundling them into their existing sites, depending on one's outlook, to publish in these traditional outlets.

These acquisitions serve to create wider 'moats' that help ward off potential competitors, which have also changed the work process of journals as well as their ability to collect data about their authors (Anderson, 2018a). Turnitn.com is one example of how the usage of a tool can be expanded to create a more sustainable business model. The program was first used for copy-detection and then created features that provided the ability to use macros to give predetermined comments, all of which could be integrated into learning management systems. Later, they purchased a start-up for evaluating essays. With these additions, teachers were provided with a suite of tools, so they were less likely to give up the product or turn to another, perhaps less expensive choice.

MOOCs now employ various cost structures to raise revenues to make them more appealing to investors. FutureLearn, which was once totally funded by the Open University, received a large grant to diversify its sustainability. Coursera is now considered a hot startup in Silicon Valley (Adams, 2018). While these MOOCs could incorporate literacy instruction into these models, there is little indication that they are doing so. Flipped learning has also attracted new sources of potential revenue, such as training courses, conferences and journals.

As has been the case in the past (e.g. Dear, 2017), large companies have focused on the profit potential of these spaces (e.g. 'Flipped Classroom Market to 2023 with Key Players like Cisco, Dell, Adobe, Desire2Learn, Echo360, Panopto, OpenEye, Saba Software', 2018). New technologies have always impacted publishing, teaching and learning spaces, pressuring the less sustainable spaces to either find new sources of funding or disappear. Some tools often succumb to business pressures. I lost access to Xtranormal, an animation tool for designing videos, when the company went out of business and later had to pay for Screencast-O-Matic to make videos since the free model was not easily adaptable. Other spaces can retain a low-cost structure that can allow for wider usage. Blogging, for example, relies on platforms having free access. Multimodal projects, such as digital storytelling, use tools that are bundled with other software, and open access tools such as Audacity, another free tool for recording podcasts. However, there are more expensive programs for editing movies, and often significant costs for using intellectual property, which is an important consideration in the design of digital spaces.

The Possible Futures for Digital Literacy Spaces

There is no question that there has been resistance to digital literacies over whether these literacies are really 'writing'. Such resistance has placed greater importance on implementation. Regardless of how these digital spaces and literacies are implemented, their impact on teaching literacy can be substantial. Implementing these technological spaces must take account of the needs of the students, the goals of the curricula and the constraints from departments, institutions and governments. Speaking of MOOCs, but applicable to these literacies, Levine (cited in Krause, 2014) argues that these technologies can begin the conversation across all writing programs about both in-class and online writing, and, what may be of particular value to teachers of multilingual writing, how literacy approaches developed in a culture may be applicable to other cultures.

The answers to these questions in the future can depend on changes in these literacy spaces. Coursera sponsors a series of courses on English for Research Publication Purposes Specialization created in Russia (https://www.coursera.org/specializations/english-for-research-publication-purposes) that seem to address some of the language problems students may have when publishing. The Open University's Innovative Pedagogy 2019 (https://iet.open.ac.uk/file/innovating-pedagogy-2019.pdf) provides new spaces and learning approaches that someday might contribute to new designs of literacy spaces, but for now, literacy is seldom even mentioned. While much learning in online spaces has been influenced by in-class pedagogies, there has also been a reverse trend of moving pedagogies from the Web to the classroom.

In these literacy spaces, teachers often ask why they are implementing these technologies. How will they improve the writing process? Are there developments that can only be obtained through the implementation of digital literacies? New developments in technology can impact the literacy discussed in ways that can affect how traditional rhetorical concepts are viewed. The genres of writing, for example, occurring in these spaces are similar to those found in the classroom, although this relationship can vary from space to space. Teachers who want to teach argumentation, for example, now have a greater variety of texts to draw on, whether images or blogs, that shift writers into what Canagarajah (2018) calls a *bricoleur*. Moreover, the issues surrounding the roles of literacies in these spaces are comparable to those that teachers, students and administrators face with their use of technology, such as the amount of data mined about the students, which has increased with the growing concerns with privacy and the lack of access.

The proliferation of tools that can be incorporated into these spaces, each with their own affordances, has often been exploited in these digital literacy spaces. Different platforms have been used for supporting collaboration in different ways and for different purposes. Wikis (Kessler, 2009), Google docs (Abrams, 2019), as well as various graphic representations of data, can support different approaches to collaboration. Concordance programs have been implemented to help students with lexical and grammatical choices (Bloch, 2010; Yoon, 2008), although again the differences in their affordances can greatly impact their usability. A simple and free program like Google Ngram (https://books.google.com/ngrams), for example, can help students judge the appropriateness of their choices, particularly in areas such as collocation that are difficult to teach. Grammar checking tools, such as those built into Microsoft Word or externally used ones such as GradeProof (https://gradeproof.com/) and Grammarly (https://www.grammarly.com/), can help correct lower-level lexical and syntactic problems. Word recognition programs, such as those built into word processing programs or stand-alone programs such as Text Aloud, can help some students identify the problems in their texts without help from the teacher.

The goals for our multimodal assignments often used the tools associated with creating digital stories, since it was important to understand the affordances of tools such as Audacity for creating a podcast or Movie Maker for mixing the podcast with images. Both teachers and students need to understand the affordances of these tools in developing the agency and voice throughout the topics that the students choose. In part, some challenges were legacies of the development of these spaces before being integrated into the classroom. Other forms of literacies are developing, often from outside the classroom, which will make the academic writing classroom more chaotic if these changes are incorporated.

New forms of literacies, such as blogs and digital stories, are beginning to have greater value in academic writing. Their impact has affected traditional literacy practices in areas such as citing sources. However, they also raise problems. The affordances of the tools used with these literacies, such as Turnitin's ability to harvest student writing or Proctorio's monitoring of test-taking (e.g. Morrison & Heilweil, 2020), can impact the design and pedagogy of these spaces, sometimes with consequences beyond the control of the teacher. While we may have hoped that implementing these tools reflected our goals for the academic writing class, we soon found that we could not completely control how students learned or what literacies they used, which was a valuable lesson for teaching in digital spaces where both groups can break the rules to create new forms.

The evolution of all these spaces inevitably leads to new pedagogical problems, such as providing feedback and assessment, for which new tools, including voice and video, are implemented. The designs of these new literacy spaces may raise new problems for students regarding sharing their work outside the classroom, finding new resources for their projects and connecting to other students, teachers or researchers to share these resources. New technologies are being developed and implemented to address these issues, but they may require teachers and students to acquire new skills and utilize resources in new or different ways.

Their implementation incorporates issues in design that Norman (2007, 2013) has discussed, which can both constrain and support new designs. Regardless of the design, there are questions over the determinism these technologies may bring to learning to write; that is, how they impact the pedagogies they were implemented to support. Controversies over technology in society inevitably spill into the writing classroom and become more pervasive as new technologies are adapted into our daily lives. Using Facebook, Google and Twitter has not meant that the issues surrounding them, such as privacy or metrics, will die away when they move inside the classroom. Snapchat, Instagram and WeChat, as well as other programs used for communicating, have all impacted the literacies that students are bringing into the classroom and how different forms of writing are valued but are still constrained by their business models as well as privacy concerns.

The problems that writing teachers often face may not change in digital spaces although the spaces and corresponding tools may be very different. These changes will not become simpler to address with the evolution of new tools and new spaces. New technologies will inevitably be introduced that may further complicate the design of these spaces. The future of all these spaces may include a greater role for data analytics, for example, in evaluating the value of research, how students are using the technologies they have access to and the degree to which technology is impacting their learning behaviors. The collection of data has raised various ethical issues both inside and outside the classroom (Downes, 2020), often related to their lack of transparency. Of all the data collected, which data is most valuable for teachers in the design of digital spaces? Even traditional means of assessment such as end-of-class surveys can provide some data to help teachers assess technological usage and remediate problems. Such data can be shared with students for remediating classroom design. The resulting changes in all these areas of design and usage may be inevitable although the consequences are not clear.

The Consequences of Digital Designs on Literacy Spaces

One of the most exciting consequences of these digital spaces is how they support students crossing the borders of different literacies. The introduction of these new technological spaces can support writers and teachers in crossing the boundaries between these digital and textual literacies by remixing different forms of textual and visual literacies. Their interoperability means that the spaces, as well as the tools used for creating them, will be more familiar. Writing therefore become more multimodal; for example, students may already be familiar not only with multimodal literacies but also with the tools used as they cross these boundaries.

The 2020 Horizon Report lists artificial intelligence and the growing importance of open standards as the two main technological trends for the future, what '7 Things You Should Read About NGDLE' (2018) refers to as the next-generation digital learning environment (NGDLE), which may provide a more integrative environment than current learning management systems. Some technologies have either been introduced or conceptualized as part of the writing process. Controversial tools, such as Turnitin and other copy-detection programs, have been used by publishers, teachers and students for detecting copying, even though they raise new controversies about the relationship between teacher and student in these digital spaces as well as new concerns about student privacy.

Artificial intelligence and natural language processing can be used by students in revising programs such as GradeProof to search for lexical and syntactic problems as well as by publishers for evaluating copy. Coursera uses natural language processing for peer review by comparing current submissions with past ones. Blockchain, which was designed primarily for business, has been growing in popularity and may be used in education for making and evaluating connections, although its uses are unclear (Weller, 2020). Szafir and Mutlu (2013) suggest ways that artificial intelligence can be used in the design of technologically enhanced literacy spaces.

Students have attempted in a number of ways to take more control over the design process. To counter the chaotic discussion boards, the participants could create their own literacy spaces, such as blogs or Twitter, to post comments. New technologies have led to new tools for these problems. Georgia Tech, for example, developed a tool using artificial intelligence to respond to questions on the discussion boards. Publishers have begun to use artificial intelligence to evaluate the writing of proposals. At the same time, artificial intelligence can be used for surveillance and is still constrained by the same questions that technology has always had to address, what has been referred to as 'garbage in/garbage out' in making decisions that humans have always made.

New technologies are continually being developed as the nature of the university evolves (Davidson, 2017), which raise new and old questions on teaching writing. These programs may improve as new algorithms are developed and computational power increases, but their impact may still be limited by how learning theories and design problems are addressed. Do the new algorithms incorporated in proofreading programs relieve the anxiety some students have with using English? Can these connections provide students with a greater sense of identity or at least relieve some of the stress associated with writing? How will spaces like the flipped classroom and the MOOC evolve as new technologies are introduced? What new tools will be developed for the writing classroom? Will these new forms of communication mean that the languages most connected with literacy will change? What are the ethical considerations associated with each of these spaces and technologies?

Both teachers and students will need to consider the ethical issues associated with every form of technology: the privacy concerns, the use of intellectual property and the changing relationships between teachers and students, all of whom will be tasked with not only answering these questions but also assessing how well they are answered. Therefore, the goal here is to place teachers and students at the center of a discussion of literacy since they are the ones who understand best the answers to these questions.

As old tools vanish or become obsolete and new tools emerge, these new or evolved spaces and their learning experiences will also change, again reflecting the power of Raymond's (1999) 'commons' metaphor for allowing increased participation among teachers to remediate the weaknesses of these spaces. That is how teachers can play a central role as designers of these literacy experiences but also how these spaces will develop. While these digital spaces are constructed to improve learning, their future will be greatly affected by which tools are available and how these tools are designed, understood, implemented and modified.

Writing teachers will always be concerned with how these tools impact the languages these spaces most value. Such changes are at the heart of Crystal's (2011) argument that these new technologies reflect linguistic and literacy evolutions. Discussion of multimodality provides different perspectives on what translingualism can mean in multilingual composition (e.g. Wysocki *et al.*, 2019). While teachers still have a powerful role in instantiating these new forms of language in the classroom, they can still be constrained by the institutional and disciplinary goals. However, these tools do not determine either teaching or learning but are used only for supporting the goals for expression or creativity that were designed into the course. As Lessig (1999) has argued, tools are always constrained by their architecture, as well as the technical and social backgrounds of the teachers and students, which contributes to the often chaotic nature of the digital classroom.

An individual classroom tool can provide efficiency as well as support to the writing process. A new app may provide greater efficiency but not change the relationships within the classroom. The tools discussed here, however, still do not bring the same efficiency as do the tools often found in our homes and our classrooms. However, these technologies may have features, such as Zoom's ability to create small groups, that teachers may exploit. In some ways, the 'chaos' found in our classrooms is antithetical to the efficiency of the tools found in the home or classroom, so teachers must be 'agile' to respond to this chaos.

This book has just begun to explore the possibilities for teaching multilingual writing. Many questions remain. How disruptive will these spaces be for multilingual writing? Many of the new technologies, even those yet unproven, can disrupt learning. They all, however, place new demands on teachers/facilitators. These new technologies have placed new burdens for understanding the potential of each technology's affordances in the writing process as their meanings evolve.

The new spaces have made the terms used to describe learning similarly contested and raise another set of questions for teachers to struggle with: for example, what does it mean when we discuss hybrid learning? Does it mean hybridity as in an automobile where electricity or gas is used depending on the driving conditions? Or does hybridity mean a mixing of two forms, the brick-and-mortar space with the digital space so that new literacy forms emerge? These literacy forms reflect how some issues found in digital spaces are also found in writing classes. These challenges can change how information is delivered but need to be carefully evaluated by teachers who may not have the criteria or the background to evaluate them. Terms such as 'Ed Tech 2.0' or 'Flipped Learning 3.0' have been used to differentiate our current technologies from those used in the past 20 years. Ed Tech 3.0 has emerged as data becomes more distributed and more devices are used for creating and distributing information.

The design of these digital spaces has challenged many of the dichotomies that have developed in discussing multilingual research. Concepts such as 'guide/sage' and 'digital native/digital immigrant' have been challenged by the new roles for both teachers and students. Both teachers and students may need to adjust their 'mindsets' (e.g. Dweck, 2007) to adapt to these different approaches to literacy. Teachers cannot avoid the chaos often associated with these spaces, which challenges them to keep up with the changes in pedagogies and technologies. Teachers often lack technical and financial support in the design of online spaces (Jaschik & Lederman, 2018), which can leave them floundering.

The issues that teachers face in these digital spaces are sometimes the same issues in traditional classrooms. Changing social and political factors can impact how these technologies are implemented. As teachers face the challenges of pandemics or other global challenges, technologies become more important in teaching writing. New sources of data and how technologies can aid in its access can greatly affect the publishing space. In their book on online writing instruction, Borgman and McArdle (2020) use 'golf' as a metaphor for addressing technology. Golf is a useful metaphor for teachers as we realize that our own skills are constantly evolving (hopefully) and that some of us will never play as well as professionals, but the game remains interesting and challenging for everyone. However, improving one's game is not only about acquiring skills but also having the possible financial resources to buy equipment as well as negotiating a new set of hype, rules and constraints.

As the contexts for these new literacies emerge, these issues will also evolve – how audiences are viewed with multimodal literacies or what assessments can best exploit the affordances of the technologies – are just two of many issues that have been reimagined. Throughout this book, the future in designing digital literacy spaces has been shown to be already present but not distributed equally across disciplines. Current approaches are largely classroom centered, but with a recognition, as Heath (1983) argued, that new literacies can be found everywhere and can be brought into the classroom both as alternative forms and in relation to existing literacies.

These controversies will impact literacy teaching both online and in classrooms as students continuously cross the boundaries between print and digital spaces. These boundaries are not only theoretical but also physical, as the designs challenge traditional views of classroom spaces, labs, learning management systems and gated journals. This approach requires teachers to commit to the development of a new curriculum as well as their own personal growth. However, it must respond to the needs of students, not only for understanding content but also for their social interactions. Technology is not a replacement for teaching but can require even more training. Teacher training requires investment in professional development, which includes providing teachers with more time for reflecting, training and collaborating with students, technical designers and administrators. Since teachers may not always have the funding for professional development, various technological spaces, such as MOOCs, have been created for increasing professional development.

What then should be included in professional development: for example, how can teachers connect to each other for learning and support or how can they measure the results of this professional development. Teachers do not have to be 'techies' to implement these literacies, although having support networks is important, rather they need to be able to adapt to the possible chaos resulting from these changes. Whether the teacher is a planner or likes to quickly improvise, the key is to be willing to constantly revise their designs. New approaches to designing literacy spaces, such as webinars (e.g. the Electronic Village Online) and websites such as the Flipped Global Network, which provides a magazine (https://flr.flglobal.org/ and a website (https://flglobal.org/elements10b/) and the Flipped Learning Network (https://flippedlearning.org/) can support teacher development by providing opportunities to connect with like-minded teachers. Traditional discussion boards sponsored by the Consortium on Graduate Communication or the second language writing intersection (slw-is) provide spaces where teachers can connect with each other. MOOCs still offer limited opportunities for professional development. The digitization of literacies has become one of the greatest challenges for teachers to keep up with the latest technologies and participate in discussions of the latest issues while addressing the same problems writing teachers have always addressed.

In the end, the values of these digital literacies are how students learn, which can vary across ability, age and background, and how teachers design and teach. Do students learn better individually or in groups? How much autonomy should the spaces provide? What new forms of literacies will be developed and how will they be valued? The answers to such questions are not determined by the architecture of the space but can be impacted by it. Implementing these literacies requires a change in 'mindsets' (e.g. Dweck, 2007) for valuing them. However, as Chen et al. (2015) found, changing these attitudes requires both a sense of obtaining an immediate return and hoping for future development, that is what do the teachers and students bring to the context and how what they bring needs to develop. Given the evolution of the technologies and controversies regarding these spaces, it may be difficult for both teachers and students to perceive both the possibilities and limitations.

This book has focused on the design of spaces, not on the tools used to design the spaces, but still recognizing the value of the tools. The book did not discuss the use of many tools that some teachers may feel are useful, such as Twitter. On the other hand, many of the tools discussed here can be used across spaces, both online and in class, although each brings its own affordances that can shape the literacies created in the spaces. Teachers can structure their literacy spaces without overwhelming themselves or their students with new technologies. Inevitably the technologies will change, and pedagogies will change with them. Teachers' roles will change as well, as my own experiences illustrate. I shared with my students the criticism of my earlier book on technology that I had ignored Facebook, a technological space I have never completely understood. After class, a Libyan student shared with me some remarkable videos of the civil war in Libya that had been posted on Facebook.

The COVID-19 pandemic dramatically increased the need to create digital spaces for remote or online learning. Moving face-to-face classes online has highlighted issues concerning how the design of digital spaces incorporates economic and racial factors already existing in society. These issues had been previously discussed but without the immediacy to address them that the pandemic brought, particularly in global spaces (Bates, 2020). Coursera has reported large increases in enrollment, though not necessarily for literacy. A report by Bay View Analytics (2020) on the shift in American universities to online teaching showed variations in how instructors were using technology, often depending on their prior experiences.

The COVID-19 pandemic has raised greater concerns about the mental health of students in these digital spaces ('Powering What's Next for Higher Education', 2020), a factor that needs to be considered at both the social and cognitive levels of their designs. In our assessment of our students in the publishing space, they expressed how they missed even the limited social interaction of face-to-face classes while supporting the flexibility of the Zoom tutorials. Different spaces incorporate different tools with different affordances that can impact writing. Clearly, teaching in a time of crisis, such as caused by the COVID-19 virus, has placed a greater focus on digital spaces as courses for every level of student have moved online.

The technological designs of these spaces is continually changing. Many uses of technology depend on our understanding of these technologies, as well as blending in-person and online spaces; however, I do not see the future clearly enough to conceive of technological spaces in these ways, and probably few creators of technologies did either. Mark Zuckerberg, the creator of Facebook, probably did not foresee it being used as my students did. Even Steve Jobs may not have initially realized how his design of the Mac or the iPhone as a 'cathedral' might evolve into being a 'commons' as new generations participate in their usages.

It is important that teachers remain in touch with their students through both formal and informal means of instruction and assessment, as they might in any literacy space. Teachers may find themselves in the same dilemma over whether these spaces positively contribute to the literacy development of their students even though in many cases they may not know. The goal was not to make students literate but to help them explore the different contexts and goals for multiple literacies. The students enter these spaces with different technological and personal backgrounds, so they may not have the same motivations for improving their literacies. Teachers may encounter the hype that comes with each new technology and therefore must critically evaluate each new iteration of a space. Implementing some technologies may transform these spaces into 'dystopias', bringing new concerns regarding privacy and disinformation (e.g. Weller, 2020), as illustrated by the controversy over the harvesting of data by grammar-checking programs or monitoring programs for online testing. Watters (2020) warns that the original meaning of 'Luddism' referred not to the technology but to how it is used, a concern we have today with our implementations. Many of the issues that are faced in our day-to-day lives can be found in our universities, The ease with which institutions, whether universities or corporations, can collect student data is one such development, which may change as literacy spaces become 'commons' where more teachers, students and forms of information can interact without the walls and information silos prevalent today. These spaces can contain the same factors that traditional spaces do: the student–teacher relationships, the nature of the assignments and course requirements.

These spaces were designed to help students see the disruptions in their views of literacy, from both in-class and global perspectives. Corporations such as Coursera are eager to participate in these disruptions, particularly for students outside of traditional universities, although without the concern for pedagogy that it is hoped these spaces can provide. How these spaces develop, whether cooperatively or in competition, may be both unpredictable and unstoppable. This change may be the most challenging issue for teachers.

References

2017 Horizon Report (2017, Feb. 15). See https://library.educause.edu/resources/2017/2/2017-horizon-report.

2018 Global State of Peer Review (2018) Publons. See https://publons.com/static/Publons-Global-State-Of-Peer-Review-2018.pdf.

2019 Higher Education Edition (2019) Educause Horizon Report. See https://library.educause.edu/-/media/files/library/2019/4/2019horizonreport.pdf?la=en&hash=C8E8D444AF372E705FA1BF9D4FF0DD4CC6F0FDD1.

2020 Educause Horizon Report™ | Teaching and Learning Edition (2020) See https://library.educause.edu/-/media/files/library/2020/3/2020_horizon_report_pdf.pdf?la=en&hash=08A92C17998E8113BCB15DCA7BA1F467F303BA80.

'7 Things You Should Know About the HyFlex Course Model' (2010) Educause. See https://library.educause.edu/resources/2010/11/7-things-you-should-know-about-the-hyflex-course-model.

'7 Things You Should Know About Flipped Classrooms' (2012) Educause Learning Initiative. See https://library.educause.edu/resources/2012/2/7-things-you-should-know-about-flipped-classrooms.

'7 Things You Should Read About NGDLE' (2018) Educause. https://library.educause.edu/resources/2018/1/7-things-you-should-read-about-ngdle.

'7 Things You Should Know About … Domain of One's Own' (2019) Educause. See https://library.educause.edu/-/media/files/library/2019/10/eli7170.pdf.

'A Review of Flipped Classroom Research, Practice, and Technologies' (2014) The International Higher Education Teaching and Learning Association. See https://www.hetl.org/a-review-of-flipped-classroom-research-practice-and-technologies.

'A mystery: "none of the authors listed had any involvement with or knowledge of the article"' (2020) Retraction Watch. See https://retractionwatch.com/2020/03/25/a-mystery-none-of-the-authors-listed-had-any-involvement-with-or-knowledge-of-the-article/#more-119156.

Abasi, A.R., Akbar, N. and Graves, B. (2006) Discourse appropriation, construction of identities, and the complex issue of plagiarism: ESL students writing in graduate school. *Journal of Second Language Writing* 15, 102–117.

Abrams, Z.I. (2019) Collaborative writing and text quality in Google Docs. *Language Learning & Technology* 23, 22–42. See https://www.lltjournal.org/item/3105.

'Action Agenda for the future of the TESOL profession' (2017) TESOL International Association. See https://www.tesol.org/docs/default-source/advocacy/action-agenda-final-web.pdf?sfvrsn=2.

Adams, S. (2018, Oct 16) This company could be your next teacher: Coursera plots a massive future for online education. *Forbes*. See https://www.forbes.com/sites/susanadams/2018/10/16/this-company-could-be-your-next-teacher-coursera-plots-a-massive-future-for-online-education/#655768192a39.

Adler-Kassner, L. and Wardle, E. (2015) *Naming What We Know: Threshold Concepts of Writing Studies*. Ogden, UT: Utah University Press.

Agarwal, A. (2018) Reimagine Education. Open edX conference. See https://www.youtube.com/watch?v=ZvJpdRWLA_w.

Ahearn, A. (2018, Nov 28) Stop asking about completion rates: Better questions to ask about MOOCs in 2019. Edsurge. See https://www.edsurge.com/news/2018-11-28-stop-asking-about-completion-rates-better-questions-to-ask-about-moocs-in-2019.

Alexander, B. (2017) *The New Digital Storytelling: Creating Narratives with New Media*. Santa Barbara, CA: Praeger.

Almquist, M., von Allmen, R.S., Carradice, D., Oosterling, S.J., McFarlane, K. and Wijnhoven, B. (2017) A prospective study on an innovative online forum for peer reviewing of surgical science. *PLoS ONE* 12 (6) See https://journals.plos.org/plosone/article?id=10.1371/journal.pone.0179031.

Amaya-Rios, J., Secker, J. and Morrison, C. (2016) Lecture recording in higher education: Risky business or evolving open practice. University of Kent. See https://ukcopyright-literacy.files.wordpress.com/2016/11/lecture-recording-survey-report-final1.pdf.

Anderson, C. (2006) *The Long Tail: How Endless Choice is Creating Unlimited Demand*. London: Random House.

Anderson, K. (2018a, June 19) Interview: The BMJ's patient review initiative – A novel expansion of peer review. Scholarly Kitchen. See https://scholarlykitchen.sspnet.org/2018/06/19/interview-bmjs-patient-review-initiative-novel-expansion-peer-review/?informz=1.

Anderson, K. (2018b, Aug 7) Denialism on the rocks: It just got a lot harder to pretend that predatory publishing doesn't matter. Scholarly Kitchen. See https://scholarlykitchen.sspnet.org/2018/08/07/denialism-rocks-justgot-lot-harder-pretend-predatory-publishing-doesnt-matter.

Anderson, R. (2017a, Dec 4) The University of California and Elsevier: An interview with Jeff MacKie-Mason. Scholarly Kitchen. See https://scholarlykitchen.sspnet.org/2019/05/06/the-university-of-california-and-elsevier-an-interview-with-jeff-mackie-mason/.

Anderson, R. (2017b, July 25) Cabell's new predatory journal blacklist: A review. Scholarly Kitchen. See https://scholarlykitchen.sspnet.org/2019/05/01/cabells-predatory-journal-blacklist-an-updated-review/?informz=1.

Anderson, R. (2017c, Dec 4) Federal Trade Commission and National Institutes of Health take action against predatory publishing practices. Scholarly Kitchen. See https://scholarlykitchen.sspnet.org/2017/12/04/federal-trade-commission-national-institutes-health-take-action-predatory-publishing-practices/?informz=1.

Anderson, R. (2018a, July 18) One author's novel approach to article self-publishing: An interview with Allyson Mower. Scholarly Kitchen. See https://scholarlykitchen.sspnet.org/2018/07/18/one-authors-novel-approach-article-self-publishing-interview-allyson-mower.

Anderson, R. (2018b) Do you have concerns about Plan S? Then you must be an irresponsible, privileged, conspiratorial hypocrite. Scholarly Kitchen. See https://scholarlykitchen.sspnet.org/2018/11/26/do-you-have-concerns-about-plan-s-then-you-must-be-an-irresponsible-privileged-conspiratorial-hypocrite/?informz=1.

Anderson, R. (2018c, Aug 6) Interpreting Elsevier's acquisition of Aries systems. Scholarly Kitchen. See https://scholarlykitchen.sspnet.org/2018/08/06/interpreting-elseviers-acquisition-aries-systems/?informz=1.

Anderson, R. (2019a, Jan 15) Sherlock Holmes and the case of the baffling funder mandate. Scholarly Kitchen. See https://scholarlykitchen.sspnet.org/2019/01/15/sherlock-holmes-and-the-case-of-the-baffling-funder-mandate/?informz=1.

Anderson, R. (2019b, May 1) Cabell's predatory journal blacklist: An updated review. Scholarly Kitchen. See https://scholarlykitchen.sspnet.org/2019/05/01/cabells-predatory-journal-blacklist-an-updated-review/?informz=1.

Anderson, J. and Rainie, L. (2018) The future of well-being in a tech-saturated world. Pew Research Center. See https://www.pewresearch.org/internet/2018/04/17/the-future-of-well-being-in-a-tech-saturated-world.

Angélil-Carter, S. (2000) *Stolen Language? Plagiarism in Writing*. Harlow: Longman.

Anson, C.M. and Moore, J.L. (2017) *Critical Transitions: Writing and the Question of Transfer*. Boulder, CO: University of Colorado Press. See https://wac.colostate.edu/docs/books/ansonmoore/transfer.pdf.

Anson, C.M., Dannels, D.P. and Laboy, J.I. (2016) Students' perceptions of oral screencast responses to their writing: Exploring digitally mediated identities. *Journal of Business and Technical Communication* 30, 378–411.

Arfstom, K.M. (2013, Oct 16) Flipped learning in the UK – two examples. See https://oerhub.net/blogs/flipped-learning-in-the-uk-two-examples.

Arfstom, K.M., Hamdan, N., McKnight, K. and McKnight, P. (2013) A review of flipped learning. See http://www.flippedlearning.org/cms/lib07/VA01923112/Centricity/Domain/41/LitReview-FlippedLearning.pdf.

Asadi, A., Nader, N., Rezvani, M.J. and Asadi, F. (2018) Fake/bogus conferences: Their features and some subtle ways to differentiate them from real ones. *Science and Engineering Ethics* 24, 779–784.

Atkinson, D., Crusan, D., Matsuda, P.K., Ortmeier-Hooper, C., Ruecker, T., Simpson, S. and Tardy, C. (2015) Clarifying the relationship between l2 writing and translingual writing: An open letter to writing studies editors and organization leaders. *College English* 77, 383–386.

Aufderheide, P. and Jaszi, P. (2012) *Reclaiming Fair Use: How to Put Balance Back in Copyright*. Chicago, IL: University of Chicago Press.

Baker, W. (2014) Interpreting the culture in intercultural rhetoric: A critical perspective from English as a *lingua franca* studies. In D. Belcher and G. Nelson (eds) *Critical and Corpus-Based Approaches to Intercultural Rhetoric* (pp. 22–45). Ann Arbor, MI: The University of Michigan Press.

Baldwin, M. (2018) Scientific autonomy, public accountability, and the rise of 'peer review' in the Cold War United States. *Isis* 109 (3), 538–558.

Ball, C., Morrison, A. and Eyman, D. (2018) The rise of multimodality in academic publishing. In M.J. Curry and T. Lillis (eds) *Global Academic Publishing: Policies, Practices, and Pedagogies* (pp. 166–183). Bristol: Multilingual Matters.

Bar-Ilan, J. and Halevi, G. (2018, June 27) Retracted papers keep being cited as if they weren't retracted. Two researchers suggest how Elsevier could help fix that. Retraction Watch. See https://retractionwatch.com/2018/06/27/retracted-papers-keep-being-cited-as-if-they-werent-retracted-two-researchers-suggest-how-elsevier-could-help-fix-that/#more-67350.

Barlow, J.P. (1994) The economy of ideas. *Wired*. See https://www.wired.com/1994/03/economy-ideas.

Basken, P. (2017a, Sept. 12) Why Beall's list died — and what it left unresolved about open access. *The Chronicle of Higher Education*. See https://www.chronicle.com/article/Why-Beall-s-List-Died-/241171.

Basken, P. (2017b, Sept 22) Why Beall's blacklist of predatory journals died. *The Chronicle of Higher Education*. See http://www.universityworldnews.com/article.php?story=20170920150122306.

BasuMallick, C. (2019, Feb 19) 4 MOOC trends we expect to see in 2019. *Hrtechnologist*. See https://www.hrtechnologist.com/articles/learning-development/4-mooc-trends-we-expect-to-see-in-2019.

Bates, T. (2013) Discussing design models for hybrid/blended learning and the impact on the campus. See http://www.tonybates.ca/2013/05/08/discussing-design-models-for-hybridblended-learning-and-the-impact-on-the-campus.

Bates, T. (2016) Are you ready for blended learning? See http://www.tonybates.ca/2016/12/12/are-we-ready-for-blended-learning.

Bates, T. (2020, Apr 27) Crashing into online learning: A report from five continents – and some conclusions. *Online Learning and Distance Education Resources*. See https://www.tonybates.ca/2020/04/26/crashing-into-online-learning-a-report-from-five-continents-and-some-conclusions/.

Batson, T., Paharia, N. and Kumar, M.S.V. (2008) A harvest too large? A framework for educational abundance. In T. Liyoshi and M.S.V. Kumar (eds) *Opening Up Education: The Collective Advancement of Education through Open Technology, Open Content, and Open Knowledge* (pp. 89–103). Cambridge, MA: MIT Press. See https://oerknowledgecloud.org/sites/oerknowledgecloud.org/files/0262033712chap6.pdf.

Bawarshi, A.S. and Reiff, M.J. (2010) *Genre: An Introduction to History, Theory, Research, and Pedagogy*. West Lafayette, IN: Parlor Press.

Bazerman, C. (1988) *Shaping Written Knowledge: The Genre and Activity of the Experimental Article in Science*. Madison, WI: The University of Wisconsin Press.

Bazerman, C. (2013) *A Rhetoric of Literate Action. The WAC Clearinghouse*. See https://wac.colostate.edu/books/perspectives/literateaction-v1/.

Beall, J. (2012, Sept. 12) Predatory publishers are corrupting open access. *Nature*. See https://www.nature.com/news/predatory-publishers-are-corrupting-open-access-1.11385.

Beall, J. (2013) The open access movement is not really about open access. *TripleC: Communication, Capitalism & Critique* 11, 589–597.

Belcher, D. (2017) On becoming facilitators of multimodal composing and digital design, *Journal of Second Language Writing* 38, 80–85.

Belcher, W.L. (2009) *Writing Your Journal Article in 12 Weeks*. Thousand Oaks, CA: Sage.

Benchekroun, S. and Knepper, M. (2020, Mar 25) Coronavirus is a wakeup call for academic conferences. Here's why. Scholarly Kitchen. See https://scholarlykitchen.sspnet.org/2020/03/25/guest-post-coronavirus-is-a-wakeup-call-for-academic-conferences-heres-why/?informz=1.

Bennett, S.K. and Kervin, K.L. (2008) The 'digital natives' debate: A critical review of the evidence. *British Journal of Educational Technology* 39, 775–786.

Bensen, P. and Voller, P. (2014) *Autonomy and Independence in Language Learning*. London: Routledge.

Bergmann, J. (2017, Apr 6) Flipped Learning 3.0: New data on engagement, interaction and retention [video]. See http://www.jonbergmann.com/flipped-learning-3-0-new-data-on-engagement-interaction-and-retention.

Bergmann, J. (2018, May 10) Do you know what you don't know about flipped learning? *The Flipped Learning 3.0 Magazine*. See http://flr.flglobal.org/?p=8784.

Bergmann, J. (2019) The global elements of effective flipped learning [video]. See https://flglobal.org/elements41/.

Bergmann, J. and Sams, A. (2012) *Flip your Classroom: Reach Every Student in Every Class Every Day*. Eugene, OR: International Society for Technology in Education.

Bergmann, J. and St Clair Smith, E. (2017) *Flipped Learning 3.0: The Operating System for the Future of Talent Development*. Irving, CA: Flipped Learning Global Publishing.

Berkenkotter, C. (2012) Genre change in the digital age: Questions about dynamism, affordances, evolution. In C. Berkenkotter, V.K. Bhatia and M. Gotti (eds) *Insights into Academic Genres* (pp. 31–45). Bern: Peter Lang.

Berners-Lee, T. (1999) *Weaving the Web: The Original Design and Ultimate Destiny of the World Wide Web*. New York: Harper Collins.

Biagioli, M. (2003) *Scientific Authorship: Credit and Intellectual Property in Science*. London: Routledge.

Biber, D. and Barbieri, F. (2007) Lexical bundles in university spoken and written registers. *English for Specific Purposes* 26 (3), 263–286.

Binfield, P. (2013) Open access megajournals – Have they changed everything? *OA Week*. See http://www.openaccessweek.org/events/open-access-megajournals-have-they-changed-everything-1.

Blankstein, M and Wolff-Eisenberg, C. (2019) Ithaka S+R US faculty survey 2018. See https://sr.ithaka.org/wp-content/uploads/2019/03/SR-Report-US-Faculty-Survey-2018-04122019.pdf.

Bloch, J. (2001) Plagiarism and the ESL student: From printed to electronic texts. In D. Belcher and A. Hirvela (eds) *Linking Literacies: Perspectives on L2 Reading–Writing Connections* (pp. 209–228).

Bloch, J. (2007a) Abdullah's blogging: A Generation 1.5 student enters the blogosphere. *Language, Learning and Technology* 11, 128–141. See https://www.lltjournal.org/item/2577.

Bloch, J. (2007b) *Technology in the L2 Composition Classroom*. Ann Arbor, MI: University of Michigan Press.

Bloch, J. (2008a) Plagiarism in an intercultural rhetoric context: What we can learn about one from the other. In U. Connor, E. Nagelhout and W. Rozycki (eds) *Contrastive Rhetoric: Reaching to Intercultural Rhetoric* (pp. 257–274). Amsterdam: John Benjamins.

Bloch, J. (2008b) Blogging as a bridge between multiple forms of literacy: The use of blogs in an academic writing class. In D. Belcher and A. Hirvela (eds) *Oral/Written Connections* (pp. 288–309). Ann Arbor, MI: University of Michigan Press.

Bloch, J. (2010) A concordance-based study of the use of reporting verbs as rhetorical devices in academic papers. *Journal of Writing Research* Special Corpus Issue. See http://www.jowr.org/articles/vol2_2/JoWR_2010_vol2_nr2_Bloch.pdf.

Bloch, J. (2012) *Plagiarism, Intellectual Property and the Teaching of L2 Writing*. Bristol: Multilingual Matters.

Bloch, J. (2015) The use of digital storytelling in an academic writing course: The story of an immigrant. In M. Roberge, K.M. Losey and M. Wald (eds) *Teaching U.S-Educated Multilingual Writers: Practices from and for the Classroom* (pp. 178–204). Ann Arbor, MI: University of Michigan Press.

Bloch, J. (2016) The challenge and opportunity for MOOCs for teaching writing. *Journal of Academic Writing* 6. See http://e-learning.coventry.ac.uk/ojs/index.php/joaw/article/view/301.

Bloch, J. (2018) Digital storytelling in the L2 academic writing classroom: Expanding the possibilities. *Dialogues* 2. See https://dialogues.ojs.chass.ncsu.edu/index.php/dialogues/article/view/30.

Bloch, J. (2019) Digital storytelling in the L2 graduate classroom: Expanding the possibilities of personal expression and textual borrowing. In S. Khaddka and J.C. Lee (eds) *Bridging the Multimodal Gap* (pp. 182–200). Ogden, UT: Utah University Press.

Bloch, J. and Wilkinson, M.J. (2013) *Teaching Digital Literacies*. Alexandria, VA: TESOL Press.

Blood, R. (2000) Weblogs: A history and perspective. *Rebecca's Pocket*. See http://www.rebeccablood.net/essays/weblog_history.html.

Bloom, B.S., Engelhart, M.D., Furst, E.J., Hill, W.H. and Krathwohl, D.R. (1956) *Taxonomy of Educational Objectives: The Classification of Educational Goals. Handbook I: Cognitive Domain*. New York: David McKay Company.

Blum, S.D. (2009) *My Word!: Plagiarism and College Culture*. Ithaca, NY: Cornell University Press.

Bocanegra-Valle, A. (2014) 'English is my default academic language': Voices from LSP scholars publishing in a multilingual journal. *Journal of English for Academic Purposes* 13, 65–77.

Boelens, R., De Wever, B. and Voet, M. (2017) Four key challenges to the design of blended learning: A systematic literature. *Educational Research Review* 22, 1–18.

Borgman, J. and McArdle, C. (2020) *Personal, Accessible, Responsive, Strategic: Resources and Strategies for Online Writing Instructors*. Fort Collins, CO: WAC Clearinghouse. See https://wac.colostate.edu/books/practice/pars/.

Bornmann, L. and Mutz, R. (2015) Growth rates of modern science: A bibliometric analysis based on the number of publications. *Journal of the Association for Information Science and Technology* 66, 2215–2222.

Bowen, T. and Whithaus, C. (2013) *Multimodal Literacies and Emerging Genres*. Pittsburgh, PA: University of Pittsburgh Press.

boyd, d. (2014) *It's Complicated: The Social Lives of Networked Teens*. New Haven, CT: Yale University Press. See https://seeingcollaborations.files.wordpress.com/2014/08/itscomplicated.pdf.

Boyle, J. (2010) *The Public Domain: Enclosing the Commons of the Mind*. New Haven, CT: Yale University Press.

Brand, S. (1985) Information wants to be free. *Whole Earth Review* 49.

Brandt, D. (2001) *Literacy in American Lives*. New York: Cambridge University Press.

Bravo, G., Grimaldo, F., López-Iñesta, E., Mehmani, B. and Squazzoni, F. (2019) The effect of publishing peer review reports on referee behavior in five scholarly journals. *Nature Communications* 10, 1–8.

Budapest Open Access Initiative (2012, Sep. 12) See https://www.budapestopenaccessinitiative.org/boai-10-recommendations.

Bruner, J. (1994) The remembered self. In U. Neisser and R. Fivush (eds) *The Remembering Self: Construction and Agency in Self-Narrative* (pp. 41–54). Cambridge: Cambridge University Press.

'Building your blockchain advantage' (2019) Educause Horizon Report. See https://library.educause.edu/-/media/files/library/2019/4/2019horizonreport.pdf?la=en&hash=C8E8D444AF372E705FA1BF9D4FF0DD4CC6F0FDD1.

Buranen, L. (1999) But I *wasn't* cheating. Plagiarism and the cross-cultural mythology. In L. Buranen and A. Roy (eds) *Perspectives on Plagiarism and Intellectual Property in a Postmodern World* (pp. 63–74). Albany, NY: State University of New York Press.

Bush, V. (1945) As we may think. *The Atlantic*. See https://www.theatlantic.com/magazine/archive/1945/07/as-we-may-think/303881.

Canagarajah, S. (2010) The tyranny of the new referee: TQ editor's pondering. See http://www.personal.psu.edu/asc16/blogs/TQeditor/2010/02.

Canagarajah, A.S. (2013) Negotiating translingual literacy: An enactment. *Research in the Teaching of English* 48, 40–67.

Canagarajah, A.S. (2015) 'Blessed in my own way': Pedagogical affordances for dialogical construction in multilingual student writing. *Journal of Second Language Writing* 27, 122–139.

Canagarajah, A.S. (2016) TESOL as a professional community: A half-century of pedagogy, research, and theory. *TESOL Quarterly* 50, 7–41.

Canagarajah, A.S. (2018) Translingual practice as spatial repertoires: Expanding the paradigm beyond structuralist orientations. *Applied Linguistics* 39, 31–54.

Carbone, N. (2014) Here a MOOC, there a MOOC. In S. Krause and C. Lowe (eds) *Invasion of the MOOCs: The Promises and Perils of Massive Open Online Courses* (pp. 193–203). Anderson, SC: Parlor Press.

Cargill, M. and O'Connor, P. (2006) Developing Chinese scientists' skills for publishing in English: Evaluating collaborating-colleague workshops based on genre analysis. *Journal of English for Academic Purposes* 5, 207–221.

Carr, N. (2011) *The Shallows: How the Internet is Changing the Way We Think, Read and Remember*. New York: Norton.

Casanave, C.P. (2017) *Controversies in Second Language Writing* (2nd edn). Ann Arbor, MI: University of Michigan Press.

Casanave, C.P. and Vandrick, S. (2003) *Writing for Scholarly Publication*. Mahwah, NJ: Erlbaum.

Castelló Badia, M. (2019) Students' research writing: Why, when and how. Presented at the 10th Conference of the European Association for the Teaching of Academic

Writing. Chalmers University of Technology, Göteborg Sweden. See https://2019. eataw.eu/video-recordings-and-session-material.

Cayley, R. (2020) Using genre to teach the publication-based thesis. In L.E. Bartlett, S.L. Tarabochia, A.R. Olinger and M.J. Marshall (eds) *Diverse Approaches to Teaching, Learning, and Writing Across the Curriculum: IWAC at 25* (pp. 153–163). Ft. Collins, CO: WAC Clearinghouse. See https://wac.colostate.edu/docs/books/iwac2018/chapter9.pdf.

Cazden, C., Cope, B., Fairclough, N. and Gee, J. (1996) A pedagogy of multiliteracies: Designing social futures. *Harvard Educational Review* 66, 60–92.

Chae, B. and Jenkins, M. (2015) A qualitative investigation of faculty open educational resource usage in the Washington Community and Technical College System: Models for support and implementation. See https://drive.google.com/file/d/0B4eZdZMtpULyZC1NRHMzOEhRRzg/view?pli=1.

Chandrasoma, R., Thompson, C.M. and Pennycook, A. (2004) Beyond plagiarizing: Transgressive and nontransgressive intertextuality. *Journal of Language, Identity, and Education* 3, 171–193.

Chen, P., Ellsworth, P.C. and Schwarz, N. (2015) Finding a fit or developing it: Implicit theories about achieving a passion for work. *Personality and Social Psychology Bulletin* 41, 1411–1424.

Chesbrough, H. (2006) *Open Innovation: The New Imperative for Creating and Profiting from Technology.* Cambridge: Harvard Business Press.

Christensen, C. (1997) *The Innovator's Dilemma: When New Technologies Cause Great Firms to Fail.* Cambridge: Harvard Business Review Press.

Cheng, L., Ritzhaupt, A.D. and Antonenko, P. (2018) Effects of the flipped classroom instructional strategy on students' learning outcomes: a meta-analysis. *Education Tech Research Development.* See https://link.springer.com/article/10.1007/s11423-018-9633-7.

Cheng, S.C., Hwang, G.J. and Lai, C.L. (2020) Critical research advancements of flipped learning: A review of the top 100 highly cited papers. *Interactive Learning Environments* 1–17.

Clark, R., Kau, A. and Delgado, E. (2018a) Do adaptive lessons for pre-class experience improve flipped learning? 2018 AASEE Conference & Exposition. See http://www.asee-se.org/proceedings/ASEE2018/papers2018/14.pdf.

Clark, R., Kau, A., Lou, Y., Scott, A. and Besterfield-Sacre, M. (2018b) Evaluating blended and flipped instruction in numerical methods at multiple engineering schools. *International Journal for the Scholarship of Teaching & Learning* 12. See https://digitalcommons.georgiasouthern.edu/ij-sotl/vol12/iss1/11.

Clarke, M. (2018, Oct 4) Navigating the big deal: A guide for societies. Scholarly Kitchen. See https://scholarlykitchen.sspnet.org/2018/10/04/navigating-the-big-deal/.

Cochran, A. (2018, Dec 7) Plan S: A mandate for gold OA with lots of strings attached. Scholarly Kitchen. See https://scholarlykitchen.sspnet.org/2018/12/07/plan-s-a-mandate-for-gold-oa-with-lots-of-strings-attached/?informz=1.

Cochran, A. (2020, Mar 11) Making a plan when planning is impossible. Scholarly Kitchen. See https://scholarlykitchen.sspnet.org/2020/03/11/making-a-plan-when-planning-is-impossible/.

Cochran, A. and Wulf, K. (2019, Apr 24) Editing is at the heart of scholarly publishing. Scholarly Kitchen. See https://scholarlykitchen.sspnet.org/2019/04/24/editing-is-at-the-heart-of-scholarly-publishing/?informz=1.

Colvard, N.B., Watson, C.E. and Park, H. (2018) The impact of open educational resources on various student success metrics. *International Journal of Teaching and Learning in Higher Education* 30 (2), 262–276.

Comer, D.K. (2014) Learning how to teach … differently: Extracts from a MOOC instructor's journal. In S. Krause and C. Lowe (eds) *Invasion of the MOOCs: The Promises and Perils of Massive Open Online Courses* (pp. 130–149). Anderson, SC: Parlor Press.

Comer, D.K. and White, E.M. (2016) Adventuring into MOOC writing assessment: Challenges, results, and possibilities. *College Composition and Communication* 67, 318–359.

Connor, U. (2011) *Intercultural Rhetoric in the Writing Classroom*. Ann Arbor, MI: University of Michigan Press.

Coombes, C., Anderson, N.J. and Stephenson, L. (eds) (2020) *Professionalizing Your English Language Teaching*. New York: Springer.

Corcoran, J.N., Englander, K. and Muresan, L-M. (2019) Diverse global perspectives on scholarly writing for publication. In J.N. Corcoran, K. Englander and L.-M. Muresan (eds) *Diverse Global Perspectives on Scholarly Writing for Publication* (pp. 1–16). Abingdon: Taylor & Francis.

Cormier, D. (2008a, June 3) Rhizomatic education: Community as curriculum. *Dave's Educational Blog*. See http://davecormier.com/edblog/2008/06/03/rhizomatic-education-community-as-curriculum .

Cormier, D. (2008b, Oct 2) The CCK08 MOOC: Connectivism course, 1/4 way. *Dave's Educational Blog*. See http://davecormier.com/edblog/2008/10/02/the-cck08-mooc-connectivism-course-14-way.

Crane, D. (1972) *Invisible Colleges: Diffusion of Knowledge in Scientific Communities*. Chicago, IL: University of Chicago Press.

Cronin, C. (2017) Open education, open questions. *Educause Review*. See https://er.educause.edu/articles/2017/10/open-education-open-questions.

Crotty, D. (2016, Aug 31). When bad science wins, or 'I'll See It When I Believe It'. *Scholarly Kitchen*. See https://scholarlykitchen.sspnet.org/2016/08/31/when-bad-science-wins-or-ill-see-it-when-i-believe-it.

Crotty, D. (2017, Oct) Study suggests publisher public access outpacing open access: Gold OA decreases citation performance. Scholarly Kitchen. See https://scholarlykitchen.sspnet.org/2017/10/04/study-suggests-publisher-public-access-outpacing-open-access-gold-oa-decreases-citation-performance/?informz=1.

Crotty, D. (2018, Aug 19) Revisiting: Six years of predatory publishing. Scholarly Kitchen. See https://scholarlykitchen.sspnet.org/2018/08/14/revisiting-six-years-predatory-publishing/.

Crowther, K. (2017) Composing communities: Blogs as learning communities in the first-year composition classroom. In K. Crowther (ed.) *First-Year Composition Classroom* (pp. 117–127). Fort Collins, CO: WAC Clearinghouse.

Crusan, D. (2010) *Assessment in the Second Language Writing Classroom*. Ann Arbor, MI: University of Michigan Press.

Crystal, D. (2011) *Internet Linguistics: A Student Guide*. London: Routledge.

Crystal, M. (2019, May 22) *PLOS* journals now OPEN for published peer review. *The Official PLOS Blog*. See https://blogs.plos.org/plos/2019/05/plos-journals-now-open-for-published-peer-review/.

Cuban, L. (2001) *Oversold and Underused*. Cambridge, MA: Harvard University Press.

Cunningham, U. (2016) Language pedagogy and non-transience in the flipped classroom. *Journal of Open, Flexible, and Distance Learning* 20, 44–58.

Curry, M.J. and Lillis, T. (2004) Multilingual scholars and the imperative to publish in English: Negotiating interests, demands, and rewards. *TESOL Quarterly* 38, 663–688.

Curry, M.J. and Lillis, T. (2006) Professional academic writing by multilingual scholars: Interactions with literacy brokers in the production of English-medium texts. *Written Communication* 23, 3–35.

Curry, M.J. and Lillis, T. (2010) Academic research networks: Accessing resources for English-medium publishing. *English for Specific Purposes* 29, 281–295.

Curry, M.J. and Lillis, T. (2016) Academic writing for publication in a multilingual world. In R. Manchón and P.K. Matsuda (eds) *Handbook of Second and Foreign Language Writing* (pp. 201–222). Berlin: De Gruyter Mouton.

Curry, M.J. and Lillis, T. (2018) *Global Academic Publishing: Policies, Perspectives and Pedagogies.* Bristol: Multilingual Matters.

Curry, M.J. and Lillis, T. (2019) Unpacking the lore on multilingual scholars publishing in English: A discussion paper. MDPI, 7. See https://www.mdpi.com/2304-6775/7/2/27/htm.

Czerniewicz, L., Deacon, A., Walji, S. and Glover, M. (2017) OER in and as MOOCs. In C. Hodgkinson-Williams and P.B. Arinto (eds) *Adoption and Impact of OER in the Global South* (pp. 349–386). Cape Town: African Minds.

Daiute, C. (1985) *Writing and Computers.* Reading, MA: Addison-Wesley.

Davidson, C. (2012, May 9) Why flip the classroom when we can make it do cartwheels? Fast Company. See https://www.fastcompany.com/1679807/why-flip-the-classroom-when-we-can-make-it-do-cartwheels.

Davidson, C. (2017) *The New Education: How to Revolutionize the University to Prepare Students for a World in Flux.* New York: Basic Books.

Davis, P. (2009, June 10) Open access publisher accepts nonsense manuscript for dollars. Scholarly Kitchen. See https://scholarlykitchen.sspnet.org/2009/06/10/nonsense-for-dollars.

Davis, P. (2010, Aug 10) The mismeasure of man, funds, and open access experiments. Scholarly Kitchen. See https://scholarlykitchen.sspnet.org/2010/08/10/mismeasure-of-oa/.

Davis, P. (2016, Aug 23) Scientific reports on track to become largest journal in the world. Scholarly Kitchen. See https://scholarlykitchen.sspnet.org/2016/08/23/scientific-reports-on-track-to-become-largest-journal-in-the-world.

Davis, P. (2018, May 21) Journals lose citations to preprint servers. Scholarly Kitchen. See https://scholarlykitchen.sspnet.org/2018/05/21/journals-lose-citations-preprint-servers-repositories/?informz=1.

Davis, P. (2019, Jan 3) Poor financials push *PLOS* to ponder prospects. Scholarly Kitchen. See https://scholarlykitchen.sspnet.org/2019/01/03/poor-financials-pushes-plos-to-ponder-future-prospects/?informz=1.

Dear, B. (2017) *The Friendly Orange Glow: The Untold Story of the PLATO System and the Dawn of Cyberculture.* New York: Pantheon.

Deckert, G.D. (1993) Perspectives on plagiarism from ESL students in Hong Kong. *Journal of Second Language Writing* 2, 131–148.

Denbo, S. (2020, Mar 4) Open peer review in the humanities. Scholarly Kitchen. See https://scholarlykitchen.sspnet.org/2020/03/04/guest-post-open-peer-review-in-the-humanities/?informz=1.

Department of Education (2019) Realising the potential of technology in education: A strategy for education providers and the technology industry. See https://assets.publishing.service.gov.uk/government/uploads/system/uploads/attachment_data/file/791931/DfE-Education_Technology_Strategy.pdf.

Diwanji, P., Hinkelmann, K. and Friedrich, H. (2018) Enhance classroom preparation for flipped classroom using AI and analytics. *Proceedings of the 20th International Conference on Enterprise Information Systems (ICEIS 2018)* 1, 477–483. See https://www.scitepress.org/papers/2018/68076/68076.pdf.

Doctorow, C. (2002, May 31) My blog, My outboard brain. See http://archive.oreilly.com/pub/a/javascript/2002/01/01/cory.html.

Dodds, F. (2019, Sept 2) The future of academic publishing: Revolution or evolution revisited. *Wiley Online Library.* See https://onlinelibrary.wiley.com/doi/abs/10.1002/leap.1258.

Dorman, E. and Webb, M. (2017) The flipped experience for Chinese university students studying English as a foreign language. *TESOL Journal* 8, 102–141.

Dove, A. (2018) The successes and lessons learned of flipped learning. In E. Langran and J. Borup (eds) *Proceedings of the Society for Information Technology & Teacher Education International Conference* (pp. 1794–1801). Washington, DC: Association for the

Advancement of Computing in Education (AACE). See https://www.learntechlib.org/primary/p/182771/.

Downes, S. (2001) Learning objects: Resources for distance education worldwide. *The International Review of Research in Open and Distributed Learning* 2. See http://www.irrodl.org/index.php/irrodl/article/view/32/378.

Downes, S. (2011) *Free Learning: Essays on Open Educational Resources and Copyright*. See http://www.downes.ca/files/books/FreeLearning.pdf.

Downes, S. (2019) A look at the future of open educational resources. *The International Journal of Open Educational Resources*. See https://www.ijoer.org/a-look-at-the-future-of-open-educational-resources/.

Downes, S. (2020) *Ethics, Analytics, and the Duty of Care*. See https://downes.pressbooks.com/chapter/chapter-three/.

Dweck, C. (2007) *Mindset: The New Psychology of Success*. New York: Ballantine Books,

Eddy, S.L. and Hogan, K.A. (2014) Getting under the hood: How and for whom does increasing course structure work. *CBE Life Sciences Education* 13, 453–468. See http://www.lifescied.org/content/13/3/453.full#content-block.

Edington, M. (2018) Loving our modesty. *Journal of Scholarly Publishing* 49, 287–304.

Eisenstein, E. (1980) *The Printing Press as an Agent of Change*. Cambridge: Cambridge University Press.

Elbow, P. (1991) Reflections on academic discourse: How it relates to freshman and colleagues. *College English* 53, 135–155.

Elbow, P. (2007) Voice in writing again: Embracing contraries. *College English* 70, 168–188.

Elgort, I. (2017) Blog posts and traditional assignments by first- and second-language writers. *Language, Learning, & Technology* 21, 52–72.

Elola, I. and Oskoz, A. (2017) Writing with 21st century social tools in the L2 classroom: New literacies, genres, and writing practices. *Journal of Second Language Writing* 36, 52–60.

Emerson, L. (2016) *The Forgotten Tribe: Scientists as Writers*. Ft. Collins, CO: WAC Clearinghouse. See https://wac.colostate.edu/docs/books/emerson/tribe.pdf.

Esposito, J. (2013, Dec 16) Parting company with Jeffrey Beall. Scholarly Kitchen. See https://scholarlykitchen.sspnet.org/2013/12/16/parting-company-with-jeffrey-beall.

Esposito, J. (2017, Apr 26) Decline and fall of the editor. Scholarly Kitchen. See https://scholarlykitchen.sspnet.org/2017/04/26/decline-fall-editor.

Esposito, J. (2018a, June 20) Counting the holes in the swiss cheese: 'Read and Publish' discovers America. Scholarly Kitchen. See https://scholarlykitchen.sspnet.org/2018/06/20/counting-holes-swiss-cheese-read-publish-discovers-america/?informz=1.

Esposito, J. (2018b, July 16) Why hasn't the academy taken back control of publishing already? Scholarly Kitchen. See https://scholarlykitchen.sspnet.org/2018/07/16/hasnt-academy-taken-back-control-of-publishing-already/?informz=1.

Esposito, J. (2019a, Mar 5) Revisiting: Governance and the not-for-profit publisher. Scholarly Kitchen. See https://scholarlykitchen.sspnet.org/2019/03/05/revisiting-governance-and-the-not-for-profit-publisher-2/?informz=1.

Esposito, J. (2019b, May 6) The new 'University Journals' in the marketplace. Scholarly Kitchen. https://scholarlykitchen.sspnet.org/2019/05/06/the-new-university-journals-in-the-marketplace/?informz=1.

'Faculty views on the teaching tools of tomorrow. How digital textbooks and tech innovation impact professors' work' (2018) *The Chronicle of Higher Education*. See http://results.chronicle.com/LP=1817.

Farr, M. (1993) Essayist literacy and other verbal performances. *Written Communication* 10 (1), 4–38.

Farrow, R. (2014) OER impact: Collaboration, evidence, synthesis. See http://conference.oeconsortium.org/2014/wp-content/uploads/2014/02/Paper_51-OER-Impact.pdf.

Fasel, I. and Hartse, J.H. (2018) Reconsidering 'predatory' journals open access journals in the age of globalized English-language academic publishing. In M.J. Curry and T. Lillis (eds) *Global Academic Publishing: Policies, Perspectives, and Pedagogies* (pp. 200–213). Bristol: Multilingual Matters.

Feenberg, A. (1999) *Questioning Technology*. London: Routledge.

Ferguson, R., Coughlan, T., Egelandsdal, K., Gaved, M., Herodotou, C., Hillaire, G., Jones, D., Jowers, I., Kukulska-Hulme, A., McAndrew, P., Misiejuk, K., Ness, I.J., Rienties, B., Scanlon, E., Sharples, M., Wasson, B., Weller, M. and Whitelock, D. (2019) *Innovating Pedagogy 2019: Open University Innovation Report 7*. Milton Keynes: The Open University. See https://iet.open.ac.uk/file/innovating-pedagogy-2019.pdf.

Ferric, F.C., Bennett, J.W. and Casadevall, A. (2013) Males are overrepresented among life science researchers committing scientific misconduct. *mBio*. https://mbio.asm.org/content/mbio/4/1/e00640-12.full.pdf.

Fitzpatrick, K. (2011) *Planned Obsolescence: Publishing Technology and the Future of the Academy*. New York: New York University Press.

Fitzpatrick, K. (2016, Apr 11) Academia, not edu. See https://kfitz.info/academia-not-edu.

Flaherty, C. (2019a, Aug 26) Questionable rejection. *Inside Higher Education*. See https://www.insidehighered.com/news/2019/08/26/sociologist-says-journal-rejected-her-paper-because-shes-shared-it-elsewhere.

Flaherty, C. (2019b, Oct 23) Where research meets profits. *Inside Higher Education*. See https://ahrecs.com/resources/where-research-meets-profits-inside-higher-ed-colleen-flaherty-october-2019.

Flaherty, C. (2020, May 11) Big proctor. *Inside Higher Education*. See https://www.insidehighered.com/news/2020/05/11/online-proctoring-surging-during-covid-19.

'Flipped Classroom Market to 2023 with Key Players like Cisco, Dell, Adobe, Desire2Learn, Echo360, Panopto, OpenEye, Saba Software' (2018) Big Market Research. See https://www.openpr.com/news/1366832/Flipped-Classroom-Market-to-2023-with-Key-Players-like-Cisco-Dell-Adobe-Desire2Learn-Echo360-Panopto-Open-Eye-Saba-Software.html.

'Flipped Classroom Trends: A Survey of College Faculty' (2015) Faculty Focus. See https://www.facultyfocus.com/wp-content/uploads/2015/08/Flipped-Classroom-Trends_FFReport-2015.pdf.

Flower, L.S. and Hayes, J.R. (1980) The cognition of discovery: Defining a rhetorical problem. *College Composition and Communication* 31, 21–32.

Flowerdew, J. (2000) Discourse community, legitimate peripheral participation, and the nonnative-English-speaking scholar. *TESOL Quarterly* 34, 127–150.

Flowerdew, J. (2015) Some thoughts on English for research publication purposes and related issues. *Language Teaching* 48, 250–262.

Flowerdew, J. and Dudley-Evans, T. (2002) Genre analysis of editorial letters to international journal contributors. *Applied Linguistics* 23, 463–489.

Flowerdew, J. and Wang, S.H. (2016) Author's editor revisions to manuscripts published in international journals. *Journal of Second Language Writing* 32, 39–52.

Foer, F. (2017) *World Without Mind: The Existential Threat of Big Tech*. New York: Penguin.

Fox, H. (1994) *Listening to the World: Cultural Issues in Academic Writing*. Urbana, IL: NCTE.

Freeman, D. (1983) *Margaret Mead and Samoa*. Cambridge, MA: Harvard University Press.

Freeman, J. (2016) Designing and building a graduate communication program at the University of Toronto. In S. Simpson, N.A. Caplan, M. Cox and T. Philips (eds) *Supporting Graduate Student Writers* (pp. 222–238). Ann Arbor, MI: The University of Michigan Press.

Friend, C. (2020) Double-Open Peer Review: Shaping the Teaching Community. *Hybrid Pedagogy*. See https://hybridpedagogy.org/double-open-peer-review/.

Fund, S. (2018, May 14) From supermarkets to marketplaces: The evolution of the open access ecosystem. Scholarly Kitchen. See https://scholarlykitchen.sspnet.org/2018/05/14/guest-post-supermarkets-marketplaces-evolution-open-access-ecosystem.

Gardner, C.C. and Gardner, G.J. (2016) Fast and furious (at publishers): The motivations behind crowdsourced research sharing. *College & Research Libraries* 78, 2. See https://crl.acrl.org/index.php/crl/article/view/16578/18024.

Gardner, J.N. and Barefoot, B.O. (2017) *Your College Experience: Strategies for Success* (13th edn). Boston, MA: Bedford/St. Martins.

Garfield, E. (2005) The Agony and the Ecstasy: The History and Meaning of the Journal Impact Factor. Paper presented at the International Congress on Peer Review and Biomedical Publication Chicago, 16 September 2005. See http://garfield.library.upenn.edu/papers/jifchicago2005.pdf,

Gass, S., Winke, P., Isbell, D.R. and Ahn, J. (2019) How captions help people learning languages: A working-memory, eye-tracking study. *Language, Learning, & Technology* 31, 84–104.

Gee, J. (2003) *What Video Games Have to Teach Us About Learning and Literacy*. London: Palgrave/MacMillan.

Gee, J. (2004) *Situated Language and Learning: A Critique of Traditional Schooling*. New York: Routledge.

Geisler, C. (2016) Opening: Toward an integrated approach. *Journal of Writing Research* 7, 417–424.

Gentil, G. and Séror, J. (2014) Canada has two official languages — or does it? Case studies of Canadian scholars' language choices and practices in disseminating knowledge, *Journal of English for Academic Purposes* 13, 17–30.

Gere, A.R. (1994) Kitchen tables and rented rooms: The extra curriculum of composition. *College Composition and Communication* 45, 75–92.

Gerstein, J. (2011) The flipped classroom model: A full picture. See http://usergenerat-ededucation.wordpress.com/2011/06/13/the-flipped-classroom-model-a-full-picture.

Gibson, J.J. (1977) The theory of affordances. In R. Shaw and J. Bransford (eds) *Perceiving, Acting, and Knowing: Toward an Ecological Psychology* (pp. 67–82). Hillsdale, NJ: Erlbaum.

Gibson, W. (1999) 'The Science in Science Fiction' on Talk of the Nation, NPR (30 Nov.).

Gilliland, B., Oayama, A. and Stacey, P. (2018) Second language writing in a MOOC: Affordances and missed opportunities. *TESL-EJ*. See http://www.tesl-ej.org/wordpress/issues/volume22/ej85/ej85a3.

Gilster, P. (1997) *Digital Literacy*. New York: John Wiley.

Godwin-Jones, R. (2018) Second language writing online: An update. *Language Learning & Technology* 22, 1–15.

Gonzalez, J. (2014, Mar 24) Modifying the flipped classroom: The 'in-class' version. *Edutopia*. See https://www.edutopia.org/blog/flipped-classroom-in-class-version-jennifer-gonzalez.

Gonzalez, L. (2015) Multimodality, translingualism, and rhetorical genre studies. *Composition Forum* 31. See https://compositionforum.com/issue/31/multimodality.php.

Goody, J. (1977) *The Domestication of the Savage Mind*. New York: Cambridge University Press.

Graff, G. (2003) *Clueless in Academe: How Schooling Obscures: The Life of The Mind*. New Haven, CT: Yale University Press.

Graff, H.J. (1991) *The Legacies of Literacy*. Bloomington, IN: Indiana University Press.

Graff, H.J. (2015) *Undisciplining Knowledge*. Baltimore, MD: Johns Hopkins University Press.

Greenfield, G. and Hibbert, P. (2017) Reflective and reflexive practices in the flipped classroom. In C. Reidsema, L. Kavanagh, R. Hadgraft and N. Smith (eds) *The Flipped*

Classroom: Practice and Practices in Higher Education (pp. 75–86). Singapore: Springer.

Greeno, J. (1994) Gibson's affordances. *Psychological Review* 2, 336–342.

Groom, J. (n.d.) A domain of one's own. See https://www.youtube.com/watch?v=PHLZF WGou_M.

Guerin, C. (2016) Connecting the dots: Writing a doctoral thesis by publication. In C. Badenhorst and C. Guerin (eds) *Research Literacies and Writing Pedagogies for Masters and Doctoral Writers* (pp. 31–50) Leiden: Brill Publishers.

Guerra, J.C. and Shivers-McNair, A. (2017) Toward a new vocabulary of motive. In B. Horner and L. Tetreault (eds) *Crossing Divides: Exploring Translingual Writing Pedagogies and Programs* (pp. 19–30). Ogden, UT: Utah University Press.

Guinda, C. and Hyland, K. (2012) *Stance and Voice in Written Academic Genres*. London: Palgrave/MacMillan.

Gustafsson, M., Ericksson, A. and Karlsson, A. (2016) Facilitating writing in the tension between quasi-generic and the multidisciplinary: Chalmers University of Technology. In S. Simpson, N.A. Caplan, M. Cox and T. Philips (eds) *Supporting Graduate Student Writers* (pp. 255–271). Ann Arbor, MI: The University of Michigan Press.

Haas, C. (1989) Does the medium make a difference? Two papers with pen and paper and with computer. *Human-Computer Interactions* 4, 169–189.

Haas, C. and Flower, L. (1988) Rhetorical reading strategies and the construction of meaning. *College Composition, & Communication* 39, 67–183. See https://www.jstor.org/stable/358026?seq=1#metadata_info_tab_contents.

Habermas, J. (2001) The public sphere. In S. Seidman (ed.) *On Society and Politics: A Reader* (pp. 231–236). Boston, MA: Beacon Press.

Hafner, C.A. (2015) Remix culture and English language teaching: The expression of learner voice in digital multimodal compositions. *TESOL Quarterly* 49, 486–450.

Hafner, C.A. and Ho, W.V.J. (2020) Assessing digital multimodal composing in second language writing: Towards a process-based model. *Journal of Second Language Writing* 47. See https://doi.org/10.1016/j.jslw.2020.100710.

Hafner, C.A., Chik, A. and Jones, R.H. (2015) Digital literacies and language learning. *Language Learning & Technology* 19, 1–7.

Halasek, K., McCorkle, B., Selfe, C.L., DeWitt, S.L., Delagrange, S., Michaels, J. and Clinnin, K. (2016) A MOOC with a view: How MOOCs encourages us to reexamine pedagogical doxa. In S. Krause and C. Lowe (eds) *Invasion of the MOOCs: The Promises and Perils of Massive Open Online Courses* (pp. 156–166). Anderson, SC: Parlor Press.

Hall, J. (2018) The translingual challenge: Boundary work in rhetoric & composition, second language writing, and WAC/WID. Writing across the disciplines. See https://wac.colostate.edu/docs/atd/trans/hall2018.pdf.

Hanauer, D.I. and Englander, K. (2011) Quantifying the burden of writing research articles in a second language: Data from Mexican Scientists. *Written Communication* 28, 403–416.

Hanauer, D.I., Sheridan, C.L. and Englander, K. (2019) Linguistic injustice in the writing of research articles in English as a second language: Data from Taiwanese and Mexican researchers. *Written Communication* 36, 136–154.

Hardin, G. (1968) The tragedy of the commons. *Science* 162, 1243–1248. See https://science.sciencemag.org/content/162/3859/1243.

Harnad, S. (1995) A subversive proposal. In A.S. Okerson and J. O'Donnell (eds) *Scholarly Journals at the Crossroads: A Subversive Proposal for Electronic Publishing*. Publishing Association of Research Libraries. See https://www.google.com/books/edition/Scholarly_Journals_at_the_Crossroads/InDgAAAAMAAJ?hl=en&gbpv=1&printsec=frontcover.

Harnad, S. (2011) Open access is a research community matter, not a publishing community matter. See https://eprints.soton.ac.uk/272403/1/harnad-LLinE-1.pdf.

Harnad, S. (2014) The post-Gutenberg open access journal. In B. Cope and A. Phillips (eds) *The Future of The Academic Journal* (2nd edn, pp. 179–194). Amsterdam: Elsevier.

Hart-Davidson, B. (2014) Learning many-to-many: The best case for writing in digital environments. In S.D. Krause and C. Lowe (eds) *Invasion of the MOOCs: The Promises and Perils of Massive Open Online Courses* (pp. 212–222). Anderson, SC: Parlor Press.

Harvey, H.B. and Weinstein, D.F. (2017) Predatory publishing: An emerging threat to the medical literature. *Academic Medicine* 92, 150–151.

Harwood, N. and Hadley, G. (2004) Demystifying institutional practices: Critical pragmatism and the teaching of academic writing. *English for Specific Purposes* 23, 355–357.

Head, K. (2014) The hidden costs of MOOCs. In S. Krause and C. Lowe (eds) *Invasion of the MOOCs: The Promises and Perils of Massive Open Online Courses* (pp. 45–55). Anderson, SC: Parlor Press.

Heath, S.B. (1983) *Ways with Words: Language, Life and Work in Communities and Classrooms.* New York: Cambridge University Press.

Hegarty, B. (2015) Attributes of open pedagogy. A model for using open educational resources. *Educational Technology* 3–13. See https://upload.wikimedia.org/wikipedia/commons/c/ca/Ed_Tech_Hegarty_2015_article_attributes_of_open_pedagogy.pdf.

Heilwell, R. (2020, May 4) Paranoia about cheating is making online education terrible for everyone. Vox. See https://www.vox.com/recode/2020/5/4/21241062/schools-cheating-proctorio-artificial-intelligence.

Herring, S. (1999) Interactional coherence in CMC. *Journal of Computer-Mediated Communication* 4. See https://academic.oup.com/jcmc/article/4/4/JCMC444/4584407.

Herrington, R. (2020, Apr 20) Copyright, creative commons, and confusion. Scholarly Kitchen. https://scholarlykitchen.sspnet.org/2020/04/20/copyright-creative-commons-and-confusion/?informz=1.

Hessler, B. and Lambert, J. (2017) Threshold concepts in digital storytelling: Naming what we know about storywork. In G. Jamisson, P. Hardy, Y. Nordkvelle and H. Pleasants (eds) *Digital Storytelling in Higher Education* (pp. 19–35). Basel: Springer Nature.

Hewings, A. (2012) Stance and voice in academic discourse across channels. In K. Hyland and S. Guinda (eds) *Stance and Voice in Written Academic Genres* (pp. 187–201). Basingstoke: Palgrave Macmillan.

Hinchliffe, L.J. (2019, Feb 19) Is hybrid a valid pathway to open access? Publishers argue yes, in response to Plan S. Scholarly Kitchen. See https://scholarlykitchen.sspnet.org/2019/02/19/is-hybrid-valid-pathway-to-open/.

Hinchliffe, L.J. (2020a, Mar 9) Subscribe to open: A mutual assurance approach to open access. Scholarly Kitchen. See https://scholarlykitchen.sspnet.org/2020/03/09/subscribetoopen/?informz=1.

Hinchliffe, L.J. (2020b, Apr 7) Seeking sustainability: Publishing models for an open access age. Scholarly Kitchen. See https://scholarlykitchen.sspnet.org/2020/04/07/seeking-sustainability-publishing-models-for-an-open-access-age/?informz=1.

Hirvela, A. and Du, Q. (2013) Why am I paraphrasing?': Undergraduate ESL writers' engagement with source-based academic writing and reading. *Journal of English for Academic Purposes* 12, 87–98.

Holland, T. (2018, Nov 13) The public necessity of student blogging. *Hybrid Technology.* See https://hybridpedagogy.org/public-necessity-student-blogging/.

Hook, D., Hahnel, M. and Calvert, I. (2019, Jan 26) The ascent of open access. *Digital Science.* See https://digitalscience.figshare.com/articles/The_Ascent_of_Open_Access/7618751.

Horner, B., Selfe, C. and Lockridge, T. (2014, Oct 6) Thinking about multi (or trans-) modality, and trans (or multi-)linguality: Power, ideology, and emerging questions. *Digital Rhetoric Collective.* See http://www.digitalrhetoriccollaborative.

org/2014/10/06/thinking-about-multi-or-trans-modality-and-trans-or-multi-lingual-ity-power-ideology-and-emerging-questions/.

Howard, R.M. (2007) Understanding 'Internet plagiarism'. *Computers and Composition* 24, 3–15.

Howard, R.M. (1999) *Standing in the Shadow of Giants: Plagiarists, Authors, Collaborators*. Westport, CT: Greenwood Publishing Group.

Howard, R.M. and Robillard, A.E. (2008) *Pluralizing Plagiarism: Identities, Contexts, Pedagogies*. Portsmouth, NH: Heinemann.

Howard, R.M., Serviss, T. and Rodrigue, T.K. (2010) Writing from sources, writing from sentences. *Writing & Pedagogy* 2, 177–192. See http://justinlewis.me/wp-content/uploads/2013/09/Howard-Serviss-Rodrigue-Writing-from-Sources.pdf.

'Hydroxychloroquine-COVID-19 Study Did Not Meet Publishing Society's "Expected-Standard"' (2020) Retraction Watch. See https://retractionwatch.com/2020/04/06/hydroxychlorine-covid-19-study-did-not-meet-publishing-societys-expected-standard/.

Hyland, K. (1998) *Hedging in Scientific Research Articles*. Amsterdam: John Benjamins.

Hyland, K. (1999) Disciplinary discourses: Writer stance in research articles. In C. Candlin and K. Hyland (eds) *Writing: Texts, Processes, and Practices* (pp. 99–121). London: Longman.

Hyland, L. (2012) Welcome to the machine: Thoughts on writing for scholarly publication. *Journal of Second Language Teaching and Research* 1, 58–66.

Hyland, K. (2015) *Academic Publishing: Issues and Challenges in the Construction of Knowledge*. London: Oxford University Press.

Hyland, K. (2016a) Academic publishing and the myth of linguistic injustice. *Journal of Second Language Writing* 31, 58–69.

Hyland, K. (2016b) Language myths and publishing mysteries: A response to Politzer-Ahles et al. *Journal of Second Language Writing* 34, 9–11.

Hyland, K. and Jian, F. (in press) 'This work is antithetical to the spirit of research': An anatomy of harsh peer reviews. *Journal of English for Academic Purposes*.

Hull, G.A. and Nelson, M.E. (2005) Locating the semiotic power of multimodality. *Written Communication* 22, 224–261.

Hull, G.A. and Katz. M.L. (2006) Crafting an agentive self: Case studies of digital storytelling. *Research in the Teaching of English* 41, 43–81.

'"I was Shocked. I Felt Physically Ill". And Still, She Corrected the Record' (2020) Retraction Watch. See https://retractionwatch.com/2020/03/26/i-was-shocked-ifelt-physically-ill-and-still-she-corrected-the-record/.

Irfanunallah, H. (2019, Mar 25) What does Bangladesh tell us about research communication? Scholarly Kitchen. See https://scholarlykitchen.sspnet.org/2019/03/25/guest-post-what-does-bangladesh-tell-us-about-research-communication/.

Ivanič, R. (1998) *Writing and Identity: The Discoursal Construction of Identity in Academic Writing*. Amsterdam: John Benjamins.

Ivanič, R. and Camps, D. (2001) I am how I sound: Voice as self-representation in l2 writing. *Journal of Second Language Writing* 10, 3–33.

Jaschik, S. (2015, Nov 2) The language of protest. *Inside Higher Education*. See https://www.insidehighered.com/news/2015/11/02/editors-and-editorial-board-quit-top-linguistics-journal-protest-subscription-fees.

Jaschik, S. (2017, Sept 5) Harvard professor tells students they should come to class. *Inside Higher Education*. See https://www.insidehighered.com/news/2017/09/05/professor-who-teaches-harvards-largest-class-says-students-should-show.

Jaschik, S. and Lederman, D. (2016) The 2016 *Inside Higher Ed* survey of faculty attitudes on technology. *Inside Higher Education*. See https://www.insidehighered.com/booklet/2016-survey-faculty-attitudes-technology.

Jaschik, S. and Lederman, D. (2018) 2018 survey of faculty attitudes on technology. *Inside Higher Education*. See https://www.insidehighered.com/booklet/2018-survey-faculty-attitudes-technology.

Jenkins, H. (2006) *Participatory Culture: Where Old and New Media Collide*. New York: New York University Press.

Jenkins, H. (2009) *Confronting the Challenges of Participatory Culture: Media Education for the 21st Century*. Cambridge, MA: MIT Press. See http://digitallearning. macfound.org/atf/cf/%7B7E45C7E0-A3E0-4B89-AC9C-E807E1B0AE4E%7D/JEN-KINS_WHITE_PAPER.PDF.

Jenkins, H., Ito, M. and boyd, d. (2016) *Participatory Culture in a Networked Era: A Conversation on Youth, Learning, Commerce, and Politic*. Malden: MA: Polity Press.

Johns, A. (2017) Augmenting argumentation in second language writing. *Journal of Writing Research* 36, 79–80.

Johnson, G. (2018, May 24) A case for flipping learning—without videos. Edsurge. See https:// www.edsurge.com/news/2018-05-24-a-case-for-flipping-learning-without-videos.

Johnson, R. and Chiarelli, A. (2019, Oct. 16) The second wave of preprint servers: How can publishers keep afloat? Scholarly Kitchen. See https://scholarlykitchen.sspnet. org/2019/10/16/the-second-wave-of-preprint-servers-how-can-publishers-keep-afloat/?informz=1.

Kahle, D. (2010) Designing open educational technology. In T. Iiyoshi and M.S.V. Kumar (eds) *Opening Up Education: The Collective Advancement of Education through Open Technology, Open Content, and Open Knowledge* (pp. 27–45). Cambridge, MA: MIT Press. See https://florida.theorangegrove.org/og/file/86b3ba4b-3cb8-75fb-712e-b5c1beb17833/1/Open.pdf#page=49.

Kaplan, R.B. (1966) Cultural thought patterns in intercultural learning. *Language Learning* 16, 1–20.

Karatsolis, A. (2016) Disciplines and levels of participation. *Journal of Writing Research* 7, 425–452.

Keck, C. (2010) How do university students attempt to avoid plagiarism? A grammatical analysis of undergraduate paraphrasing strategies. *Writing & Pedagogy* 2 (2), 192–222.

Keck, C. (2014) Copying, paraphrasing, and academic writing development: A re-examination of L1 and L2 summarization practices. *Journal of Second Language Writing* 25, 4–22.

Kent, C. (n.d.) Artificial Intelligence in education. *European Ed Tech Network*. See file:///C:/Users/cherepaha/Dropbox/articles/Evidence_Summary_Artificial_Intelligence_in_education.pdf.

Kessler, G. (2009) Student-initiated attention to form in wiki-based collaborative writing. *Language Learning & Technology* 13, 79–95. See http://resourcesfortefiteachers. pbworks.com/f/Student-Initiated+Attention+to+Form+in+WikiBased+Collaborative+Writing.pdf.

King, A. (1993) From sage on the stage to guide on the side. *College Teaching* 41, 30–35. See https://faculty.washington.edu/kate1/ewExternalFiles/SageOnTheStage.pdf.

Knobel, M. and Lankshear, C. (eds) (2007) *A New Literacies Sampler*. London: Peter Lang Publishing.

Koebler, J. (2020, Apr 9) The viral 'study' about runners spreading coronavirus is not actually a study. *Vice*. See https://www.vice.com/en_us/article/v74az9/the-viral-study-about-runners-spreading-coronavirus-is-not-actually-a-study.

Kop, R. (2011) The challenges to connectivist learning on open online networks: Learning experiences. *International Review of Research in Open and Distance Learning* 12 (3). See http://www.irrodl.org/index.php/irrodl/article/view/882/1823.

Kostka, I. and Marshall, H.W. (2018) Flipped learning in TESOL: Past, present, and future. In J. Perren, K. Kelch, J.-S. Byun, S. Cervantes and S. Safavi (eds) *Applications of CALL Theory in ESL and EFL Environment* (pp. 223–243). Hershey, PA: IGI Global.

Krause, S.K. (2014) MOOC assigned. In S.K. Krause and C. Lowe (eds) *Invasion of the MOOCs: The Promises and Perils of Massive Open Online Courses* (pp. 122–129). Anderson, SC: Parlor Press.

Krause, S. and Lowe, C. (2014) *Invasion of the MOOCs: The Promises and Perils of Massive Open Online Courses*. Anderson, SC: Parlor Press.

Kress, G. (2003) *Literacy in the New Media Age*. London: Routledge.

Kress, G. (2005) Gains and losses: New forms of texts, knowledge, and learning. *Computers and Composition* 22 (1), 5–22.

Krumholz, H. (2015) The end of journals. *Circulation: Cardiovascular Quality and Outcomes* 8, 533–534. See http://circoutcomes.ahajournals.org/content/8/6/533.long.

Kuhn, T. (1962) *The Structure of Scientific Revolutions*. Chicago, IL: University of Chicago Press.

Kulkarni, S. (2015, Aug 18) Springer retracts 64 papers from its journals alleging fake reviews. *Editage Insights*. See https://www.editage.com/insights/springer-retracts-64-papers-from-its-journals-alleging-fake-reviews/1439909698.

Kupferschmidt, K. (2020, Feb 26) 'A completely new culture of doing research'. Coronavirus outbreak changes how scientists communicate. *Science*. See https://www.sciencemag.org/news/2020/02/completely-new-culture-doing-research-coronavirus-outbreak-changes-how-scientists.

Kuteeva, M. and Mauranen, A. (2014) Writing for publication in multilingual contexts. *Journal of English for Academic Purposes* 13, 1–4.

Laakso, M., Welling, W., Bukvova, H., Nyman, L., Bjork, B. and Hedland, T. (2011) The development of open access journal publishing from 1993 to 2009. *PLOS*. See http://journals.plos.org/plosone/article?id=10.1371/journal.pone.0020961.

Lage, M.J., Platt, G.J. and Treglia, M. (2000) Inverting the classroom: A gateway to creating an inclusive learning environment. *The Journal of Economic Education* 31, 30–43.

Lambert, C. (2012) Twilight of the lecture. *Harvard Magazine*. See http://harvardmagazine.com/2012/03/twilight-of-the-lecture.

Lambert, J. (2013) *Seven Stages: Story and the Human Experience*. Berkeley, CA: Digital Diner Press.

Lambert, J. (2020) *Digital Storytelling: Story Work for Urgent Times*. Berkeley, CA: Digital Diner Press

Lappalainen, P.H. (2016) Pedagogical design promoting writing productivity on the doctoral level – a case study from Finland. *Journal of Academic Writing* 6 (1), 108–121.

Latour, B. (1987) *Science in Action*. Cambridge, MA: Harvard University Press.

Latour, B. and Woolgar, S. (1979) *Laboratory Life*. Beverly Hills, CA: Sage Publications.

Lave, J. and Wenger, E. (1991) *Situated Learning: Legitimate Peripheral Participation*. Cambridge: Cambridge University Press.

Lea, M. and Street, B. (2006) The 'Academic Literacies' model: Theory and applications. *Theory into Practice* 45, 368–377.

Lederman, D. (2006, June 1) Student plagiarism, faculty responsibility. *Inside Higher Education*. See https://www.insidehighered.com/news/2006/06/01/student-plagiarism-faculty-responsibility.

Leis, A., Tohei, A.A. and Cooke, S. (2015) The effects of flipped classrooms on English composition writing in an EFL environment. See https://www.researchgate.net/publication/281102795_The_Effects_of_Flipped_Classrooms_on_English_Composition_Writing_in_an_EFL_Environment.

Leki, I. (2007) *Undergraduates in a Second Language: Challenges and Complexities of Academic Literacy Development*. Mahwah, NJ: Erlbaum.

Lessig, L. (1999) *Code and Other Laws of Cyberspace*. New York: Basic Books.

Lessig, L. (2002) *The Future of Ideas: The Fate of the Commons in a Connected World*. New York: Vintage Books.

Lessig, L. (2004) *Free Culture: How Big Media Uses Technology and the Law to Lock Down Culture and Control Creativity*. New York: Penguin. See http://www.free-culture.cc/freeculture.pdf.

Lessig, L. (2009) *Remix: Making Art and Commerce Thrive in The Hybrid Economy*. New York: Penguin.

Levi-Strauss, C. (1964) *The Raw and the Cooked*. Chicago, IL: The University of Chicago Press.

Levine, A. (2014) A MOOC or not a MOOC: ds106 questions the form. In S. Krause and C. Lowe (eds) *Invasion of the MOOCs: The Promises and Perils of Massive Open Online Courses* (pp. 29–38). Anderson, CA: Parlor Press

Levy, R. and Yong, D. (2014, Apr 25) Can flipped classroom help students learn? We are trying to find out. *Slate*. See http://www.slate.com/articles/technology/future_tense/2014/04/ flipped_classrooms_can_they_help_students_learn.htm.

Li, Y. and Casanave, C.P. (2012) Two first-year students' strategies for writing from sources: Patchwriting or plagiarism? *Journal of Second Language Writing* 21 (2), 165–180.

Lieberman, M. (2017) Trial and error: To flip or not to flip? *Inside Higher Education*. See https://www.insidehighered.com/digital-learning/article/2017/11/01/professor-flips-class-mixed-results?utm_source=Inside+Higher+Ed&utm_campaign=aca409df29-IDL20171101&utm_medium=email&utm_term=0_1fcbc04421-aca409df29-197342173&mc_cid=aca409df29&mc_eid=22aa5fb9fc.

Lieberman, M. (2018, Sept 21) Furor over blended and active learning. *Inside Higher Education*. See https://www.insidehighered.com/digital-learning/article/2018/09/21/ blended-learning-model-university-central-florida-draws-business Lessons learned in flipping the classroom.

Lillis, T and Curry, M.J. (2006) Professional academic writing by multilingual scholars: Interactions with literacy brokers in the production of English-medium texts. *Written Communication* 23 (1), 3–35.

Lillis, T. and Curry, M.J. (2014) *Academic Writing in A Global Context: The Politics and Practice of Publishing in English*. London: Routledge.

Lim, J. and Polio, C. (2020) Multimodal assignments in higher education: Implications for multimodal writing tasks for L2 writers. *Journal of Second Language Writing* 47, 1–8. doi:10.1016/J.JSLW.2020.100713.

Littlewood, W. (1999) Defining and developing autonomy in East Asian contexts. *Applied Linguistics* 20, 71–94.

Lo, C.K., Hew, K.F. and Chen, G.W. (2017) Toward a set of design principles for mathematics flipped classrooms: A synthesis of research in mathematics education. *Educational Research Review* 22, 50–73.

Lockwood, R.B. (2014) *Flip It!: Strategies for the ESL Classroom*. Ann Arbor, MI: University of Michigan Press.

Lowry, R.J. (1973) *AH Maslow: An Intellectual Portrait*. Boston, MA: Thomson Brooks/Cole.

Lu, M.Z. and Horner, B. (2016) Introduction: Translingual work. *College English* 78, 207–218.

McCabe, D.L., Treviño, L.K. and Butterfield, K.D. (2001) Cheating in academic institutions: A decade of research. *Ethics and Behavior* 11, 219–232.

McCool, J.H. (2017, Apr 6) Why I published in a predatory journal. *The Scientist*. See https://www.the-scientist.com/critic-at-large/opinion-why-i-published-in-a-predatory-journal-31697.

McGlynn, T. (2017) Why blogging is still good for your career. *The Chronicle of Higher Education*. See https://www.chronicle.com/article/Why-Blogging-Is-Still-Good-for/241523.

McKenzie, L. (2018a, Jan. 18) The evolution of the 'Monkey Cage'. *Inside Higher Education*. See https://www.insidehighered.com/news/2018/01/18/ how-academic-blog-monkey-cage-became-part-mainstream-media.

McKenzie, L. (2018b, Aug ry pub20) The end of a blogging era at Harvard. *Inside Higher Education*. See https://www.insidehighered.com/news/2018/08/20/ end-era-old-harvard-blogging-site.

McKenzie, L. (2018c, Oct 4) Publishers escalate legal battle against ResearchGate. *Inside Higher Education*. See https://www.insidehighered.com/news/2018/10/04/ publishers-accuse-researchgate-mass-copyright-infringement.

McKenzie, L. (2018d, Dec 13) Heavyweight showdown over research access. *Inside Higher Education*. See https://www.insidehighered.com/news/2018/12/13/university-california-challenges-elsevier-over-access-scholarly-research.

McKenzie, L. (2019, Sept 17) Arizona State moves on from global freshman academy. *Inside Higher Education*. See https://www.insidehighered.com/digital-learning/article/2019/09/17/arizona-state-changes-course-global-freshman-academy.

McKenzie, L. (2019a, Mar 1) UC drops Elsevier. *Inside Higher Education*. See https://www.insidehighered.com/news/2019/03/01/university-california-cancels-deal-elsevier-after-months-negotiations.

McKenzie, L. (2019b, Nov 22) A new kind of 'Big Deal' for Elsevier. *Inside Higher Education*. See https://www.insidehighered.com/news/2019/11/22/new-kind-big-deal-elsevier-and-carnegie-mellon-university.

McLaughlin, J.E., Roth, M.T., Glatt, D., Gharkholonarehe, N., Davidson, C.A., Griffin, L.M., Esserman, D.A. and Mumper, R.J. (2014) The flipped classroom: A course redesign to foster learning and engagement in a health professions school. *Academic Medicine* 89, 236–243.

MacWilliam, T., Aquino, R.J. and Malan, D.J. (2013) Engaging students through video: Integrating assessment and instrumentation. *Journal of Computing Sciences in Colleges* 28 (6), 169–178. Harvard University Library, Cambridge, MA. See https://dash.harvard.edu/bitstream/handle/1/10629764/ccscne13.pdf?sequence=1.

Mackness, J. and Bell, F. (2016) The ideals and reality of participating in a MOOC. *Research Gate*. See https://www.researchgate.net/publication/235886519_The_Ideals_and_Reality_of_Participating_in_a_MOOC.

Malczyk, B.R. (2019) Introducing social work to Hyflex blended learning. *Journal of Teaching in Social Work* 39, 414–428.

Manca, A., Martinez, G., Cugusi, L., Dragone, D., Mercuro, G. and Deriu, F. (2017, Jan 20) Predatory open access in rehabilitation. *Archives Physical Medicine and Rehabilitation* 98, 1051–1056.

Mao, L.M. (1995) Individualism or personhood: A battle of locution or rhetoric? In J.F. Reynolds (ed.) *Rhetoric, Cultural Studies, and Literacy* (pp. 127–135). Hillsdale, NJ: Lawrence Erlbaum.

Marcus, A. (2018, Dec 11) Amid ethics outcry, should journals publish the 'CRISPR babies' paper? *STAT*. See https://www.statnews.com/2018/12/11/should-journals-publish-crispr-babies-paper.

Marcus, A and Oransky, I. (2011, Dec 22–29) This paper is not sacred. *Nature* 480, 449–450.

Martindale, T. and Wiley, D.A. (2005) Using weblogs in scholarship and teaching. *TechTrends: Linking Research and Practice to Improve Learning* 49, 55–61.

Maslow, A.H. (1962) *Toward a Psychology of Being*. Princeton, NJ: D. Van Nostrand Company.

Maslow, A.H. (1966) *The Psychology of Science: A Reconnaissance*. New York/London: Harper & Row.

Maslow, A.H. (1971) *The Farther Reaches of Human Nature*. New York: The Viking Press.

Matalene, C. (1985) Contrastive rhetoric: An American writing teacher in China. *College English* 47, 789–808.

Matsuda, P. (2006) The myth of linguistic homogeneity in U.S. college composition. *College English* 68, 637–651.

Matsuda, P.K. (2014) The lure of translingual writing. *PMLA* 129, 478–483.

Matzke, A. and Garrett, B. (2018) Studio bricolage: Inventing writing studio pedagogy for local contexts. In M. Sutton and K. Chandler (eds) *The Writing Studio Sampler: Stories About Change. Perspectives on Writing* (pp. 43–60). Fort Collins, CO: The WAC Clearinghouse and University Press of Colorado. See https://wac.colostate.edu/books/perspectives/studio.

Maycock, K.W., Lambert, J. and Bane, D. (2018) Flipping learning not just content: A 4-year action research study investigating the appropriate level of flipped learning. *Journal of Computer Assisted Learning* 34, 661–672.

Mazur, E. (2009) Farewell, lecture? *Science* 323, 50–51.

Meadows, A. (2019, Jan 17) Mixed realities, virtual reality, and augmented reality in scholarly publishing: An interview with Markus Kaindl and Martijn Roelandse. Scholarly Kitchen. See https://scholarlykitchen.sspnet.org/2019/01/17/mixed-realities-virtual-reality-and-augmented-reality-in-scholarly-publishing-an-interview-with-markus-kaindl-and-martijn-roelandse/?informz=1.

Medawar, P. (1984) *Pluto's Republic: Incorporating the Art of the Soluble and Induction and Intuition in Scientific Thought*. Oxford: Oxford University Press.

Mehring, J. and Leis, A. (2018) *Innovations in Flipping the Language Classroom: Theories and Practices*. Singapore: Springer Nature.

Meyer, J.H.F. and Land, R. (2003) Threshold concepts and troublesome knowledge: Linkages to ways of thinking and practicing within the disciplines. In G. Gibbs (ed.) *Improving Student Learning: Improving Student Learning Theory and Practice* (pp. 412–424). Oxford: Oxford Centre for Staff.

Michael, A. (2018, Feb 22) Open access technology options. Scholarly Kitchen. See https://scholarlykitchen.sspnet.org/2018/02/22/open-access-technology-options/?informz=1.

Michael, A. (2019, Oct 24) Beyond the APC. Scholarly Kitchen. See https://scholarlykitchen.sspnet.org/2019/10/24/ask-the-chefs-oa-business-models/.

Miller, A. (2014, Jan 21) 5 tips for flipping your PBL classroom. *Edutopia*. See https://www.edutopia.org/blog/5-tips-flipping-pbl-classroom-andrew-miller.

Milligan, C., Littlejohn, A., and Margaryan, A. (2013) Patterns of engagement in connectivist MOOCs. *MERLOT Journal of Online Learning and Teaching* 9. See http://jolt.merlot.org/vol9no2/milligan_0613.htm.

Minai, N.Z. (2018, Aug 16) Challenges for academics in the global south — Resource constraints, institutional issues, and infrastructural problems. Scholarly Kitchen. See https://scholarlykitchen.sspnet.org/2018/08/16/guest-post-challenges-academics-global-south-resource-constraints-institutional-issues-infrastructural-problems/?informz=1.

MIT Opencourseware (2013, Sept 5) Massachusetts Institute of Technology. See http://ocw.mit.edu/index.htm.

Monteiro, K. and Hirano, E. (2020) A periphery inside a semi-periphery: The uneven participation of Brazilian scholars in the international community. *English for Specific Purposes* 58, 15–29.

Morozov, E. (2014) *To Save Everything, Click Here: The Folly of Technological Solutionism*. New York: Public Affairs.

Morris, S.M. and Stommel, J. (2017) A guide for resisting EdTech: The case against Turnitin. *Hybrid Pedagogy*. See http://www.digitalpedagogylab.com/hybridped/resisting-edtech.

Morris, S.M. and Stommel, J. (2018, Sept 11) An urgency of teachers. *Hybrid Technology*. See http://hybridpedagogy.org/an-urgency-of-teachers.

Morrison, S. and Heilweil, R. (2020, Dec 18) How teachers are sacrificing student privacy to stop cheating. *Recode*. See https://www.vox.com/recode/22175021/school-cheating-student-privacy-remote-learning.

Mudditt, A. (2018, Jan. 18) Countering the über-brands: The case for the megajournal. Scholarly Kitchen. See https://scholarlykitchen.sspnet.org/2018/01/18/countering-uber-brands-case-megajournal/?informz=1.

Mudditt, A. (2019, June 3) Plan S and the transformation of scholarly communication: Are we missing the woods? Scholarly Kitchen. See https://scholarlykitchen.sspnet.org/2019/06/03/plan-s-and-the-transformation-of-scholarly-communication-are-we-missing-the-woods/?informz=1.

Myers, G. (1990) *Writing Biology: Texts in the Social Construction of Scientific Knowledge*. Madison, WI: University of Wisconsin Press.

Myers, G. (2010) *Discourse of Wikis and Blogs*. London: Continuum.

'National Council of Teachers of English' (2015) See OpenEducationResources_Infographic_v4.pdf.

Nelson, M.E. (2006) Mode, meaning, and *synaesthesia* in multimedia l2 writing. *Language Learning & Technology* 10, 56–76.

Nelson, M.E., Hull, G.A. and Roche-Smith, J. (2008) Challenges of multimedia self-presentation: Taking, and mistaking, the show on the road. *Written Communication* 25, 415–440.

New London Group (1996) A pedagogy of multiliteracies: Designing social futures. *Harvard Educational Review* 66, 60–92. See http://newarcproject.pbworks.com/f/Pedagogy%2Bof%2BMultiliteracies_New%2BLondon%2BGroup.pdf.

Niyazov, Y., Vogel, C., Price, R., Lund, B., Judd, D., Akil, A., Mortonson, M., Schwartzman, J. and Shron, M. (2016) Open access meets discoverability: Citations to articles posted to Academia.edu. *PLoS ONE*. See https://journals.plos.org/plosone/article?id=10.1371/journal.pone.0148257.

Norman, D. (2007) *Emotional Design: Why We Love (Or Hate) Everyday Things*. New York: Basic Books.

Norman, D. (2013) *The Design of Everyday Things: Revised and Expanded Edition*. New York: Basic Books.

North, S.A. (1987) *The Making of Knowledge in Composition*. Portsmouth, NH: Heinemann.

Nowacek, R.S. (2011) *Agents of Integration: Understanding Transfer as a Rhetorical Act*. Carbondale, IL: Southern Illinois University Press.

O'Reilly, T. (2005) What is web 2.0: Design patterns and business models for the next generation of software. See http://www.oreillynet.com/pub/a/oreilly/tim/news/2005/09/30/what-is-web-20.html?page=1.

Odlin, T. (2015) Language transfer and the link between comprehension and production. In L. Yu and T. Odlin (eds) *New Perspectives on Transfer in Second Language Learning* (pp. 207–225). Bristol: Multilingual Matters.

Olson, D.R. (1994) *The World on Paper: The Conceptual and Cognitive Implications of Writing and Reading*. Cambridge: Cambridge University Press.

Ong, W.J. (1982) *Orality and Literacy: The Technologizing of the Word*. London: Routledge. See file:///C:/Users/cherepaha/Dropbox/articles/9780203103258_googlepreview.pdf.

'Open Educational Resources Why They Have Yet to Reach Their Full Potential (2018) *The Chronicle of Higher Education*. See http://images.results.chronicle.com/Web/TheChronicleofHigherEducation/%7B0cbd562d-5eee-4c74-88e4-4894148213e1%7D_2018_Principles and Practices in Electronic Portfolios.

Ostrum, E. (2015) *Governing the Commons: The Evolution of Institutions for Collective Action*. Cambridge: Cambridge University Press.

Ouellette, M.A. (2008) Weaving strands of writer identity: Self as author and the NNES 'plagiarist'. *Journal of Second Language Writing* 17, 255–273.

Ozdemir, M., Izmirli, S. and Sahin-Izmirli, O. (2016) The effects of captioning videos on academic achievement and motivation: Reconsideration of redundancy principle in instructional videos. *Educational Technology & Society* 19, 1–10.

Page, B. (2015, Oct 15) Green OA 'will hit publishers'. *The Bookseller*. See http://www.thebookseller.com/news/green-oa-will-hit-publishers-314667.

Palfrey, J. and Gasser, U. (2010) *Interoperability*. New York: Basic Books.

Palfrey, J. and Gasser, U. (2012) *Interop*. New York: Basic Books.

Palmeri, J. (2012) *Remixing Composition: A History of Multimodal Writing Pedagogy*. Carbondale, IL: Southern Illinois University Press.

Paltridge, B. and Starfield, S. (2016) *Getting Published in Academic Journals: Navigating the Publication Process*. Ann Arbor, MI: University of Michigan Press.

Panetta, K. (2018, Aug 18) 5 Trends emerge in the Gartner Hype Cycle for emerging technologies, 2018. *Gartner*. See https://www.gartner.com/smarterwithgartner/5-trends-emerge-in-gartner-hype-cycle-for-emerging.

Papadapoulos, C. and Roman, A.S. (2010) Implementing an inverted classroom model in engineering statistics: Initial results. American Society for Engineering Statistics. Proceedings of the 40th ASEE/IEEE Frontiers in Education Conference, Washington, DC, October.

Papert, S. (1980) *Mindstorms: Children, Computers, and Powerful Ideas*. New York: Basic Books.

Pecorari, D. (2001) Plagiarism and international students: How the English-speaking university responds. In D. Belcher and A. Hirvela (eds) *Linking Literacies: Perspectives on L2 Reading-Writing Connections* (pp. 229–245). Ann Arbor, MI: The University of Michigan Press.

Pecorari, D. (2003) Good and original: Plagiarism and patchwriting in academic second-language writing, *Journal of Second Language Writing* 12 (4), 317–345.

Pecorari, D. (2008) *Academic Writing and Plagiarism: A Linguistic Analysis*. London: Continuum.

Pecorari, D. (2015) Plagiarism in second language writing: Is it time to close the case? *Journal of Second Language Writing* 30, 94–99.

Pecorari, D. (2016) Writing from sources, plagiarism and textual borrowing. In R.M. Manchón and P.K. Matsuda (eds) *Handbook of Second and Foreign Language Writing* (pp. 229–247). Berlin: Walter de Gruyter.

Pecorari, D. and Shaw, P. (2012) Types of student intertextuality and faculty attitudes. *Journal of Second Language Writing* 21, 149–164.

Pecorari, D. and Petrič, B. (2014) Plagiarism in second language writing. *Language Teacher* 47 (3), 269–302.

Pennycook, A. (1996) Borrowing others' words: Text, ownership, memory, and plagiarism. *TESOL Quarterly* 30, 201–230.

Perez, M.M., van Den Noorgate, W. and Desmet, P. (2013) Captioned listening for L2 listening and vocabulary: A meta-analysis. *System* 41, 720–739.

Perkins, D.N. and Salomon, G. (1988) Teaching for transfer. *Educational Leadership* 46, 22–32.

'Perspectives: COVID-19, and the Future of Higher Education' (2020) Bay View Analytics. See http://onlinelearningsurvey.com/covid.html.

Petrou, C. (2020, May 7) The megajournal lifecycle. Scholarly Kitchen. See https://scholarlykitchen.sspnet.org/2020/05/07/guest-post-the-megajournal-lifecycle/?informz=1.

Pettit, E. (2018, Aug 1) These professors don't work for a predatory publisher. It keeps claiming they do. *The Chronicle of Higher Education*. See https://www.chronicle.com/article/These-Professors-Don-t-Work/244120.

Phillipson, R. (1992) *Linguistic Imperialism*. Oxford: Oxford University Press.

Pitts, A. (2018, Sept. 18) Think sci-hub is just downloading PDFs? Think again. Scholarly Kitchen. See https://scholarlykitchen.sspnet.org/2018/09/18/guest-post-think-sci-hub-is-just-downloading-pdfs-think-again/?informz=1.

Piwowar, H., Priem, J., Larivière, V., Alperin, J.P., Matthias, L., Norlander, B., Farley, A., West, J. and Haustein, S. (2018) The state of OA: A large-scale analysis of the prevalence and impact of Open Access articles. *PeerJ*. See https://www.ncbi.nlm.nih.gov/pmc/articles/PMC5815332.

Politzer-Ahlesa, S., Holliday, J., Girolamod, T., Spychalskae, M. and Berkson, K.H. (2016) Is linguistic injustice a myth? A response to Hyland (2016). *Journal of Second Language Writing* 34, 3–8.

Porter, J.E. (2016) Framing questions about MOOCs and writing courses. In S. Krause and C. Lowe (eds) *Invasion of the MOOCs: The Promises and Perils of Massive Open Online Courses* (pp. 14–28). Anderson, SC: Parlor Press.

Posner, R.A. (2007) *The Little Book of Plagiarism*. New York: Pantheon Books.

'Powering What's Next for Higher Education' (2020) *Inside Higher Education*. See https://www.insidehighered.com/system/files/media/IHE_COVID-19_Pt2_NewSurveyof-Presidents_20200427.pdf.

Powers, S. and Doctorow, C. (2002) *Essential Blogging: Selecting and Using Weblog Tools*. Sebastopol, CA: O'Reilly Media.

Poyndor, R. (2019, Nov 18) Open access: Could defeat be snatched from the jaws of victory? See https://richardpoynder.co.uk/Jaws.pdf.

'Predatory Journals: No Definition, No Defense' (2019, Dec 11) *Nature* 576, 210–212. See https://www.nature.com/articles/d41586-019-03759-y.

'Predatory Publishing: Red Flags' (2020) Himmelfarb Health Science Library. See https://guides.himmelfarb.gwu.edu/PredatoryPublishing/RedFlags.

Prensky, M. (2001) Digital natives, digital immigrants. See http://www.marcprensky.com/writing/Prensky%20-%20Digital%20Natives,%20Digital%20Immigrants%20-%20Part1.pdf.

Prensky, M. (2011) *From Digital Natives to Digital Wisdom: Hopeful Essays for 21st Century Education*. Thousand Oaks, CA: Corwin. See http://marcprensky.com/writing/Prensky-Intro_to_From_DN_to_DW.pdf.

'Principles and Practices in Electronic Portfolios' (2015) See https://ncte.org/statement/electronicportfolios/.

'Probe into Carlo Croce Reached "Defensible and Reasonable" Decisions, Says External Review' (n.d.) Retraction Watch. See https://retractionwatch.com/2018/03/05/probe-into-carlo-croce-reached-defensible-and-reasonable-decisions-says-external-review/.

'Promoting Integrity in Research and Its Publication' (2017) Committee on Publication Ethics. See https://publicationethics.org.

Pyne, D. (2017) The rewards of predatory publications at a small business school. *Journal of Scholarly Publishing* 48, 137–160.

Raine, D. and Gretton, S. (n.d.) The flipped classroom: A teaching enhancement fund report. University of Leicester. See https://www2.le.ac.uk/offices/lli/recognition-for-teaching/teaching-excellence-microsite/reports-resources/the-flipped-classroom.

Ravitch, D. (2019, Dec 31) Diane Ravitch's blog. See https://dianeravitch.net/2019/12/31/audrey-watters-the-most-important-post-of-the-decade-the-100-worst-edtech-disasters-of-the-decade/.

Ray, M. (2016) An expanded approach to evaluating open access journals. *Journal of Scholarly Publishing* 47, 307–327.

Raymond, E.S. (1999) *The Cathedral and the Bazaar*. Sebastopol, CA: O'Reilly & Associates. See https://monoskop.org/images/e/e0/Raymond_Eric_S_The_Cathedral_and_the_Bazaar_rev_ed.pdf.

Redden, E. (2007, May 24) Cheating across cultures. *Inside Higher Education*. See http://www.insidehighered.com/news/2007/05/24/cheating (accessed 25 June 2007).

Redden, E. (2017, Feb 24) Teaching and integrating international students. *Inside Higher Education*. See https://www.insidehighered.com/news/2014/02/20/gathering-senior-international-educators-integration-international-students-was.

Reid, G., Snead, R., Pettiway, K. and Simoneaux, B. (2016, Mar 28) Multimodal communication in the university: Surveying faculty across disciplines. *Across the Disciplines* 13. See http://wac.colostate.edu/atd/articles/reidetal2016.cfm.

Reidsema, C., Khosravi, H., Fleming, M., Kavanagh, L., Achilles, N. and Fink, E. (2017) Analyzing the learning pathways of students in a large flipped engineering course. *ASCILITE 2017*. See http://2017conference.ascilite.org/wp-content/uploads/2017/11/Full-Reidsema.pdf.

Resnick, D.P. (1990) Historical perspectives on literacy and schooling. *Daedalus* 119, 5–32.

'RIP OAPL: An Academic Publisher Vanishes' (2018, Oct. 11) *Discover Magazine*. See http://blogs.discovermagazine.com/neuroskeptic/2018/10/15/rip-oapl-academic-publisher/#.W84_pGhKiJb.

Rittman, M. (2018, Oct 12) Opening up peer review. *MDPI*. See http://blog.mdpi.com/2018/10/12/opening-up-peer-review.

Robillard, A.E. (2008) Situating plagiarism as a form of authorship: The politics of writing in a first-year writing course. In A.E. Robillard and R.M. Howard (eds) *Pluralizing*

Plagiarism: Identities, Contexts, Pedagogies (pp. 27–42). Portsmouth, NH: Boynton/Cook.

Roehling, P.V. (2018) *Flipping the College Classroom*. Cham: Palgrave/Macmillan.

Rogerson, A.M. and McCarthy, G. (2017) Using Internet based paraphrasing tools: Original work, patchwriting or facilitated plagiarism. *International Journal for Educational Integrity* 13 (2). See https://edintegrity.springeropen.com/articles/10.1007/s40979-016-0013-y.

Roll, N. (2017) New salvo against Turnitin. *Inside Higher Education*. See https://www.insidehighered.com/news/2017/06/19/anti-turnitin-manifesto-calls-resistance-some-technology-digital-age.

Rose, M. (1989) *Lives on the Boundary: A Moving Account of The Struggles and Achievements of America's Educational Underclass*. New York: Penguin Books.

Rosenthal, D. (2018) Blockchain for peer review. DSHR's blog. See https://blog.dshr.org/2018/05/blockchain-for-peer-review.html.

Ross-Hellauer, T. (2017, Sept 29) Disambiguating post-publication peer review. ScienceOpen.com. See https://blog.scienceopen.com/2016/09/disambiguating-post-publication-peer-review/.

Rowbottom, D.P. (2007) Demystifying threshold concepts. *Journal of Philosophy of Education* 41, 263–270.

Rowe, N. (2019) Language editing & peer review [video]. See https://www.youtube.com/watch?v=Pw3UcCosgb4.

Rozycki, W. and Johnson, N.H. (2013) Non-canonical grammar in best paper award winners in engineering. *English for Specific Purposes* 32, 157–169.

Salager-Meyer, F. (2012) The open access movement or 'edemocracy': Its birth, rise, problems and solutions. *Ibérica* 24. See https://www.researchgate.net/publication/289017346_The_open_access_movement_or_edemocracy1_Its_birth_rise_problems_and_solutions.

Salager-Meyer, F. (2014) Writing and publishing in peripheral scholarly journals: How to enhance the global influence of multilingual scholars? *Journal of English for Academia Purposes* 13, 78–82.

Salager-Meyer, F. (2018) Open Access: The next model for research dissemination? In M.J. Curry and T. Lillis (eds) *Global Academic Publishing: Policies, Perspectives and Pedagogies* (pp. 184–199). Bristol: Multilingual Matters.

Sapp, D.A. (2002) Towards an international and intercultural understanding of plagiarism and dishonesty in composition: Reflections from the People's Republic of China. *Issues in Writing* 13 (1), 58–79.

Saunders, M.E., Duffy, M.A., Heard, S.B., Kosmala, M., Leather, S.R., McGlynn, T.P., Ollerton, J. and Parachnowitsch, M.L. (2017) Bringing ecology blogging into the scientific fold: Measuring reach and impact of science community blogs. *Royal Society Open Science*. See http://rsos.royalsocietypublishing.org/content/royopensci/4/10/170957.full.pdf.

Schimmer, R., Geschuhn, K.K. and Vogler, A. (2015) Disrupting the subscription journals' business model for the necessary large-scale transformation to open access. See http://hdl.handle.net/11858/00-001M-0000-0026-C274-7.

Schonfeld, R.C. (2017) When is a publisher not a publisher? Cobbling together the pieces to build a workflow business. Scholarly Kitchen. See https://scholarlykitchen.sspnet.org/2017/02/09/cobbling-together-workflow-businesses.

Schonfeld, R.C. (2018a, Dec 10) Elsevier Chairman YS Chi: An interview. Scholarly Kitchen. See https://scholarlykitchen.sspnet.org/2018/12/10/elsevier-chairman-ys-chi-interview/?informz=1.

Schonfeld, R.C. (2018b, Dec 11) Why Is the digital preservation network disbanding? Scholarly Kitchen. See https://mail.google.com/mail/u/0/#inbox/WhctKJVBHkBWf-HKHMpxFwftrzHwknnRKZmFGGJljtgxHdLrDzCBgsBftHdxJxlZzFmqjwNV.

Schonfield, R.C. (2019a, Apr 15) Open access publishing: New evidence on faculty attitudes and behaviors. Scholarly Kitchen. See https://scholarlykitchen.sspnet.org/2019/04/15/open-access-publishing-new-evidence/?informz=1.

Schonfield, R.C. (2019b, Oct 2) The research data sharing business landscape. Scholarly Kitchen. See https://scholarlykitchen.sspnet.org/2019/10/02/research-data-sharing-business-landscape/?informz=1.

Schreiber, B.R. (2015) 'I am what I am': Multilingual identity and digital translanguaging. *Language Learning & Technology* 19, 69–87.

Scribner, S. and Cole, M. (1981) *The Psychology of Literacy*. Cambridge, MA: Harvard University Press.

Searls, D. (2020, Mar 27) Zoom needs to clean up its privacy act. Doc Searls Weblog. See https://blogs.harvard.edu/doc/.

Secker, J. (2017) The trouble with terminology: rehabilitating and rethinking 'Digital Literacy'. In K. Reedy and J. Parker (eds) *Digital Literacy Unpacked* (pp. 3–16). London: Facet Publishing.

Selber, S. (2004) *Multiliteracies for a Digital Age*. Urbana, IL: NCTE Press.

Selfe, C.L. (2009) The movement of air, the breadth of meaning: Aurality and multimedia composing. *Composition and Communication* 60, 616–663.

Selfe, C.L. and Selfe, R.J., Jr. (1994) The politics of the interface: Power and its exercise in electronic contact zones. *College Composition and Communication* 45, 480–504.

Selinker, L. (1972) 'Interlanguage'. *International Review of Applied Linguistics* 10, 209–241.

Senske, N., (2017). Five years of flipped classrooms: Lessons learned. *Architecture Conference Proceedings and Presentations*. 109. See https://lib.dr.iastate.edu/arch_conf/109

Setren, E., Greenberg, K., Moore, O. and Yankovich, M. (2019) Effects of the flipped classroom: Evidence from a randomized trial (Ed Working Paper: 19–113). Annenberg Institute at Brown University. See http://www.edworkingpapers.com/ai19-113.

Shah, D. (2018, May 21) The second wave of MOOC hype is here, and it's online degrees. Edsurge. See https://www.edsurge.com/news/2018-05-21-the-second-wave-of-mooc-hype-is-here-and-it-s-online-degrees.

Shamseer, L., Moher, D., Maduekwe, O., Turner, L., Barbour, V., Burch, R., Clark, J., Galipeau, J., Roberts, J. and Shea, B.J. (2017) Predatory and legitimate biomedical journals: Can you tell the difference? A cross-sectional comparison. *Biomedical Ethics*. See https://bmcmedicine.biomedcentral.com/articles/10.1186/s12916-017-0785-9.

Shapiro, S. (2014) 'Words that you said got bigger': English language learners' lived experiences of deficit discourse. *Research in the Teaching of English* 48, 386–406.

Shen, C. and Bjork, B. (2015) 'Predatory' open access: A longitudinal study of article volumes and market characteristics. *BMC Medicine* 13. See https://bmcmedicine.biomedcentral.com/articles/10.1186/s12916-015-0469-2.

Shi, L. (2004) Textual borrowing in second-language writing. Written Communication 21, 171–200.

Shi, L. (2006) Cultural backgrounds and textual appropriation. *Language Awareness* 15, 264–282.

Shi, L. (2010) Textual borrowing and citation behaviors of university undergraduates. *Applied Linguistics* 31, 1–24.

Shi, L. (2016) Textual appropriation in two discipline-specific undergraduate writings. *Writing & Pedagogy* 8 (1), 91–116. See https://journals.equinoxpub.com/index.php/WAP/article/view/27207.

Shipka, J. (2013) Including, but not limited to, the digital: Composing multimodal texts. In T. Bowen and C. Whithaus (eds) *Multimodal Literacies and Emerging Genres* (pp. 73–89). Pittsburgh, PA: University of Pittsburgh Press.

Shirky, C. (2009) *Here Comes Everybody: How Change Happens When People Come Together*. New York: Penguin.

Siemens, G. (2005) Connectivism: A learning theory for the digital age. See https://jotamac.typepad.com/jotamacs_weblog/files/Connectivism.pdf.

Siemens, G. (2012, July 25) MOOCs are really a platform. *eLearnspace*. See http://www.elearnspace.org/blog/2012/07/25/moocs-are-really-a-platform.

Simpson, S., Caplan, N.A., Cox, M. and Phillips, T. (2016) *Supporting Graduate Student Writers*. Ann Arbor, MI: University of Michigan Press.

Smallhorn, M. (2017) The flipped classroom: A learning model to increase student engagement not academic achievement. *Student Success* 8, 43–53. See https://studentsuccessjournal.org/plugins/generic/pdfJsViewer/pdf.js/web/viewer.html?file=https%3A%2F%2Fstudentsuccessjournal.org%2Farticle%2Fdownload%2F502%2F368%2F.

Smith, R. (1999) Opening up BMJ peer review. *British Medical Journal* 318, 23–27.

Smith, A. and Olmstead, K. (2018) Declining majority of online adults say the Internet has been good for society. *Pew Research Center*. See https://www.pewresearch.org/internet/wp-content/uploads/sites/9/2018/04/PI_2018.04.30_Internet-Good-Bad_FINAL.pdf.

Smithers, M. (2011, Mar 11) Is lecture capture the worst educational technology? Higher Ed I.T. blog. See website http://www.masmithers.com/2011/03/11/is-lecture-capture-the-worst-educational-technology.

Solomon, D.J., Laakso, M and Bjork, B-C. (2016) Converting scholarly journals to open access: A review of approaches and experiences. In P. Suber (ed.) *Digital Access to Scholarship at Harvard*. See https://dash.harvard.edu/bitstream/handle/1/27803834/DASH%20Version-Journal-flipping-final-Aug4-2016-print-2.pdf?sequence=3&isAllowed=y.

Somers, J. (2018, Apr 5) The scientific paper is obsolete. *The Atlantic*. See https://www.theatlantic.com/science/archive/2018/04/the-scientific-paper-is-obsolete/556676.

Sorokowski, P., Kulczycki, E., Sorokowska, A. and Pisanski, K. (2017, Mar 17) Predatory journals recruit fake editor. *Nature* 543. See http://www.nature.com/news/predatory-journals-recruit-fake-editor-1.21662.

Spack, R. (1997) The acquisition of academic literacy in a second language: A longitudinal case study. *Written Communication* 14, 3–62.

'Speak Up Survey' (2013) Project Tomorrow. See http://www.tomorrow.org/speakup.

Squazzoni, F., Grimaldo, F. and Marušić, A. (2017) Publishing: Journals could share peer-review data. *Nature* 546. See https://www.nature.com/articles/546352a.

Starfield, S. and Paltridge, B. (2019) The many roles of the journal editor. In P. Habibe and K. Hyland (eds) *Novice Writers Writing for Publication* (pp. 253–270). London: Palgrave/MacMillan.

Steele, C.N. (2016) The digital barbershop: Blogs and online oral culture within the African American Community. *Social Media + Society* 1–10. See http://journals.sagepub.com/doi/pdf/10.1177/2056305116683205.

Steen-Utheim, A.T. (2017) A qualitative investigation of student engagement in a flipped classroom. *Teaching in Higher Education* 23 (3), 307–324. See http://dx.doi.org/10.1080/13562517.2017.1379481.

Stephens, W. (2018) *Privacy's Blueprint: The Battle to Control the Design of New Technologies*. Cambridge, MA: Harvard University Press.

Stewart, B. (2015) Open to influence: What counts as academic influence in scholarly networked Twitter participation. *Learning, Media, & Technology* 40, 287–309.

Straumsheim, C. (2013, Oct 30) Still in favor of the flip. *Inside Higher Education*. See http://www.insidehighered.com/news/2013/10/30/despite-new-studies-flipping-classroom-still-enjoys-widespread-support#ixzz2q1V7ydq0.

Straumsheim, C. (2017, Jan. 18) No more 'Beall's list'. See https://www.insidehighered.com/news/2017/01/18/librarians-list-predatory-journals-reportedly-removed-due-threats-and-politics?utm_source=Inside Higher Ed&utm_campaign=b7df7f04e5-.DNU20170118&utm_medium=email&utm_term=0_1fcbc04421-b7df7f04e5-197342173&goal=0_1fcbc04421-b7df7f04e5-197342173&mc_cid=b7df7f04e5&mc_eid=22aa5fb9fc (accessed 18 January 2017).

Strayer, J. (2012) How learning in an inverted classroom influences cooperation, innovation, and task Orientation. *Learning Environments* 15, 171–193.

Street, B. (1984) *Literacy in Theory and Practice*. Cambridge: Cambridge University Press.

Suber, P. (2012) *Open Access*. Boston, MA: MIT Press. See https://mitpress.mit.edu/sites/default/files/titles/content/9780262517638_Open_Access_PDF_Version.pdf.

Suber, N.P. (2016) *Knowledge Unbound: Selected Writings on Open Access, 2002–2011*. Cambridge: MIT Press.

Sun, Z., Xie, K. and Anderman, L.H. (2018) The role of self-regulated learning in students' success in flipped undergraduate math courses. *The Internet and Higher Education* 36, 41–53.

Sunderland-Smith, W. (2005) Pandora's box: Academic perceptions of student plagiarism in writing. *Journal of English for Academic Purposes* 4, 83–95.

Sunderland-Smith, W. (2008) *Plagiarism, The Internet and Student Learning: Improving Academic Integrity*. New York: Routledge.

Surowiecki, J. (2004) *The Wisdom of the Crowds*. New York: Doubleday.

Sutton, M. and Chandler, S. (eds) (2018) *The Writing Studio Sampler: Stories About Change. Perspectives on Writing*. Fort Collins, CO: The WAC Clearinghouse and University Press of Colorado. See https://wac.colostate.edu/books/perspectives/studio.

Swales, J. (1991) *Genre Analysis: English in Academic and Research Settings*. Cambridge: Cambridge University Press.

Swales, J. (1996) Occluded genres in the academy: The case of the submission letter. In E. Ventola and A. Mauranen (eds) *Academic Writing: Intercultural and Textual Issues* (pp. 25–58). Amsterdam: John Benjamins.

Swales, J.M. (2009) Worlds of genre: Metaphors of genre. In C. Bazerman, A. Bonini and D. Figueiredo (eds) *Genre in A Changing World* (pp. 3–16). Fort Collins, CO: WAC Clearinghouse and Parlor Press.

Swales, J.M and Feak, C.B. (2012) *Academic Writing for Graduate Students, 3rd edition: Essential Skills and Tasks*. Ann Arbor, MI: University of Michigan Press.

Sweet, B.V. (1984) *Literacy in Theory and Practice*. Cambridge: Cambridge University Press.

Swope, J. (2013, Nov 25) What do we know about MOOC students so far?: A look at recent user data. *MOOC News and Reviews*. See http://moocnewsandreviews.com/what-do-we-know-about-mooc-students-so-far/#ixzz5nlEabrHR.

Szafir, D. and Mutlu, B. (2013) ARTFul: Adaptive review technology for flipped learning. *Proceedings of the SIGCHI Conference on Human Factors in Computing Systems*, 1001–1010.

Taczak, K., Robertson, L. and Yancey, K.B. (2020) A framework for transfer: Students' development of a 'Theory of Writing'. In J.-A. Kerr and A.N. Amicucci (eds) *Stories from First-Year Composition: Pedagogies that Foster Student Agency and Writing Identity* (pp. 159–176). Ft. Collins, CO: The WAC Clearinghouse; University Press of Colorado. See https://wac.colostate.edu/docs/books/stories/chapter9.pdf.

Talbert, R. (2014, May 5) Flipped learning skepticism: Do students want to have lectures? *The Chronicle of Higher Education*. See http://flexible.learning.ubc.ca/news-events/flipped-learning-skepticism-do-students-want-to-have-lectures/.

Talbert, R. (2017) *Flipped Learning: A Guide for Higher Education Faculty*. Sterling, VA: Stylus Publishing.

Talbert, R. (2019, Aug 16) My year as an embedded academic. See https://www.youtube.com/watch?time_continue=591&v=flgliMh98kQ.

Talbot, R. (2017) *Flipped Learning: A Guide for Higher Education Faculty*. Sterling, VA: Stylus.

Tao, T. (2020, Feb 5) India's fight against predatory journals: An interview with Professor Bhushan Patwardhan. Scholarly Kitchen. See https://scholarlykitchen.sspnet.

org/2020/02/05/indias-fight-against-predatory-journals-an-interview-with-professor-bhushan-patwardhan/.

Tardy, C.M. (2016) *Beyond Convention: Genre Innovation in Academic Writing*. Ann Arbor, MI: University of Michigan Press.

Tardy, C.M. (2019) We are all reviewer #2: A window into the secret world of peer review. In P. Habibe and K. Hyland (eds) *Novice Writers Writing for Publication* (pp. 271–289). London: Palgrave/MacMillan.

Tasi, F.S. (2013) The state of massive open online courses (MOOCs) in engineering education: Where do we go from here? Paper presented at the 120th ASEE Annual Conference & Exposition, Atlanta, GA. See https://www.asee.org/file_server/papers/attachment/file/0003/3914/6416.pdf.

Taylor & Francis (2014) Open Access Survey. See http://www.tandf.co.uk/journals/explore/open-access-survey-june2014.pdf.

Tennant, J.P., Waldner, F., Jacques, D.C., Masuzzo, P., Collister, L.B. and Chris, H.J. (2016) The academic, economic and societal impacts of Open Access: An evidence-based review. *F1000 Research*. See https://f1000research.com/articles/5-632.

'Text recycling guidelines' (2018, Feb 2) Committee on Publication Ethics. See https://publicationethics.org/resources/guidelines-new/text-recycling-guidelines-editors-0.

Tham, J., McGrath, M., Duin, A.H. and Moses, J. (2018) Immersive technologies and writing pedagogy. *Computers and Composition* 50, 1–7.

'The Hard Choices of Academic Technology' (2019) *The Chronicle of Higher Education*. See http://images.results.chronicle.com/Web/TheChronicleofHigherEducation/%7B0 2b593e6-6402-46fb-8bb5-a3320ddad521%7D_TechDecisions_ResearchBrief_Workday_v4.pdf.

'The Impact of OER: Achievements and Challenges' (2019) UNESCO. See https://iite.unesco.org/wp-content/uploads/2019/04/Understanding_the_impact_of_OER_2019_final.pdf.

Toulmin, S.E. (1958) *The Uses of Argument*. Cambridge, MA. Cambridge University Press.

Turkle, S. (2017) *Alone Together: Why We Expect More From Technology and Less From Each Other*. New York: Basic Books.

Twomey, T. (2009) What's the deal with Turnitin? In T. Twomey, H. White and K. Sagendorf (eds) *Pedagogy, not Policing: Positive Approaches to Academic Integrity at the University* (pp. 149–155). Syracuse, NY: The Graduate School Press of Syracuse University.

'Understanding the Impact of OER Achievements and Challenges' (2019) OER Africa. See https://www.saide.org.za/documents/Understanding_the_impact_of_OER_2019-1.pdf.

Vandergriff, I. (2016) *Second Language Discourse in the Digital World: Linguistic and Social Practices In and Beyond the Networked Classroom*. Amsterdam: John Benjamins.

Veletsianos, G. (2020) *Learning Online: The Student Experience*. Baltimore, MD: Johns Hopkins University Press. See https://muse.jhu.edu/chapter/2541444/pdf.

Vines, T. (2018, Sept. 20) Plan T: Scrap APCS and fund open access with submission fees. Scholarly Kitchen. See https://scholarlykitchen.sspnet.org/2018/09/20/plan-t-scrap-apcs-and-fund-open-access-with-submission-fees.

Vines, T. (2019, Aug 15) Two new initiatives at *eLife* to start the Eisen era. Scholarly Kitchen. See https://scholarlykitchen.sspnet.org/2019/08/15/two-new-initiatives-at-elife-to-start-the-eisen-era/?informz=1.

Vygotsky, L. (1934/1986) *Thought and Language*. Cambridge, MA: MIT Press.

Wakeling, S., Spezi, V., Fry, J., Creaser, C., Pinfield, S. and Willet, P. (2017) Open access megajournals: The publisher perspective (Part 1: Motivations). *Learned Publishing*. See https://onlinelibrary.wiley.com/doi/full/10.1002/leap.1117.

Wakeling, S., Willett, P., Creaser, C., Fry, J., Pinfield, S., Spezi, V., Bonne, M., Founti, C. and Perea, I.M. (2019) 'No comment'? A study of commenting on PLOS articles. *Journal of Information Science*. See https://journals.sagepub.com/doi/pdf/10.1177/0165551518819965.

Warner, J. (2019, Sept 9) AI in education hype: Feel like I've seen this play before. *Inside Higher Education*. https://www.insidehighered.com/blogs/just-visiting/ai-education-hype-feel-ive-seen-play.

Warschauer, M. (2002) Languages.com: The internet and linguistic pluralism. In I. Snyder (ed.) *Silicon Literacies: Communication, Innovation and Education in the Electronic Age* (pp. 62–74). London: Routledge.

Watters, A. (2013a, Apr 10) The early days of videotaped lectures. *Hybrid Technology*. See https://hybridpedagogy.org/the-early-days-of-videotaped-lectures/.

Watters, A. (2013b, Nov 18) 'Zombie Ideas' (Ed-Tech ideas that refuse to die even though we know they're monstrous). *Hack Education*. See http://2013trends.hackeducation.com/zombies.html.

Watters, A. (2018, Jan 5) PLATO and the history of education technology (that wasn't). See http://hackeducation.com/2018/01/25/plato.

Watters, A. (2019, Dec 31) The 100 worst ed-tech debacles of the decade. See http://hack-education.com/2019/12/31/what-a-shitshow.

Watters, A. (2020, Sep 14) Hack Education: 'Luddite Sensibilities' and the Future of Education. *National Education Policy Center*. See https://nepc.colorado.edu/blog/luddite-sensibilities.

Weinberger, D. (2002) *Small Pieces Loosely Joined*. New York: Perseus Books.

Weller, M. (2012, Apr. 29) The virtues of blogging as scholarly activity. *The Chronicle of Higher Education*. See https://www.chronicle.com/article/The-Virtues-of-Blogging-as/131666.

Weller, K., Mahrt, M. and Puschmann, C. (2014) *Twitter and Society*. New York: Peter Lang.

Weller, M. (2018a, July 2) Twenty years of EdTech. *Educause*. See https://er.educause.edu/articles/2018/7/twenty-years-of-edtech.

Weller, M. (2018b, June 21) 25 years of EdTech: 2010 – Connectivism. *The Ed Techie*. See http://blog.edtechie.net/pedagogy/25-years-of-edtech-2010-connectivism.

Weller, M. (2020) *25 Years of Ed Tech*. Edmonton: AU Press. See https://www.aupress.ca/app/uploads/120290_99Z_Weller_2020-25_Years_of_Ed_Tech.pdf.

Wellmon, C. and Piper, A. (2017) Publication, power, and patronage: On inequality and academic publishing. *Critical Inquiry*. See https://criticalinquiry.uchicago.edu/publication_power_and_patronage_on_inequality_and_academic_publishing.

Wharton, E. (1912) *The Reef*. New York: D. Appleton & Company. See https://www.gutenberg.org/ebooks/283.

Wheeler, S. (2017, Oct 29) Reasons to be blogging …. 1 2 3 …. See http://www.steve-wheeler.co.uk/2017/10/reasons-to-be-blogging-1-2-3.html.

Whitehouse, T. (2019, Oct 7) A look at the user-centric future of academic research software: And why it matters, Part 1: Trends. Scholarly Kitchen. See https://schol-arlykitchen.sspnet.org/2019/10/07/guest-post-a-look-at-the-user-centric-future-of-academic-research-software-and-why-it-matters-part-1-trends/?informz=1.

Wiley, D. (2007) On the sustainability of open educational resource initiatives in higher education. OCED. See https://www.oecd.org/education/ceri/38645447.pdf.

Wiley, D. (2019, Aug 15) Everything old is new again: Textbooks, the printing press, the internet, and OER. *iterating* toward *openness*. See https://opencontent.org/blog/archives/6104.

Wiley, D. and Green, C. (2012) Why openness in education? In D. Oblinger (ed.) *Game Changers: Education and Information Technologies* (pp. 81–89). Washington, DC: Educause. See https://library.educause.edu/resources/2012/5/chapter-6-why-openness-in-education.

Wilhite, A.W. and Fong, E.A. (2012) Coercive citation in academic publishing. *Science* 335, 542–543.

Willinsky, J. (2006) *The Access Principle: The Case for Open Access in Research and Scholarship.* Cambridge, MA: MIT Press.

Willinsky, J. (2017) *The Intellectual Properties of Learning.* Chicago, IL: University of Chicago Press.

Willinsky, J. and Moorhead, L. (2014) How the rise of open access is altering journal publishing. In B. Cope and A. Phillips (eds) *The Future of the Academic Journal* (2nd edn, pp. 195–222). Amsterdam: Elsevier.

Wilsdon, J., Allen, L., Belfiore, E., Campbell, P., Curry, S., Hill, S.A., Jones, R., Kain, R.J.P., Kerridge, S., Thelwall, M., Tinkler, J., Viney, I., Wouters, P., Hill, J. and Johnson, B. (2015) The metric tide: Report of the independent review of the role of metrics in research assessment and management. See https://responsiblemetrics.org/wp-content/uploads/2019/02/2015_metrictide.pdf.

Wilson, E. (2018, Sept 24) Why a society publisher is moving toward read and publish models. Scholarly Kitchen. See https://scholarlykitchen.sspnet.org/2018/09/24/guest-post-why-a-society-publisher-is-moving-toward-read-and-publish-models/.

Wilson, J.A. and Soblo, H. (2020) Transfer and transformation in multilingual student writing. *Journal of English for Academic Purposes* 44, 1–13.

Woodworth, E.L. (2014) I open at the close: A post-MOOC meta-happening reflection and what I'm going to do about that. In S. Krause and C. Lowe (eds) *Invasion of the MOOCs: The Promises and Perils of Massive Open Online Courses* (pp. 180–192). Anderson, SC: Parlor Press.

Wu, T. (2010) *The Master Switch: The Rise and Fall of Information Empires.* New York: Vintage.

Wulf, K. (2017, July 26) Missing the target: The UK Scholarly Communications Licence. *Scholarly Kitchen.* See https://scholarlykitchen.sspnet.org/2017/07/26/missing-target-uk-scholarly-communications-license/.

Wulf, K. and Meadows, A. (2016, Mar 21) Seven things every researcher should know about scholarly publishing. Scholarly Kitchen. See https://scholarlykitchen.sspnet.org/2016/03/21/seven-things-every-researcher-should-know-about-scholarly-publishing.

Wysocki, R., Udelson, J., Ray, C.E., Neuman, J.S.B., Matravers, L.S., Kumari, A., Gordon, M.L.P., Scott, L.P., Day, M., Baumann, M., Alvarez, S.P. and DeVoss, D. (2019) On multimodality: A manifesto. In S. Khadka and J.C. Lee (eds) *Bridging the Multimodal Gap* (pp. 17–29). Louisville, CO: Utah State University Press.

Yabro, J., Arfstrom, K.M., McKnight, K. and McKnight, P. (2014) Extension of a review of flipped learning. *Flipped Learning Network.* See http://flippedlearning.org/wp-content/uploads/2016/07/Extension-of-FLipped-Learning-LIt-Review-June-2014.pdf.

Yancey, K.B. (1998) *Reflection in the Writing Classroom.* All Utah State University Press Publications. Provo: UT. See https://digitalcommons.usu.edu/usupress_pubs/120.

Yancey, K.B. (2004) Made not only in words: Composition in a new key. *College Composition and Communication* 56, 297–321.

Yancey, K.B. (2015) *Writing in the 21st Century.* National Council of Teachers of English. See at https://cdn.ncte.org/nctefiles/press/yancey_final.pdf.

Yancey, K.B. (2019) Blogging multimodality: A multiyear study of graduate-student composing process. In S. Khadka and J.C. Lee (eds) *Bridging the Multimodal Gap* (pp. 123–139). Louisville, CO: Utah State University Press.

Yancey, K.B., Robertson, L. and Taczak, K. (2014) *Writing Across Contexts: Transfer, Composition, and Sites of Writing.* Provo, UT: Utah State University Press.

Yong, D., Levy, R. and Lape, N. (2015) Why no difference? A controlled flipped classroom study for an introductory differential equations course. *Primus* 25, 907–921.

Yoon, H. (2008) More than a linguistic reference: The influence of corpus technology on L2 academic writing. *Language Learning & Technology* 12, 31–48.

Young, J.R. (2012, Aug 16) Dozens of plagiarism incidents are reported in Coursera's free online courses. *The Chronicle of Higher Education.* See https://www.chronicle.com/article/Dozens-of-Plagiarism-Incidents/133697.

Young, J.R. (2019, Mar 20) Could remixing old MOOCs give new life to free online education? Edsurge. See https://www.edsurge.com/news/2019-03-20-could-remixing-old-moocs-give-new-life-to-free-online-education.

Young, R.E. (1976) Invention: A topographical survey. In G. Tate (ed.) *Teaching Composition: Ten Bibliographic Essays* (pp. 1–44). Fort Worth, TX: Texas Christian University Press.

Zappe, S.E., Leicht, R.M., Messner, J.L. and Lee, H.Y. (2009) 'Flipping' the classroom to explore active learning in a large undergraduate course. *American Society for Engineering Education.* See https://peer.asee.org/flipping-the-classroom-to-explore-active-learning-in-a-large-undergraduate-course.

Zittrain, J. (2009) *The Future of the Internet: And How to Stop It.* New Haven, CT: Yale University Press.

Index